The Eclipse of the Legality Principle in the European Union

EUROPEAN MONOGRAPHS

Editor-in-chief Professor David O'Keeffe

In this series *European Monographs* this book *The Eclipse of the Legality Principle in the European Union* is the seventy-fifth title. *The titles published in this series are listed at the end of this volume.*

The Eclipse of the Legality Principle in the European Union

Edited by

Leonard Besselink

Frans Pennings

Sacha Prechal

Wolters Kluwer

Law & Business

Published by:
Kluwer Law International
PO Box 316
2400 AH Alphen aan den Rijn
The Netherlands
Website: www.kluwerlaw.com

Sold and distributed in North, Central and South America by:
Aspen Publishers, Inc.
7201 McKinney Circle
Frederick, MD 21704
United States of America
Email: customer.serivce@aspenpublishers.com

Sold and distributed in all other countries by:
Turpin Distribution Services Ltd.
Stratton Business Park
Pegasus Drive, Biggleswade
Bedfordshire SG18 8TQ
United Kingdom
Email: kluwerlaw@turpin-distribution.com

Printed on acid-free paper.

ISBN 978-90-411-3262-8

Printed in Great Britain.

List of Contributors

Leonard Besselink	Professor of European Constitutional Law at Utrecht University
Evelien Brouwer	Assistant Professor of Constitutional and Administrative Law at Utrecht University
Susanne Burri	Associate Professor of Gender and Law at Utrecht University, Europa Institute
Ton Duijkersloot	Assistant Professor in Administrative and Constitutional Law at Utrecht University
Hanneke van Eijken	PhD student in European Law at Utrecht University, Europa Institute
Lyana Francot-Timmermans	Assistant Professor of Legal Theory, Department of Legal Theory, Utrecht University
Teun Jaspers	Emeritus Professor of Labour Law and Social Security Law at Utrecht University, Europa Institute
Gerdy Jurgens	Professor of Administrative Law at Utrecht University
Saskia Lavrijssen	Associate Professor of Public Economic Law at Utrecht University, Europa Institute
Tony Marguery	Assistant professor of European Law, Utrecht University, Europa Institute
Reile Meyers	PhD student in Labour Law at Utrecht University, Europa Institute
Annetje Ottow	Professor of Public Economic Law at the Europa Institute, Utrecht University and Associate Member of the Board of the Dutch Telecommunications Regulator (OPTA).
Frans Pennings	Professor of Labour Law and Social Security Law at Utrecht University, Europa Institute; Professor of International Social Security Law at Tilburg University

Sacha Prechal	Judge in the Court of Justice of the European Union; Professor of European Law, Europa Institute, Utrecht University.
Albertine Veldman	Associate Professor of Labour Law and Social Security Law at Utrecht University, Europa Institute
Maartje Verhoeven	Assistant Professor European and Administrative Law, Utrecht University, Europa Institute
Sybe de Vries	Associate Professor in European Law, Utrecht University, Europa Institute
Ubaldus de Vries	Associate Professor at Department of Legal Theory, Utrecht University and member of the Working Group Reflexive Modernisation and Law.
Rob Widdershoven	Professor of European Administrative Law at Utrecht University
Paulien Willemsen	Assistant Professor of Administrative Law at Utrecht
Aleidus Woltjer	Assistant Professor of Constitutional and Administrative Law, Utrecht University

Summary of Contents

Table of Contents

List of Abbreviations

AB	Administratiefrechtelijke Beslissingen (Journal on Case Law)
AC	Law Reports Appeal Cases
ACER	Agency for the Cooperation of Energy Regulators
AFM	Autoriteit Financiële Markten (Financial Markets Authority)
ALL E.R.	All England Reports
ARSP	Archiv für Rechts- und Sozialphilosophie
AZR	Ausländerzentralregister
BEREC	Body of European Regulators for Electronic Communications
B.vE	Bundesgesetz über die verdeckte Ermittlung
BVerfG	Bundesverfassungsgericht
BverwGE	Bundesverwaltungsgericht
BImSchG	Bundes-Immissionsschutzgesetz
CBP	College Bescherming Persoonsgegevens
CC	Conseil constitionnel
CEBS	Committee of European Banking Supervisors
CEEP	European Centre of Employers and Enterprice Providing Public Service
CEIOPS	Committee of European Insurance and Occupational Pension Supervisors
CESR	Committee of European Securities Supervisors
CFI	Court of First Instance (Court of Justice EU)
CLA	Collective Labour Agreement
CLP	Current Legal Problems
CML.Rev.	Common Market Law Review
CLWP	Commission's Legislative and Work Programme
DNB	De Nederlandsche Bank
DPC	Data Protection Convention

DuD	Zeitschrift Datenschutz und Datensicherheit
EACH	European Association of Central Counterparty Clearing Houses
EC	European Commission
ECA	European Collective Agreement
ECJ	European Court of Justice
ECHR	European Convention of Human Rights
ECtHR	European Court of Human Rights
ECLAN	European Criminal Law Academic Network
ECR	European Court of Justice Reports
ECSA	European Community Shipowners Association
ECSDA	European Central Securities Depositories Association
EDPS	European Data Protection Supervisor
EEA	European Economic Area
EES	European Employment Strategy
EESC	European Economic and Social Committee
EGAOB	European Group of Audit Oversight Bodies
EIPA	European Institution of Public Administration
EJSB	Eurojust Joint Supervisory Board
EJSS	European Journal Social Security
ElRev	European Law Review
EP	European Parliament
ESC	European Social Charter
ESD	European Social Dialogue
ETF	European Training Foundation
ETUC	European Trade Union Confederation
EWC	European Works Council
FESE	Federation of European Securities Exchanges
FSA	Financial Services Authority
GALA	(Dutch) General Administrative Law Act
GG	Grundgesetz
HMSO	Her Majesty's Stationery Office
HRA	Human Rights Act
ICESCR	International Covenant on Economic, Social and Cultural Rights
IGC	Intergovernmental Conference
ILO	International Labour Organization
IWCFC	Interim Working Committee on Financial Conglomerates
JB	Jurisprudentie Bestuursrecht
JBPlus	Jurisprudentie Bestuursrecht Plus
JHA	Justice and Home Affairs
JIT	Joint Investigation Teams
LJN	Landelijk Jurisprudentie Nummer
M&M	Markt & Mededinging
MiFID	Markets in Financial Instruments
MoU	Memorandum of Understanding

NCA	National Competition Authority
NJ	Nederlandse Jurisprudentie
NJV	Nederlandse Juristen-Vereniging
NJW	Neue Juridische Wochenschrift
NRA	National Regulatory Authority
NTB	Nederlands Tijdschrift Bestuursrecht
NTER	Nederlands Tijdschrift voor Europees Recht
NVzW	Neue Zeitschrift für Verwaltungsrecht
NYR	Not Yet Reported
OECD	Organisation for Economic Co-operation and Development
OJ	Official Journal of the EC
OMC	Open Method of Coordination
OVG	Oberverwaltungsgericht
PJCC	Police and Judicial Cooperation in Criminal matters
QB	Law Reports Queen's Bench
REALaw	Review of European Administrative Law
SCE	European Cooperative Society (Societas Cooperativa Europaea)
SDC	Social Dialogue Committee
SE	European Company (Societas Europaea)
SEA	Single European Act
SEW	Tijdschrift voor Europees en economisch recht (Dutch Magazine)
SME	Small and Medium Enterprise(s)
SPA	Social Policy Agreement
TCN	Third Country National
TEC	Treaty of the European Communities
TEEC	Treaty on the European Economic Community
TEU	Treaty on the European Union
TFEU	Treaty on the Functioning of the European Union
TILEC	Tilburg Law and Economics Center
UEAPME	European Association of Craft, Small and Medium-sized Enterprises
UNICE	Union of Industrial and Employers' Confederations of Europe
VIS	Visa Information System
VwVfG	Verwaltungsverfahrensgesetz
Wash. and Lee L. Rev.	Washington and Lee Law Review
Wft	Wet op het financieel toezicht
WL	Westlaw
WLR	Weekly Law Reports
WPPJ	Working Party on Police and Justice
WRR	Wetenschappelijke Raad voor het Regeringsbeleid

Preface

For lawyers legality seems a very well known phenomenon, as it is a basic notion in many areas of law. It means that a particular rule or act has to be based on acts adopted by Parliament. Sometimes it even has a more specific meaning in specific areas of law.

In this study we studied legality, however, from a different perspective: that of the European Union, and, in more specifically, that of the multi-layered legal order. Is legality a useful concept in this perspective and what does it mean in this context?

Twenty-one outstanding legal scholars, most of them working at the Europa Institute of Utrecht University have studied and discussed this issue in the past three years. On 5 November 2009 the Europa Institute organized a conference on this topic on the basis of the papers which had so far been prepared.

Mark van Hoecke, University Professor of Legal Theory at the University of Gent; Linda Senden, Professor of European Law at the University of Tilburg; Arjen Meij, Visiting Professor at the Utrecht University (G.J. Wiarda chair); Stephen Weatherill, Jacques Delors Professor of European Community Law at the University of Oxford commented on the papers. These comments have been very useful for the finalization of this book. The organizers received a welcome grant from the Wiarda institute for the organization of this conference.

Finally we have to thank Fiona McGrath, PhD student at the School of Social and Political Science, University of Edinburgh who corrected mistakes in the language of the papers.

Utrecht, 29 September 2011

Leonard Besselink, Frans Pennings and Sacha Prechal

Part I
Introduction: Transformation

Chapter 1

Introduction: Legality in Multiple Legal Orders

Leonard Besselink, Frans Pennings & Sacha Prechal

1. PLURALITY OF LEGAL ORDERS

Public law in Europe is characterized by the simultaneity of multiple overlapping, colluding and competing norms and legal orders within single jurisdictions. In this collection of essays, we focus on the consequences that this has for the operation and concept of legality.

The simultaneity of multiple overlapping, colluding, competing and sometimes colliding norms and legal orders within single jurisdictions is most evident in the European Union (EU). The Member States are each based on national constitutional premises that are the foundation of their respective political and legal orders. The very aim and purpose of their membership is that these national legal orders participate in the broader legal order of the EU. It is, moreover, a condition of their membership that they also have formally and substantively bound themselves to observe the human rights standards contained in the European Convention of Human Rights, a treaty which the European Court of Human Rights has repeatedly referred to as 'a constitutional instrument of European public order'.

These three legal orders are mutually anchored: one cannot do without the other. Most Member State constitutions refer formally or substantively to the EU

Leonard Besselink, Frans Pennings & Sacha Prechal (eds), *The Eclipse of the Legality Principle in the European Union*, pp. 3–9.

to express the participation of their national constitutional orders in that of the EU. In turn, the Treaty of the EU has declared the constitutional principles of liberty, democracy, and the respect of human rights, which are common to the Member States, to be the foundation of the Union itself – principles which the Union is bound to respect.[1] The EU Treaty has now incorporated the Charter of Fundamental Rights into its primary sources, which makes it explicit that the EU institutions or the Member States must never fail to meet the substantive minimum European Convention on Human Rights (ECHR) standards, and also that EU fundamental rights must be interpreted in accordance with the rights common to the constitutional traditions of the Member States.[2] Moreover, the EU Treaty carries the obligation of formally acceding to the ECHR.[3]

While once upon a time the political order and liberty of citizens could largely be delimited in terms of legal orders that coincided with national boundaries, this is no longer the case. The very fact of EU membership implies that public decision-making no longer mainly takes place within the boundaries of the State political system, either in the national, regional or local contexts, but now also takes place in the multitude of EU arenas formed by the institutions and their political environments that impact directly on the national and sub-national contexts at which their decision-making is, in most cases, ultimately targeted.

2. LEGALITY IN EUROPE

These three legal orders have consequences for legality within Member States and each of them imposes requirements regarding legislation and legality. The reason for taking a closer look at legality as an object of study is twofold. Firstly, legality has played a central role in our understanding of the Rule of Law in Europe, and must be considered one of its pillars. Secondly, legality is rooted in the idea and concept of the nation-State as it arose in the French Revolution. Its importance as a principle at the basis of modern European States crucially hinged on the idea of the sovereignty of the nation and of the State embodying that nation.

Clearly, the nation-State is no longer the mainstay of political communities. This is not so much because of the fact that in few European States the nation and the State coincide (some important EU Member States are, to a greater or lesser extent, socially, culturally and linguistically multi-national States, and even States which ostensibly think of themselves as embodying a nation in a socio-cultural sense in reality have significant minorities in their midst, minorities which enjoy a constitutionally entrenched formal status). A much more important reason is

1. Previously Art. 6 (1) EU Treaty as interpreted by the ECJ in *Kadi* (Court of Justice 3 Sep. 2008, Joined Cases C-402/05 P and C-415/05 P), para. 303; now in Art. 2 EU Treaty, which expands the list of principles to 'the values of respect for human dignity, freedom, democracy, equality, the rule of law and respect for human rights, including the rights of persons belonging to minorities'.
2. Article 52(3) and (4) of the Charter.
3. Article 6(1) and (3) TEU.

precisely that EU membership has created a situation in which the State is no longer the only source of legality. Apart from other factors (such as the development of the Welfare State aimed at protecting citizens from welfare risks), it is the multiplicity of legal orders claiming simultaneous validity and application that has arguably contributed to the diminished role of the principle of legality. This, then, leads to the question of whether the principle of legality as a cherished foundation of the democratic State, based on the rule of law, has been eclipsed in the overlapping multiple legal orders of Europe. To what extent has legality as we knew it from within the State context been obscured behind and within other legal orders, especially the EU? What has been offered in return, and can that compensate for the functions and purposes which legality served?

Before we embark on the route towards answering such questions, we need to take a step back and make some introductory remarks regarding the concept of legality and its status as a constitutional principle common to the Member States of the EU. Firstly, it is not self-evident that legality is, at its core, a concept that is, common to the constitutional orders of the EU Member States. Secondly, we need to distinguish the various functions of the principle of legality, in particular the requirement that the exercise of public authority be based on an act of parliament. These functions are manifold. Confusing them can easily create misunderstandings when assessing the scope and meaning of current developments.

3. A CONSTITUTIONAL PRINCIPLE COMMON TO THE MEMBER STATES

First then, an introductory remark on the commonality of the notion of 'legality'. The notion of legality in public law is very much the product of the French Revolution. The *Déclaration des Droits de l'Homme et du Citoyen* of 1789 starts with the liberty of the citizens and declares that the limits imposed on liberty *ne peuvent être déterminé que par la Loi* (Article 4). This requirement is explained by that other fundamental tenet of the *Déclaration*:

4. *LA LOI EST L'EXPRESSION DE LA VOLONTÉ GÉNÉRALE*[4]

Based on ideas of popular sovereignty, legality has taken shape as a distinctly European concept: to be more precise, it has taken shape as a particularly continental European concept. In the UK the ideas of the French Revolution never took root, if only because Napoleon never passed by. This may explain why in the British constitutional doctrine there is no 'principle of legality' which prescribes that the exercise of public authority over citizens, whether in

4. The Act is the expression of the general will. Arts 4 and 6 of the *Déclaration*, which is still a valid part of the French Constitution via its preamble, on the basis of its interpretation by the *Conseil constitutionnel*, CC, 16 Jul. 1971, Decision no. 71-44 DC, *Liberté d'association*.

the form of administrative acts or as a form of binding regulation, requires a basis in an act of parliament. The idea of the common law, as established through the courts of law, has been too strong for there to be an articulation of a principle of legality in these terms. In the French Revolution, on the contrary, is was precisely the resistance against this lawmaking role of the courts that resulted in the articulation of the primacy of the legislature. And it is this, in continental legal orders, that gives the principle its fundamental constitutional nature, albeit with a different scope in different systems and particular branches of the law.

And yet the British courts and legal doctrine would fully assent to the principle that the liberty of citizens can only be restricted by act of parliament. It has been a fundamental tenet that the common law assumes the liberty of citizens. Indeed, for many decades this has been the very reason why the British have resisted the idea that they need to incorporate the bills of rights from human right treaties into national law, as this would be based on the false assumption that the liberty of British citizens depends on and extends no further than those bills of rights determine, which would contradict liberty as regulated by the common law. The constitutional basis of the idea of legality is not popular sovereignty, but the liberty as regulated by common law liberty and the doctrine of the sovereignty of Parliament.

This may go a long way to explaining why in British doctrine 'legality' does not quite have the specific and pregnant connotation it has had in continental Europe, but more easily dissolves into the broader notion of 'lawfulness' than in continental European understanding. We must, on the other hand, immediately add that in continental countries – and several contributions in this volume testify to this – it is precisely the multiplicity of legal sources of constitutional nature and rank which has made the idea of legality as embodied in the legislative decisions of the democratic representative bodies more relative. Many lawyers on the continent would argue that lawfulness is the prime category of the rule of law, not legality.

Be this as it may, for the purposes of this collection of essays we focus on legal developments with regard to the notion and principle of legality in Europe. As one of the contributions in this volume proves, this does not preclude its relevance for the United Kingdom, since all of the functions of the legality requirement are shared there with the rest of Europe.[5]

5. FUNCTIONS OF LEGALITY

We distinguish here three types of function of the concept of legality:

- the democratic function of *legitimating* the existence of public authorities, their powers and the exercise thereof within the limits of the set legal rules;
- the instrumental function of *attributing* public authorities with powers and responsibilities in line with preferences and the local situation, and in accordance with a prevalent distribution of powers;

5. See the contribution by Verhoeven, Willems and Jurgens in this volume.

- the normative function of *regulating* the use public authorities can make of such powers.

The *legitimating* function is highly prominent as the original function of legality. Starting off from the French Revolutionary idea of the sovereignty of the people, it went through different historical phases. One such phase is the German distinction between a substantive and formal concept of *Gesetz*, originating in the nineteenth century discussion on the nature of the relation between the Monarchy and Parliament in Prussia: when is the government empowered to act autonomously? What rules can it set? What is the power of Parliament in this respect? Can the government do without its cooperation? When does it need parliamentary authorization, and what things can Parliament only do in terms of setting the law? All these questions were discussed in nineteenth century Germany, and they still dominate the constitutional framework and practice of the EU Member States today, now a matter discussed in the context of EU legislative powers.[6] At least potentially, the matter has been complicated due to the fact that the sources of legislative authority derive legally from different legal orders, from the EU as well as from national institutions. This raises some intricate questions on the relationship between the legitimacy of legislative measures as they become operative in the national context but that originate from outside that context. Where does the power to exercise public authority come from? Who has legitimate power to perform legislative acts, and through these to create the basis for the exercise of public power over citizens?

The issue is closely connected with, but distinct from, the attributive function of the concept of legality – that the function of legislation is to designate the public authorities and determine which powers are attributed to them. It is this type of legislative act that makes for the legality of the exercise of such powers by public authorities. It articulates the basis of the authority, what the scope of the power is, and who can exercise it lawfully. It is through this function of legality that responsibility is allocated and, hence, it makes it possible for mechanisms of accountability to operate.

Legality also serves a normative, regulatory function in as much as it regulates the exercise of public authority. It creates legal certainty, and prevents arbitrariness and other forms of abuse of power. It makes the exercise of power foreseeable, and the requirement of a basis in enacted laws makes it possible in principle for citizens to create transparency.

The question of whether these various functions are still fulfilled by the principle of legality within legal orders, whether they are still operative in the context of the EU, and in the context of the overlapping, interacting and mutually dependent legal orders of Union and Member States, is at the background of all essays contained in this volume.

6. See Alexander Türk, *The Concept of Legislation in European Community Law: A Comparative Perspective* (The Hague: Kluwer, 2006).

6. STRUCTURE OF THE BOOK

The book is in five parts. This introductory chapter of Part I is followed by a contextual chapter of a theoretical nature (Chapter 2). Developments with regard to legality are determined not merely by one legal order influencing the other. Legality is too fundamental a concept to escape from other societal developments. One of these is the development of what has come to be known as the risk society. The authors illustrate the interdependency between social developments (risks) and legal developments (the changing perspectives on legality) through the prism of the principle of precaution as this is used in EU decision-making.

Among the prime functions of legality are the attribution of specific powers to public authorities and, next, the conditions under which these powers may be exercised. These are discussed in a variety of legal orders in Part II of this book. It starts with a contribution on the scope of the principle that the exercise of public authority must rest on an act of Parliament in Germany and the United Kingdom, countries with very different historical backgrounds as regards the concept and principle of legality (Chapter 3). The comparative look at two different national legal systems in the EU illustrates how different the issues already may be at national level

Chapter 4 discusses the attribution and regulation of powers across the EU and national legal orders and analyses the extent to which the EU can provide a legal basis for action of Member State authorities in the absence of such a basis within Member State legal orders. Chapter 5 looks more specifically at the position of independent regulatory authorities, an area that is, profoundly influenced by EU law and its interpretation by the European Court of Justice (ECJ). This (case) law has sparked off a lively debate on the constitutional position of independent 'regulators' and the tensions between European and national constitutional principles, the legality principle included.

Part III of the book contains three essays that focus on legality in relation to the qualitative requirements applying to legislation. Regulatory functions of legality are prominent in these three essays. Requiring a basis for the exercise of public authority can become an empty formality if the legal basis is mere an empty shell empowering any institution to make any legislation or exercise authority otherwise.

Chapter 6 (Woltjer) investigates the requirements that the case law of both the ECJ and the European Court of Human Rights imposes in this regard. The ECJ guarantees the observance of 'the law', as the EU Treaty puts it. The European Convention allows for restrictions to be provided 'by law'. In both cases this is a European concept that had to abstract from the concrete forms and status of legislation that exist in the European States that are a party to the Convention. Nevertheless, the case law analysed makes it clear that 'law' which affects and curbs the exercise of rights, including fundamental rights, must live up to substantive requirements.

Chapter 7 (Burri) is a case study of EU equality treatment legislation. This is a field of EU law which has had a primary impact on Member State law in the sensitive area of equal treatment. Starting from a more limited field of equal pay and sex discrimination, it has developed into an encompassing sector of EU law in which it has been necessary to come up with repeated attempts at codification and consolidation. This chapter looks into the question of whether the legislative results are coherent, as would be one of the main virtues of legality.

Chapter 8 (Jaspers and Meyers) also is a case study. It analyses the legislative quality, in terms of technical quality, transparency, legal certainty, enforceability and implementation of EC Directives in the field of workers' involvement.

Part IV of the book deals with legality and non-legislative instruments. Government of citizens and other private parties was, throughout the nineteenth century, conceived of as mainly a matter of legislation, and ideally in the form of commands and prohibitions. Newer forms of governance have been seeking alternative methods of seeking compliance to norms by its addressees. Often these are non-legislative, soft law instruments. Resorting to these instruments evidently raises questions on the impact these instruments have on the functions of and the requirements that ensue from the legality principle. Chapters 9 to 11 study in this context the so-called Open Method of Coordination, the Social Dialogue, and also the expanding use of supervisory agencies. The three contributions show, *inter alia*, how the use of these instruments may result in the extension of competences and may affect the quality of the provisions at issue, which, under certain circumstances, at least de facto if not de jure, impose obligations.

The fifth and last Part of the volume gathers contributions on mechanisms that, particularly at EU level, contribute to a more or less silent extension of powers. Chapter 12 looks into the matter of how the ECJ, through interpretation of a number of key concepts and by extending its own mandate, broadens the scope of EU law. This, in turn, often results in various forms of competence creep. The principle of attributed powers – which might be considered the counterpart of the principle of legality in the EU law context – is apparently not able to stop this process. Chapter 13 imports additional problems by concentrating on the law in the context of the areas of Freedom, Security and Justice, more particularly the consequences for public prosecution offices. The chapter shows, *inter alia*, that what is going on in relation to public prosecutors is a de facto harmonization and considerable impact on the national criminal justice systems. However, the legitimation of the process in particular is very weak. The last chapter (Chapter 14) takes the prominent role of the EU in the field of data protection as its focus and, more particularly, looks at the role of the principle of purpose limitation, the function of which is similar to legality in restricting the exercise of power, and in particular its erosion, thus providing public powers to expand.

Parallel to the extension of powers, the mechanisms of competence creep also seem to undermine the principle of legality and its attributive, regulatory and legitimizing functions. Due to the reality of multiple legal orders these processes also have an impact on national and sub-national levels, and at the end of the day, on private individuals.

This volume winds up with a concluding chapter providing a *synthesis and the main findings* concerning the main theme: the eclipse of legality in Europe.

Chapter 2

As Good as It Gets: On Risk, Legality and the Precautionary Principle

Ubaldus de Vries & Lyana Francot-Timmermans

1. INTRODUCTION

Legality offers legal certainty in the sense that it prohibits the exercise of arbitrary power. As an aspect of the rule of law it provides boundaries to the State's playing field (only if and when foreseen by law, the State may act). The Precautionary principle stipulates that the absence of scientific certainty is no reason not to act to prevent (environmental) harm. Here, uncertainty is the basis for action (in the end the Principle seeks to reduce uncertainty, but it is uncertain if the desired result is within reach). The Precautionary principle potentially expands the possible actions of the State. The certainty-uncertainty axis exposes a tension between legality and the Precautionary principle. It is this tension that is, subject to analysis in this contribution.

2. PATIENT ZERO

The world seemed to be relieved when the source of the Mexican flu virus could be traced; it was a cute ten-year-old Mexican child.[1] The relief had little to do with the

1. M. Lacey, 'From Edgar, 5, Coughs Heard around the World', *The New York Times*, 28 Apr. 2009, <www.nytimes.com/2009/04/29/world/americas/29mexico.html?_r=1>, 17 Nov. 2009.

Leonard Besselink, Frans Pennings & Sacha Prechal (eds), *The Eclipse of the Legality Principle in the European Union*, pp. 11–34.

cuteness of the boy and more to do with the fact that science was able to locate the source of the pandemic. It seemed that locating the source meant control over its spread. This is, of course, against better judgment. What the Mexican flu threat shows is our interdependency of a global scale. Across the world instances of the virus in humans were reported and all these instances were, in one way or the other, interrelated. The reactions were of a precautionary nature and rightly so. Nation-States – at least those who have the means – had antiviral medication produced in mass quantities and geared their researchers towards developing the antidote. Precautionary measures also entailed the quarantining of Mexicans who had flown abroad without showing any symptoms of the flu.[2] As if nationality alone could be a source of infection. Of course, it is not only viruses that become global. More typical of our contemporary society is globalization at a structural level, found not only in transport, trade, agriculture, tourism, but also in human rights, the war on terror, immigration and other areas.

It shows that processes of globalization are multidimensional and capture economic, political, cultural, social and legal dimensions. It puts a strain on the *raison d'être* of the modern State. This strain is not only related to territory and territorial boundaries, but perhaps more importantly, to the institutions such as the rule of law, that determine the playground of the modern State – a playground that can be bigger than its territory. These institutions both grant and curb the power of the State. Pivotal is the concept of legality as an aspect of the rule of law, or its European continental twin brother, *Rechtsstaat.* The rule of law is understood in this contribution as possessing four interrelated characteristics. It entails the aspect of legality, suggesting that power can only be legally exercised on the basis of rules that themselves have been formulated on the basis of a known procedure. This procedure refers to the second characteristic, which entails the democratic element. It suggests that the rule-making procedure is democratic and that those who make and/or apply the rules are democratically elected. The third characteristic refers to the distribution of this rule-based power among different institutions: legislative (the aforementioned rule-makers), executive and judicial powers. Finally, the contents of the rules are based upon, or stem from, certain fundamental values or organizing principles for society. These principles find expression first and foremost in human rights. These four characteristics of the rule of law are connected to the notion of the nation-State; from within the nation-State the concept of the rule of law was developed into the above four characteristics. This article puts a special emphasis on legality.

Although the nation-State still performs an important role on the world stage, globalization, in all its dimensions, not only puts a strain on the nation-State and its functions, but riddles it with uncertainties. Social theories that describe our contemporary age perceive these uncertainties in terms of global risks and fears, to an extent that these risks both contribute to and result from increasing global interdependencies – not only among States, but also among other social actors,

2. M. Lacey & A. Jacobs, 'Even as Fears of Flu Ebb, Mexicans Feel Stigma', *The New York Times*, 4 May 2009, <www.nytimes.com/2009/05/05/world/asia/05china.html>, 17 Nov. 2009.

such as organizations, groups and individuals.[3] Traditionally, law is an instrument that contributes to reducing uncertainty.[4] Law customarily addresses the problem of uncertainty by attributing responsibility or liability through employing a conditional normativity on the basis of an 'if... then...' formula. This requires linear causality. The problem – indeed, the central problem – of global risk is that linear causality cannot be established. This poses a problem for the law. This problem is tackled through the implementation of a contemporary version of the principle of *prudentia*, *viz.* the Precautionary principle.[5] Central to the Principle is the absence of legal causality as a condition for distributing responsibility. It may well be that the Precautionary principle contributes to solving the problem of uncertainty. As any principle of this kind comes with its own side effects, a fierce academic debate is ongoing.[6]

In this Chapter we are not concerned with the question of whether the Precautionary principle contributes in its application to resolving the contemporary problems encapsulated in the notion of modern risk. Rather, the article assumes that it does, but that it puts, as a side effect, the notion of legality under strain. It does so as it allows the withdrawal of legislative procedures from the requirements of legality and, hence, it allows the withdrawal of regulation and its application from parliamentary and legal control. In doing so, it defeats the very purpose of legality: to establish legal certainty in the relationship between citizens and State.

Uncertainty is a social phenomenon of all times, but what is new is our heightened awareness of how uncertainty may threaten our daily life. In contemporary society our heightened awareness of uncertainty is, amongst other things, expressed in our awareness of certain types of risks that threaten our daily lives and activities, such as those illustrated by past events – for example, the disasters in Bhopal, Chernobyl and, more recently, the train disaster in Viareggio, Italy. It is the concept of modern risk that will be our focus of attention in the remainder of this article. Indeed, the article starts with a societal diagnosis aiming to clarify the concept of modern risk in a globalizing world. The diagnosis builds upon the work of Beck, in particular his work on the risk society, the term he coined in 1986 in *Risikogesellschaft – Auf dem Weg in eine andere Moderne.*[7] The article then sketches the Precautionary principle as a response to the problem of risk and does so from a European legal perspective. It addresses the different interpretations of the Principle and the criticisms the Principle provokes. In the next section,

3. On the relevance of the different social actors in the world risk society, see also L. Francot & B. de Vries, 'No Way Out? Contracting about Modern Risks', ARSP 95 (2009): 199–215.
4. See N. Luhmann, *Law as a Social System*, trans. K.A. Ziegert (Oxford: Oxford University Press, 2004), 94.
5. C. Tinker, 'State Responsibility and the Precautionary Principle', in: *The Precautionary Principle and International Law – The Challenge of Implementation*, ed. D. Freestone & E. Hey (The Hague: Kluwer Law International, 1996).
6. See for example, D. Freestone & E. Hey (eds), *The Precautionary Principle and International Law – The Challenge of Implementation* (The Hague: Kluwer Law International, 1996).
7. U. Beck, *Risikogesellschaft – Auf dem Weg in eine andere Moderne* (Frankfurt am Main: Suhrkamp, 1986).

we analyse the extent to which the rule of law is under siege in the risk society, with a particular emphasis on the concept of legality. The article suggests that the concept of legality is not threatened by the nature of the risk society itself, but by the responses to the problem of risk, such as the Precautionary principle. More abstractly, the article suggests that legality as a modern concept addressing the problem of State power and subordination is ill-equipped to deal with the responses to contemporary social problems relating to the ecological environment and, by implication, the welfare and health of man and woman. It is this that this article seeks to highlight, with the aim of provoking a discussion as to how answers can be found with regard to the exercise of legality and to whom it applies in a globalize world in which the role of the modern State is changing profoundly.[8]

3. SOCIAL DIAGNOSIS: UNCERTAINTY IN A GLOBAL WORLD

The extensive world-wide legal debate[9] about the pros and cons of the Precautionary principle implies that the description of world society as a risk society, a description coined by Ulrich Beck as far back as 1986, is adequate and to the point. 'Risk society' does not merely pertain to the idea that we live in a society of risks, but also suggests a society consisting of global interdependencies on all levels of social action.[10] The central problem of the risk society gave – initially in Germany – rise to the development and application of *prudentia*, in the shape of the Precautionary principle in respect of environmental protection. The ensuing legal debate

8. See also J. Fulcher, 'Globalisation, The Nation-State and Global Society', *The Sociological Review* 48 (2000): 522–43.
9. The literature on the Precautionary principle is endless. The following texts are illustrative and include texts – (governmental) reports, books, articles – from different jurisdictions: C.R. Sunstein, *Laws of Fear – Beyond the Precautionary Principle* (Cambridge: Cambridge University Press, 2005); A. Trouwborst, Precautionary Rights and Duties of States, *Nova et Vetera Iuris Gentium Series* 25 (Leiden/Boston: Martinus Nijhoff Publishers, 2006) (content available online at <http://igitur-archive.library.uu.nl/dissertations/2006-0629-204021/full.pdf>); European Environment Agency, 'Late Lessons from Early Warnings: The Precautionary Principle 1896–2000 – Environmental Issue Report, no. 22' (Copenhagen: EEA, 2001); N. de Sadeleer, 'The Precautionary Principle in EC Health and Environmental Law', *European Law Journal* 12 (2006): 139–72; M.B.A. van Asselt & E. Vos, 'The Precautionary principle and the Uncertainty Paradox', *The Journal of Risk Research* 9 (2009): 313–36; E. Vos & G. van Calster (eds), *Risico en Voorzorg in de Rechtsmaatschappij* (Groningen/Antwerpen: Intersentia, 2004); WRR, *Onzekere Veiligheid – Verantwoordelijkheden rond Fysieke Veiligheid* (Amsterdam: Amsterdam University Press, 2008); R. Pieterman & T. Arnoldussen, 'Het Voorzorgsbeginsel: over Ideologie en Onzekerheid', *Rechtsfilosfie en Rechtstheorie* 37 (2008): 230–251; F.B. Cross, 'Paradoxical Perils of the Precautionary Principle', Wash. and Lee L. Rev. 53 (1996): 851–925; C.F. Cranor, 'Learning from the Law to Address Uncertainty in the Precautionary Principle', *Science and Engineering Ethics* 7 (2002): 313–327; P. Sandin, 'Dimensions of the Precautionary Principle', *Human and Ecological Risk Assessment* 5 (1999): 889–907; E. Fisher, 'Is the Precautionary Principle Justifiable', *Journal of Environmental Law* 13 (2001): 315–334.
10. U. Beck, *Cosmopolitan Vision* (London: Polity Press, 2006), 22 et seq.

has focused on (the application of) the Principle, underexposing to a certain extent this central problem, as it fails to address and analyse the structural features of the problem. For us, a proper understanding of these structural features is essential, as they determine the relationship between the Precautionary principle and the rule of law.[11] It demands first and foremost an analysis of the central problem: uncertainty, in particular uncertainty in terms of risk.[12]

3.1. The Processes of Modernization: Uncertainty and Scarcity

Ulrich Beck argues that the central problem of contemporary society is constituted by risk. Risk has existed in all ages, but Beck targets a new type of risk. This risk is distinguished from so-called traditional risk, such as adverse consequences that are the result of meteorological conditions, for example, crop failures. The potato-crop failure in Ireland in the nineteenth century is a striking example, leading to the dissemination of the population and mass emigration to the United States.[13] Traditional risk was perceived as risk of an exogenous character that we cannot control. This lack of control suggests that this kind of risk is not man-made but perceived as an Act of God or a manifestation of Mother Nature.

This man-made aspect is a central feature of modern risk. Beck presents modern risk as the side-effect of the processes of modernization. In doing so, Beck distinguishes between first and second modernity. First modernity is constituted by the fundamental belief in the notion of progress through reason. The belief in progress fuelled the twin processes of industrialization and democratization, addressing the twin problems of scarcity and tradition, and culminating – at least in Western Europe – in the industrial society and the Welfare State.[14] These processes were both situated in, and circumscribed by, the nation-State. The process of industrialization can be characterized as being concerned with the production of wealth through the technological application of science and scientific discoveries. The process of democratization served, among many other things, the just distribution of this wealth, as well as the emancipation of humans as autonomous individuals, freeing them from tradition and political subordination.

Law made important contributions in respect of the efficient production and distribution of wealth. It regulated production and distribution through rules based

11. Indeed; a reflexive understanding of law, demands a proper understanding of its environment, that is, society. See also L. Francot & U. de Vries, 'Legal Education Re-enchanted', *European Journal of Legal Education* 3 (2006): 3–20.
12. We present risk as a feature of uncertainty. For a deeper understanding of the notion of uncertainty and how it pertains to modern risk, see also L.M.A. Francot-Timmermans & U.R.M.T. de Vries, 'Normativity in the Second Modernity', *Rechtstheorie* 39 (2008): 477–494.
13. P. Gray, *The Irish Famine* (Paris: Gallimard, 1995); Ch. Kinealy *This Great Calamity: The Irish Famine 1845–52* (London: Gill and Macmillan, 1995).
14. See U. Beck, *The Reinvention of Politics* (London: Polity Press, 1997), 13 and U. Beck, *Risk Society – Towards a New Modernity*, trans. M. Ritter (London: Sage, 1992), 19 et seq.

on concepts such as the freedom to contract, ownership and possession, legal personality and liability. Law reflects and gives voice to the developing liberal theory of the time. This can also be observed in the role of the State. This role was, initially, a restricted one, and was concerned with allowing the market to function and with rights (to life, liberty and property) to be protected from internal and external threats. Indeed, law served to improve the position and power of the autonomous individual to which the recognition of civil and political rights attest, but it did so merely in a formal way. Like the market, the State too was subject to regulation, encapsulated in the notions of the rule of law and democracy. The sharp distinction between the private and the public resonates in the two main bodies of modern law, particularly so in continental Europe: private and public law. The concept of State sovereignty was the guiding force behind the development of modern international law.[15]

The distinction between the public and the private became blurred as a result of what is termed in the Netherlands, the '*Sociale Quaestie*'.[16] It denotes the extreme poverty and social immobility of the working classes across Europe during the late era of first modernity. This situation eventually gave rise to social democracy and culminated in the Welfare State.[17] Law, here, did not merely codify important concepts of first modernity into manageable rules, but was employed as a tool to give shape to society as prescribed by the State. It saw the rise of socio-economic rights, allowing an effective use of civil and political rights. It saw an extensive system of social security based on law, as well as the introduction of many legal measures that sought to protect the weaker party in all kinds of contractual agreements, that is, rental agreements, labour agreements, consumer and credit contacts, etc. In more abstract terms, one saw the juridification of an ever-increasing variety of social interaction, aiming to mould social interaction into a 'designed society' based upon, and subordinated by, rules. The early developments in respect of European integration can also be understood in terms of 'design', while at the same time contributing to the erosion of the concept of State sovereignty.

3.2. Second Modernity: Uncertainty and Risk

Second modernity can be characterized by the radicalization and transformation of the processes of industrialization and democratization. Beck characterizes this radicalization of contemporary society in the second modernity by reference to

15. See also D. Held, 'Law of States, Law of Peoples: Three Models of Sovereignty', *Legal Theory* 8 (2002): 3–4.
16. On the 'sociale kwestie', see amongst others, A. de Swaan, *In Care of the State – Health Care, Education and Welfare in Europe, and the USA in the Modern Era* (Oxford: Oxford University Press, 1988).
17. This phase is deemed a phase of the first modernity because the production and distribution of wealth remained the central feature.

the processes of 'forced individualization' and 'multidimensional globalization'.[18] The former refers to the perception that individualization is no longer or not only a matter of an individual choice, but is caused by developments and decisions that are not under the control of the individual. Multidimensional globalization refers to the idea that structural societal developments and the side effects they produce are global in nature. If, for instance, global free trade refers to the free movement of goods and services, it implies by necessity the free movement of its adverse side effects, for example, the spread of diseases such as bird flu or BSE. Globalization is not restricted to the economic dimension but also includes political, cultural and moral dimensions.

What this radicalization discloses is society's confrontation with self-produced side effects.[19] The nature of these side effects, which, in respect of industrialization Beck conceptualized in the notion of 'risk', causes him to speak of society as a 'world risk society'.[20] It confronts society in the second modernity with an additional fundamental problem. While first modernity was characterized by the problem of producing and distributing wealth, delineated by the borders of modern States, second modernity has to deal with the production and distribution of the side effects of wealth production and distribution that transcend the nation-State. Beck formulates this as follows:[21]

> How can the risks and hazards systematically produced as part of modernization be prevented, minimized, dramatized, or channelled? When do they finally see the light of day in the shape of 'latent side effects', how can they be limited and distributed away so that they neither hamper the modernization process nor exceed the limits of that which is 'tolerable' – ecologically, medically, psychologically and socially?

3.3. The Nature of Modern Risk

In Beck's view 'risk' has become or will become the new fundamental distribution problem, complementing the distribution problem of first modernity. The latter problem is resolved, at least in the affluent West, within the nation-State by means of the economic notion of the free market and the political notions of rule of law and democracy, as was shown above. Societies are now transforming from

---

18. U. Beck & E. Grande, *Das Kosmopolitische Europa* (Frankfurt am Main: Suhrkamp, 2004) 50.
19. Indeed, as Francot (one of the authors of this chapter) observes, the second paradigm shift in social systems theory introduced the concept of 'self-referentiality' into societal theory. This introduction demarcates a break with the occidental tradition in which the ability of reflection was a privilege of human beings or 'subjects'. This string of thought also attributes the ability of reflection to complex, non-living systems, such as society. In L. Francot-Timmermans, *Normativity's Re-entry – Niklas Luhmann's Social Systems Theory: Society & Law* (Nijmegen: Wolf Publishers, 2008), 29.
20. U. Beck, *Cosmopolitan Vision* (Cambridge: Polity Press, 2006) 22 & 34. See also U. Beck, *World Risk Society* (Cambridge: Polity Press, 1999).
21. U. Beck, *Risk Society*, 19. see n. 14

industrial societies of States towards an integrated and interdependent world risk society. The nature or characteristics Beck ascribes to modern risk illustrate this transformation.

3.3.1. Characteristics

Risk is self-produced and self-inflicted systematically, exactly because it is a side effect of industrialized activity, that is, systemized wealth production. This suggests, in terms of responsibility, that modern (Western) society itself is responsible for the production of modern risk. The effects are not so limited. Risk lies in the future – often in the present of next generations – and is immanently global. The second feature of modern risk is its 'global' character. It may well be that risk is produced locally (and thus everywhere), but its effects are global as well as local.[22] The third feature is the existence of unequal social risk positions. People are affected by risk in different ways. Some can protect themselves against risk or at least be able to minimize their effects, whilst others are at the mercy of risk. This seems to mirror the division of traditional class society, but as risk is global, the differentiation of social positions is global too, taking place among, within and across nation-States.[23] The 'globality' of risk implies, furthermore, that in terms of the distribution problem, distribution cannot be achieved within the borders of a nation-State alone, but must also be global. The distribution of risk is a global problem foretelling a new and global '*Verelendung*'. A fourth feature of modern risk is its invisibility. Risk cannot be seen, heard, felt, tasted or smelled. Modern risk is a construction of scientific knowledge and exists in chemical and mathematical formulae or simply in ideas and suppositions. It implies that those in scientific and political key positions can determine what the risks are. Consequently, if something is not defined as such, it is not deemed to be a risk. It also remains problematic to determine when and how the effects of risk materialize, if ever, and to what extent. It merely exists in probabilities and estimations – in uncertainty. In the end, risk binds the future to the present without us being able to determine, but in vague terms, cause and effect. Indeed, a final feature Beck attributes to risk refers to the problem of causality and, hence, the problem of responsibility, as causality is always considered to be a key aspect of responsibility. The problem is that it becomes increasingly more difficult to determine what actions of which actors cause which effects; it becomes increasingly more difficult to determine causality in the production of risk (and its effects) and, hence, to determine who is to be held responsible and why. Although one may conclude that the whole of Western society is responsible, it is of no use in respect of the

22. If globalization refers to the free transfer of goods throughout the world, it implies also the global transfer of risk. Illustrative in this respect are the recent crises in food products, such as the BSE crisis and the bird flu crises. The effect of risk though – its materialization – may be local again: the individual who gets infected somewhere, say in the South-East of Turkey. Thus, risk exists in global threats & local manifestations.

23. Contrary to Beck, we suggest that risk exacerbates this differentiation rather than having an equalizing effect, see : L. Francot & B. de Vries 'No Way Out', 205, see n. 3.

distribution problem. In the end, risk is the result of organized irresponsibility. Or, following Beck:[24]

> Corresponding to the highly differentiated division of labor [*sic*], there is a general complicity, and the complicity is matched by a general lack of responsibility. Everyone is cause and effect, and thus non-cause. [. . .] This reveals in exemplary fashion the ethical significance of the system concept: one can do something and continue doing it without having to take personal responsibility for it.

To sum up: modern risk, which is, by its nature systematically man-made and self-inflicted, is global in its reach and invisible sensorily, leading to unequal social risk positions and resulting both in and from organized irresponsibility due to weak causality. One final characteristic of risk is the magnitude of its manifestation in the shape of disasters, catastrophes and calamities as shown, for example, by the Chernobyl-disaster, the catastrophe in Bhopal and the BSE crisis in the UK.

3.3.2. The Problem of Risk

Second modernity is faced with the question of how to deal with risk. Contrary to wealth, risk as such cannot be distributed because it is invisible aside from existing as scientific formulae. Part of the solution is found in the attribution of responsibility for risk and for the consequences of risk when it materializes in the shape of a disaster, for example. Law is immanently able to attribute responsibility – this is what it does. Another part of the solution lies in the attempt to prevent or minimize the production of risk. Considering the characteristics of modern risk, this is a difficult task. The Precautionary principle can be understood, however, as providing the framework for legal responses to this problem, attempting to distribute modern risk through minimizing its production by means of a normative judgment in the absence of conclusive scientific evidence about its acceptance. This is how the legal system may deal with the 'scientific deficit' in respect of modern risk. As the legal system has to act within the framework of an informational void, it puts legality under strain because power can only be exercised on the basis of rules, and the formulation and application of rules require information for them to be effective and legitimate. To understand the nature of this strain, a closer analysis of the Precautionary principle is demanded.

4. THE PRECAUTIONARY PRINCIPLE

The Precautionary principle can be regarded as a modern interpretation of the notion of *prudentia*, which, in its essence, means that when acting or making decisions, caution should be exercised. One of the first modern interpretations can be found in Germany as a way of dealing with industrial threats to the

---

24. U. Beck, *Risk Society*, 31 (emphasis in the original). See n. 14.

environment. In particular, Germany endorsed the Principle in respect of clean air as early as 1974.[25] In other national jurisdictions explicit reference to the Principle is also made. In Belgian law, the Precautionary principle has been adopted in respect of the protection of the maritime environment in the seas within the Belgian jurisdiction.[26] In the UK, the Principle is found in policy documents on sustainable development.[27] In France, legislation invokes the Precautionary principle quite explicitly in order to protect the natural environment.[28] In the US, the Precautionary principle has been applied in legislation banning, for example, animal carcinogens in foodstuffs and the use of chlorofluorocarbons.[29,30]

4.1. Global and European Context

In this Chapter we seek to concentrate on the adoption of the Principle on the global and European stage, in respect of environmental protection and preservation, and (also by implication) public health and safety. We do so as we are, amongst other things, concerned with the impact of globalization on legality that is, traditionally a State-bound principle. As risk constitutes a global phenomenon it demands a global response. There are numerous examples of international treaties endorsing the Principle.[31] Perhaps the ones that resonate most are the Rio Declaration and, in Europe, the EC Treaty. They illustrate this global response and illustrate what could be termed the 'globalization of law'. Principle 15 of the Rio Declaration states:[32]

> In order to protect the environment, the precautionary approach shall be widely applied by States according to their capabilities. Where there are threats of serious or irreversible damage, lack of full scientific certainty shall not be used as a reason for postponing cost-effective measures to prevent environmental degradation.

---

25. 'Clean Air Act, 1974' (original: Bundes-Immissionsschutz-Gesetz (BIMSchG), 1974).
26. B.S. 12 maart 1997. *Wet van 20 januari 1999 ter bescherming van het maritieme leefmilieu in de zeegebieden onder de rechtsbevoegdheid van België* (Art. 4).
27. Department of the Environment, *UK Strategy on Sustainable Development* (London: HMSO, 1990) and Department of the Environment, *Better Quality of Life: A Strategy for Sustainable Development* (London: HMSO, 1994).
28. See for example, Loi no. 95–101, 2 Février 1995, relating to the reinforcement of the protection of the environment (Loi Barnier). In 2005, the French Parliament passed the *Chartre de l'environnement*, in which the Precautionary principle is laid down in Art. 5.
29. See for an overview, EEA, 'Late Lessons from Early Warnings', 11–12, see n. 9
30. In the Netherlands the Precautionary principle does not feature explicitly in Dutch environmental law. It is introduced through European legislation; see: N. Teesing, R. Uylenburg & C. T. Nijenhuis, *Toegang tot het Milieurecht*, 5th ed. (Den Haag: Kluwer, 2009) 15. However, policy is informed by the Principle, for example, in respect of electromagnetic fields in mobile phone transmitters; see: TK 2008–2009, 27.562, no. 37 (parliamentary report). Furthermore, the Principle has been subject to a governmental study: WRR, *supra* n. 9.
31. EEA, *supra* n. 29, 14.
32. 'Rio Declaration on Environment and Development' (New York: UN, 1992) <www.un.org/documents/ga/conf151/aconf15126-1annex1.htm>, 18 Nov. 2009.

The Principle is also endorsed by the European Commission as an 'essential policy instrument'.[33] Furthermore, it has been codified in the Treaty on the Functioning of the European Union (TFEU) Treaty in Article 191, paragraph 2:

> Community policy on the environment shall aim at a high level of protection taking into account the diversity of situations in the various regions of the Community. It shall be based on the Precautionary principle and on the principles that preventive action should be taken, that environmental damage should as a priority be rectified at source and that the polluter should pay.

In Article 191 the Precautionary principle is explicitly named as an instrument to deal with risks that pose a threat to the environment. Paragraph 1 provides that Union policy in respect of the environment must contribute to pursuing at least four objectives: preserving, protecting and improving the quality of the environment, protecting human health, prudent and rational utilization of natural resources, and promoting measures at international level to deal with regional or worldwide environmental problems. The Principle can be traced elsewhere too, albeit implicitly, for example, in the area of public health and consumer safety.[34]

Article 192 suggests that the Precautionary principle is a guiding principle for the Council in its legislative capacity rather than being a directing principle for Member States when developing and drafting environmental policy and legislation.[35] Nevertheless, any legislation emanating from the Council overrides national legislation,[36] effectively imposing the Precautionary principle at the national level across the European Union (EU). To be more precise, directing principles of the EC Treaty do not apply directly to Member States, or so it is said. Nevertheless, according to De Sadeleer, this must be nuanced, taking into account whether areas are subject to secondary legislation and/or whether these areas are harmonized.[37] He sums it up stating that, 'as a general principle, the precautionary principle binds the Member States in so far as they act within the scope of EU law'.[38]

---

33. More generally, the Precautionary principle is understood as a policy instrument or guideline. See for example, K. von Moltke, 'The Relationship between Policy, Science, Technology, Economics and Law in the Implementation of the Precautionary Principle', in: D. Freestone & E. Hey (eds), *supra* n. 6, 106.
34. See Arts 168 and 169 TFEU.
35. See also S. Lierman, 'Het Voorzorgsbeginsel en Gezondheidsbescherming, Oude Wijn in Nieuwe Zakken?' in: *Risico en Voorzorg in de Rechtsmaatschappij*, ed. E. Vos & G. van Calster (Groningen/Antwerpen: Intersentia, 2004), 53.
36. See Case 6/64, *Costa/ENEL* [1964] ECR 585.
37. N. de Sadeleer, *Implementing the Precautionary principle – Approaches from the Nordic Countries, the EU and the USA* (London: Earthscan, 2007), 14.
38. *Ibid.*, citing J. Scott, 'The Precautionary Principle before the European Courts', in: Principles of European Environmental Law, ed. R. Macrory (Groningen: Europa Law Publishing, 2004) 54. A recent paper suggests that the Principle is evolving towards a rule; see: E.C. Fisher, 'Opening Pandora's Box: Contextualising the Precautionary principle in the European Union', in: *Uncertain Risks Regulated: National, EU and International Regulatory Models Compared*, ed. E. Vos, M. Everson & J. Scott (London: Cavendish, 2009), 21–46.

4.2. The Precautionary Principle in the Literature

The above descriptions of the Precautionary principle are definitions that present the Principle as a guideline for policymakers and law makers on how to deal with developments in the field of environmental pollution, food safety, nanotechnology, etc. Indeed, the Rio Declaration refers to it as an 'approach'.[39] The essential feature is the scientific uncertainty about risk – the presence of a scientific deficit of full certainty. A more general description of the Precautionary principle, stressing this point, is found in the academic literature.[40] A concise description is the one given by Fisher, stating that it is:[41]

> A principle that in cases where there are threats to human health or the environment the fact that there is scientific uncertainty over those threats should not be used as the reason for not taking action to prevent harm.[42]

Indeed, the literature stresses scientific uncertainty as an important feature, if not the distinguishing feature of the Principle. Freestone, for example, refers to the Precautionary principle as an innovative principle because it changes the role of scientific data. He repeats the adage that taking regulatory measures should not be obstructed by the absence of scientific evidence about the effects of such activities if there is a threat of environmental damage.[43] Another feature that is, stressed by Freestone is that the Principle allows the use and application of a wide variety of measures, rather than dictating a particular measure. Indeed, he makes the point that the Principle can be characterized as '*addressing the manner in which policy makers for purposes of protecting the environment, apply science, technology and economics*'.[44] To this end, the Principle is goal-oriented: preventing harm, either to the environment, as Freestone states, or otherwise, such as with public health or food safety. It suggests the Principle to be understood as a duty to take precautionary action, avoiding risk from occurring or, alternatively, to prevent risks from materializing in real damage. Similarly, Tinker suggests that in practice the Principle can be regarded as implying 'a substantive duty of care which requires

39. Some suggest that there is a difference between the Precautionary principle and the precautionary approach and that this difference lies in a more flexible application when referred to as 'approach'; see: S. Marr, *The Precautionary principle in the Law of The Sea – Modern Decision Making in International Law* (The Hague: Kluwer, 2003), 17 et seq.
40. For a more extensive overview, see: O. Renn, *Risk Governance: Coping with Uncertainty in a Complex World* (London: Earthscan, 2008), 78 et seq.
41. Fisher (2001) *supra* n. 9, 316.
42. An even more general definition would merely speak of threats: 'A principle that in cases where there is a threat the fact that there is scientific uncertainty over the threat and its consequences should not be used as a reason for not taking action to prevent possible harm.'
43. David Freestone cited in P. Birnie, A. Boyle & C. Redgwell, *International Law and the Environment*, 3rd ed. (Oxford: Oxford University Press, 2008), 155.
44. D. Freestone & E. Hey 'Origins and Development of the Precautionary Principle', in: D. Freestone & E. Hey (eds), *supra* n. 6, 12.

undertaking environmental impact assessments or other regulatory investigations prior to permitting given actions'.[45]

It is the 'vagueness' of what the Principle demands that causes the literature to also be concerned with how strong or weak the Precautionary principle is in official formulations, such as treaties and other legislative instruments. Whether the Principle is formulated weakly or strongly has an impact upon what precisely it expects regulators to do and in which areas the Principle could or should apply. There seems to be some form of consensus in the literature that considers the Precautionary principle to be a weak principle,[46] a guiding principle.[47] This weak-strong axis is important in the context of this Chapter as it suggests a parallel with legality. The manner in which the Principle is formulated (strong-weak) suggests the extent to which it can, in its application, meet the demands of legality, or, indeed, can undermine these demands, creating more room for arbitrary State intervention. In this sense, Nollkaemper suggests that in the application of the Principle a balance must always be found between, for example, as he does, ecological and economic interests:[48]

> The absolute objective of the Precautionary principle should not be pursued blindly and unconditionally. At times, risks that threaten environmental interests may be a price worth paying to serve other environmental or societal interests.

It is this balancing act which is our focus: how can, in the application of the Precautionary principle, a balance be struck between meeting environmental and other such concerns and meeting the demands of legality? It suggests first, that a further analysis into the legal status of the Precautionary principle is needed.

4.3. The Legal Status of the Precautionary Principle

The discussion about the Principle being weak or strong relates to the legal status of the Principle. How should we interpret the Principle in legislative terms? It implies a variety of questions. One is, in respect of Article 15 of the Rio Declaration, the extent to which States are bound to use and apply the Precautionary principle. Some suggest that the Precautionary principle, at least under the Rio Declaration, enjoys the status of a rule of customary international law. It is formulated in obligatory terms and is widely endorsed by States around the world and is applied or adopted by many (other) international organizations as a matter of policy as well as a matter of law, considering the adaptation of the Principle in treaties and other such texts.[49]

---

45. C. Tinker, *supra* n. 5, 55.
46. *Ibid.*, 57.
47. See also Sunstein, *Laws of Fear*, 23 et seq., see n. 9.
48. A. Nollkaemper, 'What You Risk Reveals What You Value', and Other Dilemmas Encountered in the Legal Assaults on Risks', in: D. Freestone & E. Hey (eds), *supra* n. 6, 73.
49. P. Birnie, *supra* n. 43, 159–160.

In the absence of a wide consensus about what exactly the Principle demands, though, the Precautionary principle cannot be understood as a hard-and-fast legally binding rule. Indeed, Birnie et al. suggest that it is 'far from evident that the precautionary approach [...] has or could have the normative character of the rule of law'.[50] They give a number of plausible reasons. One is that it is far from certain what the meaning of the Principle is, or its application and consequences in order to consider it as rule of international law. Furthermore, it has not been endorsed as such by major courts, such as the International Court of Justice or the Court of Justice of the European Community. Indeed, the latter refers to it as a legal principle. This is, Birnie et al. continue,[51] also reflected in the very general terms in which the Principle is formulated, only stating that scientific uncertainty is not an excuse for complacency. More is needed to turn a general rule of conduct into a legal rule. Others agree, arguing that State practice makes it evident that the Precautionary principle is a principle of customary international law.[52] Yet others consider the Principle rather to be a matter of soft law and not even a principle of international law.[53]

Is it merely a matter of semantics or is the distinction important? We consider the distinction and representation of the Principle as either a rule of law, a principle of law or a matter of soft law important. As a principle, it allows States and other legal actors to justify policy decisions that may go against, for example, traditional economic interests. Indeed, the Principle, in this way, echoes how actors use – strategically or otherwise – other global principles such as the principle of sustainable development.[54] The principle, so used as an expression of an aspiration, cannot be but a principle one ought to agree with. In this context the Precautionary principle '*does have a legally important core on which there is international consensus*'.[55] The Precautionary principle forms the basis for action, both politically and legally. To this end, it may be relied upon by decision makers and courts as an imperative for action (to protect/prevent/remedy). When we consider the Precautionary principle in this way, surely it has consequences that impact upon legality.

One consequence is, as noted by Birnie et al., that the Principle allows for the redefining of existing rules of law for them to play a different role. One example is that the Principle allows that there is no longer a need to prove causality – there is no need to prove that real damage would otherwise occur – in order to take preventive action. The mere possibility (rather than probability) of damage suffices to demand action. Hence, the identification of risk is enough to demand action or, to formulate it differently, allows States and other international legal organizations to take action.[56] And the more politically explosive these risks are, the more

50. *Ibid.*, 160–161
51. *Ibid.*
52. See: J. Cameron & J. Abouchar, 'The Status of the Precautionary Principle in International Law', in: D. Freestone & E. Hey (eds), *supra* n. 6, 30.
53. See: C. Tinker, *supra* n. 5, 53.
54. P. Birnie, *supra* n. 43, 163.
55. *Ibid.*
56. See also D. Freestone & E. Hay, *supra* n. 44, 13.

discretion States assume to deal with such risks. Indeed, Tinker goes as far as to suggest that a reactive model (after a damage occurring event) of distributing responsibility no longer suffices to sufficiently safeguard global environmental interests, and that a preventative model is necessary, of which the Precautionary principle forms an important cornerstone.[57] The suggestion that the Precautionary principle puts legality under strain will be the subject of a more detailed analysis below. Before doing so, the article sketches what the authors assume legality to mean and how the concept fits in within the general or overriding concept of the rule of law.

5. LIBERTY AND THE RULE OF LAW

Beck, as was described above, distinguishes between two phases within the process of modernization: first and second modernity. First modernity formulated answers to the problem of scarcity and (political) subordination and saw in the twin-processes of industrialization and democratization the solutions to these problems. Liberty and the rule of law can be regarded as two of the organizing principles that underscore the process of democratization. Indeed, our understanding of the rule of law pertains to our understanding of liberty.[58] Liberty qualifies State power.[59]

The modern concept of liberty suggests, as a point of departure, that the State is not to meddle in the private affairs of citizens unless their actions cause harm, that is, real (physical) damage to life, liberty and possessions. Indeed, the harm principle, as perhaps the expression of liberal thought, qualifies the rule of law as a functional principle. The rule of law is not merely an expression of the idea that (State) power cannot be exercised arbitrarily, but the subordination of power to rules is functional:[60] it allows individual liberty as the fundamental organizing principle of early modern society. Legality is, in our view, the pivotal element of the rule of law and is embedded within this concept together with three other fundamental elements of modern society: democracy, separation of powers and respect for human rights. Hence, we employ a so-called '*thick*' description of the rule of law.[61]

---

57. See: C. Tinker, *supra* n. 5, 54.
58. See also R. Unger, *Law in Modern Society* (Washington: Free Press, 1976), referring to society as a voluntary association.
59. The harm principle may be regarded as an expression of this qualification as expounded by its main proponent John Stuart Mill; see: J.S. Mill, *On Liberty* (London: Parker and Son, 1859) 22. See also K.K. Jensen, 'The Moral Foundation of the Precautionary Principle', *Journal of Agriculture and Environmental Ethics* 15 (2002): 39–55.
60. See also A.V. Dicey, *An Introduction to the Study of the Law of the Constitution* (London: Macmillan, 1885).
61. See also B.Z. Tamanaha, 'A Concise Guide to the Rule of Law', in: *Re-locating the Rule of Law*, ed. G. Palombella & N. Walker (Oxford: Hart Publishers, 2008), 3–16. Indeed, within the literature there is an intense discussion about how to describe and characterize the rule of law. See for example, the first issue of the newly established *Hague Journal on the Rule of* Law,

The principle of legality suggests that State power can only be legally exercised on the basis of rules (legislation) that themselves have been formulated on the basis of a known procedure laid down in rules. Furthermore, legality demands legislation that be general, clear and precise, promulgated, prospective, practicable and stable in that it lasts and serves the notion of legal certainty.[62] Thus, legality, according to us, implies a procedural aspect as well as formal characteristics. The former establishes a legal basis to the exercise of power. The latter refers to certain qualitative criteria that legislation must possess. These 'Fuller-criteria', so to speak, encapsulate this aspect, in particular with regard to legislation that pertains to regulate the relationship between citizen and State.

Legality, in respect of its formal or procedural aspect, ties in with the democratic element. This element suggests that the rule-making procedure is democratic and that those who make and/or apply the rules are democratically elected. Thus, legislation is subject to a parliamentary procedure through which the proposed piece of legislation is discussed, debated, and if necessary, amended, before it is voted upon by a majority. It provides legislation legitimacy. Even more so because those who have decided democratically upon the legislation are themselves democratically elected. Collectively, by deciding upon the legislation, they delegate, as it were, the executive the power to execute the law. They even may delegate law-making powers to the executive to enable it to execute the law – so-called secondary legislation. The distinction between primary and secondary legislation will discussed below in more detail.

The third element refers to this delegation/distribution of this rule-based power among different institutions. Rule-makers delegate executive powers, formulated in the rules, to the executive, who they can hold to account for the manner in which they execute policy on the basis of that legislation. The judiciary can also be delegated this task under a system of judicial review, enabling individual complainants to seek redress if and when the executive function harms their interests. This institutional differentiation can be regarded as a strict separation of powers, as suggested by Montesquieu in his *L'Esprit de Lois* or, in a more contemporary understanding, it can be regarded as a system of checks and balances, allowing institutions to share power and/or to subject themselves to each others' control and supervision. Indeed, such an elaborate system of controlling power may be of more benefit than simply relying on the democratic element alone.

Finally, the contents of the rules are based upon, or stem from, certain fundamental values or organizing principles of the nation-State society. These principles find expression in, among others things, human rights and emanate from the liberal spirit that the thicker version of the rule of law exudes. The principles suggest that States exercise their power with respect for, and in furtherance of, civil political and socio-economic rights respectively. It means that

---

in particular, R. Peerenboom, 'The Future of Rule of Law: Challenges and Prospects for the Field', *Hague Journal on the Rule of Law* 1 (2009): 5–14.

62. See L.L. Fuller, *The Morality of Law*, revised ed. (New Haven: Yale University, 1969), in particular Ch. 2.

the exercise of State power is not only subjected to rules to prevent abuse, but that it is also instrumental/functional in that it should promote these human rights, both through non-interference and promotion.

6. BALANCING TWO PRINCIPLES

The above functional interpretation of the rule of law assumes that the rule of law served to address the problems of first modernity, as described by Beck. The question arises as to whether the rule of law can serve this function in respect of the responses, encapsulated in the Precautionary principle, to the problems of contemporary society in second modernity (the problem of modern risk). We observe a tension between the Precautionary principle as a response to the contemporary problem of modern risk, and the principle of legality that seeks to prevent the arbitrary use of State power (however functional/instrumental the exercise of that power may be). As a matter of extreme position, the question could be: what has priority? Is it legality or ecological survival? Or could the two be reconciled in one way or the other? A number of options present themselves. However, before addressing these options, we first seek to return to what, in our view, is the bottom line of the two principles at stake; what is the primary function of the principle of legality and precaution?

6.1. Regulating Relations

The primary function of legality refers to the relationship it seeks to regulate. The relationship is the one that exists between the citizen and the State or, in more general terms, legality regulates the relationship between those in power and those subjected to that power. In modern Western States the principle of legality protects the citizen against the arbitrary use of power, or, more precisely, it demands a legal basis (which by itself must be of a certain standard) to legitimize State action. In this way, legality provides certainty for citizens as to, for example, the distinction between the public and the private sphere and the certainty that if power is exercised, it is legitimate or, at least, its legitimacy can be challenged, for example, through judicial review proceedings. Hence, legality transforms the uncertainty of arbitrariness into the certainty of legitimate power. This in itself does not curb the field of play of power. In this way, legality is what could be termed a procedural instrument to curb power; it does not, however, make clear what the contents of the rules ought to be, upon which power can be exercised. The contents of these rules have, on the whole, liberal roots, of which the harm principle is exemplary when it comes to defining the relationship between State and citizen.[63]

63. The harm principle justifies as well as limits State interference also in respect of interaction among citizens.

The harm principle, in its essence, suggests that man is free in his actions only insofar he does not harm others. At least this is the version as espoused by one of its main proponents, John Stuart Mill: '*that the only purpose for which power can be rightfully exercised over any member of a civilized community, against his will, is to prevent harm to others*'.[64] It is a liberal principle that allows the organization, through law, of social relations, in particular there where damage ensues or could ensue; it allows the attribution of responsibility on the basis of linear causality *ex post facto*. Indeed, most civil liability regimes across Western societies use the harm principle as their point of departure. Furthermore, in addition to regulating private relations between citizens, the harm principle allows also States to interfere when damage ensues, or it is likely that damage will ensue, from the action of one or more if the State does not interfere. It coincides with the *raison d'être* of the State: to provide security and safety for its citizens. To this end, the harm principle is a negative duty on the part of the State: a duty not to interfere unless there is a real likelihood of damage, and this interference, by virtue of the principle of legality, must be based on law.[65]

This description of the harm principle shows that the Precautionary principle seems, in many ways, a pendant or reinterpretation of the harm principle.[66] It, too, demands action of the State to prevent real damage from occurring. The difference though, is, it is suggested, that the Precautionary principle entails a positive duty in the absence of a real likelihood of damage. Indeed, it demands action in the absence of linear causality. Whereas the harm principle places an emphasis on liberty, the Precautionary principle emphasizes the need for (collective) security and protection against dangers that are not easily proven, but rather presumed. It may even be argued that, contrary to the harm principle, the Precautionary principle is ill-equipped to prevent the exercise of arbitrary State power. Indeed, the literature, discussed above, seems to suggest that the Precautionary principle applies without reference to the demands of legality. Would this imply that in the application of the Precautionary principle legality has become an outdated concept?

6.2. AN OUTDATED CONCEPT?

Thus, one option is to conclude that the requirement of legality is an outdated one. This may seem an outrageous statement, but not if one considers the complexity of

64. Mill, *supra* n. 59, 22.
65. To note: we do not suggest that the harm principle remains the only guidance for legitimate state intervention. State intervention is rationalized on many other grounds, such as the offence principle (Feinberg), paternalism (Dworkin) or the maintenance of some public morality (Lord Devlin). An elaborate analysis of these positions is provided in F. Schauer & W. Sinnott-Armstrong, *Philosophy of Law – Classic and Contemporary Readings with Commentary* (Oxford: Oxford University Press, 2002), Ch. 4 in particular. The point here is that the harm principle serves as a counterpoint for the precautionary principle in order to illustrate its primary function.
66. Linking harm with precaution, see also Jensen, *supra* n. 59, 39–55.

society with which law is confronted, both in qualitative and quantitative terms. There is an ever-increasing development to (super) specialization and differentiated expertise in an attempt to foresee everything and make it subject to regulation. This is no longer a realistic option (if it ever was).[67] This is particularly the case in respect of ecological problems presented as risks: uncertain future events with uncertain consequences. However, considering the huge ecological problems contemporary society has generated, action is demanded, which cannot be stalled or prevented by considerations as to how power ought to be exercised. At least this could be the argument. Too much is at stake and the general welfare of all is served rather than the interests of a political elite. There seems to be an implicit understanding in the literature that attributes environmental interests (preventing environmental destruction and threats to public health and safety) a higher priority than the interests legality seeks to serve (preventing the abuse of power for the sake of individual liberty and freedom of choice). Perhaps this consensus of prioritization is understandable, as it seems that we are confronted with a simple choice: liberty or ecological survival of the planet and its humanity. The choice is simple, as the first is useless without the second. Although this polarization may enjoy some intuitive appeal, it carries with it the danger that it makes the problem of risk the sole problem of contemporary society or, alternatively, that it conveniently transforms all problems into problems of ecological risk, rather than accepting that there are many other different problems, including the problems constitutive of first modernity, such as the ongoing scarcity in different parts of the world, unjust distribution, and the misery of those who are subordinated by religious fanatics, totalitarianism and dictatorship.

Furthermore, it also opens up the possibility for the justification of any State action. This danger is not merely imaginary. Illustrative are the many measures taken to combat terrorism. An example is the US control over European bank transactions through 'Swift'.[68] Similar to these anti-terrorism measures, the effectiveness of measures to protect the environment, based on the Precautionary principle, is uncertain to say the least. Sunstein convincingly argues that in its strong version, the Precautionary principle has a '*paralysing*' effect.[69] We do not argue, then, that one should not act – this is the whole point of the Precautionary principle – but that something must exist that is, able to delimit action and to prevent States and other political actors from having a limitless playing field to exercise power. The Precautionary principle allows States to exercise power to safeguard environmental, ecological or other such interests, and they can do so on the premise that an apparent risk exists about which there is scientific uncertainty in respect of its existence in the first place, as well as about the nature and

67. This observation echoes the argument of Zygmunt Bauman that 'solid modernity' strived to establish a universal ethical code and was doomed to fail; see Z. Bauman, *Postmodern Ethics* (Oxford: Blackwell, 1993), 14.

68. E. Lichtblau & J. Risen, 'Bank Data Is Sifted by U.S. in Secret to Block Terror', *The New York Times*, 23 Jun. 2006. <www.nytimes.com/2006/06/23/washington/23intel.html> (25 Nov. 2009).

69. Sunstein, *Laws of Fear*, 26. see n. 9.

extent of its consequences if and when it manifests itself in the shape of a disaster. It is not, however, a sufficient legal basis for the legitimate exercise of power.

6.3. Legality Under Siege

Legality is under siege and the Precautionary principle illustrates or shows that legality is besieged from within and relates to the material and formal/procedural characteristic of legality.

6.3.1. 'Internal' Legislation

Legality is not an outdated concept when it comes to addressing the problems of contemporary society. Legality still serves its function, but in doing so, it demands reconsideration about its scope and application. Legality formulates a legal basis for State action and sets criteria for the evaluation of both the legal basis and State action. The Precautionary principle urges the State to take action without specifying the particular course and scope of action. Considering the complexity of the problem the Precautionary principle seeks to address, the legal basis for action (which legality demands) is complex and this also carries with it the danger that it escapes parliamentary and legal control. This can be illustrated by the shifting perspective of legislation, both in respect of the material and formal aspects.

Traditional legislation pertained to prescriptions regulating the relationship among citizens and the relationship between citizens and the State. This type of legislation must meet the so-called fuller criteria to meet the material aspect of legality: to provide legal certainty for citizens in respect of how to regulate their conduct. The last decades have seen a huge shift in the subject of legislation and, hence, its object. Indeed, Kryger concludes that much legislation nowadays is 'internal, that is, concerned at least initially with administrative agencies'.[70] This type of legislation formulates a particular objective and, subsequently delegates to all kinds of administrative agencies the task of developing executive policy and translating this policy into action to address the objective. This changing objective of legislation implies that this type of legislation escapes the material aspects of legality.

In more abstract terms, legislation can be distinguished into legislation based on a conditional programme and legislation based on goal-directed programmes.[71] The former has the logical structure of an implication, in terms of an 'if... then...' statement.[72] Here, the 'if' refers to a fact, and if this fact occurs,

---

70. M. Krygier, 'The Rule of Law: Legality, Teleology, Sociology', in: *Re-locating the Rule of Law*, ed. G. Palombella & N. Walker (Oxford: Hart Publishing, 2009), 45–70.
71. See N. Luhmann, *supra* n. 12, 196 et seq. See also L. Francot-Timmermans, *supra* n. 19, 95 et seq.
72. The idea of legislation as conditional programmes has also been described in M. Weber, *Rechtssoziologie*, ed. J. Winckelmann (München: Luchterhand, 1960).

'then' the rule applies. It is, as a matter of tautology, a normative programme and can be precise and general, etc. Law always reacts '*ex post facto*'.[73] This does not mean it has no preventative function. If fact A occurs through action B, then rule X applies, and say the actor is liable, the actor can forgo doing B as he knows he will be held liable. As the Precautionary principle refers to uncertain and future events, it cannot be captured in a conditional programme. The latter goal-directed programme or purpose-specific programme departs from the 'if... then...' logic and is legislation that formulates a particular objective for, for example, a government agency to achieve. It does not prescribe the actions that ought to be undertaken to meet the objective; that would be a matter of executive policy. They bring about a (normative) evaluation of actions that may pertain to the objective. The purpose-specific programme regulates result-driven instrumental action. A legislatively described objective, according to Willke, is sought to be achieved by variable employable means.[74] Much legislation, pertaining to environmental protection and incorporating the Precautionary principle is of this type. Another feature is that the details of such legislation are worked out in secondary legislation. This 'procedural tinkering' threatens legality.

6.3.2. Procedural 'Tinkering'

Legality does not merely denote the idea that political power can be exercised only on the basis of material criteria, but also that legislation comes into being on the basis of pre-prescribed rules (which themselves have been laid down in legislation, for example, a constitution). It suggests that all legislation comes into being through a similar procedure. The academic literature on the whole, it is suggested, focuses on what can be termed primary legislation or statute law, which comes into being through a democratic process of deliberation and decision-making. However, more and more, this type of legislation merely indicates but in vague terms the goal of the statute and the instruments by which this goal could be achieved. Indeed, it is purpose-specific legislation, delegating powers to the executive in order to effectively implement the statute. These types of statutes could be termed 'skeleton statutes' or framework legislation: statutes that lay down certain general rules pertaining to a particular goal or policy, rules that are worked out in detailed, practical rules through a myriad of secondary legislation.[75] Secondary legislation is legislation that comes into being as the result of an executive process. What we mean is that this type of legislation is formulated on the basis of primary legislation for the purpose of executing policy to meet the goals set out in the primary legislation, usually formulated in a vague and open

73. N. Luhmann, *supra* n. 12, 198.
74. H. Willke, *Ironie des Staates* (Frankfurt am Main: Suhrkamp, 1992), 179.
75. There is some resemblance to those statutes in American law, referred to as 'framework statutes', constituting institutions and procedures for the sake of constitutional policies, in similar ways the (American) Constitution does; see: E.A. Young, 'Toward a Framework Statute for Supranational Adjudication', *Emory Law Journal* 57 (2007): 98–99.

way – for example, 'to serve environmental protection', 'to promote public health', and so forth. We consider the connection between primary and secondary legislation to be problematic. The connection exists not only at State level (statute – ministerial regulation), but also at European level (directive/regulation – statute/ministerial regulation) and international level. This changing perspective of legislation and procedural tinkering ties in with the role and function of newly developed and new developing regulatory agencies which are better able to deal, as the argument goes, with regulatory and supervisory tasks that demand special expertise.[76]

This development in legislation has also been observed in the Netherlands.[77] Reasons for this development are manifold. One is that what framework legislation seeks to regulate themes addressed in European legislation, demanding implementation through national rules. In addition, framework legislation allows for flexibility. It allows the executive (to which law making powers have been delegated by statute) to take into account changing circumstances and new scientific developments when making the general rules concrete and fit for practical application. It allows the executive to anticipate and react to these circumstances and developments swiftly and adequately, or so the argument goes.

There are concerns about the growing use of this type of legislation. Of great concern is the lack of political or parliamentary control in the decision-making procedure as to how the delegated rules are formulated, what these rules are, and pertain to. The danger is that the lack of parliamentary control is exacerbated by the complicatedness of the subject mater dealt within these framework statutes. The lack of specialized expertise of members of parliament (and the lack of time) allows the executive to make rules that deeply affect society without proper parliamentary control. This becomes even more problematic in the area of environmental legislation, for example, because expert findings are deemed highly provisional and are said to lack sufficient consensus in respect of the scientific findings.[78]

As the legal system has to act within the framework of an informational void, it puts legality under strain because power can only be exercised on the basis of rules and the formulation and application of rules require information for them to be effective and legitimate. The danger, furthermore, is that too much reliance is placed on the knowledge of experts who seek to determine risks and their consequences, while knowing that their information is doubtful. Experts are said to be mistaken about '*the empirical accuracy of their implicit value premises,*

76. It is beyond the scope of this contribution to address this further. See amongst others, G. Majone, 'From the Positive to the Regulatory State: Causes and Consequences of Changes in the Mode of Governance', *Journal of Public Policy* 17 (1997): 139–167 and F. Gilardi *Delegation in the Regulatory State: Independent Regulatory Agencies in Western Europe* (Cheltenham: Edwin Elgar, 2009). For a different perspective; see: H. Wilke *Supervision des Staates* (Frankfurt am Main: Suhrkamp, 1997).
77. Reported upon in respect of animal welfare In B. de Vries & T. Hol, *Idealia en Realia rond de Omgang met Productiedieren* (Den Haag: Boom Juridische Uitgevers, 2006), 55 et seq.
78. The controversy about bio-fuel illustrates this point.

specifically, in their assumptions if what appears acceptable to the population'.[79] The informational void that legislators suffer from allows, in the first place, experts to determine risk, and this determination need not to be scientifically inspired but can be also normatively inspired. It causes risk to '*develop an incredible political dynamic*'.[80]

Finally, legislation no longer comes into being solely within the realm of the State. One could speak of a layered structure of legislative action, spread across global, regional (European) and local levels (which in themselves are further differentiated as shown above).[81]

If this were true, and much empirical research should be carried out here, it would truly mean an erosion of the modern concept of legality. We argue here that it is inevitable, considering the problem as described above, that the Precautionary principle calls for this type of framework legislation. We fear that legality here, in the guise as we know it, does not sufficiently safeguard against the abuse of power, and that application of the Precautionary principle could undermine the (legal) certainty legality seeks to provide for. Protection against the State could be in danger of being subordinated to protection against risk. What is demanded now is striking a balance between the two principles. It cannot be, at least according to these authors, that the principle of legality is subordinated to the Precautionary principle, as this would create too much room for arbitrariness. It withdraws power from control and it becomes impossible to evaluate the extent to which the exercise of power contributes to resolving the problem for which it is exercised or used in the first place – addressing the problem of modern risk through the application of precaution. This balancing act must take place first within the confines of the modern State, but on the proviso that it takes into account the changing role of the State in the era of globalization.

7. CONCLUSION

Contemporary society is confronted with the problem of our awareness of modern risk as the side effect of the successes of modernization. These risks pose a threat to our natural environment and, by implication, to us. Something needs to be done and this something exists in finding ways of dealing with risk. The Precautionary principle is a solution for dealing with modern risk. It suggests that political actors can exercise power (take action) to deal with risks in the absence of scientific certainty about these risks and their materialization. The Principle itself does not prescribe the type of action. Considering the perceived magnitude of the problem – ecological survival – the question arises as to what extent the Principle allows the exercise of political power without adhering to the precepts of legality

79. Beck, *Risk Society*, 58, see n. 14.
80. *Ibid.*, 77.
81. A more detailed example of this layered structure of legislation and its implications; see B. De Vries & T. Hol, *supra* n. 77, 73 et seq.

on the basis that it is an outdated concept merely serving the projects of first modernity. This would deny the essence of the rule of law, which lies in the prevention of the arbitrary use of political power for whatever reason. We must now realize that political power, at least in Western society, should not merely be geared towards wealth production and wealth distribution, but also towards the side effects of this production and distribution. Subordinating political power to certain rules ensures that while addressing the problem through the Precautionary principle, the interests of all concerned – ultimately the whole of humanity – are taken into account rather than just the interests of certain elites. It demands a reconsideration of legality in respect of its material and formal aspects at all levels – global, European and national – where political actors, in an integrated way, employ the Precautionary principle. More precisely, reconsidering legality demands taking issue with the uncertainty the processes of globalization bring about. Following Beck, we have conceptualized uncertainty in terms of modern risk. Law is considered to be a mechanism to reduce uncertainty. Legality in its turn frames State power in respect of this reduction. Modern risk escapes linear causality and consequently, legal causality becomes problematic, as the distribution of responsibility for risk requires linear causality. The Precautionary principle could be considered a way out of this dilemma. However, we have argued that although the Principle seeks to reduce uncertainty in respect of risk, it increases uncertainty in respect of power, as it erodes legality in withdrawing rule-making from the requirements of legality and democratic control. This is what we have sought to highlight in this essay.

Part II

Legality and the Attribution of Powers to Public Authorities

Chapter 3
Administrative Powers in German and in English Law

Gerdy Jurgens, Maartje Verhoeven & Paulien Willemsen

1. INTRODUCTION

The principle of legality is present in all Member States of the European Union. Although the background and the objective of this Principle are comparable, the precise content and scope of the Principle may differ from country to country. In this contribution we focus on an important aspect of the principle of legality: the foundation of governmental power. The central question in this article is whether and to what extent governmental actions require a – specific or otherwise – statutory basis in German law and in English law. Therefore sections 2 and 3 give an impression of German law and English law on this point. A conclusion and some final observations are laid down in section 4.

2. GERMANY

2.1. Introduction

To answer the central question of this article, it is important to give an impression of the precedence of statutory law and the requirement of a statutory basis for

Leonard Besselink, Frans Pennings & Sacha Prechal (eds), *The Eclipse of the Legality Principle in the European Union*, pp. 37–53.

governmental action in Germany. The precedence of statutory law implies that rules of statutory law have priority over delegated legislation. The requirement of a statutory basis means that actions by administrative authorities have to be based on a statutory law, either directly or indirectly. There is an important link between these principles. In the German system the protection by the requirement of a statutory basis can only be given if there is precedent of statute law.

Before going into the technicalities of the precedence of statutory law and the requirement of a statutory basis, it should be mentioned that both rules could not exist without a certain hierarchy of norms in the legal system. Section 2.2 therefore gives a short synopsis of the hierarchy of norms in Germany.

2.2. Hierarchy of Norms

The German legal system basically consists of two levels: the level of the *Bund* and the level of the *Länder*. Both these levels have their own hierarchy of norms, which are, however, comparable to each other. First there is the Constitution, then there are the statutory norms (either of the *Bundestag* or one of the *Landestage*), and lastly there is the delegated legislation (either of administrative authorities of the *Bund* or administrative authorities of the *Länder*).[1] The relationship between the law of the *Bund* and the *Länder* is governed by Article 31 GG: '*Bundesrecht bricht Landesrecht*'.

The German system places the statutory rules directly below the Constitution. These statutes, adopted by parliament, are considered to be 'statutes in the formal sense of the word' – that is, to say, acts which have been established in the formal process of law making involving the participation of parliament, as opposed to a 'legislation in substance' that concerns an act of a competent authority that provides general binding rules. Hence, a statute in the substantive sense of the word has a broader meaning, not only including acts of parliament, but also regulations adopted by ministers or decentralized authorities.

In Germany, the legislature is free to choose on which subjects it is willing to adopt parliamentary statutes, although the Constitution may oblige it to legislate in certain fields. Under certain circumstances, the German legislature is then allowed to delegate the power to regulate to administrative authorities.

The lower layer of the pyramid of legal norms in the German legal order consists of delegated legislation adopted by the executive branch. Different legal instruments fall within the scope of the general notion of 'delegated legislation'. In Germany, administrative authorities adopt generally applicable rules in the form of *Verordnungen* and *Satzungen*. *Verordnungen* are generally applicable rules, adopted by administrative authorities such as the government or individual ministers, on the basis of a statutory authorization to do so on a specific topic.

1. F. Ossenbühl, 'Rechtsquellen und Rechtsbindung der Verwaltung', in: *Allgemeines Verwaltungsrecht*, ed. P. Badura et al. (Berlin: De Gruyter Rechtswissenschaften Verlags-GmbH, 2002), 189.

Satzungen are adopted by administrative authorities in the exercise of their autonomous powers. This applies, for instance, to municipalities, but also to universities and the chambers of independent professions. *Verordnungen* are superior to *Satzungen*.[2]

Within the legal order of either the *Bund* or one of the *Länder*, a fixed hierarchical pattern exists. The highest source of law is the Constitution, followed by formal statutes and by statutory regulations (*Rechtsverordnungen*), which are based on these formal statutes.

2.3. The Precedence of Statutory Law

The precedence of statutory law (*Vorrang des Gesetzes* or *Gesetzesvorrang*) derives from the fact that both administrative authorities and courts are bound by 'statute and law'.[3] This concept includes the whole body of material legislative provisions that govern the relationship between State and citizen and the relations between citizens.[4] EC law is also included in this body of law, since '*Gesetz*' incorporates every part of written law, both of German and EC origin.[5]

Article 20 III GG requires all administrative authorities to act in accordance with the law. In other words, it prohibits the administrative authorities from taking decisions or adopting secondary law, such as, for instance, regulations or administrative guidelines that are in conflict with statutory law, including the *Grundgesetz*.[6]

The precedence of statutory law thus implies that acts of the executive have to conform with higher ranking rules of law. If necessary, this should be achieved by interpretation in conformity with the Constitution or the other higher-ranking law that is, applicable, such as EC law.[7] Nevertheless, when the administration violates the principle of precedence of statutory law and adopts an act that is, inconsistent with higher-ranking law, the act concerned is unlawful. In some cases this unlawfulness leads to the conclusion that the act concerned is null and void (this applies to the '*untergesetzliche*' *Rechtsverordnungen*[8] and *Satzungen*[9]), whereas in other cases (such as the *Verwaltungsakt*) the unlawfulness – for reasons of legal certainty – does not automatically lead to a nullity, but only creates the possibility for

2. *Ibid.*
3. H. Schulze-Fielitz, 'Gesetz und Recht', in: *GG Kommentar*, ed. H. Dreier (Tübingen: Mohr Siebeck Verlag, 2007), 221.
4. BVerfG 78, 214 (227): such as 'Verfassungsrecht, förmliche Gesetze, Rechtsverordnungen, autonome Satzungen und auch Gewohnheitsrecht'.
5. H.D. Jarass, in: H.D. Jarass & B. Pieroth (eds) *GG Kommentar* (Tübingen: Mohr Siebeck Verlag, 2009), 494; BverwGE 74, 241 (248 f).
6. F.E. Schnapp, in: *Grundgesetz Kommentar*, ed. I. Von Münch & P. Kunig (München: C.H. Beck, 2000), 21; Schulze-Fielitz (2007), *supra* n. 3, 217.
7. H.D. Jarass (2009), *supra* n. 5, 494.
8. Schulze-Fielitz (2007), *supra* n. 3, 224.
9. BVerwGE 112, 373 (380 ff).

citizens whose rights may have been infringed upon to apply an action for judicial review of the administrative act concerned.[10]

2.4. Requirement of a Statutory Basis

The combination of the precedence of statutory law and the requirement of a statutory basis means that the national administrative authorities do not only have to execute the law, but also that they are limited in how they can do this. Some acts can only be committed when they are based on a statutory authorization in which the administrative competence is well circumscribed. In the words of Maurer: 'The power does not encompass the competence to use all those means which seem necessary or suitable for the fulfilment of the problems. Interventions in the rights of the citizen need an (additional) legal authorization.'[11]

2.4.1. Field of Application: *Eingriffsverwaltung* and *Leistungsverwaltung*

The exact scope of application of the principle or requirement of a statutory basis is the subject of an ongoing discussion in scholarly writing in Germany. In this regard, it is important to distinguish between *Eingriffsverwaltung* and *Leistungsverwaltung*. On the one hand, *Eingriffsverwaltung* – or intervening administration – concerns actions by administrative authorities that affect the rights and freedoms of citizens. *Leistungsverwaltung* – or service administration – on the other hand, concerns beneficial actions for individuals, such as the grant of subsidies or other forms of aid.

The requirement of a statutory basis with regard to actions by administrative authorities that intervene in the rights and freedoms of individuals is generally accepted. This can be explained by the history of the requirement of a statutory basis. To recall the historical circumstances in which the requirement arose, the aim of the liberal constitutional movement, which at the end of the eighteenth century sought to limit the power of the sovereign through a separation of powers, was to secure the individual rights of citizens. Hence, the Executive could only encroach upon the sphere of individual rights if Parliament, as the representative of the citizens concerned, had previously given its consent through legislation.[12] Up to now, it is generally agreed that the requirement of a statutory basis applies to actions by the Administration which interfere with rights and freedoms of citizens.

---

10. W. Erbguth, *Allgemeines Verwaltungsrecht* (Baden-Baden: Nomos, 2005), 63; K.-P. Sommermann, in: *GG Commentar*, ed. H. von Mangold, F. Klein & C. Starck (München: Vahlen, 2005), 112.
11. H. Maurer, *Allgemeines Verwaltungsrecht* (München: C.H. Beck, 1995), 507: 'Die Zuständigkeit umfasst nicht die Befugnis, alle diejenigen Mittel, die zur Aufgabenerfüllung notwendig oder gar zweckmässig erscheinen, einzusetzen. Eingriffe in die Rechte des Bürgers bedürfen einer (züsatzlichen) gesetzlichen Ermächtigung.'
12. J. Schwarze, *European Administrative Law* (London: Sweet & Maxwell, 2006), 215.

This does not mean, however, that such a basis cannot give the authority concerned quite some discretion.

The applicability of the requirement of a statutory basis to service administration (*Leistungsverwaltung*) however, is less self-evident. At its introduction in the eighteenth century, the requirement of a statutory basis did not apply to that area. A statutory basis was required with regard to interventions on personal freedoms and property (*Eingriffsverwaltung*). However, outside this area the monarch continued to enjoy unfettered powers of decision-making [13]

Nowadays, opinions differ. The classic doctrine[14] takes the position that the historical background and function of the requirement of a statutory basis imply that a written basis in statutory law is only required with regard to administration intervening in rights and freedoms.

On the other hand, the 'Overall Requirement Doctrine' holds that the requirement of a statutory basis also applies to forms of service administration.[15] This Overall Requirement Doctrine has its basis in Austrian and Swiss scholarly writing,[16] and was introduced in Germany by Jesch, who argued that because Parliament is democratically legitimized, it is the highest organ of the State.[17] Hence, every executive action requires an authorization by this highest organ, regardless of the specific character and purpose of this action.

Rupp's argument rests on a more general basis. He assesses the question of what the precise contents of 'intervention in the rights and freedoms of citizens' are in the context of the principle of the rule of law. Rupp argues that the contents of these rights and freedoms in the liberal era might have been limited to the 'self-possessed living space', but that since the introduction of the Social State in Germany, rights and freedoms have a broader goal than in the liberal age: freedom not only means the absence of governmental interferences, but also the possibility of taking advantage of beneficial actions of the government, such as social security.

All this shows the ongoing debate in German literature concerning the question of what extent service administration requires a statutory basis. Some say that such a requirement does no more than limit the executive branch with regard to decisions with positive effects on citizens. If one opts for this doctrine, one only withholds the chances of citizens of profiting from beneficiary decisions that lack a statutory basis because the legislature has not yet taken any action. It is, however, generally accepted in the literature that service administration requires a statutory basis in situations in which third parties are involved (e.g., a competitor of

13. Dietrich Jesch, *Gesetz und Verwaltung* (Tübingen: Mohr Siebeck Verlag, 1961) 1 et seq. and 108 et seq.
14. 'Klassische rechtsstaatliche Gesetzesvorbehalt' or 'klassischen Eingriffsvorbehaltes'.
15. This doctrine is called Totalvorbehalt des Gesetzes; W. Wolff, *Allgemeines Verwaltungsrecht* (Baden-Baden: Nomos, 2004), 85.
16. See also Öhlinger on the (comparable) Austrian situation: T. Öhlinger, 'Legalitätsprinzip und Europäische Integration', in: *Österreichische Parlamentarische Gesellschaft (Hg.): 75 Jahre Bundesverfassung. Festschrift aus Anlaß des 75. Jahrestages der Beschlussfassung über das Bundes-Verfassungsgesetz* (Wien: Verlag Österreich, 1997), 635.
17. Dietrich Jesch, *Gesetz und Verwaltung* (Tübingen: Mohr Siebeck Verlag, 1961) 24 et seq.

the company that receives a subsidy). In practice, most forms of *Leistungsverwaltung* now have a statutory basis.

In between the two extremes, German legal writing also features the doctrine of extended legislation,[18] in which the question of what statutory basis is required depends on the subject matter. This seems closely related to the theory of substantiality,[19] according to which only the most fundamental interventions should be governed by formal laws adopted by Parliament itself, hence, in that case delegation to the administrative authorities to adopt rules in a *Rechtsverordnung* or *Satzung* is not allowed. In particular interventions in the rights and freedoms of citizens require a statutory basis in formal law in this respect[20] (see also below).

The principle of the *Vorbehalt des Gesetzes* is known as the positive element of the principle of legality. It requires acts of the Administration to be based on a statutory authorization in which the administrative competence is well-circumscribed. The principle was developed to set a clear limit to the power of monarchs that ruled Germany – 'no action without a statute'.[21] Hence the Executive could only encroach upon the sphere of individual rights after gaining the consent of Parliament as the representative of the citizens.[22]

The requirement of a statutory basis is not explicitly codified in Article 20 III GG, but nevertheless derives from this provision, which states, among other things, that 'the fact that the Executive and the Judiciary are bound by statute and law, hence the precedence of the statutory law, would lose its meaning if the Constitution itself did not already require that State action in certain fundamental areas is only lawfully allowed if it is legitimized by the formal law'.[23] Moreover, the principle is also incorporated into the *Grundgesetz* with regard to specific topics such as the powers of the municipalities (Article 28 II 1 GG), the powers of the *Bundespräsident* with regard to the conclusion of international treaties (Article 59 II 1 GG), and the power of the *Bundesregierung*, the *Bundesminister* or *Landesregierungen* to issue *Rechtsverordnungen* (Article 80 1 I GG).[24]

18. Erweiterten Gesetzgebung.
19. Wesentlichkeitstheorie.
20. BVerfGE 34, 165 (192 f.), NJW 1973, 133; BVerfGE 40, 237 (248) = NJW 1976, 34; BVerfGE 49, 89 (124 f.) = NJW 1979, 359 – Mühlheim/Kärlich; BVerfGE 101, 1 (34) = NJW 1999, 3253 – Legehennen-Verordnung; M. Hilf & K. Classen, 'Der Vorbehalt des Gesetzes im Recht der Europäischen Union', in: L. Osterloh, K. Schmidt & H. Weber (eds) *Festschrift für Peter Selmer zum 70. Geburtstag* (Berlin: Duncker & Humblot, 2004), 72.
21. 'Kein Handeln ohne Gesetz', D. Triantafyllou, *Vom Vertrags- zum Gesetzesvorbehalt* (Baden-Baden: Nomos, 1996), 113.
22. J. Schwarze, *European Administrative Law* (London: Sweet & Maxwell, 2006), 215.
23. 'Die Bindung der vollziehenden Gewalt und der Rechtsprechung an Gesetz und Recht, der Vorrang des Gesetzes also, würden ihren Sinn verlieren, wenn nicht schon die Verfassung selbst verlangen würde, daß staatliches Handeln in bestimmten grundlegenden Bereichen nur Rechtens is, wenn es durch das förmliche Gesetz legitimiert wird.' See BVerfGE 40, 237 [248f.] See in more detail, M. Vögler, 'Rückforderung vertraglich gewährter Subventionen ohne Rechtsgrundlage? – Zum Warnow-Werft-Beschluss des OVG Berlin-Brandenburg', NVzW (2007): 296–297.
24. See more extensively: Schulze-Fielitz (2007), *supra* n. 3, 227.

2.4.2. Parliamentary Reservation

The requirement of a statutory basis also implies that powers in some subject matters are not transferable to the Administration, to that extent the principle also incorporates a prohibition for the parliamentary legislature to delegate[25] – the so-called parliamentary reservation or *'Parlamentsvorbehalt'*.[26] In the words of the BVerfG: 'This principle requires state action in certain fundamental areas to be legitimized by formal law. The legislature is obliged to take all essential decisions independently, and may not leave them to other norm givers.'[27] This so-called theory of substantiality applies, for instance, to restrictions to fundamental rights, budgetary decisions and putting armed forces into action. Nevertheless, the *Parlementsvorbehalt* does not apply to all subjects, as that was not the intention of the makers of the Constitution:[28]

> The concrete order of the distribution and the balance of state power which the Basic Law wants to protect, may not be avoided by a Gewaltenmonismus in the form of an all-embracing parliamentary reservation erroneously derived from the democracy principle.

The requirement of the statutory law can therefore be met either directly by law (*'durch Gesetz'*), when the legislature directly lays down the exact scope of the power of the Administration), or indirectly on the basis of the law (*'aufgrund eines Gesetzes'*), when the legislature only lays down the conditions, but leaves it to the administrative authorities to lay down more specific rules. In case of a subject matter which falls within the scope of the *Parlementsvorbehalt*, it is clear that only the first option (*durch Gesetz*) meets the requirements.

2.4.3. Implied Powers

The existence of so-called 'implied powers' would be contrary to the requirement of a statutory basis, particularly with regard to intervening administration.

25. Sommermann (2005), *supra* n. 10, 113.
26. See more extensively F. Ossenbühl, in *HStR III*, § 62, Rn. 9.
27. 'Dieser Grundsatz verlangt, daß staatliches Handeln in bestimmten grundlegenden Bereichen durch förmliches Gesetz legitimiert wird. Der Gesetzgeber ist verpflichtet, alle wesentlichen Entscheidungen selbst zu treffen, und darf sie nicht anderen Normgebern überlassen.' See BVerfGE 98, 218 (251); compare also BVerfGE 33, 125 (Facharzt: Vorgaben für Eingriffe in die Berufsfreiheit durch Satzung), BVerfGE 47, 46 (Sexualkundeunterricht: Der Gesetzgeber muss die Entscheidung über die Einführung des Sexualkundeunterrichts an öffentlichen Schulen selbst treffen), BVerfGE 49, 89 (Kalkar: Wesentliche Entscheidungen und Bestimmtheitsanforderungen im Technikrecht (AKW Kalkar)) and BVerfG NJW 1998, 2515, 2520 (Rechtschreibreform: zählt nicht zu den 'wesentlichen' Entscheidungen, die der Gesetzgeber selbst hätte treffen müssen).
28. 'Die konkrete Ordnung der Verteilung und des Ausgleichs staatlicher Macht, die das Grundgesetz gewahrt wissen will, darf nicht durch einen aus dem Demokratieprinzip fälschlich abgeleiteten Gewaltenmonismus in Form eines allumfassenden Parlamentsvorbehalts unterlaufen werden.' See BVerfGE 68, 1 (87).

Moreover, the requirement of the (democratic) legitimacy of administrative acts prevents the existence of implied powers in Germany. The doctrine of the so-called 'public law claim to compensation' (*öffentlich-rechtlichen Erstattungsanspruch)* may be the closest to such an implied power. This doctrine, which is rather controversial in German scholarship,[29] asserts the unwritten right of administrative authorities to reclaim money that has been paid without a legal basis – for example, in the case of unlawful subventions or State aid. The legal basis of this unwritten right is debatable, and only generally accepted in three cases under German law: first, if the claim is codified – for example, in Article 49a 1 S. 2 VwVfG; second, in the case of application of the so-called 'reverse theory'[30] – a benefit that has been granted by an administrative decision (*Verwaltungsakt*) can be reclaimed by *Verwaltungsakt* after the repeal of the beneficial decision; and finally, the application is accepted in cases of relations of subordination, as in the case of public servants or soldiers. In the last two cases and particularly in the second one with regard to the 'reverse theory', the 'public law claim to compensation' might be considered an implied power. Nevertheless, one should keep in mind that this truly is an exception in the German legal system, because of the strength of the requirement of a statutory basis, and the density of statutory provisions for actions of the Administration.

2.4.4. Indefinite Legal Terms

A somewhat comparable phenomenon is that of vague legal notions or indefinite legal terms (*unbestimmte Rechtsbegriffe*). On the basis of a vaguely formulated competence various decisions can be taken. The question is: can they be legitimized? When the legislature uses indefinite legal terms the result is, for all intents and purposes, a stepping back by the legislature. That is, to say, the more indefinite a term is, the more room is left to the Administration for elaboration and interpretation of delegated legislation. The same is the case with discretion, but an important difference is that according to German law in the case of discretion, to allow for a flexible approach the legislature has given the Administration room to deal with concrete cases. When the legislature uses indefinite legal terms however, in the German legal view this is not the case. Indefinite terms are, for example, public safety and public interest. To achieve uniformity in administrative activity, the interpretation of these terms is often guided by administrative guidelines. Nevertheless, courts tend to review indefinite terms without restriction.[31] According to the courts there is only one correct decision. Actually this is just a question of competence. The fact is that there is a stepping back on the part of the legislature. The courts cover this up by their approach that there is just one correct decision.

29. Hartmut Maurer, *Allgemeines Verwaltungsrecht* (München: C.H. Beck, 2000), § 28 Rn. 20.
30. 'Kehrseitentheorie'; BVerwGE 40, 85.
31. M. Schröder, 'Administrative Law in Germany', in: *Administrative Law of the European Union, its Member States and the United States* (Antwerpen – Groningen: Intersentia Uitgevers, 2007), 128.

2.5. Use of Private Law

In German law all governmental bodies can use private law instruments, as long as this is not prohibited by law. When the administration uses private law, it cannot however escape its constitutional obligations. The Administration is especially obliged to observe fundamental rights, particularly the rights of freedom and equality and the principle of proportionality or reasonableness because it is exercising executive power within the meaning of Article 1(3) of the Basic Law. Schröder remarks that the remainder is contentious as to the extent and way the Administration is bound to public law.[32]

3. THE SOURCES OF GOVERNMENTAL POWER IN ENGLISH LAW[33]

3.1. Introduction

As noted above, for the sources of powers in English law it is very important to distinguish between the powers of central government and the powers of other statutory bodies. In short: statutory bodies only possess statutory powers whereas central government also has other sources of power, such as the royal prerogative power and a so-called third source of power.

3.2. Statutory Power

The supremacy or sovereignty of Parliament is one of the pillars of the unwritten British Constitution. The importance of the sovereignty of Parliament for the whole English legal system can hardly be underestimated. Lacking any written constitution which defines the limits of governmental power, the powers of government in the United Kingdom are only subject to the approval of Parliament. Parliament's law-making power does not derive from any document that confers and constrains these powers, but is pre-existing and is accepted as a fundamental rule of the common law. The sovereignty of Parliament explains, for example, why historically primary legislation was not amenable to judicial review at all. The Human Rights Act 1988 (HRA 1988), which introduced a judicial 'declaration of incompatibility' between a parliamentary statute and a European Convention right, thus can be considered as a major constitutional change in the United Kingdom. This is only one illustration of how the supremacy of Parliament is challenged nowadays by European influences

32. Schröder (2002), *supra* n. 31, 117.
33. The United Kingdom has three different legal systems: the legal systems of England and Wales, of Northern Ireland and of Scotland. When we write about English law we refer to the legal system of England and Wales. The legal system of Northern Ireland is mainly the same as the English legal system. The Scottish legal system however is rather different. Section 3 is based on a research project concerning a comparison between Dutch law and English law by G.T.J.M. Jurgens and F.J. van Ommeren, publication is forthcoming.

like European Union Law and the European Convention on Human Rights (ECHR), although it should be added that Parliament itself has accepted these confinements, since European Union law and the ECHR law derive their legal effect in the English legal system by Act of Parliament. The concept of sovereignty of Parliament is traditionally also seen as the foundation of judicial review of administrative decisions: the court's task is to supervise whether public authorities do not act ultra vires (outside the powers entrusted to them by Parliament).[34]

The Executive – central and local – acquires its powers from Acts of Parliament. English legal doctrine however shows relatively little concern with the nature and the scope of the statutory basis. In as far as attention is paid to this topic, this occurs in the context of case law concerning the question of whether or not a governmental body has acted ultra vires, that is, has exceeded the boundaries drawn by Parliament. From the outset it is clear that the requirements are not too strict. Although there are a lot of very detailed statutory power-conferring provisions, Acts of Parliament can also contain very broad and far-reaching statutory powers. A well-known example can be found in section 111 of the Local Government Act 1972:

> Without prejudice to any powers exercisable apart from this section but subject to the provisions of this Act and any other enactment passed before or after this Act, a local authority shall have power to do any thing (whether or not involving the expenditure, borrowing or lending of money or the acquisition or disposal of any property or rights) which is calculated to facilitate, or is conducive or incidental to, the discharge of any of their functions.

From a continental point of view, such provision would hardly be seen as a power-conferring provision. It only refers in general terms to the functions of local authorities and it does not – as would be the case in a power-conferring provision in a continental legal system – articulate any specific legal instrument; the local authority is empowered 'to do any thing'.

Statutes do not only have a broad scope, they can also imply powers that they do not expressly articulate. A well-known case in which the court recognized an *implied power* of a local authority is *Attorney-General v. Crayford Urban District Council.*[35] The case concerned the powers of a local council against the tenants of council houses that were provided by the local authority. For this case it was relevant that section 111(1) of the Housing Act 1957, stated:

> The general management, regulation and control of houses provided by a local authority under this Part of this Act shall be vested in and exercised by the authority (. . .)

---

34. At the present time different visions of the foundations of judicial review are discussed. See for example, the debate started in 1987 by Dawn Oliver concerning the foundations of judicial review: D. Oliver, 'Is the ultra vires rule the basis of judicial review?', PL (1987): 543–569. See for the debate between the supporters of the ultra vires model and the rights-based approach (also called common law constitutionalism): C. Forsyth (ed.), *Judicial Review and the Constitution* (Oxford: Hart Publishing, 2000). See also M. Elliott, *The Constitutional Foundations of Judicial Review* (Oxford-Portland: Hart Publishing, 2001).
35. [1962] 2 All ER 147.

From this statutory clause, in particular the words 'general management', local authorities derived the power to recommend their tenants to insure themselves at a certain insurance company. In this case the local authority had entered into an arrangement with an insurance company for the collective insurance of its tenants and invited the tenants to join the scheme. The Attorney-General sought a declaration that the authority was not empowered to effect the insurance or to collect the premiums and that those acts were ultra vires, but the court held that the insurance of the contents was fairly incidental or consequential to the general management of the council houses since it was a safeguard to secure the payment of rent in times of difficulty. Thus, since it was not expressly authorized by the statute, this power should be considered as of an implied nature. More generally, case law has determined that governmental *contractual* powers can be derived from these kind of statutory powers.[36]

Our conclusion is that at first sight the English legal system appears to be rather strict in respect of the powers of statutory authorities. In English law a local authority is a public authority created by an Act of Parliament. The actions of such public authorities are confined to those expressly or implicitly authorized by statute: every act of these authorities needs a statutory basis. However, the requirement of a statutory basis does not lead to a very strict system of exactly specified and restricted powers for the Executive: the legislature every now and again provides for broadly formulated powers and the courts accept the existence of implied powers.

As a consequence of this restriction to statutory powers, local authorities are not allowed to use their rights deriving from the ownership of land like a private (legal) person could; instead they always have to be able to point at some kind of legal provision on which their actions can be based. An example is the *Fewings* case, in which a local authority had imposed a ban on deer hunting on common land. Since statute did not provide for a power to impose such a ban, the local authority was held to act ultra vires. In Sir Thomas Bingham's words:

> To the famous question asked by the owner of the vineyard ('Is it not lawful for me to do what I will with mine own?' St. Matthew, chapter 20, verse 15) the modern answer would be clear: 'Yes, subject to such regulatory and other constraints as the law imposes.' But if the same question were posed by a local authority the answer would be different. It would be: 'No, it is not lawful for you to do anything save what the law expressly or impliedly authorizes. You enjoy no unfettered discretions. There are legal limits to every power you have.'[37]

If the conclusion of the courts is, as it was in the *Fewings* case, that the action of a statutory body lacks an express or implicit authorization by statute, this action is held to be ultra vires. It is important to note that the rule from the *Fewings* case is not to be generalized to apply to all public authorities. With regard to central government, English law acknowledges the existence of governmental powers without a statutory basis. We focus on this in the next subsection.

36. *Attorney General v. Great Eastern Railway* [1880] 5 App. Cas. 473, 478.
37. *R. v. Somerset County Council ex p. Fewings* [1995] 1 WLR 1037, at 1042.

3.3. Non-Statutory Powers: The Royal Prerogatives and the Third Source of Power

As we have seen in section 3.2 above, statute is the only source of power in English law for local and other statutory bodies. The Crown however derives powers from two other sources: the royal prerogative and the so-called third source of power.

The first non-statutory source of power we discuss is the royal prerogative. The royal prerogative is an ancient common law power which concerns the power of the Crown. Dicey describes the royal prerogative as follows:

> [T]he residue of discretionary or arbitrary authority, which at any time is legally left in the hands of the Crown (...). Every act which the executive government can lawfully do without the authority of an Act of Parliament is done in virtue of this prerogative.[38]

This citation shows that the prerogative powers have a residual nature and that these prerogatives are not footed by statute.

In theory, the prerogative is capable of being subjected to full political control, as is the case with any other act of government, but in practice political control may prove to be inadequate.[39] The power to rule without parliamentary consent is considered the hallmark of the prerogative.[40]

Under the unwritten constitution, no exhaustive list of the prerogative powers exists. Of quite a number of prerogatives it is disputed whether they are real prerogatives or implied powers which already exist under statute.[41] Well-known examples of the prerogative powers are the power to make treaties, the power to make declarations of war and peace, the power to issue passports, the power to summon and dissolve parliament and the appointment of ministers, the power to organize the civil service, etc.

A quite relevant question is what the relation is between a statute and the prerogative: which one will prevail? When the Crown holds a certain prerogative power and subsequently an Act of Parliament provides powers on the same substance (albeit under different or severe conditions), is the Crown still allowed to use its prerogative power setting aside the statutory conditions? In *Attorney General v. De Keyser's Royal Hotel Ltd* it was held that the statutory framework displaces a pre-existing prerogative power.[42]

The exercise of prerogative powers was traditionally not amenable to judicial review, however this changed in the *GCHQ* case (1984).[43] In this landmark case it

38. A.V. Dicey, *An Introduction to the Study of the Law of the Constitution* (London: Macmillan, 1964), 425.
39. H. Barnett, *Constitutional and Administrative Law*, 6th ed. (Abingdon: Routledge-Cavendish, 2006), 146.
40. T. Daintith, 'Regulation by Contract: the New Prerogative', CLP (1979): 42.
41. See for a discussion of an overview of prerogatives: Barnett (2006), *supra* n. 39, 123 et seq.
42. *Attorney General v. De Keyser's Royal Hotel Ltd* [1920] AC 508. See also *Laker Airways v. Department of Trade* [1977] QB 643.
43. *Council of Civil Service Unions v. Minister for the Civil Service Respondent* [1985] AC 374.

was held that prerogative powers are not, in principle, immune from judicial review, although there are still quite some prerogative powers which are not subjected to review because of their subject matter, such as the appointment of ministers, the dissolution of Parliament, etc.

Since prerogative powers do not have a statutory basis, from 2007 on, the government issued, as part of the constitutional reform programme, several proposals to provide a general statutory basis for some of the royal prerogatives. The purpose of these proposals is to bring them under stronger parliamentary scrutiny and control.[44]

Apart from statutory powers and prerogative powers, English law also recognizes a third type of governmental power. Following Harris we will refer to these kinds of powers as 'third source' powers. This designation is also used in English case law. Nevertheless it should be noted that several other names refer to the same subject, such as 'common law power' or 'de facto power'.

The 'third source' and the royal prerogatives have in common that they justify the exercise of governmental power without a statutory basis. However, literature stresses a distinction between third source powers and prerogative powers in the sense that prerogative powers concern powers which are exclusive to the government, whereas the third source of power is based on the principle that the executive branch of the central government is like an individual free to do what is not legally prohibited or in breach of the legal rights of others. This third source is not an exclusive source of governmental power: the government has these powers in common with every person. An authoritative description of the term 'prerogative' and of the distinction between other non-statutory powers is given by Sir William Blackstone:

> It signifies, in its etymology (from *prae* and *rogo*) something that is, required or demanded before, or in preference to, all others. And hence it follows, that it must be in its nature singular and eccentrical; that it can only be applied to those rights and capacities which the king enjoys alone, in contradistinction to others, and not to those which he enjoys in common with any of his subjects; for if once any one prerogative of the crown could be held in common with the subject, it would cease to be prerogative any longer.[45]

However, in practice both categories of non-statutory powers are often more or less identified, as Wade and Forsyth observe.[46] Harris therefore is using the designation 'the prerogative in the narrow sense' when he refers to the 'real prerogative'.[47]

Although English case law has acknowledged the existence of this third source of power, third source powers are certainly not undisputed. From the discussions of

44. 'Governance in Britain' constitutional reform programme (2007). See also the Draft *Constitutional Renewal Bill* (2008).
45. Sir William Blackstone, *Commentaries on the Laws of England* (Oxford: Clarendon Press, 1765), 239.
46. H.W.R. Wade & C.F. Forsyth, *Administrative Law*, 9th ed. (Oxford: Oxford University Press, 2004), 216.
47. B.V. Harris, 'The 'Third Source' of Authority for Government Action Revisited', LQR (2007): 226.

the third source powers it becomes clear that English law aims for governmental power being based on statutory provisions; the exercise of governmental power without a statutory basis is being articulated as problematic. This basically holds both for the royal prerogatives and for the third source powers.

Some specific examples of third source powers include the payment of pensions to widowers (whereas statute only provided for pensions for widows),[48] the disposal of a list of persons who might not be suitable to work with children and informing a future employer from that,[49] and the tapping of telephones.[50] It is interesting to note that several of these examples that were accepted under domestic law are nowadays out of date because of the force of the ECHR law,[51] which demands more specific legal rules concerning governmental actions interfering with human rights. More generally, third source powers could concern the exercise of the rights of ownership. The essence of the third source powers is that they are based on the idea that the government is allowed to do things which every person is allowed to do. The third source does not provide for a power to impose duties and burdens unilaterally; in order to alter the legal position of its citizens, the government has to assert that it acts on a legal basis (statutory or prerogative – in the strict sense). It should be noted that the exercise of third source powers is positioned in the domain of public law and held amenable to judicial review, referring to the public function of these powers.

As stated above, the acknowledgment of the third source is based on the idea that the government is free to do everything which is not legally prohibited or is not in breach of the legal rights of others. This idea is also known as 'the Ram doctrine', referring to a memorandum by Sir Granville Ram, stating that a Minister of the Crown may exercise any powers that the Crown may exercise, except in so far as the Minister is precluded from doing so, either expressly or by necessary implication.[52] Lester and Weait note that this Ram doctrine is relied upon as the basis for exercising ministerial powers without parliamentary authority. In this respect there is also reference to the legal status of the government as a corporation, which allows the government to act like any other legal person. However, these justifications are not considered by everyone to be sufficiently convincing. According to these critics the identification of government and other (natural or legal) persons does no justice to the different character and the large scope and influence of the government.[53]

Although the existence of the third source powers is recognized, these powers are not considered unproblematic. The main objection against the third source of governmental power is the absence of any pre-action control. In conferring power by statute there has been a moment at which Parliament has given attention to the

48. *R. v. Secretary of State for Work and Pensions ex p. Hooper* [2005] 1 WLR 1681.
49. *R. v. Secretary of State for Health ex p. C* [2000] WL 559.
50. *Malone v. Commissioner of Police of the Metropolis (No. 2)* [1979] 2 WLR 700.
51. See for example, ECHR 2 Aug. 1984, *Malone v. The United Kingdom*, no. 8691/79.
52. Anthony Lester & Matthew Weait, 'The Use of Ministerial Powers without Parliamentary Authority: The Ram Doctrine', PL (2003): 415–428.
53. Harris (2007), *supra* n. 47, 239.

question of what kind of power, for which authority and for what purposes it would provide this kind of power. Moreover, Parliament has been able to restrict the exercise of the conferred power to certain limits. This pre-action parliamentary authorization both serves the ideal of democracy and contributes to the predictability of governmental action and to legal certainty. When the government exercises its third source powers the restraints have to be found in positive law (legislation) that protects justifiable competing interests; these restraints are not specially designed for the exercise of governmental power. Referring to these restraints the exercise of the third source powers could however be challenged in the courts (in private law proceedings, in judicial review or even in criminal proceedings). Apart from these possibilities, there are other mechanisms for post-action accountability of the Executive. Harris refers, for example, to parliamentary scrutiny and ministerial accountability or review by the Parliamentary Commissioner for Administration.[54]

Although the exercise of third source powers is restrained in several ways and the government can be held to account by various mechanisms, various commentators have searched for a more restrictive framework in respect of the exercise of third source powers. Requiring statutory authorizations for all governmental action is however not considered to be realistic: this would most likely only result in general statutory authorizations which, from the perspective of pre-action control, scarcely add anything to the acceptance of third source powers. Thus, Harris has argued, in a model that he has called 'the conventional expectation model', the clear expectation from constitutional convention should be that Executive action should normally be authorized in advance by statute. In this model the third source could be maintained for the unforeseen, but only as a last resort – in so far as no other instruments can be provided. Harris does not however emphasize the necessity of a mass exercise of enacting statutory authorizations, which would be an immense practical task, aside from the question of whether the legislature would be able to foresee all the needed authority and therefore would, just to be sure, be driven back on the provision of general statutory authorizations. Rather, he prefers that necessary statutory authorizations be enacted 'incrementally as particular needs arose, and Parliament had helpful contexts in which to carry out its responsibilities as to pre-action accountability'.[55] The other important commentator on the third source powers is Cohn.[56] Cohn also acknowledges that there is no getting away from the acceptance of the third source of power, but she advocates constraining the third source of power further, specifically when governmental actions directly affect human rights or have 'a long-lasting bearing' on society. More recently[57] Cohn has made a plea for an 'anxious review' of third source powers

54. *Ibid.*, 238.
55. *Ibid.*, 247.
56. Margit Cohn, 'Medieval Chains, Invisible Links: on Non-statutory Powers of the Executive', (2005), 97–122.
57. Margit Cohn, 'Judicial Review of Non-Statutory Executive Powers after Bancoult: A Unified Anxious Model', PL (2009): 260–286.

(and of prerogative powers). Thus, both commentators essentially strongly prefer the principle that governmental action should be based on a statutory basis.

4. CONCLUSION AND OBSERVATIONS

The Executive has become a major player in the Social State. To some degree the stepping back by the legislature is, bearing in mind the nature and volume of governmental activity, inevitable. But it does raise the question of the democratic legitimacy of lawmaking and the aspect of legal certainty.

The first conclusions that can be drawn from the comparison of German law and English law is that in both legal systems the ideal of a statutory basis for actions of the executive is articulated. The legislature has a strong democratic legitimacy because of the imperative involvement of Parliament in legislation, and legislation offers more certainty. Administration is from a democratic viewpoint less legitimized and offers less certainty than the legislature.

The comparison also demonstrates the dilemmas that come with a strict demand of a statutory basis for governmental actions. Whenever a statutory basis is required for all, or almost all kinds of governmental actions, a discussion arises as to the requirements that have to be met by such a statutory basis. English law, which requires a statutory basis for all actions performed by local authorities and other statutory bodies, is not very strict in this respect: a more or less general description of a governmental task is sufficient, and case law shows some surprising examples of the kinds of actions which can be based on a certain statutory provision. In English law statutes do not only have a broad scope, they can also imply powers which they do not expressly articulate. English law also does not make a clear distinction between implied powers and indefinite legal terms. German law on the other hand, which demands a statutory basis for – at least – *Eingriffsverwaltung*, is much stricter concerning the requirements of such a statutory basis. The discussion as to the need for a statutory basis for *Leistungsverwaltung*, is surely influenced by the strictness of these requirements in German law. In German law the Administration does not only have to execute the law but it is also limited in how it can do this. Some acts can only be taken when they are based on a statutory authorization in which the administrative competence is specifically defined. Implied powers are really an exception in the German legal system, because of the strictness of the requirement of a statutory basis and the density of statutory provisions for actions of the Administration. German courts review the interpretation of indefinite terms by the Executive without restriction.

The comparison also demonstrates that both legal systems are struggling with the acceptance and restraining of non-statutory powers. As we have seen above, in English law the requirement of a statutory basis for governmental action is not fully applicable to the central government, whereas their actions can be based on the prerogative or the third source of power. Nowadays these kinds of powers are increasingly considered as problematic; several commentators have argued strongly in favour of extending the demand for a statutory basis to all governmental actions. It is interesting to see that the creation of general statutory authorizations for governmental action is not considered to be an adequate solution. Unlike what one would expect from the legal practice considering the statutory authorizations for statutory authorities, in this context attention is paid to the specificity of the statutory basis.

As to the 'third source of power' in English law, it is interesting to note that the continental legal systems of, for example, Germany and the Netherlands also acknowledge a comparable power for the Executive based on its status as a corporation soul. However, unlike English law the same goes for other public bodies, are capable of being subject to private legal rights and duties. The major difference with the English legal system is that the actions based on this particular status are not qualified as public law acts as is the case in English law, but as private law acts. In the continental systems legal theory is engaged on questions such as how to restrict the use of private law instruments and the applicability of public law standards to these kinds of actions. English law, looking for the creation of a statutory basis, appears to articulate this more as the responsibility of the legislature to take the necessary measures.

Chapter 4
National Legality and European Obligations

Maartje Verhoeven & Rob Widdershoven

1. INTRODUCTION

The legal order created by European union law, hereafter referred to as the European legal order, is often characterized as an integrated or composite legal order.[1] Within this legal order, the EU imposes all kinds of obligations upon the Member States, as parties to the Treaties, in the Treaties and secondary legislation. The principle of loyal cooperation obliges the Member States to take all measures necessary to meet these obligations and to apply them with regard to their citizens. In light of the principle of national institutional autonomy, the Member States are, in principle, free to decide which authority within the national legal order is empowered to apply a specific obligation, deriving from EU law.[2] Within the national legal order the principle of legality governs the attribution of powers to

1. J.H. Jans et al., *Europeanisation of Public Law* (Groningen: Europa Law Publishing, 2007) 18–22; L.F.M. Besselink, *A Composite European Constitution*, inaugural address on 10 Jan. 2007 (Groningen: Europa Law Publishing, 2007).
2. For instance Case C- 8/88, *Commission v. Germany* [1990] ECR I-2321; Case C-33/90, *Commission v. Italy* (Campania) [1991] ECR I-5987; Case C-435/92, *Association pour la protection des animaux savages* [1994], ECR I-67; Case C-344/01, *Commission v. Germany* [2004] ECR I-2081.

Leonard Besselink, Frans Pennings & Sacha Prechal (eds), *The Eclipse of the Legality Principle in the European Union*, pp. 55–72.

the different administrative authorities. In brief – the principle will be discussed in more detail in section 2 – the principle of legality requires that public authority within a Member State can only be exercised on the basis of, and in accordance with, enacted national laws. Hence, there is a dual basis of power when national authorities apply EU law:[3] the rule to be applied, or the power to be conferred, is thus created at the European level, while the power to actually apply the rule or exercise the power is conferred under national law. In other words, the substantive basis is in EU law, the institutional basis can be found in national law.

As long as the institutional, national law basis is guaranteed and has itself a basis in law, there is no problem. In practice, however, the situation is sometimes different as there is no or deficient institutional basis. This situation arises in particular when Member States fail to transpose directives, or fail to transpose them correctly, or when regulations are not made operational in national law. Therefore, this contribution focuses on these two methods of giving effect of EU law.

When the necessary national institutional basis is lacking, the question arises as to whether national administrative authorities can base powers directly on EU law. From the point of view of a strictly national principle of legality, the answer is simply no. In the composite European legal order, however, such an answer is not satisfactory, since the methods of giving effect of European law have their own 'European legality'. They have been adopted in conformity with the applicable European rules by the competent institutions, and derive legal importance in the Member States from the EU Treaties and the case law of the European Court of Justice. This European legality might be able to compensate for shortcomings with regard to national legality. Thus, a 'composite legality' may arise, in which in principle, national legality may be totally replaced by European legality.

This contribution focuses on the question of the extent to which national administrative authorities can derive their powers directly from directives and regulations. To answer this question, first the content and scope of the principle of legality are discussed in section 2. Then the question of if, and to what extent, national administrative authorities can derive powers directly from directives (section 3) and regulations (section 4) is discussed. The requirements of both EU law and Dutch law in this regard are taken into account. For the extent to which national administrative authorities can derive their powers directly from directives or regulations, section 5 discusses whether this is problematic in the light of the functions of the legality principle. Finally, the contribution is finished by a conclusion in section 6.

2. CONTENT AND SCOPE OF THE LEGALITY PRINCIPLE

As stated above, the legality principle requires that public authority can only be exercised on the basis of, and in accordance with, enacted laws. The principle is

3. See for instance, Jans (2007), *supra* n. 1, 23–29; M.J. Jacobs, W. den Ouden & N. Verheij, 'Bezint eer ge begint!', NTB 6 (2008): 160.

one of the keynote principles of the rule of law, since it guarantees that the government can only have powers with regard to citizens on the basis of the law, and it is subject to this law when it acts. Moreover, the principle can be related to the principle of democracy as the basis in the law guarantees that the government only has powers which derive from a general rule adopted by, or at least with, the assent of the representatives of the people.[4]

The principle of legality seems to be recognized as a general principle of European law by all Member States and the EU itself.[5] The precise content, however, and especially the requirements of a 'basis in the law' differ considerably. For instance, in the United Kingdom fundamental rights can be limited by every governmental rule that is, 'foreseeable and accessible',[6] which may include governmental policy rules, whereas restrictions of fundamental rights in most continental States have to be retraceable to the Constitution. Moreover, within one Member State also, various requirements with regard to the legal basis may apply to different forms of power. Roughly speaking, one may say that with regard to *Eingriffsverwaltung* – that is, to say, powers which interfere with the rights of individuals, such as freedom or ownership – more extensive formal requirements apply than with regard to so-called *Leistungsverwaltung* – powers of the government with positive consequences for individuals, such as the grant of financial aid. In the Netherlands, for instance, with regard to *Eingriffsverwaltung*, generally the rule applies that powers have to be established in a formal statute adopted by the government and parliament jointly, or on the basis of such a statute.[7] With regard to specific forms of *Eingriffsverwaltung*, the Constitution even requires that delegation is not allowed. This applies, for instance, for the levying of taxes[8] and the criminal penalization and the determination of criminal penalties.[9] With regard to *Leistungsverwaltung*, such as the grant of subsidies, a more limited requirement applies: this should be based on a 'statutory rule' (*wettelijk voorschrift*).[10] This

4. See in general on the principle of legality in Europe, J. Schwarze, *European Administrative Law* (London: Sweet & Maxwell, 2006), 212–232; compare, for instance for German law recently, H. Rieckhoff, *Der Vorbehalt des Gesetzes im Europarecht* (Tübingen: Mohr Siebeck Jus Internationale et Europaeum, 2007); for French law, J.B. Auby & L. Cluzel-Métayer, 'Administrative Law in France', in: *Administrative Law of the European Union, its Member States and the United States*, ed. R.J.G.H. Seerden (Antwerpen-Oxford: Intersentia, 2007), 77; G. Braibant & B. Stirn, *Le droit administratif Français* (Paris: Presses de Sciences Po/Dalloz, 2005), 231; for Dutch law, for example, D.J. Elzinga & R. de Lange, *Van der Pots Handboek van het Nederlandse Staatsrecht* (Deventer: Kluwer, 2006), 651; C.A.J.M. Kortmann, *Constitutioneel Recht* (Deventer: Kluwer, 2008), 51.
5. Jans (2007), *supra* n. 23. See Joined Cases 46/87 and 227/88, *Hoechst* [1989], ECR 2859. Although the latter case concerns a fine, the Court has formulated its considerations in rather broad, general terms.
6. Compare Jurgens/Verhoeven/Willemsen in this book; see the Sunday Times case of the ECHR (ECHR 26 Apr. 1979, Publ. ECHR Series A vol. 30).
7. Dutch Supreme Court 27 Jun. 1986 (Methadonbrief), NJ 1987, 898; Dutch Supreme Court 22 Jun. 1972 (Fluoridering), NJ 1973, 386.
8. Article 104 Dutch Constitution.
9. Article 16 and Art. 89, second paragraph, Constitution.
10. Compare Art. 4:23 (1) GALA.

not only includes statutes adopted by the government and parliament jointly, but also, for instance, international treaties, delegated rules of law adopted by organs of the central government, or general applicable rules adopted by decentralized authorities. The requirement of a statutory rule as legal basis for granting subsidies was introduced in the Dutch General Administrative Law Act (GALA) in 1997; beforehand subsidies could also be granted on the basis of a policy rule or a covenant. That shows that the requirements which derive from the legality principle not only differ for different governmental powers, but also from time to time.

Looking at the literature, three different functions of the legality principle can be distinguished: the function of legitimation, the function of attribution and the regulating function.[11]

Legitimation: the principle of legality guarantees that the rules to which individuals are subject can only be adopted in conformity with the right of codecision of the elected representatives of the people.[12] This way the principle safeguards the observance of the principle of democracy. The function of legitimation is also of importance with regard to positive actions by the government, such as the grant of subsidies.[13] One of the reasons for limiting the freedom of government to develop its own subsidy rules by introducing the requirement of a statutory rule in 1997 in the Netherlands was to allow the elected representatives of the people to have more influence on the governmental expenses.[14]

Attribution: the principle of legality also has a function with regard to the designation of competent bodies, since authorities only have the powers attributed to them by law. The law provides which body is competent for which power. This is important from the point of view of attribution of powers among different branches of the administration, for instance, by the principle of decentralization. Moreover, the legality principle safeguards that it is clear to the citizen as to which authority can apply which power with regard to him or her.

Regulation: finally, the principle of legality regulates the exercise of powers by the administration. It provides substantive boundaries, primarily in the statute which provides the power concerned. Moreover, the principle of speciality is related to this, which provides that authorities in which the power is assigned are not allowed to promote any other interest than the specific subject of the law concerned. Moreover, the fundamental rights and general principles of law also provide limits to the exercise of powers by authorities. Thus, arbitrary use of powers is prevented.

---

11. Compare the introduction of this book; see M.C. Burkens et al., *Beginselen van de democratische rechtsstaat* (Deventer: Tjeenk Willink, 2001), 49; N. Verheij, 'Alleen de wet heerscht over ons', *Publiek Domein* (1989), 188–197.
12. Dutch Supreme Court 22 Jun. 1972 (Fluoridering), NJ 1973, 386. Compare F.J. van Ommeren, 'Fluoridering', in *AB Klassiek*, ed. T. Barkhuysen et al. (Deventer: Kluwer, 2009), 49.
13. *Kamerstukken II* (Parliamentary Papers) 1993–1994, 23 700, no. 3, 38–40.
14. Compare for a comparative line of reasoning on the Community level Case C-106/96, *United Kingdom v. Commission* [1998] ECR I-2729, in which the Court has stated that the spending of Community budget by the Commission requires a base in a basic act of the Council.

3. THE DIRECTIVE AS DIRECT BASIS FOR POWERS OF THE ADMINISTRATION IN THE NATIONAL LEGAL ORDER

3.1. General

Article 288(3) Treaty on the Functioning of the European Union (ex Article 249(3) EC Treaty) provides: 'A directive shall be binding, as to the result to be achieved, upon each Member State to which it is addressed, but shall leave to the national authorities the choice of form and methods.' This choice is made by the Member State when it implements the directive, which, according to the Court of Justice, must be done in binding provisions of national law. This generally means that directives are transposed into general applicable rules. These rules include the designation of the authority which is competent to execute and apply the implementing legislation. Hence, the designation of the authority which is indirectly empowered to apply the directive takes place by national law, observing the national principle of legality. The directive itself, however, cannot function as a direct basis for the power of a national authority, as will be explaned below.

In the case of late transposition, incorrect transposition, or when complete application of the directive concerned is not actually ensured,[15] provisions of directives can have effect in the national legal order by means of direct effect (if the provision is unconditional and sufficiently precise) and consistent interpretation.[16] Both methods of giving effect, however, cannot lead to the creation of a new power that did not exist previously under national law. For consistent interpretation, this follows from the fact that the Court of Justice systematically rules that this obligation applies within the limits of the powers of courts and administrative authorities.[17] Hence, if no power is available under national law, consistent interpretation is not possible.

The prohibitions of horizontal and inverse direct effect provide that direct effect of directive provisions which leads to obligations for citizens, cannot be a direct basis for powers of national administrative authorities.[18] Because of these prohibitions, which mainly derive from the principle of legal certainty, a directive cannot impose obligations on citizens without transposition into national law. With regard to directive provisions which create *rights* for citizens, however, the same applies: direct effect of such provisions cannot lead to the creation of new powers of administrative authorities under national law. This follows from *Dorsch Consult*,[19] in which the Court of Justice ruled that a national appeal body,

15. Case C-62/00, *Marks & Spencer* [2002] ECR I-6325; compare R. Ortlep & M.J.M. Verhoeven, 'The Struggle of the Dutch Council of State in Applying Marks & Spencer', REALaw 1 (2008): 91–100.
16. Compare Jans (2007), *supra* n. 1, 63–112.
17. Case 14/83, *Von Colson & Kamann* [1984] ECR 1891; Case C-106//89, *Marleasing* [1990] ECR I-4135; Case C-397/01, *Pfeiffer* [2004] ECR I-8835.
18. Case 152/84, *Marshall I* [1986] ECR 723; Case C-91/92, *Faccini Dori* [1994] ECR I-3325.
19. Case C-54/96, *Dorsch Consult* [1997] ECR I-4961.

which had competence in relation to procedures for the award of public works and supply contracts, could not base the power to hear appeals relating to procedures for the award of public service contracts directly on a directly effective provision of a directive. The Court explicitly referred to the principle of national institutional autonomy in this regard.

Although both consistent interpretation and direct effect thus cannot lead to the creation of new powers on the basis of directive provisions, both methods of giving effect can regulate the contents of a national administrative power considerably. In this way they are of great importance for the regulatory function of the legality principle. The boundaries of direct effect and consistent interpretation of directive provisions in this regard will be addressed in the next paragraphs in light of case law from the Court of Justice and the Dutch administrative courts.

3.2. Direct Effect

The Court of Justice has systematically ruled that national courts are obliged to set aside national law in the case of an incompatibility between a provision of national law and a directly effective provision of a directive, and, if necessary, apply the directive provision instead. This obligation also applies to administrative authorities.[20]

European Union law limits the obligation of national courts and authorities to apply directly effective provisions of directives by the prohibition of inverse vertical direct effect and horizontal direct effect of directives. The scope of this prohibition, however, has been diminished in so-called triangular situations, when the interests of the person addressed by an administrative decision may be directly opposed to those of third parties. This regularly occurs in national administrative law cases, particularly in economic law and environmental law. The Court of Justice has decided in this regard that 'mere adverse repercussions on the rights of third parties, even if the repercussions are certain, do not justify preventing an individual from invoking the provisions of a directive against the Member State concerned'.[21] In other words: the prohibition of inverse direct effect of directive provisions does not apply when the negative consequences for one party (e.g., the owner of a permit) are the necessary consequence of the successful invokement by another private party (e.g., an environmental group) of the non-transposed directive provision against the State.

The application of directly effective provisions of directives can also be limited by national law, more specifically, the national principle of legality. This limitation does not apply when national law provides for a power on the same subject as the directive, and thus the directly effective provisions can be applied by the execution of that power. When the national regulation of the power concerned

20. Case 103/88, *Fratelli Costanzo* [1989] ECR 1839.
21. Case C-201/02, *Wells* [2004] ECR I-723 (in an environmental dispute); Joined cases C-152-154/07, *Arcor* [2008] ECR I-5959 (in a telecommunication dispute).

is incompatible with the directly effective provisions of the directive, the national rules are set aside and replaced by the directive provision. For individuals this change can, of course, imply that the power in national law is regulated in another way than might be expected on the basis of national law.

The national legality principle, however, does stand in the way of the application of directly effective provisions of directives when national law does not provide for any power at all which relates to the provision concerned. For example, when a Member State does not have any environmental legislation at all, no power will exist within which directly effective provisions of European environmental law can be applied. Although in general this does not apply in the Netherlands, a comparable situation occurred at the introduction of the Nitrates Directive. During a period of ten years, this directive had not been transposed correctly,[22] but no administrative power was available which allowed for the application of the directly effective norms provided in the directive, as Dutch law did not require a permit for the putting nitrate into the soil.[23]

Tensions with the national principle of legality can also occur when national law provides for a power which theoretically makes the application of a directive provision possible, but nevertheless which is regulated by national law in such a way that no possibility exists of incorporating the directive. In such cases, the principle of speciality is at odds with the directly effective provision of the directive. In the Netherlands, such tensions exist with regard to the application of the comprehensive mandatory enumeration which, for example, exists with regard to building permits (Article 44 of the Housing Act). These permits can only be refused by the authorities concerned when one of the grounds of refusal named in the act concerned are applicable. Should a permit then also be denied when it is clearly contrary to EU law, for example, the Habitat Directive, despite the fact that this directive is not named in the act concerned? The literature and lower administrative courts generally answer this question in the affirmative, as does the Dutch Council of State in the limited case law which exists in this regard.[24] The background of this case law lies in the European obligation to set aside national law in case of incompatibility with directly effective provisions of EU law, including directive provisions. Although we agree with this case law, the regulatory function of the speciality principle and the legality principle is considerably limited. This also diminishes the protective function of these principles.

---

22. See Case C-322/00, *Commission v. Netherlands* [2003] ECR I-11267.
23. See H.F.M.W. van Rijswick, 'Het Nederlands mestbeleid te kakken gezet', NTER 3 (2004) 48–56.
24. Dutch Council of State 16 Mar. 2005, LJN AT0540; see also District Court Zutphen 4 Jan. 2006, LJN AV0543; for an opposite view, however, *see* Council of State 28 Oct. 2005, LJN AU5387. See for more references, J. Jans, 'European Law and the Inapplicability of the "Speciality Principle"', REALaw 1 (2008): 35–49.

3.3. Consistent Interpretation

The case law of the Court of Justice obliges national courts and authorities to interpret, within the limits of their powers, national law in the light of a directive as far as possible.[25] This obligation can have far reaching consequences, but is limited by the principle of legal certainty.

The principle of legal certainty implies in the first place that consistent interpretation may not lead to the creation or aggravation of national criminal liability.[26] The Court would deem that a violation of the principle of non-retroactivity, which is safeguarded, amongst others, by Article 7 European Convention for the Protection of Human Rights (ECHR). Because of this limitation, a citizen cannot be prosecuted or punished for the violation of a provision of a European directive when this violation has not been penalized in national law. The Dutch Council of State has applied the same limitation with regard to the charge of an administrative fine.[27] This is also not allowed on the basis of consistent interpretation of the national provision. The background to this equation of administrative sanctions with criminal law may be found in the fact that administrative fines are also to be considered as *criminal charges* within the meaning of Article 6 ECHR.[28]

In the second place, the Court of Justice has derived from the principle of legal certainty that consistent interpretation *contra legem* is not allowed.[29] Thus, consistent interpretation of a provision of national law cannot lead to an interpretation which is incompatible with the provision itself. As opposed to direct effect, consistent interpretation is thus not suitable by definition to alter a comprehensive mandatory enumeration.[30] The principle of speciality thus remains upright.

Thirdly, the Dutch Council of State has ruled that consistent interpretation cannot be applied to extend the scope of a prohibition that is, linked to the requirement of a permit.[31] The Council of State regards this as incompatible with the principle of legal certainty, as this extension cannot be known by the individuals who have to comply with the prohibition. We agree to this view, which may be seen as an application of the principle of legality. As said above, the principle of legality implies that consistent interpretation can only be applied to adapt an existing national power in a European way, but not to create an entirely new power.

---

25. Case 14/83, *Von Colson & Kamann* [1984] ECR 1891; Case C-106//89, *Marleasing* [1990] ECR I-4135; Case C-397/01, *Pfeiffer* [2004] ECR I-8835.
26. Case 80/86, *Kolpinghuis* [1987] ECR 3969; Joined Cases C-387/02, C-391/02 & C-403/02, *Berlusconi* [2004] ECR I-3565.
27. Dutch Council of State 4 Mar. 2009 (Mandemakers) *AB* 2009, 156.
28. ECHR 21 Feb. 1984 (*Öztürk*), Publ ECHR Series A vol. 73.
29. Case C-105/03, *Pupino* [2005] ECR I-5285. See in Dutch case law, Council of State 29 May 2001, *JB* 2001/179; Council of State 7 Dec. 2005 (Boxtel), *AB* 2006/67; Council of State 5 Dec. 2007, *AB* 2008, 18.
30. See also Jans, 'European Law and the Inapplicability of the "Speciality Principle" ', REALaw 1 (2008): 35–49.
31. Dutch Council of State 28 Feb. 2007 (Fortis), *AB* 2007/183.

Therefore, the interpretation of national law in the light of directives assumes the existence of a national power which can be applied consistently. If such power is not available, there is nothing to interpret in the light of EU law.

When an administrative power is available under national law and the power concerned leaves quite some discretion, then generally, consistent interpretation may guarantee the effect of a directive in the national legal order. Nevertheless, this may imply that the national law is interpreted in a rather different way than before. In this regard one may point at the fact that the Dutch Supreme Court has decided in fiscal cases that the phrasing of the provision of national law is decisive enough to decide to what extent consistent interpretation is possible, and not the history of the law concerned, which may deviate from the obligation.[32] The Supreme Court rests this view on *Wagner Miret*, in which the Court of Justice stated that 'every national court must presume that the State had the intention of fulfilling entirely the obligations arising from the directive concerned'.[33] This also applies when it is clear that the legislature was not aware of any obligation whatsoever. The only reason to deviate from this obligation is in the rather theoretical case that the legislature has explicitly stated the intention that the national provision should differ from the directive. In fact, consistent interpretation would be *contra legem* in such cases, which is deemed incompatible with the principle of legal certainty by the Court.

The discussed case law proves that in the view of the Dutch Supreme Court, the duty of consistent interpretation is not limited by a prohibition of inverse vertical effect. That is, to say, in the discussed cases consistent interpretation can lead to the imposition of higher taxes than could have been expected by individuals on the basis of the legal history of the national legislation. The Dutch Council of State shares the view that consistent interpretation is also allowed in inverse vertical situations.[34] In the light of *Pfeiffer*, in which the Court of Justice explicitly established that consistent interpretation is allowed in horizontal situations, this view seems correct.[35] After all, consistent interpretation does not mean that a directive itself is applied against an individual, but the national law concerned. Therefore, less objections exist from the view of the principles of legal certainty and legality since individuals have to be prepared for the reality that judicial interpretation may sometimes lead to unexpected consequences. Thus, the foregoing shows that consistent interpretation of directives may modify the application of national powers, and limits the regulatory function of the national principle of legality in a rather far reaching manner.

32. Dutch Supreme Court 10 Aug. 2007 (Wandelviercaagse), *AB* 2007/291; Dutch Supreme Court 6 Jun. 2008 (Joustra), *AB* 2008/214.
33. Case C-334/92, *Wagner Miret* [1993], ECR I-6911.
34. Dutch Council of State 7 Dec. 2005 (Boxtel), *AB* 2006/67.
35. Case C-397/01, *Pfeiffer* [2004] ECR I-8835.

4. THE REGULATION AS DIRECT BASIS FOR POWERS OF THE ADMINISTRATION IN THE NATIONAL LEGAL ORDER

4.1. The European View

Article 288 TFEU (ex Article 249 EC) provides that a regulation 'shall have general application. It shall be binding in its entirety and directly applicable in all Member States'. This definition suggests that the founding fathers of the European Communities assumed that in principle, a regulation can be applied in a Member State without being made operational in national law. If this starting point is true, a regulation can in principle function as the direct basis for a power of a national authority. To that extent, regulations are completely equivalent to national laws.[36]

Examples of regulations which do not require any operational implementation in national law, however, are scarce and cannot be found – as far as we know – with regard to regulations which are executed by national authorities. A very uncommon example is Regulation 1/2003 on the implementation of the rules on competition laid down in Articles 81 and 82 of the Treaty.[37] This Regulation provides, in Chapter 5, for investigative powers for the Commission or its servants, which are applied mainly within the national legal orders of the Member States. Hence, the servants of the Commission can then apply these powers within the Member State without any basis in the national law of the Member State concerned.

Most regulations, however, require some implementation into national law by the Member States before they can actually be applied. The precise scope and content of the implementation depends on the regulation concerned.[38] Some regulations require that substantive provisions are completed or made concrete in national law. Many regulations require national law to provide for rules of procedure and rules on enforcement. Last but not least, as a rule, national law will establish which authority within the national legal order will execute the regulation, as most regulations do not mention by name the competent authorities in each Member State. As a rule, the application is directed to 'the competent authority' or the Member State as such. Which concrete authority is competent, then, has to be established in national law, following the rules that national law provides in this regard. This practice fits in with the idea of the principle of national institutional autonomy. Besides, it also has, we assume, a practical background,

---

36. E. Steyger, 'Wringend recht. Doorwerking van gemeenschapsrecht bezien vanuit het perspectief van de nationale overheid', in: E. Steyger, R.J.G.M. Widdershoven & A.W.H. Meij (eds), *Europees recht en het Nederlandse bestuursrecht: preadviezen VAR-Reeks 16* (Alphen a/d Rijn: Samson H.D. Tjeenk Willink, 1996), 7–96, particularly at 23 and 28. See also for the same point of view in German law, H. Rieckhoff (2007), *supra* n. 4, in which the author states that a regulation is recognized as 'Gesetz im Sinne des deutschen Gesetzesvorbehalts'.
37. PbEG 2003, L 1/1; currently concerning Arts 101 and 102 TFEU.
38. See Richard Kral, 'National Normative Implementation of EC Regulations: An Exceptional or Rather Common Matter', ELRev. 33 (2008): 243–256.

as it would be problematic for the European legislature to assign the correct authorities which are the most suitable to apply legislation in all twenty-seven Member States.

Since regulations which assign the competent national authorities by name are very scarce, hardly any case law of the Court of Justice exists which affirms the view that theoretically, regulations can be the direct basis of the powers of concrete national administrative authorities. The only case that touches upon this theme is a rather recent judgment on the *European Structural Funds*.[39]

The basis for this case was, in brief, the fact that the Dutch minister of Social affairs and Employment withdrew several awards of subsidy and claimed back the money concerned, since the grant of the subsidy was in violation with the European regulations concerning structural funds. The Dutch Council of State, which referred several preliminary questions to Luxembourg, deemed that the withdrawal and recovery of the subsidy was not allowed under national law, and that thus a legal basis to do so was lacking.[40] Therefore, the Council referred the preliminary question of whether 'a Member State or an administrative authority of that State derive a power directly – that is, to say without a basis in national law – from a regulation', more specifically, Article 23(1) of Regulation nr. 4253/88,[41] which provides that 'Member States shall take the necessary measures in implementing the operations, to recover any amounts lost as a result of an irregularity or negligence.' The answer of the Court of Justice to this question in the English version of judgment was as follows: 'Article 23(1) of Regulation nr. 4253/88 requires the Member States to recover any amounts lost as a result of an irregularity or negligence without there being any need for authority to do so under national law.'[42]

In our view, this answer suggests more than it literally says. It is clear that the regulation concerned imposes an obligation on the Member States to recover the amount lost, independent of the attribution of powers or authority in the national legal order. This is self-evident, because otherwise a Member State could escape

39. Joined Cases C-383/06 & C-385/06, *Vereniging Nationaal Overlegorgaan Sociale Werkvoorziening (ESF)* [2008] ECR I-1561.

40. Views may differ as to whether the assumption of the Council of State that the statutory basis of an administrative power elapses when the accompanying regulatory provisions of law concerned are incompatible with Community law is correct. In our view, the power as such remains unimpaired. The only consequence of the incompatibility is that the national regulatory provision has to be interpreted in accordance with Community law, or left unapplied. In terms of this book, however, this case did not concern a problem of attribution, but of regulation. This view is supported by the completion of the case by the Council of State in its decision of 24 Dec. 2008 (JB 2009, 53) in which it revitalized the national power by interpreting it in the light of the Regulation. That allowed the minister to revoke and reclaim the subsidy, as far as required by Community law. This consistent interpretation would not have been possible if the power no longer existed because of the incompatibility with Community law.

41. Dutch Council of State 30 August, *AB* 2007, 240 and 24.

42. In other language versions of the judgment, the answer seems even more pertinent. According to these versions, the Regulation in question requires the Member States to recover any amount lost (. . .), 'sans qu'une habilitation prévue par le droit national soit nécessaire' (French), 'ohne dass er einer Ermächtigung durch nationales Recht bedarf' (German) and 'zonder dat een bevoegdheidsattributie naar nationaal recht noodzakelijk is'(Dutch).

its obligations by not providing for the recovery by competent authorities in national law.[43] Nevertheless, it is problematic that it is not the Member State as such which withdraws or recovers the amount: this is done by the authorities which have been attributed the power to do so by national law. This is not only the way it works in the Netherlands, but also in the other Member States and the EU itself, in which the tasks and powers have not been attributed to the Member State or EU as such, but to the different authorities or institutions of these organizations. The Court, however, focused on the Member State, and remained silent over the possibility that national administrative authorities derive their powers directly from a regulation. In this regard, the Court took advantage of the discretionary room left by the preliminary question, which was not concentrated with administrative authorities, but with 'a Member State or an administrative authority of that State'. In this regard, the answer can also be seen as an affirmation of the principle of national institutional autonomy: the Court was very explicit on the obligations for the Member States, but avoided the question as to what extent this also applies to administrative authorities of that State. Thus, the creation of powers for administrative authorities is left to the Member States.

All in all, the *ESF* case cannot be regarded as confirmation of our view that regulations can directly provide powers for specified administrative authorities. The attributive function of the national principle of legality is left untouched to that extent. It should not be forgotten, however, that it is clear and undisputed that a regulation can be greatly modify the execution of an existing power of a national authority. Thus, the regulatory function of the national legality principle can be taken over to a greater or lesser degree by a regulation.

The extent to which a regulation takes over the regulation of national powers, depends on the contents of the regulation concerned. Some regulations provide for rules for a part of the regulated subject, and leave room for additional substantive or procedural national rules. Others, however, regulate a subject to a greater extent, or even exhaustively. In such cases, there is little or no room for supplementary national law. As far as national law that has already been adopted contrary to the regulation is concerned then, national authorities and courts can assess whether the incompatibility can be solved by means of consistent interpretation of the provisions of national law. If that is, not possible, the provisions of national law should be set aside in favour of the rules of the regulation. If a regulation regulates a power exhaustively, but does not mention the competent national authority by name, the Member States can make the regulation operational by assigning the competent authority. The execution of the power, however, is then totally regulated by the regulation.

4.2. Regulations in the Dutch Legal Order

The foregoing can be retraced in the Dutch legal order. It is undisputed that regulations can be considered as statutory rules ('wettelijke voorschriften').

43. M.L. van Emmerik, 'De Nederlandse Grondwet in een veellagige rechtsorde', Themis 169 (2008): 145–161, particularly at 151.

The concept of statutory rule is rather broad and includes not only statutes adopted by the government and parliament jointly, but also 'all rules adopted by organs which derive regulatory powers by the Constitution or a statute',[44] which includes 'resolutions by international institutions'.[45] In the explanation of Article 4:23 (1) of the GALA, which provides that subsidies may only be granted on the basis of a statutory rule, the legislature has stated that this requirement is also met when a subsidy has a basis in a European regulation.[46] That makes it clear that subsidies in principle can be granted on the sole basis of a regulation, and that as a principle, a regulation can provide national authorities with a power to grant subsidies. In practice, however, such specific empowerment is very scarce, since – as was said above – a regulation hardly ever mentions by name which national organ is competent to execute the regulation. The Dutch Council of State and the Trade and Industry Appeals Tribunal have held that if neither the regulation nor national law provides which authority is competent, the regulation cannot be applied lawfully.[47]

Other Dutch case law shows that regulations can even take over the function of formal statutes adopted by the government and parliament jointly. That follows from a judgment of the President of the Dutch Trade and Industry Appeals Tribunal,[48] which held – referring to Article 249 EC (now Article 288 TFEU) – that a regulation provided the power for the Minister of Agriculture to apply a regime of control to a company, although this power was not made operational in national law. The Minister concerned had been appointed as the competent authority for the application of the regulation, so it was clear which authority was competent.

Another example can be found in a customs case of the Haarlem District Court.[49] In this case also it was very clear which administrative organ was competent. The levy, however, was based on a Customs decree – a delegated lower decree based on the Dutch Customs Law. The provisions of the Customs decree concerned were meant to make the Community Customs Code operational in the national legal order. The applicant, thus, argued that the provisions of the Customs decree were incompatible with the legality principle as codified in Article 104 of the Constitution, which requires that taxes are levied in formal statutes adopted by the government and parliament jointly. The District Court, however, rejected this argument, as the power to levy duties was based on the EC Treaty and the

44. PG Awb I, 64. See also R. Ortlep, 'Drie Nederlandse rechtsbeginselen in communautair perspectief', JBplus (2009), 81–106, especially 82–84; R.J.G.M. Widdershoven et al., *De Europese agenda van de Awb* (Den Haag: BJu, 2007), 24–26.
45. See Art. 93 of the Dutch Constitution. 'Resolutions' is the official translation of the Dutch Ministry of the Interior and Kingdom Relations; 'binding decisions', however, seems to be more appropriate.
46. Kamerstukken II 1993–1994, 23 700, no. 3, 41.
47. Dutch Council of State 19 Apr. 2006, *AB* 2006, 296; Dutch Trade and Industry Appeals Tribunal LJN BL0650 and LJN BL0649.
48. President of the Dutch Trade and Industry Appeals Tribunal 28 Aug. 2008, *AB* 2008, 344. Compare also Dutch Trade and Industry Appeals Tribunal 25 Feb. 2009, *AB* 2009, 153 in this regard.
49. Dutch district Court Haarlem 28 Apr. 2009, LJN BI9227.

Community Customs Code based on this Treaty. This Code provides for an independent and directly applicable Community system, which renders unnecessary a statute as required in Article 104 Constitution. Thus, in such way, a regulation can bypass the rather firm requirement that the legality principle provides for the levying of taxes.

The foregoing shows that in the Dutch legal order, regulations can not only be equated to statutary rules, but also can take over the function of formal statutes. This, however, does not mean that every regulation is suitable to do so. In this regard, one may point at the judgment of the Dutch Council of State in the case of *Fleuren-Compost*.[50] In this case, the Council of State rejected an appeal against the recovery of unlawful state aid, but did annul the accompanying recovery of interest. The Council ruled that national law required a specific statutory basis for this recovery,[51] which was not available at the time.[52] According to the Council, such authority could neither be based on Article 14(2) of Regulation 659/1999, nor on the decision of the Commission ordering recovery, nor on Article 87(1) EC (now Article 107(1) TFEU).

From the point of view of national legality this judgment of the Council of State can be welcomed, although its protective importance for citizens should not be overestimated, as the Council of State did accept the recovery of interest by the Dutch state on the basis of private law. From a European law perspective, however, one can cast some doubts on the judgment, particularly since Article 14(2) of Regulation 659/1999 provides that the recovery of unlawful state aid by definition includes the recovery of interest.[53] After all, that is, the only way to rectify all financial advantages of the unlawful state aid and restore the competition.[54] The regulation system thus regards the recovery of interest as implied by the decision obliging the recovery of state aid. Since a legal basis exists for the latter, in our view the recovery of interest aid could have been based on that legal basis as well.

It is generally accepted in the Dutch legal order that a regulation can directly provide powers for administrative authorities, and can also take over the attributive function of the legality principle by attributing these powers to specific administrative authorities. This, however, applies mainly in theory, as it is generally required in practice that national law attributes the powers deriving from regulations amongst the authorities, as regulations generally do not mention the competent authorities in the Member States by name.

---

50. Dutch Council of State 11 Jan. 2006, *AB* 2006, 208.
51. Dutch Council of State 10 Jul. 2002, *AB* 2003, 123.
52. A legal base will be provided for in the bill on the recovery of illegal state aid (Kamerstukken II 2007–2008, 31418, nos 1–3).
53. Article 14(2) of Regulation 659/1999 laying down detailed rules for the application of Art. 93 of the EC Treaty prescribes: 'The aid to be recovered pursuant to a recovery decision shall include interest at an appropriate rate fixed by the Commission. Interest shall be payable from the date on which the unlawful aid was at the disposal of the beneficiary until the date of its recovery.'
54. P. Adriaanse, 'Terugvordering van onrechtmatige staatssteun. Knelpunten en oplossingen in het Nederlandse recht', in: *Europees recht effectueren*, ed. T. Barkhuysen, W. den Ouden & E. Steyger (Alphen aan den Rijn: Kluwer, 2007), 202.

That regulations can take over the regulatory function of the legality principle is not controversial at all in the Netherlands. That follows from the abovementioned judgment of the President of the Trade and Industry Appeals Tribunal, in which it was held that a minister, on the basis of a regulation, could execute a supervisory power, despite the fact that this had not been made operational in national law except for the appointment of the minister as competent organ. Besides, it has happened numerous times in the last fifty years that an administrative authority or a court has set aside a provision of national law and applied a provision of a regulation instead. This may concern all kinds of rules of national law, including general national principles of law which may have been codified or not, like the principle of legitimate expectations of the principle of legal certainty. If the regulation does not provide any room for the application of these principles, they are set aside.[55]

5. EVALUATION IN THE LIGHT OF 'COMPOSITE' LEGALITY

The preceding sections may lead to the conclusion that the national principle of legality only has a limited meaning when the application of directives and regulations is concerned. With regard to directives, the attributive function still exists, since directives cannot create new powers for national authorities (or courts) without transposition in national law. However, the regulatory function of the principle is considerably limited, since directives can modify the contents of existing powers under national law to a large extent. With regard to regulations, the regulatory function of the national legality principle is even more eroded. Moreover, regulations can also take over the attributive function, since they can directly confer powers onto national authorities. It has to be mentioned, however, that regulations can only lawfully be applied if a specific organ is appointed, either in national law or in the regulation itself. The latter, however, is very scarce in practice. The consequence of the foregoing is that only a limited discretion is left for the national parliament in the process of law making. Hence, the legitimatizing function of the national principle of legality is also affected. Therefore, this paragraph addresses the question of whether the erosion of the national principle of legality, also in the light of the concerned functions, is compensated sufficiently.

It is beyond question that the legitimizing function of the national principle of legality is of little importance when the national implementation of directives and regulations is concerned. With regard to regulations, the task of the national legislature is limited to operational sing the provisions of the regulation, which are

55. See for instance, Dutch Trade and Industry Appeals Tribunal 19 Oct. 2005, JB 2006, 24, in which this court regarded the codification of the principle of legitimate expectations in Regulation 3887/92 as exhaustive and saw no further room for the national principle of legitimate expectations. The application of a national principle can also be prevented by the principle of effectiveness. See Council of State 11 Jan. 2006, *AB* 2006, 208.

often highly detailed. No room is left for choices at the national level. Therefore, lower national regulatory instruments can be used to put regulations into operation. The transposition of directives generally provides more discretionary room for the national legislature, although often important choices are already made in the directive itself. As far as national parliaments are involved in the implementation of directives and regulations, their involvement *ex post* therefore only provides limited democratic legitimation. The question, however, is how problematic this is, as compensating mechanisms do exist at the European level.

First and foremost, the role of national parliaments is taken over by the European parliament, that in one way or another – usually through the procedure of codecision – is involved with the adoption of regulations and directives. This involvement safeguards a certain extent of democratic legitimation with regard to the contents of these regulations and directives, although the powers of the European parliament in the European legislative process are more limited than those of national parliaments in national legislative matters. Furthermore, it is important to notice that national parliaments have the possibility of influencing the contents of regulations and directives *ex ante*, before adoption.[56] As of 2006, the Commissions sends all proposals for European legislation directly to the national parliaments. They can discuss these proposals with their own governments in national parliament and can use their national powers to force their governments to put forward specific provisions in the Council.[57] Moreover, they can advise the Commission on the proposal. Under the Treaty of Lisbon, the involvement of national parliaments in the European legislative process will be further extended. Particularly important in this regard is the Protocol on the application of the principles of subsidiarity and proportionality (Protocol nr. 2), which introduces a yellow and orange card procedure. In brief, this procedure allows a group of national parliaments to enforce the consideration of a legislative proposal, or even its dismissal. These developments increase the 'composite' democratic control by the European parliament and the national parliaments on the adoption of regulations and directives.[58] In our view, this sufficiently counterbalances the loss of the legitimizing function of the national principle of legality.

As stated above, the *attributive function* of the national principle of legality is still unaffected with regard to the implementation of directives. The national legislature transposes the directive and decides which authority will be empowered to execute the national legislation concerned. In this regard, national views on the attribution of powers and decentralization are of importance. With regard to

56. Compare L.F.M. Besselink & B. van Mourik, 'THE NETHERLANDS – The Roles of the National Parliament and the European Parliament in EU Decision-Making: The Approval of the Lisbon Treaty in the Netherlands', *European Public Law* 15 (2009): 307–318. Compare also L.A.J Senden & T.A.J.A. Vandamme, 'Het Verdrag van Lissabon en het Europese mandaat van de nationale parlementen', SEW 57 (2009): 4.
57. In Protocol no. 1 of the Treaty of Lisbon this procedure is formalized.
58. L.F.M. Besselink, 'National Parliaments in the EU's Composite Constitution: A Plea for a Shift in Paradigms', in: *National and Regional Parliaments in the European Constitutional Order*, ed. Ph. Kiiver (Groningen: Europa Law Publishing, 2006), 117–131.

regulations, this may be different in theory, as regulations in principle may mention the competent national authorities by name. This, however, hardly ever happens in practice, so generally it is for the national legislature to attribute the power to execute a regulation to a specific authority. Therefore, in practice, the attributive function of the legality principle also applies with regard to regulations. That makes counterbalancing mechanisms in this regard unneccesary.

The regulatory function of the national principle of legality is limited with regard to directives. In the case of incorrect transposition of directives or incorrect application of the transposing national legislation, individuals can be faced with directive provisions which differ from national law by means of direct effect or consistent interpretation (See sections 3.2 and 3.3).[59] This is no problem with regard to direct effect, as this instrument may only be applied in favour of individuals for the sake of the legal certainty of citizens. Horizontal and inverse direct effect are thus prohibited. Consistent interpretation, however, can also be applied by the administration to the detriment of individuals. Because of legal certainty and legality, however, the instrument is limited in several ways. Consistent interpretation cannot lead to the creation or aggravation of criminal penalization, to the imposition of administrative fines or to the extension of the scope of a prohibition, which is linked to the requirement of a permit. Moreover, the possibilities of the instrument are limited by the prohibition of *contra legem* consistent interpretation; the interpretation has to fit in the existing frame of national legislation. Since consistent interpretation therefore by principle does not exceed the boundaries which the national law provides, we consider the use of the instrument to the prejudice of individuals no big problem in light of national legality.

It goes without saying that the regulatory function of the national principle of legality is eroded with regard to regulations. The administration can also apply regulations directly to the detriment of individuals. Moreover, regulations can set aside general principles of national law, irrespective of whether these are codified or not. These consequences follow from the definition of Article 288 TFEU (ex Article 249 EC), so there are no possibilities of compensation at the national level. To counterbalance this erosion of the regulatory function at the national level, it has to be emphasized that regulations have a 'European legality': they are adopted in conformity with the procedures of the EU Treaties by the competent European authorities. Moreover, the Member States are involved in the legislative process and can influence the adoption of regulations and their scope. This influence can be used to include safeguards and norms which are common in their national legal order. Finally, it is of great importance that the Court of Justice has systematically ruled that national authorities have to observe the general principles of European law when they apply regulations. This also applies when the regulation does not explicitly say so;[60] after all, the authorities then act 'in the scope of

59. In case of correct transposition of a directive, the directive is applied by means of a national statute. In that case the national principle of legality is upheld.

60. See Case C-349/07, *Sopropé* [2008] ECR I-10369. National authorities are also bound by European general principles when they apply a directive or the national statute implementing a directive. See Case C-28/05, *Dokter* [2006] ECR I-5431.

European law'. The protection that these general principles offer can be less extensive than the corresponding principles of national law,[61] but is, generally speaking, adequate. Hence, in our view, enough compensatory mechanisms exist to counterbalance the erosion of the regulatory function of the national principle of legality with regard to regulations.

6. CONCLUSION

This contribution shows that the national principle of legality has a limited importance with regard to the implementation of regulations and directives in the national legal order. This applies particularly to regulations. As directives require transposition, the national legislature then has a more important role to play, albeit though important choices with regard to the contents are often already decided on the European level. In fact, only the attributive function of this principle is unaffected. The legitimizing function and the regulatory function are eroded: rather slightly with regard to directives, and drastically with regard to regulations. This finding, however, is less dramatic than it seems, as several counterbalancing mechanisms are available. The loss of the legitimizing function of the national principle of legality is compensated by the fact that a 'composite' democratic control by the European parliament and the national parliaments exists on the adoption of European legislation. The loss of the regulatory function at the national level is counterbalanced by several mechanisms. In this regard it is particularly important that the national application of directives and regulations has to meet the requirements following from European general principles of law. This guarantees an adequate regulatory standard in Europe.

On the whole, our view is that the functions which are traditionally fulfilled by the national principle of legality are also safeguarded within the European legal order. This is guaranteed in a rather complex way, in which singular national concepts are replaced by composite concepts. These safeguard the different functions of the legality principle in a cooperation of European law and national law. This is, in our view, inevitable in a composite legal order.

61. The Dutch principle of legitimate expectations offers more protection than its European equivalent. Other European principles, like the principle of equality, the principle of proportionality and the rights of defence, offer more protection than their Dutch equivalents.

Chapter 5
The Legality of Independent Regulatory Authorities

Saskia Lavrijssen & Annetje Ottow

1. INTRODUCTION: THE PRINCIPLE OF LEGALITY

Under influence of European law and the European Union policies on market liberalization and market integration, the number of independent regulatory authorities, such as economic regulators and competition authorities, has increased tremendously in the EU Member States since the nineties. The position of independent regulatory authorities has been subject to academic and political debate in the EU Member States ever since their existence.[1] Independent regulatory authorities should act independently from the market parties and are positioned at some distance from the political arena to ensure an impartial exercise of their powers and the creation of a level playing field. At the same time they enjoy

1. R. Caranta, M. Andenas & D. Fairgrieve (eds), *Independent Administrative Authorities* (London: British Institute of International and Comparative Law, 2004); T. Zwart & L. Verhey (eds), *Agencies in European and Comparative Law* (Antwerpen: Intersentia, 2003), 113–147. See for the Dutch situation, A.T. Ottow, *Telecommunicatietoezicht, de invloed van het Europese en Nederlandse bestuurs(proces)recht* (Den Haag: SDU 2006); S.A.C.M. Lavrijssen, *Onafhankelijke mededingingstoezichthouders, regulerende bevoegdheden en de waarborgen voor good governance* (Den Haag: Boom Juridische Uitgevers, 2006) and L.F.M. Verhey & N. Verheij 'De macht van marktmeesters, markttoezicht in constitutioneel perspectief', *Toezicht, Handelingen Nederlandse Juristenvereniging* 1 (2005).

Leonard Besselink, Frans Pennings & Sacha Prechal (eds), *The Eclipse of the Legality Principle in the European Union*, pp. 73–96.

discretionary powers to make policy choices and/or to make complex legal and economic assessments at a distance from the parliament and/or the responsible minister.

Although European liberalization directives oblige the Member States to set up independent authorities and to give them some minimum powers, the principle of national institutional and procedural autonomy plays an important role in the setting up of these authorities. This principle implies that unless Community law provides otherwise, national constitutional and procedural rules apply, provided that: (i) the rules that govern a dispute or a case with a community dimension may not be less favourable than those governing similar domestic actions (*the principle of equivalence*); and (ii) the rules must not render virtually impossible or excessively difficult the exercise of rights conferred by the Community legal order (the principle of effectiveness).[2] Accordingly, national regulatory authorities (NRAs) should be embedded in the national legal systems on the basis of national constitutional and administrative law, provided that national law guarantees an effective implementation of European law and does not treat the application of European law less favourably than the application of national law in comparable cases.[3]

The principle of national institutional and procedural autonomy forms the red thread of this paper. This contribution focuses on what is left of the principle of procedural and institutional autonomy for the Member States when setting up national regulatory authorities in the implementation of European law. The national institutional principle of legality is of particular importance here. In the Netherlands the principle of legality means that unilateral administrative action impinging on the rights and freedoms of the citizens should be exercised on the basis of, and in accordance with, a legal base.[4] Although it is not entirely clear what is meant by 'a legal base', it is submitted that the principle of legality and of representative democracy in any event require that the legislator regulates the most essential parts of a law.

In the Netherlands the principle of legality is further specified by means of the principle of 'the Primacy of the Legislator' (*Primaat van de wetgever*). According to this principle, merely providing a legal basis for administrative action by the legislator is not enough. The democratically elected legislator should adequately regulate powers that are delegated to (independent) administrative authorities. In principle the legislator cannot delegate the power to adopt general binding rules or any other power implying a significant degree of discretion to independent administrative authorities.[5] The principle of the Primacy of the Legislator is not

2. Taken from: J.H. Jans, R. de Lange & S. Prechal, *Europeanisation of Public Law* (Groningen: Europa Law Publishing, 2007), 42.
3. See also Case C-82/07, *Comisión del Mercado de las Telecomunicaciones* [2008] ECR I-1265.
4. W. Voermans, *Toedeling van bevoegdheid* (Den Haag: Boom Juridische Uitgevers, 2004); F.J. van Ommeren, *De verplichting verankerd, de reikwijdte van het legaliteitsbeginsel en het materiële wetsbegrip* (Zwolle: W.E.J. Tjeenk Willink, 1996), 62 et. seq.
5. It should be noted that the legislator can delegate the power to adopt general binding rules to independent authorities under strictly circumscribed circumstances, namely when it concerns the

written down in the constitution or in a formal legal act. The principle is included and specified in the 'Directions for Legislation' (*Aanwijzingen voor de Regelgeving*).[6] The ministerial departments should take these directions into account when drafting legislation, but they do not have binding force.[7] The principle of the 'Primacy of the Legislator' can be seen as a political interpretation of the principle of legality.[8]

In the light of the aforementioned 'Dutch' interpretation of the principle of legality, the Dutch legislator and some Dutch authors have advocated the view that independent national regulatory authorities cannot be attributed powers that involve policy choices; they only implement policy decisions of the legislator and the Minister.[9] Moreover, it is argued that the powers of the independent authorities should be interpreted as strictly as possible by virtue of the principle of legality. However, research shows that the distinction between policymaking and policy implementation is difficult to make in practice and may result in too limited a formulation of the legal mandates of the authorities. This bears the risk that the independent authorities cannot adequately exercise their powers and effectively contribute to the realization of the goals of the European directives.[10]

The debate on the constitutional position of independent authorities is further complicated by recent amendments of the European directives that strengthen the political independence of the regulators vis-à-vis their Member States in the energy and the electronic communications sector (see section 4).[11]

Meanwhile, the European Court of Justice has handed down several judgments on the interpretation of the relevant European liberalization directives, which give some indications on how the constitutional position of the independent regulatory

---

power to adopt technical implementation rules or in special circumstances, provided that the rules are subject to approval by the competent minister.

6. 'Aanwijzing 124 van Aanwijzingen voor de Regelgeving', *Staatscourant* 1996, no. 177, 16.
7. Voermans (2004), *supra* n. 4, 41.
8. Lavrijssen (2006), *supra* n. 1, 73.
9. S.E. Zijlstra, 'Zbo's, marktautoriteiten en regelgevende bevoegdheid', *Tijdschrift voor Ondernemingsbestuur* 1 (2005): 2–6; H.J. de Ru 'Overheidsbemoeienis met prijzen, een algemene inleiding', in: H.J. de Ru (ed.) *Tarieven, regelgeving en toezicht* (Den Haag: Sdu, 2003); H.J. de Ru, 'Toezicht moet geen nieuwe staatsmacht worden, commentaar op de pre-adviezen voor de VAR over toezicht op markten', M&M 5 (2003a).
10. See for a discussion, Lavrijssen (2006), *supra* n. 1, 77 ff., Ottow (2006), *supra* n. 1, 86 ff.; L. Hancher, P. Larouche & S. Lavrijssen, 'Principles of Good Market Governance', *Journal of Network Industries* 4 (2003), 355–389.
11. Directive (EC) 2009/72 of the European Parliament and of the Council of 13 Jul. 2009 concerning common rules for the internal market in electricity and repealing Directive (EC) 2003/54, OJ 2009, L 211/55; Directive (EC) 2009/73 of the European Parliament and of the Council of 13 Jul. 2009 concerning common rules for the internal market in natural gas and repealing Directive (EC) 2003/55, Art. 1, para. 3 of Directive (EC) 2009/140 of the European Parliament and of the Council of 25 Nov. 2009 amending Directives (EC) 2002/21 on a common regulatory framework for electronic communications networks and services (EC) 2009/19 on access to, and interconnection of, electronic communications networks and associated facilities, and (EC) 2002/20 on the authorization of electronic communications networks and services, OJ 2009, L 337/37.

authorities should be interpreted in the light of European law. This contribution analyses the case law of the ECJ and the relevant European directives with regard to independent national regulatory authorities in the energy and electronic communications sectors to find out what the impact of European law is on their role, powers, independence and accountability. The ultimate goal of this exercise is to answer the central question of this article – whether the principle of institutional and procedural autonomy, and the principle of legality in particular, still prevails, or whether the Member States have lost a significant degree of autonomy when designing the national independent institutions that play a crucial role in the application of the European liberalization directives and the realization of their goals.

2. STRUCTURE

Section 3 gives an *overview* of the relevant European liberalization directives in the energy sector and the electronic communications sector that oblige the Member States to set up independent regulatory authorities. It will discuss the main characteristics, structure, tasks and powers of independent regulatory authorities. Section 4 discusses the importance of the independence of national regulatory authorities and the requirements that follow from European Commission law with regard to the independence of national regulatory authorities.

Section 5 analyses the way the ECJ interprets the *scope of powers* of the national authorities. It examines whether the ECJ interprets these powers in a very restrictive and literal way, taking into account national constitutional principles, such as the principle of legality, or whether it is ready to adopt a more flexible approach by interpreting the authorities' powers in the light of the goals of the relevant regulatory frameworks. Section 6 reflects on the role of the EC when it exercises its powers to control draft administrative decisions of the national regulatory authorities on the basis of European directives. In particular, it investigates the purpose of these powers and the consequences for the Member State autonomy in regulating the legal accountability of the independent regulatory authorities.

Section 7 analyses the judicial accountability of the national authorities. It investigates to what extent the authorities actions are subject to judicial review, including the interpretation of the possibilities for legal standing and the scope of review on the basis of European law. Section eight provides some conclusions with regard to the central question of this contribution – whether the principle of institutional and procedural autonomy still prevails. Can Member States still apply a restrictive interpretation of the principle of legality, meaning that independent regulatory authorities cannot be granted powers implying a significant degree of discretion and that their powers should be interpreted as strictly as possible? Or has European law curtailed the Member States' autonomy to a significant extent when setting up and regulating the accountability of independent national regulatory authorities in implementation of European law, preventing such restrictive interpretation of the principle of legality?

3. SETTING THE SCENE: THE REGULATORY BACKGROUND

Independent national regulatory authorities were often created by the Member States in order to implement the relevant European sectoral market liberalization directives. Their task is to supervise and regulate the relevant markets and to this end they should be entrusted with various powers to regulate certain matters, including tariffs and access rights, as well as to settle disputes. Extensive *ex ante* regulatory powers are considered necessary to ensure what is referred to as the introduction and promotion of 'controlled competition' in markets where national monopolists – also referred to as incumbents – traditionally enjoyed exclusive rights and privileges to supply goods and services and to operate energy and communications networks. Even after the abolition of these formal rights, many incumbents continue to enjoy significant market power, not least because they own essential infrastructure, which cannot be easily duplicated. This in turn requires regulatory solutions to ensure competition in the market.[12]

The first package of European telecommunications directives entailed an obligation for the Member States to ensure that each of the relevant tasks assigned to the NRAs in the directives were undertaken by a competent body.[13] It was mainly left to Member States to decide upon the form and powers of their NRAs, but the directives required that their independence from the industry was secured and that there were independent appeal mechanisms available for interested market parties affected by decisions of the NRAs.[14] This independence requirement was of particular importance to guarantee impartial decision-making, as the Member States themselves still had (and have) financial interests in the telecommunications market by means of their shares in the incumbents.

The energy directives merely stipulated that the Member States shall create appropriate and efficient mechanisms for regulation, control and transparency so as to avoid any abuse of a dominant position.[15] In addition, the Member States had to designate a competent body, independent of the market parties, to settle disputes concerning network access.[16] Inevitably substantial divergence emerged between the NRAs' practices across the Member States. This stimulated the Commission to

12. See for electronic communications, M. Cave, 'Broadband Regulation in Europe – Present and Future', *Competition and Regulation in Network Industries* 4 (2007): 405–424.
13. Article 5a of Directive (EC) 97/51 of the European Parliament and of the Council of 6 Oct. 1997 amending Council Directives (EEC) 90/387 and (EEC) 92/44 for the purpose of adaptation to a competitive environment in telecommunications, OJ 1997, L 295/23.
14. Articles 21 and 22 of Directive (EC) 98/30 of the European Parliament and of the Council of 22 Jun. 1998 concerning common rules for the internal market in natural gas, OJ 1998, L 204/1; Arts 20 and 22 of Directive (EC) 96/92 of the European Parliament and of the Council of 19 Dec. 1996 concerning common rules for the internal market in electricity, OJ 1996, L 27/2.
15. Article 22 of Directive (EC) 98/30 of the European Parliament and of the Council of 22 Jun. 1998 concerning common rules for the internal market in natural gas, OJ 1998, L 204/1 and Art. 22 of Directive (EC) 96/92 of the European Parliament and of the Council of 19 Dec. 1996 concerning common rules for the internal market in gas, OJ 1996 L 27/2.
16. Article 21 of Directive (EC) 98/30 and Art. 20 of Directive (EC) 96/92.

initiate further substantive harmonization of the powers of the NRAs, as well as to include common principles for fair and transparent decision-making in a second package of European directives.[17] Moreover, the Commission spurred on an early effort to coordinate the work of the different NRAs in implementing European legislation, via informal agreements and working groups.[18] Given continued resistance by the Member States to the creation of European regulatory agencies, and in line with broader moves to encourage open methods of coordination and subsidiarity, the EC essentially fostered European regulatory harmonization through the formation of formal and informal horizontal networks of NRAs In these European regulatory networks the NRAs coordinate the application of European regulations and directives by NRAs at national level to ensure a consistent interpretation and effective application of European law in the twenty-seven Member states.[19]

A third package of European directives further harmonizes the independence and powers of the national regulatory authorities (see next section). The amended energy and electronic communications legislation will require a greater political and, indeed, legal, independence for the members of the national regulatory authorities from their national governments. In the opinion of the Commission, inadequate political independence at national level hampered an effective cooperation between the national regulatory authorities within the European regulatory networks and impartial application of European law by the national authorities.

In the light of their tasks to promote competition in liberalized national markets, the individual NRAs are entrusted with substantial powers. These powers may imply a degree of discretion, in that the national authorities may make policy choices or complex economic and legal assessments. For example, the NRAs in the energy sector have the power to implement *ex ante* forms of regulation on tariffs and on the terms and conditions for third-party access to the energy networks. The NRAs in the electronic communications sector have powers to impose specific remedies on a market party having significant market power; a position which equals a dominant position within the meaning of Article 102 Treaty on the Functioning of the European Union (TFEU) (ex Article 82 EC). The NRAs must

---

17. Articles 3 to 8 of Directive (EC) 2002/21 of the European Parliament and of the Council of 7 Mar. 2002 on a common regulatory framework for electronic communications networks and services (Framework Directive), OJ 2003, L 108/33; Art. 23 of Directive (EC) 2003/54 of the European Parliament and of the Council of 26 Jun. 2003 concerning common rules for the internal market in electricity and repealing Directive (EC) 96/92, OJ 2003, L 176/37; Art. 25 of Directive (EC) 2003/55 of the European Parliament and the Council of 26 Jun. 2003 concerning common rules for the internal market in gas and repealing Directive (EC) 98/30, OJ 2003, L 176/57.
18. L. Hancher, 'The Regulatory Role of the European Union', in: H. Kassim & A. Menon (eds) *The European Union and National Industrial Policy* (London: Routledge, 1996).
19. S. Lavrijssen & L. Hancher, 'Networks on Track: From European Regulatory Networks to 'European Regulatory Network Agencies', *Legal Issues of Economic Integration* 1 (2009): 23–55; M. de Visser, Network Based Governance in EC Law, *The Example of EC Competition and Communication Law* (Oxford: Hart Publishing, 2009).

co-operate with the national competition authorities (NCAs), having concurrent powers to enforce competition law in regulated sectors.[20]

Section 4 analyses how the ECJ has interpreted the concept of independence, and how the ECJ has linked this concept to the requirements following from the EC Treaty and the European liberalization directives. Section 5 examines whether the independent status of the NRAs has affected the way in which the ECJ has interpreted the powers that were delegated to them by the Member States in implementation of EU law.

4. INDEPENDENCE

This section discusses the importance of the independence of the national regulatory authorities, as well as the independence requirements that follow from EU law. The concept of independence is linked with the principle of legality. The Dutch government and some academics argue that in case of (a certain degree) of political independence, the responsible minister has only limited powers to ensure that the national regulatory authorities apply the law in harmony with the intent and the will of the democratically elected legislator, which is one of the main purposes of the principle of legality. Therefore it is argued that the principle of legality implies that the legislator cannot delegate powers involving a significant degree of discretion to authorities that function at a distance from the political arena (see section 1).

4.1. Political Independence and Independence from Market Parties

Before analysing the European directives and case law of the ECJ with regard to the independence requirements of national regulatory authorities, it should be pointed out that independence comprises two elements.[21] The first element is uncontroversial and means that national regulatory authorities should be independent from the market parties to create a level playing field. This element of independence is laid down in the European directives and accepted and specified by the ECJ in its case law.[22]

The second type of independence is more controversial and means that national regulatory authorities should also, to some extent, be independent from the political arena. Within Organisation for Economic Co-operation and Development (OECD) countries, independence usually does not mean complete autonomy from government policy.[23] Rather, it means that national regulatory

20. Joined Cases C-359/95P and C-397/95P, *Ladbroke* ECR [1997] I-62225.
21. Ottow (2006), *supra* n. 1, 62–66.
22. Hancher, Larouche & Lavrijssen (2004) *supra* n. 10, 360–361.
23. OECD, *Telecommunications Regulations: Institutional Structures and Responsibilities*, DSI/ICCP (99) 15/FINAL, 14.

authorities are independent in implementing regulations and policies without intrusion from the executive, while they must still heed general government policy. Up until now, European law has not required the Member States to position their national authorities independently from the political arena, except that there should be a functional and legal separation between the Member States' regulatory activities and their financial interests in the relevant regulated sectors. As discussed below, however, this will change in the future.

In the legal and political science literature several arguments are put forward for (a degree of) political independence of the national regulatory authorities. First and foremost, the consistency of economic regulation, in particular with regard to innovation and efficiency incentives for regulated firms, is endangered by undue political interference. If investors are to make long-term commitments in networks and other capital-intensive industries, they need guarantees for a stable regulatory regime that is, not subject to sudden changes as a consequence of opportunistic (short term) political choices.[24] If the application of the legal acts is delegated to independent authorities, the legislator gives a sign to the market parties that in principle the basic principles, provisions and goals of the regulatory framework will be respected and applied in an impartial way. Amendments to the regulatory frameworks may only be adopted through a heavy democratic parliamentary procedure.[25]

Another argument stems from the technical nature of the decisions that have to be taken by independent regulatory authorities. The idea is that these decisions very often are not based on political choices, but on expert opinions.[26] Members of Parliament do not usually possess the required expertise. Furthermore, democratic procedures are usually slow and cumbersome and therefore not suited to adopt technical decisions in a specific case. The delegation of the power to adopt these technical decisions to an independent authority may contribute to effective, efficient and fair decision-making processes.

4.2. Legal Basis

This section analyses what the legal basis is in European law for the independence requirements of national regulatory authorities. In Case C-202/88 *France v. Commission*, the ECJ already based the requirement that national regulatory authorities should be independent from the market parties on the direct applicable competition provisions of the EC Treaty (Articles 5, 81 and 82 and 86 EC; now Article 4 Treaty

24. Hancher, Larouche & Lavrijssen (2004), *supra* n. 10, 360–361; P. Vass, 'The Principles of Better Regulation-Separating Roles and Responsibility', in: *Regulated Industries — The Governance Contract*, ed. P. Vass (Bath University, Centre for Regulated Industries, 2002).
25. B.J.M. van der Meulen, 'Marktautoriteiten, Aanzet tot een interne rechtsvergelijking', in: B.J.M. van der Meulen & A.T. Ottow (eds) *Toezicht op markten*, *VAR-reeks* 130 (Den Haag: Boom Juridische Uitgevers, 2001), 49. See also Verhey & Verheij (2005), *supra* n. 1, 195–197.
26. *Ibid.*, see also Lavrijssen (2006), *supra* n. 1.

on European Union (TEU) and Articles 101, 102 and 106 TFEU). In the former case the ECJ ruled on the legality of a EC directive adopted on the basis of Article 86(3) EC (now Article 106(3) TFEU), specifying the obligations for the Member States with regard to undertakings having special or exclusive rights in the sense of Article 86(1) EC (now Article 106(1) TFEU).[27] The Court recognized that a system of undistorted competition, as laid down in the Treaty, can be guaranteed only if equality of opportunity is secured as between the various economic operators. Accordingly, a system of undistorted competition would not be realized if an undertaking marketing terminal equipment was entrusted with the task of drawing up the specifications for such equipment, monitoring its application and granting type-approval with regard to its own equipment and that of competing undertakings. Consequently, the Commission was justified in seeking to entrust responsibility for drawing up technical specifications to a body independent of public or private undertakings offering competing goods and/or services in a Article 86(3) EC (now Article 106(3) TFEU) directive.[28]

On the basis of the foregoing it may be observed that even before the adoption of the European directives obliging the Member States to set up independent regulatory authorities, the requirement of independence of the market parties existed and was binding on the Member States by virtue of the Treaty provisions on the free movement of services and goods and on competition.

4.3. Independence from Market Parties

As mentioned above, until recently EC law has only required that the Member States position the national regulatory authorities independently from the market parties to ensure the creation of a level playing field. The ECJ pointed out in Case *C-69/91 Decoster*[29] that the requirement of independence from the market parties would make it unacceptable for one directorate of a ministry to be involved in economic activities and another directorate of the same ministry in regulating them. Recently, in Case *C-82/07 Comisión del Mercado de las Telecomunicaciones*, the ECJ ruled that Directive 2002/21/EC does not require a separation of different regulatory functions; in this case the assignment of national numbering resources and the management of national numbering plans on the one hand, and the adoption of the national numbering plans on the other.[30] The ECJ also acknowledged the potentially pluralist nature of regulatory authorities which follows clearly from the very definition of national regulatory authority set out in Article 2(g) Directive 2002/21/EC. Although the Member States enjoy institutional autonomy as regards the organization and structuring of their national regulatory

27. Case C-202/88, *France v. Commission* [1991] ECR I-01223 and Case C-69/91, *Decoster* [1993] ECR I-05335.
28. See also Case C-18/88, *GB-Inno* [1991] ECR I-05941.
29. See also Case C-69/91, *Decoster* [1993] ECR I-05335.
30. Case C-82/07, *Comisión del Mercado de las Telecomunicaciones* [2008] ECR I-1265.

authorities, the ECJ stresses that such autonomy may be exercised only in accordance with the objectives and obligations laid down in that directive. Consequently, where part of the regulatory functions is to be discharged by ministerial authorities, each Member State must ensure that those authorities are neither directly nor indirectly involved in 'operational' functions (activities associated with ownership or control) within the meaning of the Directive.

In light of Case C-69/91 and Case C-82/07, it is submitted that an effective and loyal application of the independence requirement obliges the Member States to ensure that the national regulatory authorities are legally distinct from and functionally independent of all market parties. Member States that retain ownership or control of undertakings providing economic activities should ensure structural separation of the regulatory function from operational functions.

4.4. New Requirements: Political Independence

Until recently, neither the case law of the ECJ nor the European liberalization directives required political independence of the national regulatory authorities. However, some authors have argued that an effective implementation of the independence requirement following from the EC Treaty and the European directives, aimed at the creation of a level playing field, demands that the Member States provide for sufficient legal guarantees that the national authorities actually can take an impartial decision in a specific case.[31] This would mean that the possibility should be excluded that the national authorities can feel pressure from parliament or a minister and/or can receive specific directions to take a specific decision favouring national interests and undertakings above undertakings from other Member States. It should be recognized that the ECJ so far has not recognized such wide implications following from the requirement that the authorities should be independent from the market parties or the Member States' financial interests. Indeed, according to this line of reasoning, independence would amount to some degree of political independence of the national authorities, which stretches beyond the situation that the state has interests in the market itself. This would require political independence of the authorities each time they apply the relevant regulatory frameworks in a specific case.

However, the Commission, a strong proponent and advocate of greater political independence of the national authorities, tabled proposals to strengthen the national authorities' political independence in the electronic communications and energy sectors in 2007. The Commission proposals were in line with the abovementioned suggestion that NRAs should have the power to take autonomous decisions, free from political influence, when they apply the relevant regulatory frameworks in a specific case. Basically, the Commission proposed that the national authorities shall not seek or take instructions from any other body in relation to the day-to-day performance of the tasks assigned to them under national

31. Lavrijssen (2006), *supra* n. 1, 64–68. Also Ottow (2006), *supra* n. 1, 65.

law implementing community law. Moreover it gave further specifications of how this political independence should be realized.[32]

The European Parliament and the Council have accepted the core of the Commission proposals. However, they have adopted amendments clarifying that the independent authorities cannot act completely independently from *political and judicial* oversight in accordance with national constitutional traditions. In this view, national authorities should be able to take autonomous decisions; in doing so, however, they should still respect general policy guidelines of the government not directly related to the exercise of their powers in a specific case. Furthermore, their decisions may be suspended or overturned by appeal bodies, ensuring the right of effective legal protection of citizens that are affected by those decisions. The definitive text on the independence requirements of the energy directives stipulates:[33]

> Article 35
> Designation and independence of regulatory authorities
>
> 1. Each Member State shall designate a single national regulatory authority at national level.
>
> 2. (. . .)
>
> 3. (. . .)
>
> 4. Member States shall guarantee the independence of the regulatory authority and shall ensure that it exercises its powers impartially and transparently. For this purpose, Member States shall ensure that, when carrying out the regulatory tasks conferred upon it by this Directive and related legislation, the regulatory authority:
>
> (a) is legally distinct and functionally independent from any other public or private entity;
>
> (b) ensures that its staff and the persons responsible for its management:
>
> (i) act independently from any market interest; and
>
> (ii) do not seek or take direct instructions from any government or other public or private entity when carrying out the regulatory tasks. This requirement is without prejudice to close cooperation, as appropriate, with other relevant national authorities or to general policy guidelines issued by the government not related to the regulatory powers and duties under Article 37.

---

32. See Art. 2(3), Proposal for a Directive of the European Parliament and of the Council amending Directives (EC) 2002/21 on a common regulatory framework for electronic communications networks and services COM (2007) 697 final and Art. 1(12) of a Proposal for a Directive of the European Parliament and of the Council amending Directive (EC) 2003/54 concerning common rules for the internal market in electricity COM (2007) 528 Final.
33. Article 35 of Directive (EC) 2009/72 of the European Parliament and of the Council of 13 Jul. 2009 concerning common rules for the internal market in electricity and repealing Directive (EC) 2003/54, OJ 2009, L 211/55. See also Art. 39 of Directive (EC) 2009/73 of the European Parliament and of the Council of 13 Jul. 2009 concerning common rules for the internal market in natural gas and repealing Directive (EC) 2003/55, OJ 2009, L 211/94.

5. In order to protect the independence of the regulatory authority, Member States shall in particular ensure that:

(a) the regulatory authority can take autonomous decisions, independently from any political body, and has separate annual budget allocations, with autonomy in the implementation of the allocated budget, and adequate human and financial resources to carry out its duties; and

(b) the members of the board of the regulatory authority or, in the absence of a board, the regulatory authority's top management are appointed for a fixed term of five up to seven years, renewable once.

In regard to point (b) of the first subparagraph, Member States shall ensure an appropriate rotation scheme for the board or the top management. The members of the board or, in the absence of a board, members of the top management may be relieved from office during their term only if they no longer fulfil the conditions set out in this Article or have been guilty of misconduct under national law.

4.5. A Gradual Reduction of the Member States' Institutional Autonomy

Summing up, initially it followed from EU law that Member States have to position the national regulatory authorities independently from the market parties and the government or government departments for those cases in which government is a shareholder in one of the supervised undertakings. At first, it seemed that the Member States enjoyed a significant degree of discretion in complying with the independence requirement.[34] However, gradually the case law of the ECJ and the European directives have filled in how the Member States should comply with the independence requirement, in that they should ensure a legal and functional separation between the Member States' operational activities on the one hand, and their regulatory activities on the other. Furthermore, as the Commission proposals on political independence have been endorsed by the European Parliament and the Council, the Member States' institutional autonomy has been further curtailed. Although the assumption is that the national authorities should follow general policy guidelines formulated by the responsible ministers, the Member States should ensure that the national authorities can take autonomous decisions, free from political influence, in specific cases. For that purpose, the Member States have to comply with specific requirements laid down in the amended liberalization directives.

In the light of the above-mentioned link between political independence and the principle of legality, the question arises as to whether EU law also brings with it a specific interpretation of the principle of legality, according to which the increased political independence of the national regulatory authorities should

34. See also conclusion Advocate General Geelhoed, Case C-462/99, *Connect Austria* [2003] ECR I-5197.

lead to a limited formulation and interpretation of their powers. This question will be dealt with in the next section.

5. THE INTERPRETATION OF THE NATIONAL REGULATORY AUTHORITIES' POWERS

Considering that the independent national regulatory authorities must act de jure and/or de facto – to some extent at a distance from the political arena – there has been a vivid academic and political debate on the (lack of) legitimacy of the national regulatory authorities.[35] The question arises, as argued by the Dutch legislator and some Dutch scholars, as to whether under those circumstances the principle of legality requires that their powers are interpreted in a literal and restrictive way to ensure that they exercise their powers in a legitimate way.[36] Although the European requirements concerning the political independence of the national authorities are tightened with the adoption of the Commission proposals (see section 4), and it is not clear how this will affect future case law of the ECJ concerning the national authorities' powers, it will be analysed whether the current case law of the ECJ already provides indications that these powers should be interpreted in a very restrictive way on the basis of the principle of legality.

In Case C-79/00, *Telefonica España*, the ECJ attached significant importance to the goals of the Interconnection Directive (Directive 97/33/EC) for the interpretation of the concept of interconnection and the related powers for the NRAs to impose access obligations on the incumbents.[37] In the light of the goals of the relevant Directive the ECJ adopted a broad interpretation of the concept of interconnection, including access to the local loop. This case shows that the ECJ does not restrict itself to a literal intepretation of the NRAs' powers. It takes into account the context and goals of the relevant Directive when interpreting the NRAs' powers, making sure the NRAs have sufficient leeway to exercise their powers in an effective way.

In the recent Case C-55/06 *Arcor,*[38] the ECJ ruled on the question how the NRAs should interpret and apply the principle of cost orientation, enshrined in the European telecommunications directives and Regulation 2887/2000 on unbundled access to the local loop, when regulating the incumbents.[39] Pursuant to the latter regulation, the incumbents have to provide access to their local loops to new entrants on the basis of the principle of cost orientation. First the ECJ sets out which method it uses for the interpretation of the principle of cost orientation. As in Case C-79/00, *Telefonica España*, the ECJ considered that it would take account,

35. See authors cited at n. 1.
36. *Ibid.*, n. 9.
37. ECJ, Case C-79/00, *Telefonica España* [2001] ECR I-10075. See for a discussion, Ottow 2006, *supra* n. 1, 58 ff.
38. Case C-56/06, *Arcor* [2008] ECR I-2931.
39. Regulation (EC) 2887/2000 of the European Parliament and of the Council of 18 Dec. 2000 on unbundled access to the local loop, OJ 2000, L 336/ 4.

not only of the wording of that principle, but also of its context and the objectives pursued by the legislation laying down that principle. According to the ECJ, the aim of Regulation 2887/2000 is to enable both beneficiaries (new market entrants) and the notified operators (incumbents) to operate on the market so as to establish normal competition in the medium term. Subsequently the ECJ interpreted the principle in a broad way. This broad interpretation enabled the NRAs to weigh the conflicting interests of the incumbents, seeking the recovery of all their costs for providing access to the local loop, with the interest of the new entrants, seeking access to the local loop at efficient tariffs in order to be able to compete with the incumbents.[40] The ECJ explicitly recognized that, in the absence of Community legislation, it is the task of the NRAs to define the detailed rules for bringing the principle of cost orientation into practice. It confirmed that the NRAs enjoy broad discretion in applying this principle. Ultimately, the ECJ concluded that Regulation 2887/2000 grants the NRAs not only broad discretion, but also the appropriate means to enable them to examine, in the most effective way, the correct application of the principle of cost orientation laid down in Article 3(3) of that regulation.

In Case C-438/04 *Mobistar* also, which concerned the application of the principle of cost-orientation by the Belgian NRA (Institut belge des services postaux et des telecommunications) when regulating the service of number portability, the ECJ applied a teleological method for the interpretation of Article 30(2) of the Universal Service Directive (Directive 2002/22/EC[41]). According to the ECJ, number portability is intended to remove the obstacles to consumers' freedom of choice, particularly between mobile telephone operators, and thus to ensure development of effective competition in the telephone service market. With a view to achieving those aims, the Community legislator provided, in Article 30(2) of the Universal Service Directive, that NRAs are to ensure that pricing for interconnection related to the provision of number portability is cost-oriented and that direct charges to subscribers, if any, do not act as a disincentive for the use of these facilities. According to the ECJ, a restrictive interpretation of Article 30(2) of the Universal Service Directive would be contrary to the aim and purpose of that Directive, and might limit its effectiveness from the point of view of the provision of portability. So, in light of the aims of the Universal Service Directive, the ECJ adopted a broad interpretation of the principle of cost-orientation with regard to the costs that were covered by the charges for number portability. Furthermore, the ECJ also considered that the NRAs enjoy a certain discretion to assess the prices of number portability and to define the method to apply the cost-orientation principle.[42]

---

40. Case C-56/06, *Arcor* [2008] ECR I-2931, paras 70–119.
41. Directive (EC) 2002/22 of the European Parliament and of the Council of 7 Mar. 2002 on universal service and users' rights relating to electronic communications networks and services, OJ 2002, L 108/51.
42. Case C-438/04, *Mobistar Sa* [2006] ECR I-6675.

In Case C-227/07 *Commission v. Republic of Poland*,[43] the ECJ considered that the regulatory tasks of the NRAs are set out in Articles 8 to 13 of the Framework Directive (Directive 2002/21/EC).[44] Article 8(1) thereof provides that Member States are to ensure that, in carrying out those tasks, the NRAs take all reasonable measures aimed at achieving the objectives set out in paragraphs 2 to 4 of that article. Furthermore, it recalls that the Court has interpreted Article 8 as placing on the Member States the obligation to ensure that the NRAs take all reasonable measures aimed at promoting competition in the provision of electronic communications services, ensuring that there is no distortion or restriction of competition in the electronic communications sector, and removing remaining obstacles to the provision of those services at European level.[45] In this case, the ECJ consistently linked the NRAs' powers and the objectives of the regulatory framework for the regulation of the electronic communications sector. It was submitted that according to this line of reasoning, the NRAs' powers should not be interpreted in a strict and literal way. Instead, they should be interpreted in a way that enables the NRAs to pursue the objectives set out in Article 8 of the Framework Directive.

In the very recent Case C-424/07 *European Commission v. Germany*, the ECJ again confirmed that the NRAs in the communications sector enjoy a broad discretion or wide powers in order to be able to determine the need to regulate a market according to each situation on a case-by-case basis. The ECJ also considered that it is for the NRAs – and not the national legislators – to balance the objectives of Article 8(1) of the Framework Directive when defining and analysing a relevant market that may be susceptible to regulation.[46]

It is important to note that the ECJ did not rule on the allocation of the discretionary powers, between the independent authority on the one hand, and the governmental departments on the other, in any of the aforementioned cases. In light of the financial interests of the relevant governments in the incumbents however, it was submitted that at least part of the regulatory tasks had to performed by an independent NRA to ensure the impartiality of the decision-making processes. The judgments of the ECJ cases do not give any indication that the concepts of Community law should be interpreted and applied in a restrictive way, in case they have to be applied by an independent authority. Quite the contrary, the ECJ explicitly recognizes that the NRAs enjoy a degree of discretion, which is needed for an effective application of their powers, irrespective of whether or not they have to perform (at least part) of their functions independently from the political arena.

43. Case C-227/07, *Commission v. Republic of Poland* [2008] ECR I-8403.
44. Directive (EC) 2002/21 of the European Parliament and of the Council of 7 Mar. 2002 on a common regulatory framework for electronic communications networks and services (Framework Directive), OJ 2003, L 108/33.
45. Case C-380/05, *Centro Europa 7* [2008] ECR I-349.
46. Case, C-424/07 *European Commission v. Germany*, Judgment of 3 Dec. 2009, n.y.r.

5.1. Observations; Broad Interpretation of NRAs' Powers

The above-mentioned flexible and teleological approach of the ECJ in interpreting the NRAs' powers is to be welcomed. It is also positive that the ECJ explicitly recognizes that the national authorities enjoy discretion in exercising their powers. A very literal and restrictive interpretation of the NRAs' powers and the denial that they possess discretion would, in our opinion, complicate an effective exercise of their functions and the realization of the objectives of the European Directives.[47] Indeed, NRAs need a degree of discretion to exercise their powers in an effective and meaningful way. Not only do they need some leeway to make sound economic assessments before applying the often vague legal concepts to the complex factual substrates, but they should also to be able to take into account the dynamics of the market to ensure that their decisions can be attuned to the prevailing economic and technological circumstances and live up to the objectives of the regulatory frameworks.[48]

As the case law of the ECJ is binding on the Member States, the NRAs and the national courts when applying the European Directives, it is claimed that they cannot formulate or interpret the NRAs' powers in a very restrictive way on the basis of a national interpretation of the principle of legality. Indeed an effective implementation and application of European law requires that powers with a degree of discretion are delegated to the NRAs and that these powers are interpreted not only on the basis of the wording of the legal provisions but also in the light of the aims and goals of the European Directives, no matter whether those powers are exercised at some distance from the political arena or not. Therefore, it may be observed that the Member States' institutional autonomy in formulating and interpreting the NRAs' powers on the basis of specific interpretations of national constitutional principles, and the principle of legality in particular, has been significantly curtailed.

6. EUROPEAN COMMISSION AND EUROPEAN REGULATORY (NETWORK) AGENCIES

While the European liberalization directives have gradually expanded the NRAs' powers, and the ECJ has subjected them to a teleological interpretation in the light of the goals of the European Directives, the EC has sought instruments to control the way the NRAs exercise their powers. With the entry into force of the second package of liberalization directives, the EC could make use of several powers to intervene in national administrative procedures to ensure an effective and consistent application of European law by the NRAs of the Member States.[49] After the

47. Ottow (2006), *supra* n. 1, 86–110; Lavrijssen (2006) *supra* n. 1. 305–308.
48. *Ibid.*
49. S. Lavrijssen, & L. Hancher, 'European Regulators in the Network Sectors: Evolution Or Revolution?' in: *New Perspectives on Investment in Infrastructures*, ed. G. Arts, W. Dicke & L. Hancher (Amsterdam: University Press, 2008), 125–145; De Visser (2009), *supra* n. 19, Chs 4 and 5.

entry into force of the third package of liberalization directives, the abovementioned powers of the Commission will be further extended to include more national administrative decisions.[50]

Roughly, one can distinguish five specific actions that may be taken by the EC in the interest of a uniform application of European law upon notification of draft decisions by the NRAs:[51]

(i) The EC has the power to make comments with regard to draft national decisions.[52] The Knars should take the utmost account of these comments when adopting the definitive decisions. The CFI confirmed in case T-109/06 *Vodafone* that the comments made by the Commission in national administrative procedures do not produce binding effects, excluding the possibilities for legal standing on the basis of Article 230 EC. According to the CFI the Commission merely makes comments. If the NRA decides to adopt the national measure, the binding legal effects deriving from that measure are attributable to the NRA in question and not to the Commission's comments or the fact that it has not set in motion the procedure that may lead to the adoption of a veto decision.[53]

(ii) The EC may implicitly approve a draft decision by stating it has no comments; an action which, like the comments, does not produce binding effects. The statement of no comments implies that the Commission is of the opinion that the draft decision is in harmony with European law and does not frustrate the creation of the internal market. The draft decision may subsequently be adopted by the Knars.

(iii) The EC may raise serious doubts concerning a draft regulatory decision if it is of the opinion that the draft measure would create a barrier to the single market or if it has serious doubts as to its compatibility with community law. Consequently the NRA is not allowed to adopt the draft decision for a further two months.[54]

(iv) Within the above-mentioned period of two months the Commission may take a binding veto decision, obliging the NRA to withdraw the draft measure.[55]

---

50. For instance the power of the Commission to control draft measures of the telecommunications regulators will be extended to cover also the remedy stage (in addition to the relevant market and market power analysis). See Art. 7a (new) of Directive (EC) 2002/21 as amended by Directive (EC) 2009/140 and Art. 39 of Directive (EC) 2009/72.

51. See for a more detailed discussion of the instruments that the Commission may use for a consistent application of European law, De Visser (2009), *supra* n. 19, Chs 4 and 5.

52. See Art. 7, para. 3 of Directive (EC) 2002/21 as amended by Directive (EC) 2009/140 and Art. 11, paras 3 and 4 of Council Regulation 1/2003.

53. Case T-109/06, *Vodafone* [2007] ECR II-5151.

54. See Art. 7, para. 4 of Directive 2002/21/EC as amended by Directive (EC) 2009/140 and Art. 7a, para. 1 of Directive (EC) 2002/21 amended by Directive (EC) 2009/140.

55. Article 7, paras 4 and 5 of Directive (EC) 2002/21 as amended by Directive (EC) 2009/140. In some cases the European Commission may not adopt a binding veto decision, but may issue recommendations (see Art. 7a of Directive (EC) 2009/140). For similar powers of the

(v) On the basis of regulation 1/2003 the EC has the power to remove a national competition authority from a case by starting an investigation into this case itself.[56]

The ECs powers can be seen as instruments to promote the legality of the NRAs, in the sense that they aim to ensure that the NRAs in the twenty-seven Member States respect the provisions and goals of European law – the goal of market integration in particular – when applying an interpreting European law. So these instruments contribute to the legality of the NRAs for a specific aspect of the NRAs powers, namely the European law part. At the same time these powers of the EC, creating an additional European administrative control procedure on top of the national administrative procedures, can be perceived as a rather intrusive curtailment of the Member States institutional autonomy in designing the procedures with regard to the exercise of the powers of the NRAs.

The autonomy of the Member States in setting up the institutions and procedures for the application of the European liberalization directives is subject to further European harmonization. The European Parliament and the Council recently adopted European regulations formalizing the existing cooperation between the NRAs in informal European regulatory networks, by creating European independent regulatory agencies in the energy sector and the electronic communications sector to ensure a consistent application of EU law by the NRAs in the Member States.[57] The proposals of the Commission to strengthen the European coordination and cooperation between the NRAs via European regulatory agencies were very controversial. The Council and the European Parliament first adopted the proposal for a European Energy agency (Agency for the Cooperation of Energy Regulators; ACER). The primary purpose of ACER will be to assist the NRAs in exercising at Community level the regulatory tasks in the Member States and, where necessary, to coordinate their actions.[58] For that purpose it will, amongst others, have powers to adopt binding and non-binding decisions directed at the NRAs when applying the directives. The negotiations on the adoption of the proposal for a European agency in the electronic communications sector took longer and resulted in a weaker role for the agency (Body of European Regulators for Electronic Communications; BEREC). Although BEREC has various tasks to assist and guide the NRAs when exercising their powers, it has no powers to adopt decisions with binding effects.[59]

Commission in other areas see for example, Art. 39 of Directive (EC) 2009/72 and Art. 43 of Directive (EC) 2009/73.

56. Article 11, para. 6 of Council Regulation 1/2003, OJ 2003, L 1/1.
57. See extensively Lavrijssen & Hancher (2009), *supra* n. 19. See also de Visser (2009), *supra* n. 19.
58. Regulation 713/2009 of the European Parliament and of the Council of 13 Jul. 2009 establishing an Agency for the Cooperation of Energy Regulators, OJ 2009, L 211/1.
59. See Arts 2 and 3 of Regulation 1211/2009 of the European Union and of the Council of 25 Nov. 2009 establishing the Body of European Regulators for Electronic Communication (BEREC) and the Office, OJ 2009, L 337/1. Only the Office will have legal personality. See on the

7. APPEAL TO THE NATIONAL COURTS

Legal review of decisions of the NRAs is an important instrument to safeguard that the NRAs respect the principle of legality when exercising their powers. Unlike the EC (section 6), the national courts review whether all aspects of the NRAs decisions are in harmony with the law, including European law, national (procedural) law and human rights (such as the right to good governance). The judicial review ensures that the NRAs exercise their powers within the statutory provisions and do not abuse their powers. According to the autonomy principle, it is up to the Member States to design the system for legal protection against the NRAs' actions that apply European law. European law gradually curtails the Member States' autonomy in this regard, however. This section discusses how the case law of the ECJ and some EC Directives give instructions on how the judicial review has to take place.

7.1. Article 4 of the Framework Directive

In Article 4 of the Telecommunications Framework Directive, special requirements are laid down for the right of appeal against decisions of the national telecommunications independent authorities:[60]

> 1. Member States shall ensure that effective mechanisms exist at national level under which any user or undertaking providing electronic communications networks and/or services who is affected by a decision of a national regulatory authority has the right of appeal against the decision to an appeal body that is, independent of the parties involved. This body, which may be a court, shall have the appropriate expertise available to it to enable it to carry out its functions. Member States shall ensure that the merits of the case are duly taken into account and that there is an effective appeal mechanism. Pending the outcome of any such appeal, the decision of the national regulatory authority shall stand, unless the appeal body decides otherwise.
>
> 2. Where the appeal body referred to in paragraph 1 is not judicial in character, written reasons for its decision shall always be given. Furthermore, in such a case, its decision shall be subject to review by a court or tribunal within the meaning of Article 234 of the Treaty.[61]

These requirements were considered necessary, as practise had shown that the different national legal proceedings against those decisions formed an obstacle to effective supervision of the telecommunications market.

---

differences between the European agencies for the energy sector and the communications sector: Lavrijssen & Hancher (2009), *supra* n. 19.

60. Article 4 of Directive 2002/21/EC as amended by Directive 2009/140/EC.
61. See for a discussion of Art. 4, Ottow (2006), *supra* n. 1, 322; E. Pietermaat, *Mediaforum* 4 (2008): 182–183. The predecessor of Art. 4 was Art. 5*bis*, s. 3 of Directive (EC) 97/51.

The latest amendment of the Framework Directive has added some additional requirements regarding interim measures:

> Pending the outcome of the appeal, the decision of the national regulatory authority shall stand, unless interim measures are granted in accordance with national law.

This requirement is added, as in many Member States the national courts rather easily suspended the decisions of the NRAs, frustrating the application of the Directives.

7.2. Interpretation of Article 4 Framework Directive

Article 4 contains four elements regarding the right of appeal: (i) effective appeal mechanism; (ii) any user or undertaking providing electronic communications networks and/or services who is affected by a decision of a national regulatory authority; (iii) to an appeal body that is, independent of the parties involved; and (iv) ensure that the merits of the case are duly taken into account.

However, no clear instructions are given as to the interpretation of these elements. Two interpretation approaches can be followed in this context. In the first place, a stricter legal interpretation could be used. In this respect Lasok (2004) suggests that for the interpretation of the requirements of the right of appeal in Article 4 of the Framework Directive, the case law regarding Article 263 TFEU (ex Article 230 EC as amended) on the right of appeal against decisions of the European institutions at the ECJ should be followed.[62] According to this interpretation, there would only be limited possibilities for parties who are not the addressees of the administrative decisions to appeal to these decisions at the competent national court(s).[63] This approach is not self-evident however. The text of Article 4 suggests that the right to appeal is inspired by the case law of the ECJ regarding the *principle of effective judicial protection.* According to this interpretation, all parties whose rights are affected by the NRAs' decisions should have a right to appeal to the national courts to enforce and protect the rights they derive from European law. Indeed, in this context the application of Directives by NRAs in national decisions is the subject matter of the case. It does not concern the direct applicability of EU law by European institutions and the possibilities for legal standing on the basis of Article 263 TFEU (ex Article 230 EC as amended). Therefore, it is more obvious to assume that the case law on the principle of effectiveness, and not the possibilities for legal standing on the basis

62. K.P.E. Lasok, 'Appeals Under the New Regulatory Framework in the Electronic Communications Sector', paper for the EIPA seminar, Maastricht: 29 Nov. 2004.
63. Lavrijssen & Hancher (2009), *supra* n. 19, 43–44. Up until now the European courts have been very restrictive in interpreting the standing requirements for private actors on the basis of Art. 230 EC (now as amended 263 TFEU).

of Article 263 TFEU (ex Article 230 EC as amended), should be taken into account.[64]

This second, broader approach was followed by Advocate General Geelhoed in the case *Connect Austria Gesellschaft*.[65] This case concerned the application of the predecessor of Article 4, Article 5*bis*, subsection 3 of Directive 90/387/EC. The Advocate General pleaded for a broad interpretation of this right to appeal.[66] This broader view was confirmed by the ECJ in Case C-426/05 *Tele2*, where the court considered:

> 32 It follows that the requirement to provide effective judicial protection, which is at the origin of Article 4 of the Framework Directive, must apply to both users and undertakings which may derive rights from the Community legal order, in particular from telecommunications directives, and whose rights are affected by a decision taken by a national regulatory authority.[67]

As a result of this broad scope of Article 4, not only undertakings on which obligations are imposed on the basis of the telecommunications directives by the NRA, but also other users and undertakings operating in competition with the supervised company have a right to appeal (element (ii) mentioned above). According to the court, this follows not only from the text of Article 4, but also from the requirement to provide effective judicial protection.

In Case C-438/04 *Mobistar*,[68] requirements (i) and (iv) of Article 4 were subject to interpretation. The ECJ considered in this case that the national body responsible for hearing an appeal against a decision of the national regulatory authority, in accordance with Article 4 of the Framework Directive, must be able to have at its disposal all the information necessary in order to decide on the merits of the appeal in full knowledge of the facts, including information that is, subject to confidentiality. The protection of such information and business confidentiality must be guaranteed however, and must be adjusted to reconcile it with the requirements of effective legal protection and the rights to defence of the parties to the dispute. This is necessary to ensure that there is an effective appeal mechanism that permits the merits of the case to be taken duly into account.

The English language version of the Framework Directive implies that the competent appeals bodies should fully review the merits of the case, which means that they may, if necessary, substitute the NRA's assessment.[69] Therefore, the

64. See Ottow (2006), *supra* n. 1; A.T. Ottow, 'Het gevecht tegen de windmolens. De invloed van het Europese recht op het nationale procesrecht', in: *Opstellen aangeboden aan prof. Mr E.J. Dommering*, ed. N. Van Eijk & B. Hugenholtz (Amsterdam: Otto Cramwinkel, 2008), 265–279.
65. Conclusion Advocate General Geelhoed, Case C-462/99, *Connect Austria* [2003] ECR I-5197, para. 40 ff.
66. See his opinion, para. 47.
67. Case C-426/05, *Tele 2 Telecommunications Gmbh v. Telekom-Control-Kommission* [2008] ECR I-685. See for a case note: Elizabeth Pietermaat, *Mediaforum* 4 (2008): 182–183.
68. Case note A.T. Ottow, Case C-438/04, *Mobistar v. BIPT*, *Mediaforum* 10 (2006): 309–314.
69. See Art. 4 of Directive (EC) 2002/21 as amended by Directive (EC) 2009/140.

English language version seems to imply a more intensive review than the Dutch version, in which it is stated 'that the facts of the case should be duly taken into account'. In any event, one could argue that Article 4 of the Framework Directive seems to prevent the competent courts from reviewing the decisions of the NRAs merely marginally, without, however, requiring the courts to substitute the opinion of the NRAs with their own.[70] In this regard, Schimmel and Widdershoven (2009) have argued that it seems probable that the Community Courts will provide guidance as to the manner in which the national courts will have 'to take the merits of the case duly into account'.[71] They submit that it cannot in the least be excluded that the Courts will inspire themselves in this respect on their own '*Tetra Laval* standard', the standard of review that they apply when reviewing decisions of the EC that apply the European competition rules and merger control regulation.[72] If this were the case, the *Tetra Laval* standard would hence become binding upon national courts in the area of telecommunications.[73]

7.3. Observations

On the basis of the foregoing, it may be concluded that the Framework Directive increasingly harmonizes crucial aspects of judicial review of the NRAs' decisions, including the possibilities for standing and the intensity of review. Subsequently, the institutional provisions of this Directive are interpreted in a teleological way by the ECJ, ensuring the right of effective legal protection of those affected by the NRAs' decisions. So the interaction between the institutional provisions of the Directive and the subsequent case law of the ECJ interpreting those provisions lead to a significant curtailment of the Member State autonomy in regulating the judicial accountability of the NRAs, which is an important instrument in ensuring their legality. Although the ECJ has not explicitly made this link, one could argue that

70. E. Pietermaat & A. Ottow, 'De rechterlijke toetsing van OPTA's marktanalyses, Procedurele aspecten', *Mediaforum* 11/12 (2007): 347; S. Prechal, et al. *'Europeanization' of the Law: Consequences for the Dutch Judiciary* (Report for the Dutch Council of the Judiciary, October 2005), 39–40.
71. M. Schimmel & R. Widdershoven, 'Judicial Review after Tetra Laval, Some Observations from a European Adminitstrative Law Point of View', in: *National Courts and the Standard of Review in Competition Law and Economic Regulation*, ed. O, Essens, A. Gerbrandy & S. Lavrijssen (Groningen: Europa Law Publishing, 2009), 72–74.
72. Case T-5/02 *Tetra Laval v. Commission* [2002] ECR II-4381 and Case C-12/03P *Commission v. Tetra Laval* [2005] ECR I-987. Whilst the Court of Justice recognizes in the *Tetra Laval Case* that the Commission has a margin of discretion with regard to economic matters, this does not mean that the Community Courts must refrain from reviewing the Commission's interpretation of information of an economic nature. Not only must the Community Courts, *inter alia*, establish whether the evidence relied on is factually accurate, reliable and consistent, but also whether that evidence contains all the information which must be taken into account in order to assess a complex situation, and whether this evidence is capable of substantiating the conclusions drawn from it. Such a review is – according to the Court of Justice – all the more necessary in the case of a prospective analysis.
73. Schimmel & Widdershoven (2009), *supra* n. 71.

the greater possibilities for legal protection against the NRAs' decisions on the basis of EU law, may compensate for the fact that European law at the same time has decreased the role of the political arena to control the way NRAs adopt specific decisions in individual cases.

The gradual process of restricting Member State autonomy with regard to the judicial accountability of the NRAs also has its influence outside the area of electronic communications. For instance, the recently adopted energy directives now include a new provision, which provides that the Member States shall ensure that suitable mechanisms exist at national level under which a party affected by a decision of regulatory authority has a right to appeal to a body independent of the parties involved and of any government.[74]

8. CONCLUSIONS

In this article we have discerned two important trends. On the one hand, European law has gradually increased the independence requirements with which Member States should comply when setting up and regulating NRAs in implementation of European law. Initially, EC law merely required that NRAs were positioned independently from the market parties. With the entry into force of the third package of liberalization directives, Member States also have to ensure that the NRAs can take autonomous decisions in specific cases, free from political influence. However, this does not mean that the NRAs should be completely independent from the political arena; it is assumed that the national authorities should follow general policy guidelines formulated by the responsible ministers.

On the other hand, the European liberalization directives have gradually expanded the discretionary powers that have to be delegated to the NRAs. Subsequently, the ECJ has interpreted these powers in a teleological way and has recognized that the NRAs possess a significant degree of discretion when exercising their powers. Indeed, an effective implementation and application of European law requires that the NRAs' powers are interpreted, not only on the basis of the wording of the legal provisions, but also in the light of the aims and goals of the European Directives, no matter whether those powers are exercised at some distance from the political arena or not.

The above-mentioned two developments in European law restrict the Member States in applying specific national interpretations of constitutional principles. Indeed, the argument of Dutch scholars and the Dutch government that the principle of legality prohibits the legislator from delegating powers, implying a significant degree of discretion to independent NRAs does not sit well with European law. Therefore, it may be concluded that the Member States' institutional autonomy in formulating and interpreting the NRAs' powers on the basis of

74. Article 37, paras 16 and 17 Directive (EC) 2009/72 and Art. 41, paras 16 and 17 Directive (EC) 2009/73.

specific interpretations of national constitutional principles, and the principle of legality in particular, has been significantly curtailed.

At the same time, European law increasingly regulates the legal accountability of the NRAs, further curtailing the Member States' institutional and procedural autonomy. The NRAs are subject to European coordination and cooperation mechanisms, such as specific administrative control powers of the EC, ensuring that the NRAs' decisions comply with European law and do not frustrate market integration in the liberalizing sectors. The third package of European liberalization directives extends the administrative control powers of the Commission with regard to the NRAs decisions. It also further harmonizes the European coordination and cooperation in cases with cross-border effects between the NRAs of the different Member states by granting informal regulatory networks of NRAs a formal legal status through the creation of European regulatory network agencies.

Moreover, the liberalization directives increasingly provide for specific provisions regulating administrative procedures and the judicial review of the NRAs decisions, including crucial aspects of judicial review, such as legal standing and the intensity of review. As the ECJ also subjects these institutional provisions to a teleological interpretation method, ensuring the right to effective legal protection for those affected by the NRAs' decisions, the influence of European law on the judicial accountability of the NRAs is growing. One could argue that all of these trends give shape to a European interpretation of the principle of legality, which is a national constitutional principle common to the constitutional traditions of the Member States, and therefore part of European law as a general principle of law. According to this European interpretation of the principle of legality, the legality of administrative authorities will not be assured by a limited and restricted interpretation of the NRAs' powers. Instead, a mix of European and national checks and balances, including a legal base, administrative procedures, European coordination, and cooperation procedures and judicial review by national courts, will contribute to the legality of the NRAs. The practice of the NRAs and the development of the European and national checks and balances will lead to a further development of a European interpretation of the principle of legality, which will at the same time influence national interpretations of this principle, and vice versa.

Part III

Legality and Quality of Legislation

Chapter 6
The Quality of the Law as a Tool for Judicial Control

Aleidus Woltjer

1. INTRODUCTION

Imposing obligations on individuals or restrictions to their (fundamental) rights by provisions of national law may be incompatible with legal principles of European law, be it European Union law or fundamental rights and freedoms guaranteed by the European Convention on Human Rights (ECHR) and Fundamental Freedoms (hereafter referred to as ECHR), if this law is phrased in vague and overbroad terms that may give rise to arbitrary interpretation and application.

To this end, the Court of Justice of the European Union (hereafter referred to as the ECJ) requires that national law be phrased in clear, precise wording and that it be predictable in its effects as a requirement of the principle of legal certainty. The European Court of Human Rights (hereafter referred to as the ECtHR) in this regard refers to 'the quality of the law' as an indispensable element of the 'rule of law' being a fundamental principle for democratic societies, or the 'foreseeability' of the law as a criterion for legitimate restrictions of fundamental rights.

Thus, both European Courts require that (provisions of) national law be precise and clear, both in its wording and in its effects, in such a way that (re)actions of State officials become predictable and foreseeable so that an individual will be able to anticipate or respond adequately. However, the approach of both Courts seems to be different: is the quality of the law basically a requirement of a legal principle

Leonard Besselink, Frans Pennings & Sacha Prechal (eds), *The Eclipse of the Legality Principle in the European Union*, pp. 99–108.

(legal certainty) or is it an element of the fundamental character of democratic societies?

Although the Courts may use a different wording, it will be argued that the assessment of (provisions of) national law has the same effect under Community law and the Convention, thus representing a constitutional element of European law.

2. THE COURT OF JUSTICE OF THE EUROPEAN UNION

2.1. EU Law

According to Article 19 Treaty on European Union (TEU) (ex Article 220 EC), the ECJ EU shall ensure that in the interpretation and application of the EU treaties, the law is observed. 'The law' in this context is mainly primary and secondary EU law created by the EU organs based on primary EU law. It includes the international treaties concluded by the Member States within the sphere of competence of the EU, and furthermore, it also includes fundamental legal principles.[1]

The ECJ is empowered to rule on the conformity of national acts – including legal and policy provisions – of Member States with EU law. The infraction procedure of Article 258 TFEU (Article 226 EC) and the preliminary rulings procedure of Article 267 TFEU (ex Article 234 EC) may serve as a useful tool to this end. Conformity with EU law not only includes conformity with primary and secondary EU law, but also conformity with fundamental legal principles. Among these are fundamental rights, including the rights enshrined in the ECHR.[2] In this regard, the legal protection of individual rights by the ECJ has become more prominent over the years.[3]

2.2. The Approach of the ECJ

In the early eighties the ECJ ruled in the *Gondrand Frères* case (1981) that

> The principle of legal certainty requires that rules imposing charges on the tax payer must be clear and precise so that he may know without ambiguity what are his rights and obligations and may take steps accordingly.[4]

Thus, national legal provisions imposing obligations on individuals have to be clear and precise, avoiding any ambiguity, to which end the ECJ refers to the principle of legal certainty. At the same time, the wording demonstrates a striking

1. See B. Wegener, 'EGV Art. 220', rdn. 8, in Calliess/Ruffert, *EUV/EGV Kommentar*, München: Beck Verlag 2007, 1942 and 1943.
2. Article 6 TEU.
3. B. Wegener, 'EGV Art. 220', rdn. 11, in Calliess/Ruffert, *EUV/EGV Kommentar*, München: Beck Verlag 2007, 1943.
4. Gondrand Frères, CoJ EU 9 Jul. 1981, C-169/80 ECR (1981), 1931, para. 17.

parallel with the criterion of 'foreseeability' in the case law of the ECtHR, as we will see later on.

Shortly after, the ECJ pointed out in the *Deutsche Milchkontor* case (1983) that the principle of legal certainty referred to is a fundamental legal principle of Community law which is, as such, not necessarily identical to a principle in national law, but has a status of its own.[5] The requirement of national law being phrased in clear and precise terms while referring to the principle of legal certainty was repeated in the *Van Es Douane Agenten* case[6] and rephrased in the *VEMW* case with reference to predictability ('foreseeability' in terms of the ECtHR):

> With regard to the principle of legal certainty, this requires in particular that rules involving negative consequences for individuals should be clear and precise and their application predictable for those subject to them.[7]

Finally, in the *Brescia* case[8] the ECJ ruled once more that the principle of legal certainty requires that provisions of national law be clear, precise and predictable in their effects, in particular where they may have negative consequences on individuals and undertakings. This consideration was restated in the *Föster* case.[9]

Even if national legislation or action by national authorities is required by a provision of an instrument under the TFEU, such as the Framework Decision 2002/584/JHA on the European Arrest Warrant and surrender procedures between Member States, fundamental human rights and fundamental legal principles, such as the principle of legality, must be respected.[10]

Nevertheless, it may occur that a reference to the principle of legal certainty is absent and that the requirement of precise and predictable rules is used alternatively in the context of a proportionality test, as the ECJ did in the *Collins* case.[11] Here, the question of justification of indirect discrimination was at stake and therefore the Court considered factors that were suitable and necessary to achieve the legitimate aim pursued. Likewise, the ECtHR sometimes presents the requirement of the quality of the law under the heading of the proportionality test instead of the test of whether it is 'provided by law', as it did in the *S. and Marper* case (see below).

3. THE EUROPEAN COURT OF HUMAN RIGHTS

3.1. The European Convention on Human Rights

According to Article 19 of the European Convention of Human Rights, the European Court of Human Rights is set up 'to ensure the observance of the

5. Deutsche Milchkontor et al., CoJ EU 21 Sep. 1983, C-205/82 and 215/82, para. 30.
6. Van Es Douane Agenten, CoJ EU 13 Feb. 1996, C-143/93, para. 27.
7. VEMW et al., CoJ EU (Grand Chamber) 7 Jun. 2005, C-17/03, para. 80.
8. ASM Brescia, CoJ EU 17 Jul. 2008, C-347/06, para. 69.
9. Föster, CoJ EU 18 Nov. 2008, C 158/07, para. 67.
10. Advocaten voor de Wereld VZW, CoJ EU (Grand Chamber) 3 May 2007, C-303/05, para. 53.
11. Collins, CoJ EU 23 Mar. 2004, C-138/02, para. 72.

engagements undertaken by the High Contracting Parties in the Convention and the Protocols thereto'. It is not the Court's task to review national legislation, neither in general nor in detail, but to judge on the conformity of State actions (or State authorities) with the ECHR. Usually, such State actions will consist of an action, a reaction or an omission of national authorities, based on national legislation or policy and subsequent national judicial control thereof, finally constituting an alleged infringement of the ECHR. The scope of judicial power of the ECtHR is limited to the explicit (operational) provisions of the ECHR, including provisional measures based on Rule 39 of the Rules of Court. According to the ECtHR, such measures are considered to be legally binding upon State parties, because their non-observance may cause an invalidation of the right to submit individual petitions enshrined in Article 34 ECHR.[12]

The ECtHR does not consider itself as a 'fourth instance' offering redress of judgments delivered by national courts. Quite on the contrary, the ECtHR in this respect refers to the 'principle of subsidiarity', a principle that 'underpins the Convention system'.[13]

3.2. Limitation of Fundamental Rights

Under the ECHR, restrictions of fundamental rights and freedoms may be justified if they are 'provided by law' or 'in accordance with the law'.[14] In its early case law the ECtHR pointed out that the reference to 'the law' does not imply a formal requirement[15] as to the procedure for its coming into being, its promulgation or to the status of the legislature. On the contrary, any written rule, be it a constitutional rule, an Act of Parliament, a by law or even a unwritten policy rule, will be regarded as 'law' provided it is 'accessible' and 'foreseeable'.[16] The 'accessibility' of the law at hand requires that the person concerned could reasonably be aware of its existence and familiarize themselves with the contents. The 'foreseeability' requires that the person concerned is able, if need be with professional assistance, to anticipate any (re)action or measure from the State authorities, and thus take appropriate action. Such a concept of 'lawfulness', often referred to in case law of the ECtHR, was developed in the *Silver* case[17] (1983) and confirmed soon after in

12. *Mamatkulov and Askarov v. Turkey*, ECtHR (Grand Chamber) 4 Feb. 2005, appl. no. 46827/99.
13. *Burdov v. Russia* (no. 2) ECtHR 15 Jan. 2009, appl. no. 33509/04, para. 127.
14. See for example, the second paras of the Arts 8–11 ECHR.
15. According to the Court's settled case law, the concept of 'law' must be understood in its 'substantive' sense, not its 'formal' one. It therefore includes everything that goes to make up the written law, including enactments of lower rank than statutes (see in particular, *De Wilde, Ooms and Versyp v. Belgium*, 18 Jun. 1971, § 93, Series A no. 12) and the relevant case law authority (see mutatis mutandis, *Kruslin v. France*, 24 Apr. 1990, § 29 Series A no.176-A), referred to in *Dogru v. France*, ECtHR 4 Dec. 2008, appl. no. 27058/05, para. 52.
16. *Sunday Times v. UK*, ECtHR 26 Apr. 1979, appl. no. 6538/74, para. 49.
17. *Silver v. UK*, ECtHR 25 Mar. 1983, appl. nos 5947/72, 6205/73, 7052/75, 7061/75, 7107/75, 7113/75 en 7136/75, paras 86–88.

the *Malone* case[18] (1984). As to the requirement of 'foreseeability', the ECtHR recently explained in the *Dogru* case[19] that:

> the notion of foreseeability depends to a considerable degree on the content of the instrument in question, the field it is designed to cover and the number and status of those to whom it is addressed. It must also be borne in mind that, however clearly drafted a legal provision may be, its application involves an inevitable element of judicial interpretation, since there will always be a need for clarification of doubtful points and for adaptation to particular circumstances. A margin of doubt in relation to borderline facts does not by itself make a legal provision unforeseeable in its application. Nor does the mere fact that a provision is capable of more than one construction mean that it fails to meet the requirement of 'foreseeability' for the purposes of the Convention. The role of adjudication vested in the courts is precisely to dissipate such interpretational doubts as remain, taking into account the changes in everyday practice (see *Gorzelik and Others v. Poland* [GC], no. 44158/98, § 65).

4. THE QUALITY OF THE LAW ACCORDING TO THE ECtHR

Over the years, the ECtHR turned to a scrutiny of the quality of the law in cases of deprivation of liberty in the context of Article 5 ECHR. According to this Article, the deprivation of physical liberty must be in accordance with the law – that is, there must be a basis in national law. To this end, a provision in national law should be phrased in clear terms, avoiding vague notions that may give the State authorities unfettered powers and leave room for arbitrary interferences. An example of this approach may be found in the *Baranowski* case,[20] where the ECtHR stated that the law must be clear, precise and unambiguous in order to avoid any arbitrary interference by State authorities.[21] Thus the ECtHR monitors the quality of the law. In this respect, the ECtHR referred to the 'rule of law' as the leading principle for

---

18. *Malone v. UK*, ECtHR 2 Aug. 1984, appl. no. 8691/79, para. 67
19. *Dogru v. France*, ECtHR 4 Dec. 2008, appl. no. 27058/05, para. 57.
20. *Baranowski v. Poland*, ECtHR 28 Mar. 2000, appl. no. 28358/95 and *Al-Nashif v. Bulgaria*, ECtHR 20 Jun. 2002, appl. no. 50963/99.
21. *Nolan and K. v. Russia*, ECtHR 12 Feb. 2009, appl. no. 2512/04, para. 98: 'The Court must therefore ascertain whether domestic law itself is in conformity with the Convention, including the general principles expressed or implied therein. On this last point, the Court stresses that, where deprivation of liberty is concerned, it is particularly important that the general principle of legal certainty be satisfied. In laying down that any deprivation of liberty must be effected "in accordance with a procedure prescribed by law", Art. 5 § 1 does not merely refer back to domestic law; like the expressions "in accordance with the law" and "prescribed by law" in the second paras of Arts 8–11, it also relates to the "quality of the law", *requiring it to be compatible with the rule of law, a concept inherent in all the Articles of the Convention.* "Quality of law" in this sense implies that where a national law authorizes deprivation of liberty it must be sufficiently accessible, precise and foreseeable in its application, in order to avoid all risk of arbitrariness.' (emphasis added, AW).

the Member States of the Council of Europe as stated in the Preamble of the ECHR.[22] The test of the quality of the law is not limited to Article 5 ECHR, but stretches to all Articles, according to the ECtHR in a Grand Chamber judgment in the *Kafkaris* case under the heading of 'general principles'.[23] Meanwhile, the reference to the rule of law was maintained in the *Maestri* case[24] and confirmed in the *Segerstedt-Wiberg* case.[25]

The problem with this reference is the character of the Preamble of the ECHR. The Preamble may be guidance to the intentions and underlying ideas of the drafters of the Convention, but it is not legally binding and is therefore considered an additional source of interpretation. The rule of law may serve as a legal principle,[26] but its legal force, as a notion taken from the Preamble of the ECHR, may be doubtful. To put it in another way: what will be the precise

22. 'Being resolved, as the governments of European countries which are like-minded and have a common heritage of political traditions, ideals, freedom and the rule of law, to take the first steps for the collective enforcement of certain of the rights stated in the Universal Declaration.'
23. *Kafkaris v. Cyprus*, ECtHR (Grand Chamber) 12 Feb. 2008, appl. no. 21906/04, para. 116: 'The Court reiterates that where the "lawfulness" of detention is at issue, the Convention refers essentially to national law and lays down the obligation to conform to the substantive and procedural rules of national law. This primarily requires any arrest or detention to have a legal basis in domestic law but also relates to the quality of the law, requiring it to be compatible with the rule of law, a concept inherent in all the Articles of the Convention.'
24. *Maestri v. Italy*, ECtHR (Grand Chamber) 17 Feb. 2004, appl. no. 39748/98, para. 30: 'For domestic law to meet these requirements, it must afford a measure of legal protection against arbitrary interferences by public authorities with the rights guaranteed by the Convention. In matters affecting fundamental rights *it would be contrary to the rule of law, one of the basic principles of a democratic society enshrined in the Convention*, for a legal discretion granted to the executive to be expressed in terms of an unfettered power. Consequently, the law must indicate with sufficient clarity the scope of any such discretion and the manner of its exercise.' (emphasis added, AW) Compare: *Rotaru v. Romania*, ECtHR 4 May 2000, appl. no. 28341/95, para. 52 and *Hasan and Chaush v. Bulgaria*, ECtHR (GC) 26 Oct. 2000, appl. no. 30985/96, para. 84.
25. *Segerstedt-Wiberg et al. v. Sweden*, ECtHR 6 Jun. 2006, appl. no. 62332/00, para. 76: 'The Court reiterates its settled case law, according to which the expression "in accordance with the law" not only requires the impugned measure to have some basis in domestic law, but also refers to the quality of the law in question, requiring that it should be accessible to the person concerned and foreseeable as to its effects (. . .). *The law must be compatible with the rule of law, which means that it must provide a measure of legal protection against arbitrary interference by public authorities* with the rights safeguarded by para. 1 of Art. 8.' (emphasis added, AW).
26. *Mooren v. Germany*, ECtHR (Grand Chamber), 11 Jul. 2009, appl. no. 11364/03, para. 76: 'The Court must moreover ascertain whether domestic law itself is in conformity with the Convention, including the general principles expressed or implied therein. On this last point, the Court stresses that, where deprivation of liberty is concerned, it is particularly important *that the general principle of legal certainty be satisfied* (. . .). In laying down that any deprivation of liberty must be "lawful" and be effected "in accordance with a procedure prescribed by law", Art. 5 § 1 does not merely refer back to domestic law; like the expressions "in accordance with the law" and "prescribed by law" in the second paras of Arts 8–11, it also relates to the "quality of the law", requiring it to be compatible with the rule of law, a concept inherent in all the Arts of the Convention. "Quality of the law" in this sense implies that where a national law authorizes deprivation of liberty it must be sufficiently accessible, precise and foreseeable in its application, in order to avoid all risk of arbitrariness.' (emphasis added, AW).

scope of State obligations under the ECHR with regard to the rule of law? Just as the ECtHR is in search for legal certainty for the individual, State parties to the ECHR are entitled to know the scope of their legal obligations under this treaty.

Whereas the ECJ refers to recitals in an instrument's preamble (Treaty, Regulation, Directive) to define the scope and meaning of its operational provisions by applying the principle of effectiveness, the ECtHR rarely refers to the preamble of the ECHR or its protocols. Nevertheless, the result may be the same, since the ECtHR is stretching the effective interpretation of the ECHR as a 'living instrument'.

Perhaps to avoid legal disputes about the exigencies of the rule of law and possible consequences it might entail, the ECtHR is sometimes silent on the rule of law and refers to its settled case law by presenting the notion of the quality of the law as a separate element of the 'foreseeability' of the law or measure at hand.[27]

However: even a lawful action may nevertheless be arbitrary, as the ECtHR points out in the following paras 77–80: 'No detention which is arbitrary can be compatible with Art. 5 § 1, the notion of "arbitrariness" in this context extending beyond the lack of conformity with national law. As a consequence, a deprivation of liberty which is lawful under domestic law can still be arbitrary and thus contrary to the Convention. While the Court has not previously formulated a global definition as to what types of conduct on the part of the authorities might constitute "arbitrariness" for the purposes of Art. 5 § 1, key principles have been developed on a case-by-case basis. It is moreover clear from the case-law that the notion of arbitrariness in the context of Art. 5 varies to a certain extent depending on the type of detention involved (. . .). One general principle established in the case-law is that detention will be "arbitrary" where, despite complying with the letter of national law, there has been an element of bad faith or deception on the part of the authorities (. . .) or where the domestic authorities neglected to attempt to apply the relevant legislation correctly (. . .). Furthermore, in the context of sub-paragraph (c) of Art. 5 § 1, the reasoning of the decision ordering detention is a relevant factor in determining whether a person's detention must be considered as arbitrary. The Court has considered the absence of any grounds given by the judicial authorities in their decisions authorizing detention for a prolonged period of time to be incompatible with the principle of the protection from arbitrariness enshrined in Art. 5 § 1. Conversely, it has found that an applicant's detention could not be said to have been arbitrary if the domestic court gave certain grounds justifying the continued detention on remand (. . .), unless the reasons given are extremely laconic and without reference to any legal provision which would have permitted the applicant's detention. Moreover, the Court has acknowledged notably in the context of sub-paragraphs (c) and (e) of Art. 5 § 1 that the speed with which the domestic courts replaced a detention order which had either expired or had been found to be defective is a further relevant element in assessing whether a person's detention must be considered arbitrary. Thus, the Court considered in the context of sub-paragraph (c) that a period of less than a month between the expiry of the initial detention order and the issuing of a fresh, reasoned detention order following a remittal of the case from the appeal court to a lower court did not render the applicant's detention arbitrary (. . .). In contrast, a period of more than a year following a remittal from a court of appeal to a court of lower instance, in which the applicant remained in a state of uncertainty as to the grounds for his detention on remand, combined with the lack of a time-limit for the lower court to re-examine his detention, was found to render the applicant's detention arbitrary.'

27. Damian-Burueana and *Damian v. Rumania*, ECtHR 26 May 2009, appl. no. 6773/02, para. 112: '(. . .)Il convient de rappeler à cet égard que l'expression "prévue par la loi", au sens de l'article 8 § 2 de la Convention, signifie que la mesure incriminée doit avoir une base légale en droit interne, et que la loi en cause doit être accessible à la personne concernée – laquelle, de surcroît,

5. THE 'FORESEEABILITY' UNDER DIFFICULT CIRCUMSTANCES

The rule of law or the 'foreseeability' requires a certain level of quality of the law, but to what extent? Legitimate aims for restrictions may often be found in public policy, public security or national security. These notions have in common that their content lacks precision as their definitions are multiple and vague. They are meant to cover very different and unforeseen (and sometimes unpredictable) situations and are open to abuse. National security is especially surrounded by a sphere of secrecy, because democratic values such as openness and transparency do not fit in with the secret character of operations of intelligence services and the processing of information that should remain confidential. Although the ECtHR acknowledges that national security includes a wide range of situations in which action by State authorities is required and confidentiality of sources of information and means of obtaining and processing information is inevitable, the ECtHR insists that the State establishes a reasonable justification for the invocation of national security.[28] The ECtHR does not require that the State party draws up an exhaustive list of possible actions and procedures to be followed by State authorities in order to make their (re)actions 'foreseeable', but if any discretionary power is entrusted to State authorities, the limitations of those powers must be clearly indicated in order to enable judicial control and to exclude any arbitrariness. This means that State parties are obliged to indicate the nature and the intensity of State measures, as well as the period of time they will be applied. If information on individuals or groups is obtained, the nature of the information gathered must be clearly indicated, as well as who will be allowed to obtain it and to what end, how long it will be stored and who will have access to it. Finally, the requirement of an effective remedy[29] includes scrutiny by an independent and impartial body competent to review all relevant questions of fact and of law in adversarial proceedings. The use of open and vague notions in national law that gave rise to arbitrary interferences by State authorities was therefore ruled by the ECtHR in a series of cases to constitute a lack of quality of the law, and as such incompatible with the rule of law or the required 'foreseeability'.[30]

Incidentally, the ECtHR requires that (provisions of) national law be clear and precise under the test of proportionality ('necessary in a democratic society'). If the ECtHR is satisfied this requirement is met, it may decide to refrain from a 'quality

doit pouvoir en prévoir les conséquences pour elle – et être compatible avec la prééminence du droit.'

28. Association for European integration and Human Rights and *Ekimdziev v. Bulgaria*, ECtHR 28 Jun. 2007, appl. no. 62540/00.
29. Article 13 ECHR and certain elements of a fair trial from Art. 6 ECHR.
30. *Al-Nashif v. Bulgaria*, ECtHR 20 Jun. 2002, appl. no. 50963/99, paras 123 and 124; *Lupsa v. Romania*, ECtHR 8 Jun. 2006, appl. no. 10337/04; *Kaya v. Romania*, ECtHR 12 Oct. 2006, appl. no. 33970/05; *Musa et al. v. Bulgaria*, ECtHR 11 Jan. 2007, appl. no. 61259/00; *Liu and Liu v. Russia*, ECtHR 6 Dec. 2007, appl. no. 42086/05; *C.G. et al. v. Bulgary*, ECtHR 24 Apr. 2008, appl. no. 1365/07; *Liberty et al. v. UK*, ECtHR 1 Jul. 2008, appl. no. 58243/00.

of the law' test, as it did in the *S. and Marper* case.[31] Such an approach is quite odd, as the usual sequence requires that it be established that a restriction of a fundamental right is 'according to law' in the first place, with the proportionality test being applied subsequently. Nevertheless, such an application of the proportionality test bears a striking resemblance with the *Collins* case of the ECJ mentioned in section 2.2 (above, see footnote 11).

6. IS THE 'QUALITY OF THE LAW' TEST COMPATIBLE WITH THE PRINCIPLE OF SUBSIDIARITY?

Since both Courts apply a 'quality of the law' test based on the principle of legal certainty or the rule of law, the question arises as to whether such a test is compatible with the principle of subsidiarity, which at least the ECtHR has to respect on the basis of a 'principle that underpins the Convention system' (see section 3.1 above, footnote 13). According to the ECtHR the principle of subsidiarity does not refrain the Court from exercising a scrutinous test. As the ECtHR reasoned in the *Sanoma* case:[32]

> The Court's task in exercising its supervisory function is not to take the place of the competent domestic courts but rather to review under Article 10 the decisions they have taken pursuant to their power of appreciation. This does not mean that the supervision is limited to ascertaining whether the respondent State exercised its discretion reasonably, carefully or in good faith; what the Court has to do is to look at the interference complained of in the light of the case as a whole. In particular, the Court must determine whether the reasons adduced by the national authorities to justify the interference were 'relevant and sufficient' and whether the measure taken was 'proportionate to the legitimate aims pursued'. In doing so, the Court has to satisfy itself that the national authorities, basing themselves on an acceptable assessment of the relevant facts, applied standards which were in conformity with the principles embodied in Article 10.

This subsidiary principle argument was referred to in the *Lesjak* case as a 'most important' principle:[33]

> The Court would emphasize, as it did in number of its previous rulings concerning the implementation of the 2006 Act, that the subsidiary principle is one of the most important principles for the functioning of the Convention system.

---

31. *S. and Marper v. UK*, ECtHR (Grand Chamber) 4 Dec. 2008, appl. nos 30562/04 and 30566/04.
32. *Sanoma uitgevers B.V. v. the Netherlands*, ECtHR 31 Mar. 2009, appl. no. 38224/03, para. 54.
33. *Lesjak v. Slovenia*, ECtHR 21 Jul. 2009, appl. no. 33946/03, para. 60.

7. CONCLUDING REMARKS

Both the ECJ and the ECtHR apply a 'quality of the law' test in case of alleged arbitrary interferences by national authorities that have taken place while imposing obligations on individuals or restricting their fundamental rights. Both European Courts demand clear and precise wording of legal provisions so that (re)actions of national authorities become foreseeable and predictable. Both European Courts refer to foreseeability – the individual should know in advance what (re)action of the national authorities is to be expected so that he can respond accordingly. In this regard, the ECJ refers to the principle of legal certainty, that is applied as a principle of Community law, but which still remains a principle that is not clearly defined. The ECtHR refers to the element of 'foreseeability', which is not defined in the ECHR as such, but which constitutes an element of the requirement that a restriction is 'provided by law' or is 'according to law', and which has been, after all, developed in the case law of the ECtHR. The same goes for the rule of law as a fundamental requirement for democratic States. It is not defined in the operational provisions of the ECHR, but is merely mentioned in the Preamble of the ECHR. Strictly speaking, the Preamble does not have legal force. Besides, it lacks a definition that gives guidance for its interpretation. As such, it is a doubtful basis for exigencies of clear and precise wording. However, in their efforts to combat arbitrary application of national law by emphasizing the importance of the principle of legal certainty, both courts underline the practical application of the rule of law as a constitutional feature of the Member States of both the EU and the Council of Europe.

Chapter 7

Coherent Codification? A Case Study in EU Equal Treatment Legislation

Susanne Burri

1. INTRODUCTION

Since 1975, various European Union Directives have been adopted in order to combat sex discrimination in employment. Since then, the European Court of Justice has answered many preliminary questions from the national courts of Member States regarding the interpretation and application of these legal instruments. Some of these Directives are outdated compared to more recently adopted Directives, which cover not only discrimination on the grounds of sex, but also discrimination on the grounds of race or ethnic origin, religion or belief, disability, age or sexual orientation (with Article 13 Treaty of the European Communities (TEC) as legal basis). Sometimes the interpretation of crucial concepts by the ECJ – for example, the concept of pay – had the effect that some provisions of Directives were not relevant anymore. This was one of the reasons why the EU started a so-called recasting of some sex equality Directives in order to modernize, simplify and harmonize previously adopted Directives, and in order to consolidate case law of the ECJ. In 2006, the Recast Directive (2006/54/EC) on the implementation of the principle of equal opportunities and equal treatment of men and women in matters of employment and occupation was adopted.[1] In this Directive, a

1. *Official Journal of the European Union* 49, L 204, 26 Jul. 2006, 23–36.

Leonard Besselink, Frans Pennings & Sacha Prechal (eds), *The Eclipse of the Legality Principle in the European Union*, pp. 109–124.

few Directives in the field of equal pay and equal treatment of men and women in employment were consolidated. The aim of this Directive is, according to the European Commission in its initial proposal, to 'simplify, modernize and improve the Community law in the area of equal treatment between men and women by putting together in a single text provisions of Directives linked by their subject in order to make Community legislation clearer and more effective for the benefit of all citizens'.[2] According to the Commission, the proposal is also grounded in 'the general context of the new legal and political environment which aims to make the Union more open, understandable and relevant to daily life'.[3] These purposes are closely related to the regulatory function of the legality principle, particularly insofar as the exercise of consolidating and recasting the legislative instruments should render the law more accessible, foreseeable and, as such, improve legal certainty.[4]

The aim of the present contribution is to analyse the recasting process in the area of sex discrimination and to examine whether this process contributes to coherent codification, both at EU level and national level. It first describes the general requirements a recasting technique should meet in view of better law making according to the EU institutions. It then examines whether the legislative process preceding the adoption of the Recast Directive 2006/54/EC meets these requirements. Third, it analyses the (in)coherence of some provisions of Directives at EU level and the case law of the ECJ. It also looks into the transposition of the Recast Directive at national level. Finally, the pros and cons of such a recasting process and its contribution to the realization of legal certainty and coherent codification are highlighted, and the concluding remarks hopefully offer some useful recommendations for future recasting exercises.

2. RECASTING AS EU POLICY

2.1. Better Lawmaking

The recasting technique can be seen as a further step towards making Community legislation more accessible, comprehensible and consistent. Since the 1990s, explicit attention has been paid to requirements regarding technical aspects of legal texts in order to improve their quality. In 1993 a Council Resolution was adopted including rules on the quality of drafting of Community legislation.[5] This resolution requires, for example, that the wording of the act should be clear, simple, concise and unambiguous. In addition, the various provisions should be consistent with each other; inconsistency with existing legislation should be avoided, and any amendment, extension or repeal of an act should be clearly set out.

2. European Commission, COM (2004) 279, 2.
3. *Ibid.*
4. See the explicit reference to legal certainty in the Commission's proposal COM (2004) 279, 5.
5. *Official Journal of the European Union* 36, C 166, 17 Jun. 1993, 1.

In 1998, the European Parliament (EP), the Council and the European Commission (EC) adopted an Interinstitutional Agreement on common guidelines for the quality of drafting of Community legislation.[6] This document states that clear, simple and precise drafting of Community legislative acts is essential if they are to be transparent and readily understandable by the public and economic operators, and it is also a prerequisite for the proper implementation and uniform application of Community legislation in the Member States.

2.2. The Recasting Technique

Since 1994, an Interinstitutional Agreement has allowed an accelerated method for official codification of legislative texts.[7] However, according to this Agreement, the Commission is not allowed to introduce any substantive changes in the acts to be codified according to this accelerated method (see section 3). This method therefore shows shortcomings in case new amendments are adopted concerning legislative instruments subject to this procedure in the meantime. Then the whole consolidation process has to start once again. For this reason, the recasting technique makes it possible to adopt one single legislative act in order to simultaneously amend substantively a text, to codify that amendment with the unchanged provisions of the earlier act, and to repeal that earlier act. In 2001 the EP, the Council and the EC felt the need to conclude an Interinstitutional Agreement on a more structured use of such recasting techniques for legal acts.[8] This Interinstitutional Agreement lays down the procedural rules to be applied to recasting procedures and the requirements that recasting acts should meet. An important purpose mentioned in this Agreement once again is enhancing the readability and quality of Community legislation.[9] It is submitted that recasting should also enhance the consistency and uniformity of legal texts, and can therefore contribute to legal certainty, in particular the foreseeability aspects as identified in this publication.

For this contribution, the provisions in the Interinstitutional Agreement of 2001 regarding substantive amendments are particularly relevant, because the Recast Directive 2006/54 was not meant to substantially amend earlier Directives, but only to update and consolidate the earlier texts and important case law of the ECJ. Consolidating the Community *acquis* – not amending it – was the main purpose of this Directive. However, Article 33, concerning the implementation of the Directive, stipulates that the obligation to transpose the Directive into national law shall be confined to 'those provisions which represent a substantive change as compared with earlier Directives. The obligation to transpose the

6. *Ibid.*, 42, C 73, 17 Mar. 1999, 1.
7. *Ibid.*, 39, C 102, 4 Apr. 1996.
8. *Ibid.*, 45, C 77, 28 Mar. 2002, 1-3.
9. See the Interinstitutional Agreement on guidelines in the quality of drafting Community legislation of 22 Dec. 1998, *Official Journal of the European Union* 42, C 73 (17 Mar. 1999), 1.

provisions which are substantially unchanged arise under the earlier Directives'. The very fact that Article 33 is included in the Directive suggests that at least some provisions of the Directive might imply substantive changes; otherwise, such a mention would not be unnecessary. It is therefore crucial for Member States to know which provisions should be defined as a substantive amendment and which should not.

The Interinstitutional Agreement defines a substantive amendment as follows: 'any amendment which affects the substance of the earlier act as opposed to purely formal or editorial changes' (section 4). It is clear that one can have different views regarding what constitutes purely a formal or editorial change and what does not. The Agreement therefore stipulates that the proposed legislative text shall be presented in a way that 'enables the substantive amendments and the new recitals to be clearly distinguished from the provisions and recitals which remain unchanged' (section 6, (b)(i)). Furthermore, a correlation table should be included in the proposal. The Agreement further stipulates that the Article relating to the obligation to transpose a recast Directive into national law shall refer only to those provisions which have undergone substantive amendments '*and which have been precisely identified as such*' (section 7, (c)(iii); emphasis added).

Directive 2006/54/EC does not specify which provisions have undergone substantive changes. According to the correlation table, only one Article (Article 7(2)) has no correlate in earlier Directives that are part of the recasting exercise. At first sight, Directive 2006/54/EC does not, therefore, impose any further obligations on the Member States other than those arising out of earlier Directives. However, a closer look at the provisions of the Recast Directive in comparison with earlier Directives shows various clarifications and novelties, and the explanatory memorandum of the Commission's proposal highlights the 'principal innovations'.[10] This suggests that there are 'innovations,' and even more than those listed. The question of whether these 'principal innovations' represent substantive amendments or not is not explicitly addressed. Therefore the question of whether the Recast Directive implies substantive changes, and if so, what substantive changes, should be answered by a thorough analysis of the provisions of the Recast Directive in the light of earlier adopted Directives which are part of this recasting process, and the relevant case law of the ECJ. Embarking on such analysis falls outside the scope of this contribution, but attention will be paid in section 3 to a few issues in order to highlight how problematic is might be to decide whether some provisions of the Recast Directive amount to substantive changes or not.

2.3. Enforceable Rights?

The question of which legal status should be attributed to this Interinstitutional Agreement is particularly interesting when the obligations of the Member States regarding the implementation of the Recast Directive have to be defined.

10. European Commission, COM (2004) 279, 5–6.

For example, in the case of a Member State being confronted with an infringement procedure based on Article 226 EC, due to non-implementation or incorrect implementation of a provision containing an 'innovation' in the Recast Directive 2006/54/EC, could the Member State rely on the Agreement and assert that this 'innovation' does not amount to a substantive change because it is not identified as such and/or is not listed in the correlation table as a new Article? In such a case the Member State could argue that the previously implemented Directives – which are part of the recasting exercise – already meet the requirements of the Recast Directive, and that such 'innovation' does not have to be implemented separately. It is submitted that such an argument could be made and could be taken into account by the ECJ when interpreting the obligations of the Member State in question if the EC were to start an infringement procedure. Such soft law instruments could indeed be helpful when interpreting EU law as far as the obligations to implement a Recast Directive are concerned.

In the author's view however, the Interinstitutional Agreement primarily defines the obligations of the EC, the EP and the Council as regards the drafting of legal acts, and therefore does not establish enforceable rights as such for Member States. It would be for the national courts and the ECJ respectively to decide how to interpret the national law in the light of the relevant provisions of the Recast Directive, and they might decide that a provision implies a substantive change, even if a change was not identified as being a substantive change in the Commission's proposal and/or during the legislative process preceding the adoption of the Recast Directive. At the end of the day, it is the task of the ECJ to interpret the scope of the obligations of the Member States. A national court could ask a prejudicial question to the ECJ as to the obligations of the Member State regarding such 'innovations'. A closer look at the legislative process preceding the adoption of Directive 2006/54/EC brings to light the difficulties in defining which amendments to existing texts encompass a substantive change and which do not.

3. RECASTING EU SEX EQUALITY LEGISLATION

3.1. The Recast Directive

The legal basis of the Recast Directive 2006/54/EC is Article 141(3), and thus, the co-decision procedure of Article 251 EC was followed. The Directives that form part of the recasting exercise of EU sex equality legislation[11] are Directive 76/207/EEC,[12]

11. See for a recent overview, S. Burri & S. Prechal, *EU Gender Equality Law*, European Commission, Luxembourg: Office for Official Publication of the European Communities, KE-80-08-432-EN-C, 2008 (available in English, French and German); see for an electronic version, <http://ec.europa.eu/social/main.jsp?catId=641&langId=en>, 20 May 2009.
12. Council Directive 76/207/EEC, *Official Journal of the European Union* 19, L 39, 14 Feb. 1976, 40–42.

as amended by Directive 2002/73/EC,[13] on equal treatment for men and women in the access to employment, vocational training and promotion and working conditions; Directive 86/378/EEC,[14] as amended by Directive 96/97/EC,[15] on equal treatment for men and women in occupational social security schemes; Directive 75/117/EEC[16] on equal pay between men and women, and Directive 97/80/EC[17] on the burden of proof.

The objective of the Recast Directive is to combine in a single text not only the main provisions on gender equality as covered by this Directive, but also the relevant case law (preamble point 1). The Recast Directive should have been transposed in the EU Member States by 15 August 2008 (Article 33) and the Directives that are consolidated in this Directive were to be repealed one year later (Article 34). The obligation to transpose the provisions that are substantially unchanged already existed under the earlier Directives (Recital 39 and Article 33). Member States may, if necessary to take account of particular difficulties, have up to one additional year to comply with the Recast Directive (Article 33). However, the Directive does not stipulate when the Member States should communicate to the EC that they need an additional year to transpose the directive.

The Recast Directive is divided into four titles. The first title on general provisions includes a description of the aim of the Directive and definitions of different concepts, such as direct and indirect discrimination, harassment and sexual harassment. The second title includes provisions on equal pay and on equal treatment as regards access to employment, vocational training and promotion and working conditions. In the third title, provisions are brought together regarding remedies and penalties, the burden of proof, victimization, the promotion of equal treatment through equality bodies, social dialogue and dialogue with Non-Profit Organizations (NGOs). This title also includes general provisions on, for example, the prevention of discrimination, gender mainstreaming, and the dissemination of information. Final provisions regarding, for example, reporting procedures and implementation, form the last title.[18]

---

13. Directive 2002/73/EC, *Official Journal of the European Union* 45, L 269, 5 Oct. 2002, 15–20.
14. Council Directive 86/378/EEC, *Official Journal of the European Union* 29, L 225, 12 Aug. 1986, 40–42.
15. Council Directive 96/97/EC, *Official Journal of the European Union* 40, L 46, 17 Feb. 1997, 20–24.
16. Council Directive 75/117/EEC, *Official Journal of the European Union* 18, L 45, 19 Feb. 1975, 19–20.
17. Council Directive 97/80/EC, *Official Journal of the European Union* 41, L 14, 20 Jan. 1998, 6–8.
18. See also N. Burrows & M. Robinsin, 'An Assessment of the Recast of Community Equality Laws', *European Law Journal* 13, no. 2 (2007): 186–203; M.T. Lanquetin, 'L'égalité de traitement entre les hommes et les femmes en matière d'emploi et de travail: A propos de la directive 2006/54 CE du 5 juillet 2006 (directive "refonte"), *Droit Social*, no. 7/8 (2007): 861–878 and A. Masselot, 'The State of gender Equality Law in the European Union', *European Law Journal* 13, no. 2 (2007): 152–168.

3.2. Substantive Changes?

The Commission's proposal mentions a number of 'principal innovations' which concern in the first place the integration of some case law of the ECJ. Second, the scope of application of several provisions is extended, in particular, a few provisions applicable to the access to work and working conditions (Directive 76/207/EEC, as amended by 2002/73/EC) apply now to all the areas covered by the Recast Directive, thus, also, for example, to occupational social security schemes. Finally, a re-examination clause was added, which permits the Commission to propose any amendments necessary after the Commission has reviewed the operation of the Directive (by 15 February 2011 at the latest).[19]

During the legislative process, the EP proposed many amendments to the Commission's proposal.[20] Some amendments were included in the second proposal of the Commission, others were rejected.[21] It is interesting to note that the Commission rejected a few amendments of the EP, arguing that they would amount to a substantive change. For example, amendments regarding the social dialogue and obligations of employers (Article 23 of the first proposal) were rejected with the following arguments:

> These amendments have in common the objective of transforming the obligation of Member States to *encourage* certain measures to be taken either by the social partners (promote equality between women and men, conclude agreements laying down anti-discrimination rules) or by employers (planned and systematic promotion of equality, prevention of discrimination) into an obligation to *ensure* that such measures are taken. This modification cannot be endorsed as it would amount to *considerable substantive changes going beyond what can be reasonably done within the framework of a recasting exercise* (emphasis added).[22]

In the author's view such a statement shows that the Commission had no intention of including substantive changes in the Recast Directive, at least no *considerable* substantive changes. This does not, however, clarify what the obligations of Member States are as regards the issues mentioned as amounting to 'innovations' in the Commission's proposal. Are these substantive changes or not?

3.3. The Legal Obligations of Member States Arising Out of 'Principal Innovations'

None of the listed 'principal innovations' is explicitly defined as a substantive change in the Commission's first proposal. It is submitted that the codification of

19. European Commission, COM (2004) 279, 5–6.
20. European Parliament, T6-0283/2005.
21. European Commission, COM (2005) 380.
22. The Commission rejected with the same argument a proposal of the EP to modify references to parental leave (in addition, the Commission pointed at the fact that Directive 96/34/EC is no part of the recasting exercise) and a proposal to amend Art. 141(4) EC in order to place on Member States an obligation to adopt positive measures: COM (2005) 380, 13 and 15.

existing case law – if done correctly – indeed does not amount to a substantive change due to the fact that the ECJ rulings have already to be applied by the addressees of existing – and implemented – legislation. However, the codification of case law might sometimes amount to a broader protection than specific ECJ rulings. For example, the EP proposed to clarify that, for the purposes of the Recast Directive, discrimination includes less favourable treatment on the grounds of gender reassignment.[23] The Commission accepted this amendment in spirit and included in Recital 3 that:

'The Court has held that the scope of the principle of equal treatment for men and women cannot be confined to the prohibition of discrimination based on the fact that a person is of one or other sex. In view of its purpose and the nature of rights which it seeks to safeguard it also applies to discrimination arising from the gender reassignment of a person.'

According to the Commission, this Recital makes clear that discrimination of transsexuals falls within the scope of the Directive.[24] Up to now, the case law of the ECJ in relation to gender reassignment concerned pay,[25] dismissal[26] and statutory social security (Directive 79/7/EEC).[27] The inclusion of the above quoted section in the preamble of the Recast Directive makes clear that discrimination on the ground of gender reassignment is prohibited in the areas of pay, occupational social security schemes and (access to) employment, and that all the horizontal provisions of this Directive – such as the burden of proof, the right to compensation or reparation, and obligations of social partners and employers – apply also to gender reassignment. This implies a broader protection for transsexuals against discrimination than could be derived from the case law of the ECJ up to now. In the author's view however, this does not amount to a substantive change in so far as it codifies the existing approach to this issue by the ECJ, which covers not only pay, but also occupational and even statutory social security schemes. In addition, it seems quite logical that the provisions applicable to sex discrimination also apply to gender reassignment, which is considered as being discrimination based on the fact that a person is of one or the other sex, therefore constituting sex discrimination.

This having been said, it should be noted that it remains unclear whether the Member States are obliged to specify in the relevant national legislation that discrimination on the grounds of gender reassignment is prohibited. It is submitted that the transposition of this provision into national law would contribute to more clarity and legal certainty as regards the scope of application of EU anti-discrimination law. It is regrettable that it remains unclear whether Member States have to include such provisions in national law or not. This hampers a uniform transposition and application of EU law in the Member States regarding the

23. European Parliament, A-0176/2005 (Recital 2 and Art. 2(2)(d)).
24. European Commission, COM (2005) 380, 4.
25. ECJ 7 Jan. 2004, Case C-117/01, ECR 2004, I-00541 (*K.B.*)
26. ECJ 30 Apr. 1996, Case C-13/94, ECR 1996, I-02143 (*P/S*).
27. ECJ 27 Apr. 2006, Case C-423/04, ECR 2006, I-03585 (*Richards*).

prohibition of discrimination of transsexuals. It would have been preferable to define more clearly the obligations of the Member States in this respect. Providing such clarity is even more recommendable when a provision attributes rights to individuals. The same reasoning could apply to other provisions of the Recast Directive which codify existing case law that was not codified earlier in the Directives subject to this recast exercise.

The extension of some existing provisions in the field of (access to) employment to other areas could be defined as a substantive change if it adds something new to existing legislation and case law at EU level. Such extensions can contribute to coherent codification and could lead to a broader personal or material scope and/ or offer more protection.[28] An example is the burden of proof rule that applies to all areas falling within the material scope of the Recast Directive.

The obligation to review the operation of the Directive is defined as a standard clause and would therefore not represent a substantive change.

4. TRANSPOSITION OF THE RECAST DIRECTIVE INTO NATIONAL LAW

What were the main features of the transposition process of the Recast Directive in the Member States of the EU? Did the Recast Directive provide more clarity and consistency at EU level and/or at national level? What were the effects of the recasting exercise at national level? These questions were partly addressed in a report published by the EC's European Network of Legal Experts in the field of Gender Equality on the transposition into national law of the Recast Directive.[29]

4.1. The Obligations of Member States in the light of Article 33

As regards the obligation to transpose only substantive changes into national law as specified in Article 33 of the Recast Directive, the EC's European Network of Legal Experts in the Field of Gender Equality pointed out that the implementation may turn out to be complicated because the substantive changes should first be

28. The European Economic and Social Committee refers to a possible change in substance as regards the horizontal provision on Equality bodies, see: Opinion of the European Economic and Social Committee on the 'Proposal for a Directive of the European Parliament and of the Council on the implementation of the principle of equal opportunities and equal treatment of men and women in matters of employment and occupation, *Official Journal of the European Union* 48, 2005, C 157/83 at s. 3.7.
29. European Network of Legal Experts in the field of Gender Equality, S. Burri & S. Prechal, *The Transposition of Recast Directive 2006/54/EC*, European Commission 2009, available at <http://ec.europa.eu/social/main.jsp?catId=641&langId=en&moreDocuments=yes> 23 Oct. 2009. The report provides information about the transposition of the Recast Directive in the twenty-seven Member States of the EU and three EEA States: Iceland, Liechtenstein and Norway.

identified.[30] It should be recalled that apart from the mention of Article 7(2)[31] in the correlation table as being a new Article, no information at all is included in the Recast Directive itself about which amendments imply substantive changes. The Commission's proposal, while clearly mentioning in the various provisions which changes have been made compared to earlier Directives, does not once clarify whether this is a substantive change or not. It would therefore seem that it is left up to the Member States to identify such substantive changes in the light of their obligations to implement only those provisions that represent a substantive change as compared with earlier Directives (Article 33).

In the view of the authors of the Report on the transposition of the Recast Directive, a closer look at the various provisions of the Recast Directive compared to the earlier Directives shows that some 'clarifications' or 'novelties' can be identified. The independent experts mention the following issues:

- the purpose of the Directive is not only to implement the principle of equal treatment of men and women in matters of employment and occupation, but also the principle of equal opportunities (title of the Directive and Article 1);
- the Directive also applies to gender reassignment (Recital 3);
- the uniform definition of the concept of indirect discrimination in Article 2(1)(b) of the Recast Directive replaces the definition of the Burden of Proof Directive;
- the concept of positive action as described in Article 3 has been broadened in its substantive field of application because the scope of the Recast Directive is broad and also includes occupational pension schemes, for example (Recitals 21 and 22);
- Article 7(2) of the Recast Directive on the material scope of the provisions on equal treatment in occupational social security schemes is new (the text incorporates some well-established case law of the ECJ);
- the extension of the scope of the Recast Directive to the area of occupational social security schemes leads to an extension of the scope of the horizontal provisions;
- the issue of reconciliation of work, private and family life is explicitly mentioned; see in particular Recitals 11, 26, 27, Article 9(1)(g) and Article 21(2);
- this Directive lays down an obligation for Member States to assess and to report to the Commission on the exclusions from the application of the principle of equal treatment between men and women as regards genuine and determining occupational requirements, see Article 31(3);
- the availability of judicial procedures for the enforcement of obligations imposed by the Directive and where appropriate, conciliation procedures; see Article 17(1).[32]

30. Report Transposition Recast, 2.
31. The Article refers to the application of the provisions on pension schemes to civil servants.
32. Report Transposition Recast, 2–3.

Given these 'innovations', 'clarifications' and 'novelties', a few questions arise, particularly with regard to the so-called 'novelties'. Do these contribute to more clarity and therefore legal certainty at EU level?

4.2. More clarity and legal certainty at EU level?

In the first place, it is submitted that some provisions in the Recast Directive might involve a substantive change, even if this is not explicitly mentioned. For example, the principle of equal opportunities could well be understood in a much broader way than the principle of equal treatment, which has been commonly used up to now in EU sex equality legislation. However, such a principle of equal opportunities has not (yet) been clarified at EU level. The obligations of the Member States in this respect are thus, so far unclear. This definitely does not contribute to legal certainty, nor does it facilitate the monitoring task of the EC.

Second, some provisions lack clarity. For example, the Recast Directive contains the following definition of direct sex discrimination: 'where a person is treated less favourably on the grounds of sex than another is, has been, or would be treated in a comparable situation'. This definition is very similar to the definitions which were included for the first time in the 2000 Directives (the so-called Race Directive 2000/43/EC and Framework Directive 2000/78/EC) and later in the amended Equal Treatment Directive (2002/73/EC), which is part of the recasting exercise. However, the case law of the ECJ on pregnancy discrimination does not, up to now, require a comparison with another person.[33] According to this case law, adverse treatment in relation to pregnancy amounts to direct discrimination and is prohibited. Article 2(2)(c) of Directive 2006/54/EC stipulates that for the purposes of this Directive, discrimination includes 'any less favourable treatment of a woman related to pregnancy or maternity leave within the meaning of Directive 92/85/EEC'. This provision does not state explicitly that such adverse treatment amounts to direct discrimination, however the reference to women would imply that direct sex discrimination is at stake. In addition, this Article might cause some confusion as regards the protected period. According to the case law of the ECJ, Articles 2(1) and 5(1) of Directive 76/207 preclude dismissal of a female worker at any time during her pregnancy for absences due to incapacity for work caused by an illness resulting from that pregnancy.[34] The above mentioned provision refers to 'pregnancy or maternity leave within the meaning of Directive 92/85/EEC'. Pregnancy as such is not defined in Directive 92/85/EEC. However, according to Article 2(a) of this Directive, a 'pregnant worker shall mean a pregnant worker who informs her employer of her condition, in accordance with national legislation and/or practice'.

The reference to Directive 92/85/EEC might raise the question as to whether a pregnant worker who has not informed her employer of her condition and who is

33. See for example, ECJ 8 Nov. 1990, Case C-177/88, ECR 1990, I-03941 (*Dekker*).
34. ECJ 30 Jun. 1998, Case C-394/96, ECR 1998, I-04185 (*Brown*)

absent from work due to illness resulting from her pregnancy benefits from the same protection against dismissal as a female worker who has informed her employer. In other words, when does the protected period start: From the beginning of the pregnancy, or from the beginning of an absence due to a pregnancy related illness? Or only after a pregnant worker informed her employer of her condition? The relevant case law of the ECJ does not (yet) explicitly address this question; up to now it would seem that the protected period starts from the beginning of the pregnancy (see also Article 10 of Directive 99/85/EEC).[35] It is submitted that the reference to Directive 92/85/EEC has to be read in conjunction with maternity leave (see Article 8), and that 'any less favourable treatment of a woman related to pregnancy' should be interpreted broadly and that the protected period starts from the beginning of the pregnancy. This example illustrates how new definitions raise new questions. Article 2(2)(c) might perhaps simplify and modernize sex equality legislation at EU level, but it can be questioned whether it clarifies the *acquis communautaire*.

On the one hand, the Recast Directive contributes without doubt to further harmonization of central concepts and horizontal provisions in different legislative instruments aimed at combating discrimination on the grounds of sex, race and ethnic origin, religion, disability, age and sexual orientation. It thus contributes to consistency with regard to central concepts. However, in a field where existing provisions have been interpreted by the ECJ in numerous cases, slightly amending a provision could be confusing when this might amount to a different interpretation than established in earlier case law. This could be particularly problematic if the existing level of protection were not upheld. In addition, both legislation and case law in the anti-discrimination field have become rather complicated. It might, therefore be feared that minor differences in interpretation as a result of different wordings of provisions would complicate things even further, where the aim was to simplify, modernize and clarify.

4.3. Transposition at National Level

The above mentioned report of the European Network of Legal Experts in the field of Gender Equality on the transposition into national law of the Recast Directive shows that only little attention has been paid by the twenty-seven Member States and the European Economic Area (EEA) States (Iceland, Liechtenstein and Norway) to the 'clarifications' and/or 'novelties' of the Recast Directive as listed above. Many countries have not considered any transposition necessary, due to the fact that the Directives that are part of the recasting exercise have already been implemented. The main reason put forward by the national experts explaining the lack of specific transposition of the Recast Directive was that the Member States were not aware of any novelties that should be specifically transposed into national law.[36] It should be noted that existing national legislation and case law might

35. See for example, ECJ 26 Feb. 2008, Case C-506/06, ECR 2008, I-01017 (*Mayr*).
36. Report Transposition Recast, 3 and 4.

nevertheless offer even more protection against sex discrimination than required at EU level.

In the Report, three categories of countries are distinguished: First, those that have transposed the Recast Directive; second, countries where no specific transposition process has taken place yet, and third, countries where some specific provisions of the Recast Directive have been transposed. However, the authors of the Report point out that the division of the different countries into these three categories is somewhat arbitrary, since the correct transposition of the Recast Directive partly depends on the earlier implementation of the Directives that are part of the recasting exercise. It might sometimes be complex to identify the transposition of the so-called 'clarifications' and 'novelties' when no separate Act transposes the Recast Directive.[37] This is, for example, the case in France, where the main aim of the Anti-Discrimination Act of 27 May 2008 was not only to transpose the Recast Directive, but also to complete the implementation of all relevant EC Directives on discrimination (including Directives 2000/43/EC, 2000/78/EC, 2002/73/EC and 2004/113/EC), and, in addition, to transpose the Recast Directive in time. According to Laulom (the French expert of the Network), the Act intends thus to take into account the observations of the EC on the French situation and to avoid an infringement procedure, and, at the same time, to transpose the Recast Directive on time.[38] Therefore it is difficult to distinguish in the Act which provisions strictly deal with the transposition of the Recast Directive and what the missing elements are of the various transpositions of the other Directives. The fact that no correlation tables were published by the French government renders an assessment of the transposition of the Recast Directive by an independent expert even more difficult.[39] The lack of information available to the public regarding the transposition of the Recast Directive in some countries – for example, in Romania and Greece – raises even more difficulties for an independent assessment of the transposition process.

In some countries steps have been taken in order to transpose the Recast Directive. However, it should be noted that many countries have transposed the Recast Directive only *pro forma*, without any amendment of existing legislation or the adoption of new provisions. This was, for example, the case in Hungary, where the transposition was restricted to a check of existing legislation and ascertaining that it was in compliance with the provisions of the Recast Directive. The same is true for Slovenia and Spain. The Spanish government considered that with the transposition of Directive 2002/73/EC, the Recast Directive had also been transposed.[40]

In many countries, no specific transposition of the Recast Directive had taken place at the time of the Report. Most governments considered it unnecessary to explicitly and formally transpose the Recast Directive due to the fact that the

37. *Ibid.*, 3.
38. *Ibid.*, 34.
39. *Ibid.*
40. Report Transposition Recast, 3.

obligations arising out of the Directives which are part of the recasting exercise – in particular, Directive 76/207/EEC, as amended by Directive 2002/73/EC – had already been met or would be met in the near future. *Mutatis mutandis* the same reasoning was applied to the Recast Directive.

Some Member States have transposed only a few provisions, mainly because they believed that some 'clarifications' or 'novelties' did not need any specific transposition.[41] This is true, for example, for the prohibition of discrimination on the grounds of gender reassignment. Some experts mention that according to case law – in particular, the case law of the European Court of Justice – such prohibition is part of the ban on sex discrimination and that therefore no legislative provisions have been adopted regarding gender reassignment.

5. CONCLUSIONS

Sex equality legislation certainly needed an update in order to harmonize provisions and to fill gaps with other anti-discrimination Directives, particularly the so-called Race Directive (2000/43/EC) and the Framework Directive (2000/78/EC). A first step was taken with the amended second Directive (2002/73/EC), and four years later with the Recast Directive (2006/54/EC). Meanwhile, a Directive on the principle of equal treatment between men and women in the access to and supply of goods and services was adopted (2004/113/EC).[42] All these Directives now have a similar format, which reflects the efforts of the EU institutions to harmonize the anti-discrimination legislation at EU level. This certainly contributes to a more coherent codification of EU equal treatment law. However, there remain important differences in scope of application between the different Directives. These differences might even be enhanced if the proposal for a broad Directive on the principle of equal treatment between persons irrespective of religion or belief, disability, age or sexual orientation is adopted.[43]

Some sex equality legislation was left out of the recasting exercise and is not updated yet. This is the case regarding the equal treatment of women and men in statutory social security schemes and in self-employment.[44] Not including these Directives in the recasting exercise is probably linked to the fact that Member States are much more reluctant to adopt legislation in the field of statutory social security than in (access to) employment. In addition, it is not certain that the *acquis* in this field would be maintained, let alone expanded. The recasting exercise also left untouched the relation between Directives that address similar forms of discrimination, such as indirect sex discrimination in relation to part-time work.

41. *Ibid.*, 3 and 5.
42. *Official Journal of the European* Union 47, L 373/37, 21 Dec. 2004.
43. European Commission, COM (2008) 426.
44. A proposal to recall Directive 86/613/EEC is pending: Proposal for a Directive of the European parliament and of the Council on the application of the principle of equal treatment between men and women engaged in an activity in a self-employed capacity and repealing Directive 86/613/EEC, COM (2008) 636.

This can probably be explained by the fact that the Part-time Work Directive (97/81/EC) implements the agreement of the European social partners on this issue (according to Article 139 EC). Amending this Directive is thus the prerogative of the parties to this Agreement, and the EC plays a different role in this respect. The same is true for the Parental Leave Directive, which implements the framework agreement of the European social partners on parental leave (96/34/EEC).[45] The Pregnancy Directive (92/85/EEC) also has a different legal base (Article 118a EEC Treaty). Including these Directives into the recasting exercise would probably have complicated and lengthened this process.

On the other hand, leaving these Directives out of the recasting of gender equality Directives might hamper a consistent use of, for example, central concepts and the application of the so-called horizontal provisions in all the relevant Directives in the field of gender equality. The Parental Leave Directive does not, for instance, specify anything about the burden of proof[46] or the protection against victimization in concordance with the Recast Directive. The legal basis of the different legislative instruments at EU level might therefore limit the recasting possibilities and impair a uniform level of protection in related issues. In addition, the legal instruments at stake – Directives – leave discretionary powers to the Member States as regards the form and the methods (Article 249 EC), and prescribe only minimum requirements. National law might therefore reflect quite some diversity, in particular when Member States do not consider any transposition of a recast Directive necessary. This is not surprising given the fact that the aim of the Directive is to consolidate the *acquis communautaire* in this field, not to change it.

The analysis of the recasting process of (some) EU sex equality legislation with Directive 2006/54/EC in order to modernize and simplify existing provisions highlights some shortcomings. The main one is the fact that the obligations of the Member States regarding the transposition of the Recast Directive were not clearly defined. Member States have to transpose only provisions representing a substantive change, but insufficient information is provided about which provisions amount to such changes. The correlation table falls short in this respect. When the purpose of the recasting exercise is strictly limited to modernizing, simplifying and clarifying earlier Directives, no further obligations to transpose the provisions of a recast Directive arise in the author's view. The obligations for Member States are then already clearly defined in earlier Directives, and eventual infringement procedures have highlighted the lack of implementing measures. In the light of the requirement of clarity and legal certainty, it would certainly have been useful to mention either that there were no substantive changes (which would have made Article 33 in this respect unnecessary), or to include a list of the amendments amounting to a substantive change. One might expect that the Commission's

45. A proposal implementing the revised agreement of the European social partners is pending: European Commission, COM (2009) 410.
46. However, the Burden of Proof Directive (97/80/EC) applies to situations covered by, for example, Directive 96/34/EC insofar as discrimination based on sex is concerned (Arts 3(1)(a)).

proposal[47] would provide such information in the light of the above mentioned requirements of the Interinstitutional Agreement on the recasting technique of 2001.[48] The Recast Directive 2006/54/EC reflects a mixture of both approaches, which does not, in the author's view, contribute to clarity and thus, legal certainty.

The recasting of sex equality legislation also shows that harmonization of legislation at EU level might certainly, on the one hand, be useful insofar as central concepts of discrimination are, for example, defined uniformly in different equal treatment Directives. The same is true for so-called horizontal provisions. It is submitted that furthering the consistency of such definitions with existing case law might require some additional clarifying elements during the legislative process preceding the adoption of a recast Directive. On the other hand, fixing the *acquis*, in particular through codification of case law of the ECJ, might also hamper a dynamic interpretation of the issues at stake. The recasting process of EU equal treatment law also shows that the national political and legislative context might complicate the transposition process. At the end of the day, the impact of the Recast Directive (2006/54/EC) on the national law of the Member States remains quite limited.

47. European Commission, COM (2004) 279.

48. *Official Journal of the European Union* 45, C 77, 28 Mar. 2002, 1–3.

Chapter 8

The Rocky Path of EU Legislation on Workers' Involvement: Coherent Codification of the Right to Information and Consultation of Workers in European Law?

Reile Meyers & Teun Jaspers

1. INTRODUCTION: THE ISSUE OF LEGALITY IN A MULTIPLICITY OF ORDERS

In the context of the principle of legality in European law, the legislation with regard to social subjects provides for an interesting example; it illustrates very well the issues one incurs when studying the legality of legal measures in a multiplicity of legal orders. These issues exist because in the area of social issues at European level, there exist several layers of regulation that are directly related to the multiplicity of lawmakers in this field. This layered mechanism is induced by the European Union Treaty itself, therefore the legality issue is present in a prominent way. Not only does the formal question arise as to whether there exists a clear indication of who is designated to enact laws in this field, but, moreover, the question arises of coherence of the enacted legislation or rulemaking. As will be explained below (section 3), we adhere to a legality concept that is, wider than the mere formal aspect of it (to wit, the attribution of legislative power).

Leonard Besselink, Frans Pennings & Sacha Prechal (eds), *The Eclipse of the Legality Principle in the European Union*, pp. 125–149.

The question of legality in the European multi-layered legal framework dealing with our specific subject of 'information and consultation of employees on management decisions in enterprise,'[1] is challenging for various reasons. Firstly, the legal structure of legislation on this issue is a three-step process that fits perfectly in the multi-layered legal order. The Council of the EU is the assigned authority to operate as the primary legislature by virtue of Article 153 (ex 137) Treaty on the Functioning of the European Union (TFEU). However, it can only legislate by way of Directives containing minimum requirements. Therefore, the Member States operate as a subsequent legislature, by implementing the Directives in a way that they see fit, while attaining the goals laid down therein. The Directives dealing with the subject of informing and consulting workers mostly do not specify the instruments of information and consultation, and, as a consequence, the implementing national law usually does not contain any more detail. Thus, last but not least, the content of the various means by which workers' involvement is shaped actually and finally, is filled in by the private parties: the employer and the employees' representatives. In this respect, it is even more interesting to see whether, and if so, how, the parties have filled in the rights and duties.[2]

The issue at stake in this contribution has a distinct cross-border nature. Consequently, the involvement of different national systems raises the question of

1. Since we will deal with the issue of workers' involvement, we will deal with nearly all European Directives on the issue of 'information to and consultation of employees': Council Directive 98/59/EC of 20 Jul. 1998 on the approximation of the laws of the Member States relating to collective redundancies, OJ L 225, 12 Aug. 1998, 16–21; Council Directive 2001/23/EC of 12 Mar. 2001 on the approximation of the laws of the Member States relating to the safeguarding of employees' rights in the event of transfers of undertakings, businesses or parts of undertakings or businesses, OJ L 82, 22 Mar. 2001, 16–20; Directive 94/45 and 2009/38 on the establishment of a European Works Council or a procedure in Community-scale undertakings and Community-scale groups of undertakings for the purposes of informing and consulting employees (Recast), OJ L 122, 6 May 2009, 28–44; Council Directive 2001/86/EC of 8 Oct. 2001 supplementing the Statute for a European company with regard to the involvement of employees, OJ L 294, 10 Nov. 2001, 22–32; and Council Directive 2003/72/EC of 22 Jul. 2003 supplementing the Statute for a European Cooperative Society with regard to the involvement of employees, OJ L 207, 18 Aug. 2003, 25–36. (The Directive 2002/14/EC of the European Parliament and of the Council of 11 Mar. 2002 establishing a general framework for informing and consulting employees in the European Community, OJ L 80, 23 Mar. 2002, 29–34 will be touched as a point of reference in so far as it deals with the concept of workers' involvement)
2. And possibly even whether they have made use of the possibility to 'contract out'. The term 'contracting out' sees to the possibility of the parties agreeing on a level of workers' involvement that is, (much) lower than the minimum rules laid down in the directive itself. This is possible on the basis of certain directives dealing with this topic, since the legislature has clearly chosen precedence of negotiation on these matters over legislative legally binding rules. It has to be noted that this possibility of 'contracting out' is something different from the 'opt-out' option, which sees to 'an exemption granted to a country that does not wish to join the other Member States in a particular area of Community cooperation as a way of avoiding a general stalemate'. In the area of EU social policy, it refers to the choice of the UK in 1991 to not sign into the Social Charter that was to be added to the Maastricht Treaty, <http://europa.eu/scadplus/glossary/opting_out_en.htm>, 26 Feb. 2010.

whether, and if so, to what extent the EU is competent to legislate on this subject. The legal basis obviously exists but it is not clear in which way and to what extent. The question could arise as to what extent the EU can legislate on this subject. Is it an exhaustive competence? Or – in accordance with the principle of subsidiarity – does it have to be left to the Member State to flesh out? Moreover, since the national legislature is not capable – and mostly not willing- to regulate these issues in detail, the parties themselves perform this task at industry or company level. This implies the third level or layer of regulating power mentioned above. One can imagine this could at least potentially jeopardize the coherence of the law.

This is said to be beneficial to reaching a tailored solution, since a great variety of circumstances and conditions exist in enterprises or sectors and branches of industries. Another reason for this delegation is the involvement, in various degrees, of social partners in the various systems (of labour relations) existing in the Member States.[3] Sometimes the social partners have the competence to act in this field and to develop their own rules on a certain subject.[4] The multiplicity of interdependent and mutually interferential legal orders is a fact and it makes the question of legality more complicated.

The second reason for the importance of this particular subject is its political and societal sensitivity. The daily managing of the company and the decisions to be taken for that purpose are still seen as the prerogative of the management body. The entrepreneur has invested a lot in the company and thus he is entitled to take the necessary management decisions. Since the beginning of the 1900s, it slowly became generally accepted that workers' representatives were involved in the regulating of employment conditions by way of collective bargaining (resulting in collective labour agreements). Since World War II, the involvement of employees in the more general decision-making of enterprises gradually became more common and more acceptable, at least in a number of European countries.[5]

Also, gradually the EU internal market developed, and an evolution could be witnessed from conducting business at a purely national level, to expanding to the transnational and European level.[6] In contrast, the legal regulation of this phenomenon at European level has never been self-evident. Employers and their European organizations were, and still are, rather reluctant to recognize rights to information and consultation of employees. Therefore, the process of legislating on this topic is still very sensitive and the legislative proposals always represent a compromise.

This contribution will focus on the European regulatory instruments on workers' involvement in decisions at enterprise level and their transposition into the national law of the Member States. The main question we will examine is whether or not these instruments meet the criteria of the principle of legality, and, in

3. This involvement can vary from a very prominent role for the trade unions (e.g., Belgium, Italy, the UK and the Scandinavian countries) to a position a bit more on a distance (e.g., France, Germany and the Netherlands).
4. By way of collective agreements, for example.
5. Germany, Austria, The Netherlands and France were, and still are, the pioneers.
6. Both the Preambles of the EWC Directives (Directive 94/45 and Directive 2009/38) refer to this development.

particular, to what extent the various rulings are coherent, in spite of the variety of lawmakers. As said before, doubts have arisen about this. In order to assess whether the requirements for legality are met, we first have to develop these requirements. Next we will analyse the various EU Directives in this field on the basis of these criteria. In order to assess the validity of the Directives under scrutiny in terms of meeting the distinct criteria of legality, we will use two approaches:

(1) The chronological approach. This approach implies searching for a development occurring in time: has the degree of legality increased gradually? Have the legislatures learned from past experiences? Given the consolidation and the strengthening of the concept of workers' involvement in management decisions in the European context through European legislation, it can be assumed that the concept has been developed to be more in accordance with the legality principle.

(2) The second methodological approach for the analysis of the Directives is an analysis of the substance of the matters for which the information and consultation rights are provided for, and the level at which this procedure takes place. Is the level dependent on the subject at which the information and consultation is aimed? This is particularly interesting when we analyse the Directives on Collective Redundancies and the Transfer of Undertakings in comparison with Directives dealing with more general rights to information and consultation (the European Works Council and the Works Council of the SE or the Works Council in general[7]).

A final peculiarity is the national tradition and structures, or, in other words, the different manifestations of workers' involvement in the Member States. A European-wide ruling has to fit in or at least has to be adapted to these structures, traditions and specific features at national level. The Directives usually refer to these national circumstances. It cannot be denied that this approach knows both advantages and disadvantages. On the one hand, it accepts the existence of a variety of regulations and practices in the Member States according to their own structures and traditions. On the other hand, it does not contribute to the establishment of clear rules and an internally coherent system. From the requirement of improving the coherence of legislation, we will analyse whether the consecutive drafts of legislation on information and consultation procedures lead to improvements in terms of an increase of the legality value of this body of legislation.

2. THE HISTORY OF WORKERS' INVOLVEMENT RULES IN THE EU

Before we analyse the various legal instruments, we will broadly outline the history of workers' involvement in the EU and its legal roots. The genesis of the issue dates

7. We refer to the Framework Directive 2002/14/EC.

from the 1970s. It was not so much part of a discussion in the European community on Social Policy itself, but it arose in the context of proposals on the structure of the large public limited liability corporation.[8] During the period of Delors as President of the European Commission (1985–1995), the discussion became more focused on the involvement of employees and their representatives as part of a European Social Policy and on contributing to the so-called European Social Model. Some results were achieved in the1990s.[9]

This concept of involving workers' representatives in rule making fits perfectly in the policy of the EU. Since the 1980s, the Social Dialogue has been conceived as a pillar of the European Community, and later, the EU. It was introduced and adopted by the Single Act in 1986.[10] The provision dealing with this subject – Article 151 (ex 136) TFEU – mentions the promotion of the 'dialogue between management and labour' as one of the objectives of the EU in the field of social policy. This term as a general term encompasses various forms of workers' involvement, from bargaining to information and consultation. Workers can be represented by trade unions and their officials, or by works councils, whereas employers can participate in the collective bargaining independently, or as a member of an association of employers. The Social Policy Agreement concluded in 1992 extended the Social Dialogue agenda to the level of companies by inserting the right to information and consultation of workers.[11]

It should be noted however, that the involvement of workers in some social issues had already been recognized and regulated in EC legislation, even before the formal introduction of the Social Dialogue in the Single Act. Both the Directive on Collective Redundancies (1975), and the Directive on Transfers of Undertakings (1977), entail an obligation to inform and to consult the workers and their representatives before management decisions are taken or carried out. The 1975 Directive on Collective Redundancies even entails an 'obligation' for the parties concerned to try to 'reach an agreement'. It is also worth mentioning that these two Directives had an important impact on the national legislation and practice of Member States.[12]

---

8. T. Colaianni, *European Works Councils* (London: Sweet and Maxwell, 1996); T. Jaspers, 'The European Works Council Directive in its Community Context', in: *European Works Councils*, ed. F. Dorssemont & M. Rigaux (Antwerpen-Groningen: Intersentia, 1999), 15 seq.
9. See T. Colaianni, *European Works Councils* (London: Sweet and Maxwell, 1996); T. Jaspers, 'The European Works Council Directive in its Community Context', in: *European Works Councils*, ed. F. Dorssemont & M. Rigaux (Antwerpen-Groningen: Intersentia, 1999).
10. C. Barnard, *EC Employment Law*, 3rd ed. (Oxford: OUP, 2006). 11 seq.
11. The Agreement was annexed to the Protocol on Social Policy of the Treaty on European Union.
12. By a decision of the ECJ, the UK was forced to adopt legislation in order to fully implement the Collective Redundancies Directive: ECJ 8 Jun. 1994. Case C-383/92. ECR 1994 Page I-02479. Member States that could not guarantee that some kind of workers' involvement would be established (e.g., in the case of refusal to cooperate by the employer) were obliged to create a system for the designation of workers' representatives. That could imply that in sectors or enterprises where no trade union was present or active, another form of workers' representation has to be established, usually a works council. It has to be noted that both Directives were based on the provision establishing the common market: Art. 100 EC (now 115 TFEU).

If we overlook the whole body of European legislation on information and consultation, it can be stated that this issue has been high on the European agenda since the 1970s, not only on a political level, but also with regard to legislative initiatives. In the earliest Directive – that is, the Directive on Collective Redundancies – the legislation was directly targeting the involvement of employees' representatives – usually trade unions – in a process of consultation 'with a view of reaching an agreement' and aiming at the involvement of employees' representatives in regulating a situation of mass dismissal due to economic reasons.[13] In the subsequent Directive dealing with the consequences of restructuring for the workers in cases of mergers with a cross-border impact,[14] the involvement of workers in this process could be considered as a corollary to the main objective, which was the protection of the workers affected. Also in this field, the employer was obligated to inform and consult the employees' representatives – be it trade unions or works councils – before executing the measures envisaged. Another field of regulation in which the right to information and consultation of employees or their representatives has been recognized is health and safety in the workplace. In a Framework Directive (Directive 89/391/EEC), not only is the right of workers to be informed about health safety and risks and protective measures taken or to be taken by the employer secured, but it also even guarantees consultation and participation of workers and/or their representatives in health and safety policy and practice in the enterprise.

The second generation of legal instruments is specifically directed at information and consultation of employees in business matters. The European Works Council Directive, as well as its sister Directives (the information and consultation Directives for the Societas Europaea and the Societas Cooperativa Europaea) and the Framework Directive on Information and Consultation[15] are addressing the right of workers and their representatives to be informed and consulted about important management decisions. Moreover, the right to information and consultation of representatives of the employees was recognized in other EC legislation that is, not directly or mainly regulating employees' rights.[16] This is another indication of the weight that EC law was awarding (and, as the EU, is still awarding) to the 'fundamental right' of employees and their representatives to be heard in decisions by the management that could affect them.

---

13. J. Heinsius, 'The European Directive on Collective Dismissals and its Implementation Deficits Six ECJ Judgments as a Potential Incentive for Amending the Directive', *International Journal of Comparative Labour Law and Industrial Relations* 25, no. 3 (2009): 261.
14. Directive 2001/23/EC on Transfers of Undertakings.
15. Directive 2001/86/EC (SE); Directive 2003/72/EC (SCE) and Framework Directive (2002/14/EC).
16. We refer to the EC Merger Regulation No. 139/2004/EC and Directive 2004/25/EC on takeover bids. In the Regulation, the recognized representatives of the workers have the right to be heard by the Commission when it checks the concentration of undertakings in order the balance the interests of the various stakeholders concerned. The Directive grants similar rights in case of takeover bids. Both pieces of legislation refer explicitly to all of the Directives dealing with the rights of workers' representative bodies (all earlier mentioned Directives except the Health and Safety Directive).

If we take a legal approach to the structure of legislation in this field, it can be stated that the European legislature has been reluctant to regulate this subject. The choice of a Directive as the legislative instrument in combination with the option of regulating on a minimum level proves this approach. The aim of the legal basis (Article 153 TFEU (ex 137 EC)) was not a harmonization of national measures, but only the introduction of a basic notion of information and consultation of the workers in all systems of the Member States. The way to reach this goal was, and still is, left to the Member States' preference. After all, the Article explicitly mentions 'having regard to the conditions and technical rules obtaining in each of the Member States', thus emphasizing the proper competence of Member States in this field, in accordance with the subsidiarity principle.

In conclusion, it can be stated that the right to information and consultation of employees and/or their representatives is politically as well as legally well-founded. In the light of the thirty-year history of workers' involvement, it is interesting to see whether there has been a development in terms of more clear, coherent and consistent regulation. As mentioned in the introduction, we will investigate whether the learning effect can be traced chronologically, or whether the phrasing of the right to information and consultation is more linked to the subject at stake, leading to a greater variation in the codification of legal developments in the EU and its Member States.

3. LEGALITY CRITERIA

The concept of legality is usually[17] related to the issue of the attribution of legislative power to state institutions, be it the government together with the parliament, or lower state institutions. In the European context this question does not only relate to the attribution of powers, but is also geared towards 'upholding an institutional balance and the division of powers between the EU and its Member States'.[18] In the subject under scrutiny here, the concept of legality has an even broader scope: Social partners, too, have the power to make rules by way of collective agreements with binding effect towards their addressees.

In order to assess the legislation on information and consultation of employees, we will extend the scope of this principle to the question of the *legitimacy* of the intervention by lawmaking bodies. This fits in with the three main functions of the legality principle: the legitimation of public authority or the authority designated by the law; the attribution of public authority to designated public authorities or private parties, for example, the social partners in the subject at hand; and thirdly, the way in which the authority has been exercised. In literature as well

17. That is, to say, the constitutional and administrative branches of law.
18. This was also remarked by Linda Senden in her contribution to the discussion on this subject during the seminar in November 2009 in Utrecht dedicated to the main theme of this book (see Preface).

in government documents, a set of requirements has been developed which have to be fulfilled.[19]

(1) the constitutional power to legislate (*principle of legality* in the narrow sense);
(2) implementation and enforcement of the legislation (*principle of effectiveness*);
(3) the readability and intelligibility of legislative acts (*principle of legal certainty*);
(4) the duty to substantiate the need for legislation (*duty to give reasons*); presence of a sufficiently clear substantive ground for issuing the regulation (the *necessity requirement);*
(5) the duty to consult or involve interested parties during the legislative process
(6) (*democratic content*); and
(7) the duty to transparency and accessibility.

Generally speaking, these requirements can be grouped under two headings. The criteria under 1, 4 and 5 will be put together under the heading of legitimation, since they have a more political and democratic content. The three remaining criteria are of a more technical nature and can be designated as the quality requirement. In our view, a part of the assessment on the legality of the enacted laws is whether or not the rule makers have phrased the norms (the rights and duties) in a manner that is, clear, readable and intelligible, accessible (in order to be known and understood by the addressees of the norms), and finally, transparent. These conditions need to be satisfied both with regard to the way these norms are enacted as well as to their content. First, we will give a brief outline of the scope of the two sets of criteria as we interpret them. Due to the limited space available, this outline will be concise.

3.1. Legitimation

In order to assess whether a certain piece of legislation drafted by the European legislature or by the social partners (the latter parties while fleshing out the framework laid down by the EU or the Member States) is legitimized, we will divide the process into consecutive steps.

19. We refer to L.L. Fuller, *The Morality of Law* (New Haven and London: Yale University Press, 1969); [1964]): 106. See also W. Voermans, 'Concern About The Quality of EU Legislation: What Kind of Problem, by What Kind of Standards?', *Erasmus Law Review* 2, no. 01 (2009): 66. We also refer to EU documents: 'European Governance, a White Paper', COM (2001) 428 final; 'Communication from the Commission European Governance: Better lawmaking', COM (2002) 275 final. The results of an expert group: the so-called Mandelkern Group on better Regulation, final report, 13 Nov. 2001, 10, <http://ec.europa.eu/governance/better_regulation/documents/mandelkern_report.pdf>, 26 Feb. 2010. And finally we mention a Memorandum of the Dutch government of 1990: *Zicht op wetgeving* (A view on Legislation), Den Haag, *Kamerstukken II* (Parliamentary Papers) 1990/91, 22.008, IV Nr. 1–2.

The first question to be asked is whether there exists a legal basis for the legislating competence of the body. The competence of the European legislature has to be founded in the EC Treaty itself. In addition to this *constitutional power*, the scope of this competence and the legislative instrument to be used also have to be taken into account. Are these elements provided for by the Treaty? We will investigate whether the Directives and the implementing legislation by the national government and/or the social partners are fulfilling these conditions. Subsequently, the rules have to be judged on their compliance with the principles of proportionality and subsidiarity, since we are dealing with European legislation.[20] And finally, the legitimation of a European piece of legislation is dependent on whether it has passed the necessity check.

Part of the legitimation assessment related to the application of the *subsidiarity principle* is the way of legislating. According to subsidiarity principle, the aim should be to act at a level as close as possible to the citizens, and consequently involving societal organizations in the legislative process, strengthening its democratic nature and basis. In accordance with this principle, the legislation we are analysing has been subject to participation by the social partners (*the democratic principle*). The TFEU itself is taking this opportunity in Title X ('Social Policy'). Apart from the oldest Directives (on Collective Redundancies and on Transfers of Undertakings), the others were established after consultation with the social partners.

Typically, in relation to this subsidiarity principle, the *principle of proportionality* is mentioned as well: the choice of a regulatory instrument has to be identified as the most proportionate one to the aims to be achieved. This requirement is not restricted to the choice of the instrument as such, but also contains an assessment of the content of the instrument that is, used, taking into account that the law cannot surpass a minimum level. This proportionality principle can cause problems with regard to the fulfilling of the quality criteria, in particular, the clarity and the certainty requirements. It can tempt the use of vague norms and it can legitimize this use. Consequently, it can harm the effectiveness of the right to information and consultation. It will be interesting to see whether the Directives under scrutiny are suffering from this lack of effectiveness.

Finally, part of the assessment on the legitimation is the application of the *necessity requirement*: is there a clear substantive ground for issuing the regulation? Before putting a (new) policy into effect, the authorities should be convinced that it is necessary to introduce new rules. This includes a weighing up of the various instruments at their disposal. Since not many publicly accessible sources are available, it can be hard to find the reasons and grounds for legislative measures.[21]

20. A striking example of such an assessment is the decision of the Court of Justice of the EU in a case on working time: Case C-84/94, *United Kingdom of Great Britain and Northern Ireland v. Council of the European Union*, ECR 1996, Page I-05755.

21. Therefore one has to rely mainly on Preambles of the Directives, Communications of the Commission, documents and discussion papers usually provided for by the social partners, particularly the European trade unions (ETUC) and reports and documents of the EESC. However, since the coming into existence of the EU's Better Regulation Policy, more attention

Next to the primary sources,[22] the decisions of the Court of Justice of the EU[23] play an important role in clarifying the uncertainties in the texts of the Directives. By way of teleological interpretation of EU law, the European Court of Justice (ECJ) is trying to identify the very substance of a provision.[24] Since the Preambles of the amended Directives usually state that the amended Directive aims at codifying the case law of the ECJ, it can be expected that the text of the Directive is adapted to this case law. However, if the analysis shows that this is not the case, one can wonder whether the legislature may fail to meet one of the criteria mentioned above.

3.2. Quality of Law Criteria: Better Regulation

3.2.1. The Background

In its White Paper on 'European Governance' and in its 2002 Communication regarding a Strategic Review of Better Regulation, the European Commission stressed the importance and the need for an ongoing improvement of European regulation.[25] A vehement discussion has developed about the most appropriate methods for the EU to regulate issues which have a European scope: leaving more freedom to the Member States and thereby respecting national structures, or drafting more substantive legislation and guaranteeing a uniform approach for all citizens. This discussion gave rise to an Action Plan, on the basis of which the Commission is firstly striving at a more integrated approach to simplification of the legislation, with the aim 'to examine the entire body of legislation that affects a policy area to identify overlaps, gaps, inconsistencies, obsolete measures, and potential for reducing regulatory burden'.[26] In particular, transparency and legal certainty are indicated as two important goals to be reached.

It is important to point out a potential ambiguity when it comes to the notion of 'Better Regulation'. By emphasizing the objective of simplification,[27] the

has been given gradually to increasing the transparency of the EU decision-making (which is one of the goals of the Policy).

22. We refer primarily to the Preamble of the Directives, but other sources are cited in n. 23 above. Discussions in literature are helpful as well.
23. Hereinafter to be referred to as the 'ECJ'.
24. As to the subject at hand, the ECJ has played an important role by clarifying certain general and vague norms; see recently ECJ C-44/08 on Directive 98/59/EC (*Akavan Erityisalojen Keskusliitto AEK ry and Others v. Fujitsu Siemens Computers Oy*, not yet published in ECR).
25. 'European Governance, a White Paper', COM (2001) 428 final; 'Communication from the Commission, 'European Governance: Better lawmaking', COM (2002) 275 final.
26. Communication from the Commission to the European Parliament, the Council, the European Economic and Social Committee and the Committee of the Regions, 'Third strategic review of Better Regulation in the European Union', COM (2009) 15 final, 3. It seems obvious that this approach is fitting in the discussion on the value of the OMC as an alternative route to regulating European issues; see the contribution of F. Pennings in this book.
27. Simplification can be used as a requirement in so far as it contributes to the avoidance of excessive details in order to improve the effective use of the rights by the citizens, as well

Commissions might overlook the other main objective of Better Regulation: the improvement of the quality of legislation. As we will see hereafter, this could lead to a disparity and to an inherent controversy, as well as to uncertainty for the addressees of the legislation, which can be considered as a threat to the legality over all.

In its policy on Better Regulation, the Commission felt that the EU regulatory system would benefit from a less top-down approach, leading to better involvement and more openness.[28] In particular, the aim is 'to bring greater flexibility into how Community legislation can be implemented in a way which takes account of regional and local conditions'. This is thought to make EU policy easier to understand. This explains the view on the concept of European Directives which praises their ability to maintain the Member States' institutional and administrative cultures.

Next to this approach, the policy of Better Regulation has, as one of its main objectives, flexibility, and also includes a strategy for more 'open norms'. It seems that Directives in this field of social policy also contain measures that vary greatly in their open or strict character. The use of multi-interpretable, vague rules meets the need of flexibility. It is interesting to investigate the extent to which the Directives under scrutiny are contributing to this goal.

On the other hand, according to the European Commission, this approach of more flexibility should be combined with another apparent objective of the Better Regulation Policy: improvement of the coherence and the consistency of the European legislation. Using different meanings and wordings of the concept of information and consultation does not seem to contribute to attaining that objective. One can state that these two objectives not only potentially, but also actually, collide. In its White Paper on European Governance, the Commission is aware of this possible clash by referring to the need for 'the right mix between imposing a uniform approach when and where it is needed and allowing greater flexibility in the way that rules are implemented on the ground'.[29] It is hard to say in advance which of these approaches should prevail in a particular case. In our analysis of the Directives we will pay attention to this dilemma.

Another problem identified by the Commission is the detailed legislation and consequently a lack of adaptation of the legislation to local conditions and experiences. If uniform application and legal certainty is not necessary,[30] the choice of the instrument has to follow this approach. That means in the field of law we are dealing with in this contribution, that Directives with a framework character are more adequate since they are less heavy-handed, are offering greater flexibility as to their implementation, and tend to be agreed upon more quickly by the Council

as to make them less burdensome. See Mandelkern Group on better Regulation, final report, 13 Nov. 2001, 10.

28. (2001) 428, 4.
29. COM (2001) 428, 5.
30. Examples given of situations calling for Regulations are the completion of the internal market and the ensuring of timely transposition of Directives into national legislation, COM (2001) 428, 20.

and the European Parliament.[31] The European Commission is pleading for opting for Directives because, according the Treaty, the legislative proposals should be confined to containing 'the bare essentials'.[32]

3.2.2. The Quality Criteria

As part of the Good Governance policy, the High Level Group chaired by Mandelkern had phrased common principles for 'Better Regulation'. In addition to the legitimation criteria, the group has developed criteria of a more technical nature. We will base our analyses on these common principles but we will extend them by some others we derive from the literature.[33] We can distinguish three groups of criteria. We will focus on one of them in particular: the *technical criteria*. The requirement of correct *implementation and transposition* refers to careful consideration of the full consequences of the implementation, clear transposition deadlines, consideration of transitory provisions, and certainty as to the date of entry into force. It also implies a system of monitoring of the implementation and evaluation of the application in practice. We leave the assessment on the basis of this criterion aside, mainly due to the limited space we have and the necessity of doing empirical research.

The second criterion of *enforceability* we will touch upon only briefly for the same reasons. The implications of the requirement of enforceability are twofold: Firstly, the requirement implies that the European law must be clear, as well as that non-observance of the obligation to implement will be effectively sanctioned. Secondly, the law in which the European law has been transposed must provide for remedies that ensure the correct application of the law.

3.2.2.1. Technical Quality

This requirement can be summarized by terms such as accessibility, readability, and foreseeability. It is obvious that only when legislation satisfies the substantive criteria and thus leads to legal certainty is the legislation deemed to meet the legality requirement in its extended meaning as we have indicated.

A substantive criterion is that the legislation should be *accessible* and *foreseeable*.[34] Legislation should be clear to all subjects to which that legislation applies: legal certainty is needed for each subject to understand the legislation, adjust his behaviour to it and assess the consequences of his actions on the basis of that legislation. The institutions of the EU seem to realize that since their Interinstitutional Agreement of 1998 reads: 'according to the case law of the Court of Justice, the principle of legal certainty, which is part of the Community legal order,

31. COM (2001) 428, 20.
32. COM (2002) 275 final, 5. Jun. 2002.
33. See n. 20 above.
34. In the Commissions' documents it is also called *openness*.

requires that Community legislation must be clear and precise and its application foreseeable by individuals'.[35]

These criteria of accessibility and foreseeability were developed in the case law of the European Court of Human Rights.[36] This requires clear, simple and precise language with due attention to internal and external consistency. The legislation also has to take into consideration the multilingual context of the EU and the traditions and cultures existing in the various Member States. This requirement could fail to be met, since the possibility of choosing a set of minimum rules in the various Directives will allow room for differing national implementations in accordance with national legislation and the practice in each Member State.

One of the elements belonging to these quality criteria is the requirement of the coherence of the various rulings. This implies that not only should the EU legislation – that is, the body of directives concerned – be internally coherent, but also that the European legislation should be phrased in such a way that coherence, or at least a sufficient degree of coherence, exists among the Member States. That is, particularly relevant in cases of a transnational nature, for example, in cases of the restructuring of enterprises with a cross-border impact for the employees, or in cases of transnational transfers.

A specific requirement to be assessed is the *transparency* of the legislation and of the rules at a lower level.[37] Transparency refers to the way in which the rules have been developed, the background and the goals to be achieved. It also includes the identification of unforeseen effects.

4. ANALYSIS OF THE INSTRUMENTS

On the basis of the criteria listed above, we will analyse the various instruments used in the field of information and consultation of employees in management decisions. First, an assessment will be made of whether, and in which way, the Directives under scrutiny meet the legitimation criterion.

4.1. Assessment on Legitimation

Workers' involvement in business decisions, substantiated by the right to information and consultation, is to be found in various Directives. As mentioned above

35. Interinstitutional Agreement of 22 Dec. 1998 on common guidelines for the quality of drafting of Community legislation, OJ C 073, 17 Mar. 1999, 0001–0004.
36. As developed in the case law of the European Court of Human Rights in the cases *Sunday Times v. the United Kingdom* (no. 2) judgment of 26 Nov. 1991, Series A no. 217, and *Malone v. the United Kingdom*, judgment of 2 Aug. 1984, Series A no. 82 (amongst others). See also A. Woltjer in Ch. 6 of this book.
37. This means national legislation, as well as more detailed rules on enterprise level or sectoral level.

(section 2), the idea was conceived in the Collective Redundancies Directive of 1975 on the occasion of a large restructuring process conducted by the multinational *AKZO* in the Netherlands.[38] The costs of dismissal played a decisive role in the decision of the management of multinationals in which establishment workers were made redundant. The Collective Redundancies Directive thus was created in reaction to this phenomenon and strove for mandatory employee information and consultation in these situations in order to give the employees a certain role in the process of decision-making concerning the direct consequences for themselves. The later Directive on Transfers of Undertakings (1977) was inspired by the same considerations. The process of the restructuring of enterprises as a result of the removal of the trade barriers in the EC could not be stopped. In order to protect employees against the decisions most profitable for the employer but negative for the employees, the Directive did not only offer – at least for a certain period of time – protection with regard to the dismissal and the preservation of the level of employment conditions, but it also introduced the obligation of the employer to inform and consult the employees on the decisions and measures envisaged.[39]

Since the adoption of both Directives took place before the introduction of the Single Act, that is, before a social policy of the EEC had been substantiated in treaty provisions, the legal basis was found in Article 115 TFEU (ex 94 EC). The Directives were therefore based on the common market principle. Without an intervention by EC law, the differences would still remain in the Member States as regards the extent of the protection of employees in the case of mergers with a cross-border impact. These differences can have a direct effect on the functioning of the common market, and for that reason these differences should be reduced.[40] Article 94 EC (now 115 TFEU) was interpreted very broadly to include social issues which were drafted in the margin of company law issues. It is interesting to note that the application of the subsidiarity and the proportionality principles was not considered. The intervention by community law was broadly accepted. European trade unions supported this step enthusiastically. The employers eventually accepted it as a fact, but did not support it wholeheartedly. It is notable that on the occasion of the redrafting of both Directives in 1998, the legal ground did not change, nor was it even extended. No reference is made to the social paragraph of the EC Treaty as amended by the Treaty of Amsterdam.[41] This is intelligible for the case of the Directive on Transfers of Undertakings, since the core issue of that Directive is not the information and consultation obligation, but the protection of

38. The central management of *AKZO* 'chose' to shut down the plants in the countries with the lowest dismissal costs. Belgium was the country that has been hit the most. See R. Blanpain, *European Labour Law*, 10th ed. (The Hague: Kluwer Law International, 2006), 588. See also Barnard, 672.
39. Directive 77/187/EEC on Transfers of Undertakings. of 14 Feb. 1977.
40. Preamble of the Council Directive 77/187/EEC of 14 Feb. 1977.
41. References were made to the Community Charter of the Fundamental Social Rights of Workers of 1989.

workers. As to the Directive on Collective Redundancies, this is at least remarkable, since this Directive deals with information and consultation explicitly.[42]

The other four directives – the EWC directive, the SE directive, the SCE directive, as well as the Framework directive of 2002 – are the examples of the genuine 'information and consultation' EU Regulations.[43] The EWC Directive, of which the first proposal dates from 1980,[44] was a significant step in the European history of establishing information and consultation procedures; it was the only piece of legislation effectively lifting the information and consultation obligation to Community level.[45] The legal bases of these Directives are different. The EWC Directive and the Framework Directive directly refer to Article 153 (ex 137 EC) TFEU[46] being the legal basis for it, whereas the Directives on the involvement of employees in the SE and the SCE are based on the Regulations concerning the establishment of an SE or an SCE themselves. Directly or indirectly (the SE and the SCE Directives), the Directives meet the legitimation requirement, since Article 153 TFEU determines the Directive as the legislative instrument to be used. That does not change due to the fact that the Treaty provision itself leaves much freedom to the national social partners to flesh out the content, the procedure and the extent of involvement of the employees and their representatives. This is inherent in the way the Treaty deals with this competence. Moreover, it is in conformity with the double subsidiarity standard which we mentioned above[47] and which has been adopted as a principle of Community policy introducing a 'dual layer' system.[48] It has to be noted that the Directive has never been challenged on its legal basis.[49]

Assessing the legitimation of the EWC Directive, contrary to the two earlier Directives, this EWC Directive has been subject to an extensive discussion by the social partners. Even before the introduction of the involvement of social partners

42. It is also remarkable that the legal ground of this amended Directive has not been challenged before court, even by the UK, although the UK has done that in other cases such as the Working Time directive of 1993 without success; See ECJ 12 Nov. 1996. Case C-84/94, ECR I-05755.
43. If we use the term 'regulation' hereafter, we don't refer to the particular form of the European legislative measure (the Regulation), but more in a general manner. If we refer to a Regulation we will use a capital.
44. O.J. C 297, 15 Nov. 1980. 3, Bull. Supp. 3/80.
45. See T. Jaspers, 'The European Works Council Directive in its Community Context', 13 seq.
46. Actually the Directive was based on Art. 2 of the Social Policy Agreement, the wording of which is similar to Art. 153 TFEU.
47. See G.J.J. Heerma van Voss, 'The Directive on European Works Councils in Community-scale Undertakings. The introduction of "Double subsidiarity" in European Law', *Maastricht Journal of European and Comparative Law* 2, no.4 (1995): 35.
48. COM (93) 600, 6c. See also G. Falkner, *EU Social Policy in the 1990s: Towards a Corporatist Policy Community* (London: Routledge, 1998), 83.
49. However, during the process of negotiating on the Directive, the European employers' organizations were opposed to legislative action by the European Commission. However, that was more a political objection than a legal one. The legitimation of other Directives has been challenged, such as the Working Time Directive 93/1004/EEC. The UK disputed the legality of the directive before the European Court of Justice but failed; ECJ 12 Nov. 1996. Case C-84/94, ECR I-5755.

in the legislating process,[50] the social partners discussed this matter, but they were not able to agree on a jointly accepted proposal.[51] However, they did not disagree on the principle of involvement of employees and/or their representatives, but they could not achieve an agreement on the more detailed elements and the extent of the involvement.[52] Similarly, in the process of revising the EWC Directive, the consultation of social partners by the Commission started in 2004[53] and continued in a second round of negotiations in 2008[54] between the European employers associations and the European trade unions ended without result. The trade unions decided not to try to reach an agreement under Article 155 TFEU (ex 139 EC), and notified the European Commission of their wish for the latter to take unilateral legislative action. The involvement of the social partners in the preparation of the Directive contributes to its democratic content as part of the legitimation assessment, although partly because a consensus on the further details could not be reached.

The same conclusion can be drawn as to both other Directives on the involvement of employees in the Societas Europaea (SE)[55] and the Societas Cooperativa Europaea (SCE). The legal basis is not Article 153 TFEU, but Article 308 EC (now as amended Article 352 TFEU), with a specific reference to the EC Regulations establishing the SE and SCE. The explicit preference of the (European) trade unions that the involvement of employees be regulated in the Regulation itself has not been honoured. This would have led to a more democratically justifiable content; however even though they are two separate legal instruments their legal basis is not undermined, since the Directives were adopted by unanimity.[56] The ground of their severe opposition: a fear of a potential direct effect of such a provision in a Regulation, pointing to a reluctant attitude in this field to the principle of acting on a European scale.

In general, it can be concluded that all Directives are sufficiently legitimized in line with the principle of legality. They all have a legal basis for enacting legal

---

50. Firstly in the Social Agreement of 1992, inserted into the Treaty itself in 1998 (by the Treaty of Amsterdam).
51. There are good examples of successful social dialogue resulting in draft legislation, such as the Directives on Parental Leave, Part Time Work, and Fixed Term Contracts. In these three fields social partners reached an agreement and determined the content of these rulings.
52. In their study, R.Blanpain & P.Windey, *European Works Councils* (Leuven: Peeters, 1996) gave an overview of the various proposals that have been discussed between social partners.
53. European Works Councils: fully realizing their potential for employee involvement for the benefit of enterprises and their employees, <http://ec.europa.eu/social/BlobServlet?docId=2165&langId=en>, 26 Feb. 2010.
54. European Works Councils: Consultation of the European social partners on the revision of Council Directive 94/45/EC of 22 Sep. 1994 on the establishment of a European Works Council or a procedure in Community-scale undertakings and Community-scale groups of undertakings for the purposes of informing and consulting employees, C/2008/660, Brussels, 20 Feb. 2008. <http://ec.europa.eu/social/BlobServlet?docId=2159&langId=en>, 26 Feb. 2010.
55. The discussion on the issue of involvement of employees in the SE dates from the seventies of the last century; it is related to discussion on the so-called Vredeling directive. See T. Jaspers, 'The European Works Council Directive in its Community Context', 23 seq.
56. See Art. 308 EC (now, as amended Art. 352 TFEU).

measures, although these bases are different. Theoretically one might say there is a certain lack of coherence by using different legal bases for the same matter, but from a political point of view it is intelligible and acceptable. Changing the general legal basis of all the Directives to Article 153 TFEU would reopen the discussions on issues settled and agreed upon previously. This could be risky and would probably not change the progress already made as to the substance of the matter.

The 'necessity' requirement has been met as well. In the preambles of the Directives the legislature gave good reasons for enacting laws at the European level, although they could be regarded as somewhat magisterial.

Generally speaking, from a democratic point of view the support by the social partners – as well as by the European parliament, in so far as it was involved in the legislative process[57] – has contributed to the legitimation of the laws. It cannot be denied that the lack of consensus between the social partners on the details of the regulations has influenced the actual meaning and the potential impact of the right to information and consultation of employees in business matters. In line with this observation, it can be noted that the discretion the legislature has left to the Member States and – at the secondary level of the 'double subsidiarity'– to the national social partners is rather big. Apart from the fact that this has been done deliberately – due to difficulty in reaching a political consensus and again according to the subsidiarity principle – it is also a consequence of referring to the national structures, traditions and practices to be taken into account in order to adapt the European regulations to the national environment. Upholding this conclusion is only possible if the objective set by the Directives (a guarantee of an effective involvement of employees' representatives in decision making in enterprises) is achieved.[58]

4.2. Assessment on the Quality of Law Criteria

In this section we will analyse and assess whether the Directives under scrutiny are meeting the quality requirements. We will focus our analysis on some core elements and will concentrate on the earlier Directives: the Directives on Collective Redundancies, on Transfers of Undertakings, and the European Works Council Directive. This choice does not mean to imply that the other Directives are not relevant, but their fairly recent genesis mans that records of practical experience with their application are rather limited.[59] The Framework Directive and the SE and SCE Directives will be included in so far as they contribute substantially to a better understanding of the developments by applying quality criteria.

57. In the course of the decades in which the legislature was active in this field, the involvement of the Parliament became more and more important and influential.
58. The EU law requires the achievement of the objective according to Art. 288 TFEU (ex 249 EC).
59. It is worthwhile mentioning some figures: As of mid-June 2008, 146 SEs had been registered, COM (2008) 591 final, but as of October 2008, the ETUI witnessed an increase amounting to 284 SEs.

The EWC Directive, as rephrased by the Recast Directive, is a good example for showing the development in thinking and drafting of European regulations on workers' involvement. As for the other Directives, it is too early to assess whether they need to be amended, although the Commission concluded that some improvements could be made. Regarding the Framework Directive, the Commission in its Communication of March 2008[60] was concerned both about the interpretation of Directive provisions in national laws, as well as the compliance of the implementing measures with the Directive. In a report on the implementation of the Directive in the Member States, it has been pointed out that serious difficulties may arise regarding the scope of application of the Directive, because Member States can restrict the scope due to the vagueness and circularity of the definitions of 'undertaking', 'establishment' and 'employee'. Another point of discussion has to do with the discretion left to the parties to shape their arrangements. The rapporteur feels that while entrusting management and labour with defining freely and at any time through a negotiated agreement the practical arrangements for informing and consulting employees, it is too easy for Member States to disrespect the objective to be achieved.[61] One wonders whether they therefore might not respect the core issues.

In the introduction we made a distinction between two approaches: the chronological approach and the approach based on the nature and substance of the right to information and consultation. In the analysis of the Directives we will try to shed some light on whether the first road has been followed or whether the legislature has opted for the second.

4.2.1. The Requirements of Clarity, Consistency and Coherence

In section 3.2.2 clarity, consistency and coherence were listed as the main criteria for assessing of the quality of the Directives under scrutiny. It will be interesting to see whether the clarity and the consistency of the terms used in the various Directives have been improved over time. If this holds true, it proves that a so-called 'learning effect' has occurred. It can also be considered as a successful effort to 'harmonise' the various concepts as used in the Directives on this subject, resulting in more clarity and consistency. If this does not seem to be true, it could lead to a twofold conclusion. Either it is a confirmation of the hypothesis that the specific substance of the Directive concerned has been decisive for the design and the wording of that Directive, or the effort to harmonize has failed due to the political reason of not reaching a consensus or has failed on vague reasons. It has to be taken

60. COM (2008) 146 final.

61. E. Ales, 'Synthesis report on the Directive 2002/14/EC establishing a general framework for informing and consulting employees in the European Community; Studies on the implementation of Labour Law Directives in the enlarged European Union' (Cassino, Labour Asociados Consultores, 2007). See also E. Ales, 'Information and Consultation within the Undertaking: Employees' Right Or Employer's Duty? Looking for Effectiveness', in *Recasting Worker Involvement?*, ed. T. Blanke (Deventer: Kluwer, 2009), 7–21.

for granted that an inconsistency between the wording of certain terms in the various Directives cannot be avoided.

If we look at the versions of the earliest Directives, that is, the Directive on Collective Redundancies and the Directive on Transfers of Undertakings, it is clear that, over time greater clarity is being achieved with regard to the terms and concepts used, compared with the information and consultation Directives. The Directives of 1998 (Collective Redundancies) and 2001 (Transfers of Undertakings) define the core concepts in a more precise way. One of the improvements, both for reasons of clarity and also for reasons of conformity with the objective of the various Directives, is the insertion of the *requirement of timeliness* ('in good time') in all the Directives.[62]

When assessing whether the development is a result of one or the other of the approaches mentioned above, it is interesting to investigate which choice has been made. It is remarkable that the first version of the Transfers of Undertakings Directive (of 1977) already used the term 'in good time,' whereas this term is absent in the Collective Redundancies Directive of 1975 (it was added in 1992). The addition of the timeliness requirement can be seen as confirmation of the importance of this concept in making consultation with the employees' representatives effective. It strengthens the information and consultation procedure prior to the point where a decision dismissing employees collectively is made.[63] It improves the coherence of the Directives dealing with similar matters (restructuring of enterprises). It can be considered as a combination of both approaches: approximation of the respective Directives based on the substance itself, as well as for reasons of improving the coherence.

It is even more remarkable that the 1994 EWC Directive does not use this term or a similar one. In its Working Document of 1995, the European Commission supported the correct implementation of the Directive in the domestic law of the Member States, stating that although neither the Directive, nor its Annex gave guidance as to the moment at which the information and consultation should take place, the information 'should be provided in good time for works councils to consider the contents and to deliver an opinion'. It is left to the Member States' institutions (and if necessary, the national courts) implementing and applying the Directive to determine when the information and consultation takes place, given that is, should take place 'at a time such that the procedure is not devoid of all effect'.[64]

62. In its more recent decisions, the ECJ has confirmed the importance of 'timely information and consultation' of employees and has strengthened the meaning of that concept. ECJ 27 Jan. 2005, Case C-188/03 (*Junk*); and ECJ 10 Sep. 2009, Case C-44/08 (*Fujitsu Siemens*).

63. The 1975 Directive on Collective Redundancies, as well as the 1992 amendment, speak of 'starting consultations' with the workers' representatives when the employer is 'contemplating collective redundancies'. That could be interpreted as an indication that the consultation has to be started timely. The timeliness requirement has been added for reasons of strengthening this obligation. In his opinion in the Nielson case (Case 284/83 (1985) ECR 553 the Advocate-General made a suggestion in that direction.

64. Working Paper no 21, published in R. Blanpain, P. Wiley, 114/15.

It was therefore left to the Member States to give effect to this requirement in their domestic practice.

An explicit reference to the timeliness requirement is to be found in the drafts of the SE and the SCE Directive. Information and consultation should be given 'at such time' as is appropriate to enable the workers' representatives to execute effectively the rights provided for in the Directive.[65] The recent recast EWC Directive of 2009 is copying this notion. Apparently the chronological approach is used but based, one can argue, on the core content of the concept of effective information and consultation.

When we look at the specific content of both the Collective Redundancies Directive and the Transfer of Undertaking Directive, it could be argued that these two Directives have been using the notion of 'timeliness' from the beginning. The Directives would lose their effect if the information and consultation were not provided at such a moment, meaning that the rights conferred to the employees' representatives could not be exercised because the decision had already been taken and executed by the management.[66] Although it took quite some time for the legislature to improve the coherence by inserting this requirement – which is crucial for the effective application of the right to information and consultation – in all relevant Directives, it can be stated that in the end this result has been achieved.

Another element that is, of great importance for the effective exercise of the rights concerned is the meaning of the notion of '*the measure envisaged by the employer*' on which the employees have to be informed and consulted. Which managerial decision or measure qualifies for being subject to information and consultation? The phrasing of this notion is not very clear either, so again the ECJ has given some guidelines in its case law.[67] In the more recent drafts of the Directives an improvement can be noticed. They articulate explicitly that the Works Council has to be informed and consulted about *proposed* measures.[68] It indicates and supports the value that is, awarded to the so-called 'anteriority principle': in order to attain an effective use of the rights of the employees, the employer has to involve the employees' representatives in decisions or measures he is inclined to take.[69] The national

65. This wording is also used in the Framework Directive of 2002: Art. 4, para. 3.
66. In this sense, ECJ 27 Jan. 2005, Case C-188/03 (*Junk*), in which the court decided that 'the obligations to consult and to notify arise prior to any decision by the employer to terminate contracts of employment' (para. 37 Similarly the ECJ in its recent decision: ECJ 10 Sep. 2009. Case C-44/08 (*Fujitsu Siemens*), paras 48 and 49. See C. Barnard, 679.
67. See the decisions of the ECJ in its case law on the application of the EWC Directive and of the Collective Redundancies Directive. We mention as examples: Case 62/99 (Bofrost); Case C-440/00 (*Kühne & Nagel*); Case C-349/01(*ADS Anker*). Case C-188/03 (*Junk*), Case C-385/05 (CGT); C-44/08 (*Fujitsu Siemens*); C-12/08 MonoCar Styling.
68. The SE and SCE Directives are using the term 'envisaged'. The borrowing of the definitions from the 2001/86 Directive was supported by four out of six social partners consulted on the Recast, see Annex 3 to the Impact Assessment, COM (2008) 419 final.
69. In conformity with the recent decisions of the ECJ, see, *inter alia*, Case C-44/08 (*Fujitsu Siemens*). The Dutch experience could be very helpful in clarifying this notion. In its case law a special court equipped to deal with workers' involvement the '*Ondernemingskamer*'

court cases against *Renault* in 1997[70] and *Gaz de France* in 2006[71] have contributed significantly to this development; the French judges in both cases used and defined these concepts. In conclusion, it can be stated that on this topic the legislature has benefited from a progressive understanding of the notion of an effective use of these rights by the ECJ and the national courts. The clarity and the consistency of the concept show a clear evolution through the various subsequent instruments; however, this does not imply that a proper definition is provided for. The question remains as to whether that goal is possible to reach at all.

Nevertheless, some problems remain. The provisions in the Directives, although more streamlined and more elaborate due to chronological evolution (as seen above), still do not clearly stipulate the content of the rights and obligations of employees in an unequivocal way. The ECJ took on the task of creating more clarity in times when the legislature is unable to.[72] One has to wait and see whether and when the legislature will follow the approach taken by the ECJ. The research conducted by some scholars will give more insight into the way in which the Directives have been applied in the domestic law of the Member States.[73]

Apart from the timeliness concept, the most recent Directives (the SE, SCE, EWC and the Framework Directives) at least are clarifying some other terms in order to improve the effectiveness of the workers' involvement. The texts of the various provisions on information and consultation are using terms such as 'in such fashion or manner,' and 'with such content,' as are appropriate to effectively guarantee to the workers' representatives the exercise of their rights. This phrase directly refers to the definitions of 'information' and 'consultation' that should be considered as effective tools for workers' representatives to influence the decisions by the management. It therefore contributes to the achievement of the goals set by the various Directives. If we assess this development in terms of 'a learning effect', it means that in a chronological perspective, we can conclude that the more refined, sophisticated and detailed regulation of workers' involvement fits into a policy of 'better regulation' in terms of improving the quality of regulation.

(the Enterprise Section of the Amsterdam Court of Appeal of the Amsterdam High Court) has elaborated in great detail on what constitutes a 'proposed' measure.

70. See *inter alia*, F. Dorssemont & A. Jaspers, 'De "affaire Renault": een les voor later of een storm in de Europese vijver!?', *Nederlands Tijdschrift voor Sociaal Recht* (1999): 152–162; P. Lorber, 'The Renault Case: The European Works Councils Put to the Test', *International Journal of Comparative Labour Law and Industrial Relations* 13 (1997): 135–142.
71. Cour d'Appel de Paris, 21 Nov. 2006; 6; Cour de Cassation, 16 Jan. 2008,; CA Paris, 14e ch. A, 21 Nov. 2006, Sté Gaz de France c/ Comité d'entreprise européen de Gaz de France : Juris-Data n° 2006–315724. See also the Information Report 'Information and Consultation Rights in Jurisprudence (EWC Workshop)' (Brussels: 2008).
72. See *inter alia*, ECJ 27 Jan. 2005, Case C-188/03 (*Junk v. Wolfgang Kühnel*); also ECJ 10 Sep. 2009, Case C-44/08 (*Fujitsu Siemens*)
73. See F. Dorssemont, 'The European Works Councils Directive and the domestic Courts', in: *The Recast of the European Works Councils Directive*, ed. T. Blanke & F. Dorssemont (Intersentia: Antwerp – Oxford – Portland, 2010).

One can wonder whether the differing wording of similar Directive provisions will detract from the quality of the legislation. It is clear that the two Directives with a more focused matter (on Collective Redundancies, and on Transfers of Undertakings) do not use the terms 'in such fashion or manner' and 'with such content' as the other Directives do. From the point of view of consistency and coherence, it would be preferable to harmonize the way of regulating, particularly because the aims are the same. But there could be a good reason for maintaining a difference in wording. The two Directives mentioned refer directly to the subjects for which the company has to provide the necessary information and which are subject to consultation. It is therefore clear about what the employer has to give information and to consult the workers' representatives. Since the substantial scope of the Works Council Directives as well as that of the SE and SCE Directives is broad and not well defined in the body of the Directives themselves, the addition, as mentioned, is necessary in order to give more certainty as regards the effective influence of the Works Councils.

From the perspective of the substance there exists another remarkable difference as to the concepts used. We refer to *the result to be attained*. The Directive on Collective Redundancies and the Directive on Transfers of Undertakings refer to 'consultation with a view to reaching an agreement',[74] whereas the workers' involvement Directives (SE, SCE and EWC) are using more general terms: information has to be provided for in order 'to undertake an in-depth assessment of the possible impact and (...) to prepare for consultations with the competent organ', and consultation has to be undertaken aiming at 'expressing an opinion on measures envisaged by the competent organ which may be taken into account in the decision-making process'.[75] The former wording seems to contribute more to the effective exercise of the right to information and, in particular, consultation. The effectiveness of the second mode is dependent on the actual application of the concept just mentioned, in the various national laws of the Member States.[76]

An interesting example of the development of the core concept of workers' involvement in chronological as well as in substantive terms, is the EWC directive. In the 1994 version of the Directive, there is no description of 'information', let alone a definition. Only in the subsidiary requirements are the subjects listed on which the management has to give information in its annual meeting.[77] The Recast Directive has improved this substantially and is therefore a better fit

74. Article 2, para. 1 of the 98/59/EC Directive (Collective redundancies) and Art. 7, para. 2 of 2001/23/EC Directive (Transfers of undertakings).
75. Article 2 Directive 2001/86/EC (SE); Art. 2 Directive 2003/72/EC (SCE); Art. 2 Recast Directive EWC 2009/38/EC.
76. See the study by F. Dorssemont on the case law in the Member States: Dorssemont, *The European Works Councils Directive and the domestic Courts*.
77. See point 2 of the subsidiary requirements annexed to the EWC Directive 94/45/EC. In certain circumstances the management has to provide information on certain subjects listed outside the annual meeting.

with the policy on this issue.[78] As to the term of 'consultation', the former EWC directive only mentioned it in a restricted way: 'Consultation means the exchange of views and establishment of dialogue between employees' representatives and central management or any more appropriate level of management.' The Recast Directive not only rephrased the wording but also changed the concept. The non-committal exchange of views and the 'Social Dialogue' have been replaced by 'expressing an opinion on measures envisaged by the competent organ which may be taken into account in the decision-making processes'. With the last addition, more than lip service is paid to the expressing of an objective of the consultation.[79] The Framework Directive of 2002 covering the right of information to and consultation of employees in enterprise matters in general is following the same path: Article 4 mentions 'meeting the employer, obtaining a response and the reasons for that response to any opinion the works council might formulate', which aims at reaching an agreement.

A final point deals with the possibility of 'contracting out'. This could hamper the effective exercise of the right to information and consultation, and could therefore be at odds with the principles of certainty and clarity about the content of a right. The notion refers to the insertion of a contractual arrangement to be concluded between management and labour allowing the parties to 'define freely and at any time through negotiated agreement the practical arrangements for informing and consulting employees' (Article 5). This seems to give the parties a lot of freedom in a field where inequality between the powers of the parties is more rule than exception.[80] This approach has been followed in the other Directives instituting a works council.[81] However, national case law shows that the parties are not completely free in their arrangements: They have to respect the principles of the Directive. For that reason, it is vital that the judges – national as well as European – play the role of the watchdog.[82] From the point of view of the quality of legislation, one can doubt whether this approach fits into that policy.

4.2.2. Enforceability

A final point to be mentioned in this analysis is the question of whether the enforceability requirement has been fulfilled. 'Enforcement implies that compliance with EU law is monitored and non-compliance is sanctioned by national and supranational courts.'[83] Apart from assessing whether European law provides for

78. Article 2(1)(f) provides for a more detailed definition of what information should entail.
79. Similarly, as mentioned above, the effectiveness of this norm is dependent on its actual application in the various national laws of the Member States, particularly in the case law.
80. Employees (and thus also their representatives) mostly are in a dependent, subordinate position to their employer, depending on them for their jobs and wages
81. In literature, this is called contractualisation. See F. Dorssemont, *The Re-cast of the European Works Council Directive* 129 ff.
82. The judges in the Renault case of 1997, the French as well as the Belgian, have acted in that capacity. See F. Dorssemont & T. Jaspers, *De 'Affaire Renault'* 152 ff.
83. <http://ec.europa.eu/governance/better_regulation/glossary_en.htm#_E>, 26 Feb. 2010.

an effective assessment of compliance of the national law and practice with the European law, in our analysis a second method is important: the way the non-compliance is sanctioned. The sanctions must be transposed into Member State legislation and they must be made effectively available to citizens. Based on the clear case law of the European Court of Justice, it is generally accepted that the sanctions should be effective, proportionate and dissuasive.[84] In case of self-regulation (as is the case in the issue at hand), the remedies provided for have to be effective to prevent non-conformity.[85] If we look into the Directives under scrutiny, it has to be noted that they refer merely to the general wording as established in case law. They do not associate any specific sanctions with non-compliance. From the point of view of quality of regulation, this may hamper the effective use of the workers' involvement rights. It remains up to the ECJ to specify what is considered as an effective remedy.[86]

5. CONCLUSION

The analysis of the EU Directives on information for and consultation of workers in the undertaking, leads to the overall conclusion that over time, the legislation on the right to information and consultation is complying better with the legality requirements. From the chronological approach it can be stated that the so-called 'learning effect' has occurred and has resulted in more consistent and clearer legislation. The improvements are apparent. However, this does not imply that the legislation meets the legality criteria when assessed on a more detailed level. Some major aspects have been pointed out in this contribution:

In general, the legitimation criteria can be said to be met sufficiently. None of the Directives violates the necessity requirement. Although some Member States (familiar with trade unions only) doubted the competence and the necessity of the EU to legislate in that way, the legal basis of the Directives has never been challenged before a court. The participation of social partners in the legislative process is strengthening the legitimacy of the laws enacted, although the social partners could not reach a consensus on the content of a possible agreement on this topic.

When looking at the requirement of consistency of legislation, the Directives under scrutiny clearly show an evolution of convergence towards each other in the phrasing of the most important concepts. Consistent legislation was absent for a long time, resulting in legal uncertainty, inequality of treatment of workers and overall confusion. The ECJ played an important role in bringing more clarity to the

84. ECJ 10 Apr. 1984. Case 14/83 (*Von Colson*), ECR 1984, 1891. See also Deirdre Curtin, 'Effective Sanctions and the Equal Treatment Directive: the Von Colson and Harz Cases', CMLRev 22 (1985): 505.
85. See Mandelkern Group on Better Regulation, final report, 13 Nov. 2001, 14.
86. None of the Directives, except for the Framework Directive, in Art. 8(2), incorporate the fact that sanctions should be effective, proportionate and dissuasive. The others only mention this phrase in a recital of the Preambles.

concepts used, for example, in the cases of *Junk*, *Bofrost*, *CGT* and *Fujitsu Siemens*, to name only a few.

However, besides these positive developments there remain some – serious – shortcomings. The differing wording of the concepts and norms can substantially hamper their consistent application in the various Member States. Since the latter are responsible for implementing the Directives and since the EU gives them room to do this as they see fit, the application of the norms can differ substantially between Member States. In order to guarantee an effective right to information and consultation of employees, especially in a transnational environment, a clear and consistent wording of the main concepts is imperative. Differing wording is acceptable only if the full effect of the right to information and consultation is secured. Since this is not the case, as the analysis shows, the whole body of legislation is not in compliance with the legality requirements. And while it may be true that the ECJ and the national courts are very well capable and equipped to fill the gaps, this is not the best solution from a 'quality of legislation' perspective.

Another aspect that could yield an adverse result as to the legality of the legislation, is the discretion left by the Directives to the social partners to negotiate on the content of the information and consultation rights. On the one hand it does allow for more tailored solutions, fitting in the practices in a branch, sector or company of a country, but on the other hand, the possibility of 'contracting out' diminishes the very substance of the rights at stake. One wonders whether the fundamental nature of this right[87] does not oppose this practice.

A frequently used argument in favour of these two features – the use of vague norms and the possibility of freedom of negotiation *in melius* as well as *in peius* – is the reference to the nature of the matters to be regulated. Both at European and at national level, there is an apparent plea for flexibility in order to adapt the rules to the specific circumstances in the Member States. One can wonder whether this argument is convincing and sufficient. In any case, in cross-border cases or cases with a transnational impact make this reasoning difficult to maintain while aiming to guarantee the effective exercise of the rights concerned.

87. Article 27 of The EU Charter of Fundamental Rights, since the Treaty of Lisbon part of EU law, is explicitly mentioning this right of information and consultation of employees and their representatives.

Part IV

Legality and the Impact of Non-legislative Instruments

Chapter 9
The Open Method of Coordination in the Area of Social Policy and the Legality Principle

Frans Pennings

1. INTRODUCTION

The Open Method of Coordination (OMC) was developed in the 1990s in the area of employment policy. Later it was also applied in other areas: social inclusion; pensions; immigration; education and culture; and asylum. More recently its use has been suggested for other areas as well, including health care, environmental affairs and the promotion of mobility of researchers. In short, the OMC is an instrument meant to meet certain objectives defined by the Council of Ministers. It requires Member States to submit reports on the national state of affairs in the policy area concerned, and on the basis of discussions within the Council on these reports, Member States are given guidelines which require them to take measures to reach the set objectives. Subsequently the Member States have to report the results of their policies. In section 2.2 the OMC procedure will be described in more detail.

The OMC is used in particular in areas where the Treaty does not give powers to make binding rules. It enables the European institutions thus to overcome the problem of the lack of competence to make rules, while at the same time allowing them to ask Member States to undertake policy measures in such areas. Sometimes

Leonard Besselink, Frans Pennings & Sacha Prechal (eds), *The Eclipse of the Legality Principle in the European Union*, pp. 153–168.

the Treaty sets particular policy aims without giving the corresponding powers to make binding rules. Article 3 Treaty on the Functioning of the European Union is an example of such a Treaty provision that mentions several social policy aims, but gives no powers to the Council to make Regulations or Directives to realize these aims. The OMC is a useful instrument, as we will see below, to fill the gap: it leaves the room and also the responsibility to the Member States to develop their own policies where they are encouraged to take action. The obligation to report on the results of the actions taken and the recommendations following these reports make the OMC instrument far from optional.

For this reason, it is appropriate to consider the OMC in light of the functions that are traditionally attributed to the legality principle (see Chapter 1 of this book). The legality principle has to ensure that the elements of a democratic legal order are observed. We have to acknowledge, however, that these elements are not automatically guaranteed if a particular public authority is regulated by an Act. Therefore we do not only have to analyse whether authority is exercised on the basis of an Act, but we also have to consider the functions related to the principle, and whether and how they are realized.

Secondly, we have to acknowledge that the legality principle within the Nation-state may have a different meaning and function from that in the context of a multilevel legal order. The traditional meaning of the legality principle is that public authority can only be exercised on the basis of, and in accordance with, enacted laws. In the case of a multilevel order – the European Union in particular – the requirement of a legal basis for exercising authority has a reason, which is, for an important part, different from the reason why this requirement exists in national law. In the EU it serves to define the position of the stakeholders within the EU, in particular the relation between the Member States and the institutions of the Union.

The functions which have been connected to the legality principle within the nation-state context are, however, also relevant to the multilevel legal order. Therefore we will address these functions in order to see how they are satisfied in relation to the OMC. The first function of the legality principle is the attribution of public authority. Thus, we have to consider how public authority is attributed in respect of the OMC. This raises questions such as what is the legal basis for the OMC concerned, how is it drafted and does the OMC affect provisions of the Treaty where the powers to make instruments are exclusively reserved for the Member States? From the attribution function, it also follows that procedures must hold the government and administrative authorities to account for the way in which they exercise their powers. Since the OMC is applied in a multilevel legal order – that is, in the relation between the EU and the Member States – special attention is to be paid to the effects of this instrument on the various levels.

The second function of the legality principle is legitimation of public authority. This function means that democracy has to be realized through formal procedures and institutions involved in the legislative process. Alternative forms of democracy through semi-public devolution of legislative powers to functional bodies or stakeholders in sectors of society or the economy can also be required. The objective of democratic legitimacy of exercising public powers is served by the requirement of legality, if legality (in view of its function) is understood as implying a procedure that involves representative institutions, rendering the outcome of the procedure 'democratic'.

The third function of the legality principle is the regulation of the manner in which public authority is to be exercised. This implies that certain substantive standards should be satisfied. This regulation is central for the attainment of the following objectives: prevention of arbitrariness and other forms of abuse of power; legal certainty; accessibility and foreseeability. It follows from this function that rights and obligations are to be clearly and precisely identified when they affect the legal position of citizens.

I will first describe the OMC instrument in the area of employment policies (section 2). Section 3 will deal with the OMC in other areas of social policy. Section 4 will give some examples of the guidelines and recommendations following from the OMC in employment. Section 5 will analyse the OMCs in terms of the functions connected with the OMCs.

2. THE OMC FOR EMPLOYMENT POLICIES

2.1. THE LEGAL BASIS FOR THE OMC IN EMPLOYMENT

The Open Coordination Method was developed for the first time in relation to employment policy.[1] Employment policy is an important policy area for the EU, since it is part of the European Employment Strategy (EES). The EES, which was initiated in the 1990s, was initially solely part of the instruments of the European Monetarian Union. It made use of mid-term objectives, indicators and convergence aims. In 1997 the EES was made part of the Treaty of Amsterdam (Article 125 EC, now Article 145 TFEU).

A major aim of this employment strategy was to increase the employment rate in the Member States and to improve the overall economic situation. The EU was not, however, given the competence to make binding rules on the employment policies of the Member States. The OMC can be seen then as an instrument for realizing the objectives of the employment strategy, thus compensating for the lack of EU competence in this area. Article 145 TFEU does not give the powers to EU institutions to make rules which bind the Member States. Instead, according to this Article, Member States and the Community shall, in accordance with this title of the Treaty, work towards developing a coordinated strategy for employment. This strategy must be particularly aimed at promoting a skilled, trained and adaptable

1. See on the Open Coordination Method, B. Schulte, 'The new European "Buzzword": Open Method of Co-ordination', *European Journal of Social Security* 4 (2002): 343 ff.; J. Berghman & K. Okma, 'The Method of Open Coordination: Open Procedures or Closed Circuit? Social Policy Making between Science and Politics', *European Journal of Social Security* 4 (2002): 331 ff.

workforce, and labour markets responsive to economic change, with a view to achieving the objectives defined in Article 3 TFEU.

Article 146 mentions obligations for the Member States: Member States, through their employment policies, shall contribute to the achievement of the objectives referred to in Article 145 in a way consistent with the broad guidelines of the economic policies of the Member States and of the Community adopted pursuant to Article 121(2). In addition, the Member States, having regard to national practices related to the responsibilities of management and labour, have to regard promoting employment as a matter of common concern, and shall coordinate their action in this respect within the Council.

These provisions, together with Article 147, constitute the legal basis for the OMC in employment policy. In Article 148 the procedure is described in more detail. Note that the Treaty does not use the term 'Open Method of Coordination' to describe the procedure.

2.2. The Procedure for the OMC in Employment

The OMC procedure as described in Article 148 TFEU is as follows. First, each year the European Council has to consider the employment situation in the Community. On the basis of a joint annual report by the Council and the Commission, the Council adopts conclusions on this employment situation. On the basis of these conclusions, the Council, acting by a qualified majority on, *inter alia*, a proposal from the Commission, has, each year, to draw up guidelines which the Member States have to take into account in their employment policies. Subsequently, each Member State has to write an annual report on the principal measures taken to implement its employment policy in the light of these guidelines; these reports are sent to the Council and the Commission. The Council examines these reports – that is, on the employment policies of the Member States – in the light of the employment guidelines.

The Council can, if it considers it appropriate in the light of that examination, make recommendations to Member States on a proposal from the Commission. Finally, on the basis of the results of the reports, the Council and the Commission have to make a joint annual report to the European Council on the employment situation in the Community and on the implementation of the guidelines for employment.

Thus, the OMC is a cycle of guidelines, recommendations and reports:

- a report and conclusions are made by the Council on the employment situation; these set objectives, and in order to be able to measure the extent to which these are reached, common indicators are used (e.g., reaching an employment level of 70%);
- guidelines are made by the Council for Member States;
- annual reports of the Member States on the measures they have taken in light of guidelines with action plans;

- an examination by the Council of the reports (peer reviewing);
- recommendations by Council to Member States; and
- an annual report by Council and Commission on the employment situation.

2.3. The OMC as An Instrument of Soft Law

Initially, it was feared that the OMC would not have much effect. However, the Council issued detailed and specific recommendations of which I will give examples in section 4. These recommendations are to be taken into account for the next reports Member States have to write. Thus, Member States have to consider these recommendations when developing their policies, making them quite influential.

The analysis of the reports, the comparison of the results reached in the Member States, and the description of best practices of other Member States, constitute pressure on the Member States to continue to aim for the formulated objectives. We can conclude that, while having formally kept the freedom to choose the national instruments to meet the objectives of the employment strategy, Member States have to take the recommendations into account, in any case if they do not succeed in meeting the objectives of the employment strategy with their own instruments.

The OMC is a way to set Member States in motion without hard law at the EU level. It is an instrument which leaves the powers to develop a policy basically at the national level, but still has serious effects on national employment policy. In other words, the OMC is an instrument which deals in a very specific way with the subsidiarity principle.

As, from this point of view the OMC in employment was seen as successful, the Method was introduced in other areas as well.[2]

3. THE OPEN METHOD OF COORDINATION IN SOCIAL POLICY AREAS (OMC LIGHT)

3.1. Introduction

The first 'new' area where the OMC was introduced was social inclusion. Social inclusion – or 'combating social exclusion' – is important from a political point of view, as the EU is often criticized for being an economic organization only, which aims at promoting and enforcing more competition and demands the abolition of social protection rules if these impede competition. In order to mitigate these effects, the EU has to take action in the area of social policy.

The Treaty gives, in Article 3 TFEU, the obligation to the Community to promote, *inter alia*, a high level of employment and of social protection, a high level of protection and improvement of the quality of the environment, the raising

2. E. Szyszczak, 'Experimental Governance: the Open Method of Coordination', *European Law Journal* (2004): 489 ff.

of the standard of living and quality of life, and economic and social cohesion and solidarity among Member States. This Article shows that social objectives constitute a very important part of the obligations of the EU, but EU institutions have very few powers to realize these objectives.

First I will describe the competences of the Union in the area of social policy (section 3.2) and then the OMC will be discussed (section 3.3).

3.2. The Competences of the EU in the Area of Social Policy

Article 151 TFEU gives the main rules on the obligations and powers of EU in the area of social policy. According to this article, the Union and the Member States must have as their objectives the promotion of employment and improved living and working conditions so as to make possible their harmonization while the improvement is being maintained. They must also promote proper social protection, dialogue between management and labour, the development of human resources with a view to lasting high employment, and the combating of exclusion.

To this end, Article 151 continues, the Community and the Member States have to implement measures that take account of the diverse forms of national practices, in particular in the field of contractual relations, and the need to maintain the competitiveness of the Community economy. They believe that such a development will ensue not only from the functioning of the common market, which will favour the harmonization of social systems, but also from the procedures provided for in this Treaty and from the approximation of provisions laid down by law, regulation or administrative action.

Article 153 gives the powers to make instruments to realize these objectives. The Council may adopt measures designed to encourage cooperation between Member States, through initiatives aimed at improving knowledge, developing exchanges of information and best practice, promoting innovative approaches, and evaluating experiences, excluding any harmonization of the laws and regulations of the Member States.

In addition, Directives with minimum provisions can be made for this purpose, but only in a set of limited areas mentioned in the Article concerned: improvement of the working environment, working conditions, social security and social protection of workers, protection of workers where their employment contract is terminated, information and consultation of workers, representation and collective defence of interests of workers, conditions of employment for third country nationals, integration of persons excluded form the labour market, and equality of men and women. In the area of combating social exclusion and the modernization of social protection other than that of employees (mentioned in Article 153(1)), no such minimum requirements can be made. In the case of social security, the protection of workers where their employment contract is terminated, and conditions for third country nationals, unanimity in voting is required. In the area of pay, the right of association, and the right to strike, there are explicitly no powers for Union institutions to make rules.

Article 154 provides that the Commission has the task of promoting the consultation of management and labour at Community level, and has to take any relevant measure to facilitate their dialogue by ensuring balanced support for the parties. To this end, before submitting proposals in the social policy field, the Commission has to consult management and labour on the possible direction of Community action. If, after such consultation, the Commission considers Community action advisable, it has to consult management and labour on the content of the envisaged proposal. Management and labour have to forward to the Commission an opinion or, where appropriate, a recommendation. On the occasion of such consultation, management and labour may inform the Commission of their wish to initiate the process provided for in Article 155. The duration of the procedure must not exceed nine months unless the management and labour concerned and the Commission decide jointly to extend it. Article 155 provides that should management and labour so desire, the dialogue between them at Community level may lead to contractual relations, including agreements.

Thus, management and labour – often called the social partners at EU level – play a role in the development of social policies, both at the level of consultation, and legislature in lieu of the Council, although subsequently the Council has to make a Directive to give the agreement legal force in the EU and to ensure its implementation.[3]

3.3. Combating Social Exclusion

Combating social exclusion is a main objective of European social policy.[4] However, the term 'social inclusion' is far from clear.[5]

The European Commission mentioned the following objectives for combating social exclusion:

- the promotion of participation in work and the promotion of access to all sources, rights, goods and services;
- measures to prevent the risk of social exclusion;
- measures to help the most vulnerable groups to re-integrate into society ('social inclusion');
- mobilization of all the bodies concerned to combat social exclusion.

---

3. See for an extensive discussion of the relationship between this social dialogue and the legality principle, the contribution by Albertine Veldman to this volume.
4. See on this topic, D.G. Mayes, J. Berghman & R. Salais, *Social Exclusion and European Policy* (Cheltenham/Northampton: Edward Elgar Publishing, 2001); E. Apospori & J. Millar, *The Dynamics of Social Exclusion in Europe* (Cheltenham and Northampton: Edward Elgar Publishing, 2003).
5. See for a thorough analysis, K. Vlemminckx & J. Berghman, 'Social Exclusion and the Welfare State', in: D.G. Mayes, J. Berghman & R. Salais (eds), *supra* n. 4, 34 ff; P. Schoukens, 'How the European Union Keeps the Social Welfare Debate on Track: A Lawyer's View on the EU Instruments Aimed at Combating Social Exclusion', EJSS (2002), 117 ff.

For our purpose it suffices that social exclusion is more than poverty, since poverty does not necessarily mean that one cannot or does not participate in social activities or benefit from these. Also, persons with an income above subsistence level can sometimes be excluded from particular activities or benefits.

3.4. The OMC in Social Inclusion

The OMC inclusion was elaborated by a request to each Member State in 2001 to benchmark the state of social inclusion in its country by producing a two-year national action plan. Member States also had to present national level strategies for improving the situation. In 2003 the European Commission published a joint report on social inclusion in which the approaches of the Member States were compared and contrasted and recommendations were given.

In order to win the fight against social exclusion, the national measures and results were compared on the basis of so-called social inclusion indicators. These indicators are still subject to further development, but already show what results have been achieved in the Member States. The idea behind these indicators is that social exclusion is a relative concept: relevant is whether citizens have access to, among other things, work, housing and health care. The indicators have to show whether national measures are effective in ensuring access to these elements.

The OMC in social inclusion has no basis in the Treaty, as is the case with OMC in employment. Instead, the procedure can be based on Article 153(2)(a) TFEU, which provides that the Council can take measures in order to encourage Member States to cooperate by means of initiatives which increase knowledge, exchange information, and give information on examples of good results ('best practice'). Since this procedure does not provide for the power or the obligation to give recommendations and guidelines, as is the case with the OMC in employment, the OMC in social inclusion (and other OMCs in areas other than employment) are sometimes called OMC light.

4. EXAMPLES OF THE GUIDELINES AND RECOMMENDATIONS GIVEN AS PART OF THE OMC EMPLOYMENT

In order to give a picture of the guidelines which have been issued so far and to be able to provide more material for the analysis of the OMCs vis-á-vis the functions of the legality principle, it is useful to mention some examples of the guidelines and recommendations which have been made in recent years. These examples are derived from the Employment policy guidelines (2005–2008).

General recommendations made by the Commission include recommendations, *inter alia,* to improve the adaptability of workers and enterprises and the flexibility of labour markets by promoting adaptation of employment legislation, and reviewing, where necessary, the different contractual and working time arrangements. Another recommendation is to ensure employment-friendly labour cost developments and wage-setting mechanisms by reviewing the impact on employment of non-wage labour costs and, where appropriate, adjusting their structure and level, especially to reduce the tax burden on the low-paid.

In addition to these general recommendations individual recommendations were made – that is, guidelines addressed to individual Member States.[6] These individual guidelines give more specific requirements.

One example of an individual recommendation is one recommending that a Member State reduce non-wage labour costs, in particular for the low-paid, while safeguarding budgetary consolidation efforts and removing unemployment traps by reviewing the conditionality of benefits. The Member State addressed has to implement this recommendation and it has several options in doing so. It can be easily understood that the requirements are of a highly sensitive nature, since they may involve the lowering of benefits in order to avoid employment traps, or the tightening of sanctions in the case of claimants refusing work.

Another example of a guideline with of a sensitive nature is the recommendation to remove incentives for early retirement and to review the financing of social protection systems to reduce non-wage labour costs. The recommendation to encourage the social partners to take responsibility in wage setting, putting pressure on Member States to ask social partners to reduce their wage claims in collective bargaining can be also seen as an example of a sensitive recommendation. A fourth example is the recommendation to develop temporary work agencies to increase the diversity of work arrangements. A final example is the recommendation to roll out privatization programmes. These examples will be discussed in the following section.

5. THE FUNCTIONS OF THE LEGALITY PRINCIPLE VIS-À-VIS THE OMC EMPLOYMENT

5.1. Introduction

The OMCs discussed so far are, on the one hand, a way for Member States and the European Commission to exchange information. They also promote the exchange of information between the Member States themselves, and can constitute best practice and benchmarks. However, the OMC is not simply a communication instrument, it is also a steering instrument to help reach certain objectives.[7] This double role raises the question of how the functions connected with the legality principle are respected in the OMC approach.

6. Decision (EC) 2004/740 of the Council of 4 October on guidelines for the employment policies of the Member States, OJ 2004, L 326/45.
7. B. ter Haar, 'Open Method of Coordination: A New Stepping Stone in the Legal Order of International and European Relations', *Nordic Journal of International Law* 77 (2008): 236.

Although a Member State is officially not obliged to follow a recommendation, if it does not achieve the objectives that are set, it will be confronted with the question of why it failed to do so. Moreover, there may be indirect sanctions if the recommendation is not followed. If, for instance, a Member State does not fulfil the criteria set for the employment policies in the light of EMU,[8] sanctions can be imposed on this Member State and stringent requirements can be imposed. If it is claimed that a Member State has 'even been given actual support' by the recommendation and it still does not achieve the objective, this may be an important argument for imposing sanctions. Thus, the recommendations are far from a free option for Member States.

As was already mentioned in section 1, the traditional legality principle was primarily developed in order to protect citizens against the State. In the discussion on the legality principle within the EU framework, the multilevel legal order has to be kept in mind, meaning that several addressees can be distinguished apart from the individual citizens: Member States, social partners, the Council, the Commission and the European Parliament are all stakeholders.

I will discuss the functions of the traditional legality principle according to the order mentioned in the first section of this contribution. First the OMC in employment, and in section 6 the OMC light is discussed.

5.2. Attribution of Public Authority

As we have seen in section 2.2, Article 148 TFEU gives both the legal basis for the OMC in employment and the rules for its implementation. Thus, the obligations of the Member States and the recommendations made by the Council are based on a Treaty provision. Consequently, the formal requirement that the authority is based on a statutory provision is satisfied. Still, while the Treaty regulates the method of OMC, it is silent on its contents. In section 3.2 we saw that, in respect of social policy, the Treaty provides sharp rules in several areas, whether rules with minimum requirements can be made or not (Article 153(2) TFEU). In respect of social security, for instance, such a Directive has to be adopted unanimously. In the area of combating social exclusion and the modernization of social protection systems, no minimum requirements can be made, according to Article 153(2). Some areas are explicitly excluded from making rules with minimum requirements, such as pay and the right of association.

The OMC recommendations do not take such distinctions and exclusions into account. In section 4 we saw that one of the OMC employment recommendations was to review the conditionality of benefits in order to remove unemployment traps. Although the recommendation to review the conditionality of benefits is not a minimum requirement in the sense of Article 153, there is some overlap between such a requirement and this recommendation. After all, it may mean that a Member State feels indeed obliged to change its benefit system. If the reviewing of the

8. Article 128 refers to these criteria, which themselves are laid down in Art. 99(2).

conditionality of benefits is seen as a modernization of social protection systems in the sense of Article 153, we reach an area where no powers are given for minimum requirements, but the OMC applies in this area without problems.

The recommendation to encourage social partners to take responsibility in wage setting may influence collective bargaining processes, whereas Article 153(5) provides that the provisions of this Article shall not apply to pay and the right to association (which is commonly also considered as the right to collective bargaining). There is also a discrepancy with Article 153(4) TFEU: the provisions made on the basis of Article 153 do not prevent Member States from taking or maintaining measures with a higher level of protection which is compatible with the Treaty. Although this provision concerns a Directive, it can be argued that it also applies to recommendations. After all, if a Member State yields to the pressure to lower its protection, such as lowering social benefits, we cannot say that it is not prevented from maintaining a higher level.

Of course, the recommendations are of a different nature than the minimum requirements of Article 153. Member States can still decide not to follow them, they will not have direct effect in national procedures, and they are worded in such a way that there is still much discretion to develop them. Still, they touch on areas for which either no powers exist or where there are special conditions for making rules. Moreover, so far, no use of these provisions of Article 157 has been made, since there is very little support for EU law in these areas. This places the recommendations in a special light.

The question is, therefore, whether the fact that there is a legal provision dealing with the OMC is sufficient from the attribution point of view.

Therefore we will also discuss the aspects of the attribution function, mentioned in section 1. The question of whether the OMC affects provisions of the Treaty where the powers to make instruments are exclusively reserved for the Member States can be answered in the affirmative. If a Member State could completely neglect a recommendation, it could be said that there is no interference. However, the pressure can be quite high on a Member State to take action. There may, therefore, be a possible problem with the attribution of powers. After all, the unanimity rule and the involvement of the European Parliament constitute conditions for making the 'hard rules,' and some areas are excluded from being made subject to rules, whereas recommendations are made in these very areas.

From the attribution function it also follows that procedures must hold the government and administrative authorities to account for the way they exercise their powers. For this purpose, well defined functions and powers are needed. The powers in this area are not very well defined, as the Council enjoys a large discretion in making recommendations.

5.3. The Legitimation Function

The second function of the traditional legality principle is the legitimation of public authority. This function aims to realize democracy through formal procedures and institutions involved in the legislative process. For this function a procedure is required which involves representative institutions.

In the OMC in employment the Member States, the Commission and the Council are the stakeholders. We have seen that the recommendations in the OMC and the minimum requirements which can be introduced on the basis of the Article 153 procedure overlap.

In section 1, I also mentioned that the legitimation function may require alternative forms of democracy through semi-public devolution of legislative powers to functional bodies or stakeholders in sectors of society or the economy. Article 154 and 155 TFEU can be seen as elaborating this requirement by allowing social partners to advise on proposed measures or to make agreements themselves, which can later be implemented. This involvement can be necessary in order to create a larger basis for these types of measures and to make use of the knowledge of the interests of the stakeholders involved and on the effects of the measures. By their consent, the legitimacy of the instrument is deemed to increase.

However, in respect of the OMC, the social partners are not involved in making these guidelines. Nor is the European Parliament consulted. As a result, the European Parliament plays no part in the OMC procedures and practice. Nor are commissions of Parliament and other advisory bodies involved. Thus, some stakeholders who are involved in the Article 153 procedure do not play a role in the OMC. These are, in particular, the social partners and European Parliament. Their absence in the process of making the recommendations and setting priorities within the OMC framework reduces their influence in this important area significantly.

Thus, there is a tension with the legitimation function, since the OMC is a procedure that bypasses the regular procedures, and is limited to the Council, European commission and Member State concerned, rather than involving all interested stakeholders.

5.4. The Regulatory Function

The third function of the legality principle is the regulation of the manner in which public authority is exercised. It is therefore important to consider whether there is sufficient legal certainty.

The regulatory function requires legal certainty and accessibility. There may be problems in this area when it comes to the OMC. It can happen, for instance, that a Member State takes measures in order to follow recommendations without mentioning that it is doing so. It can also say that 'we are obliged to do this by Brussels'. However, although this is a problem with transparency, the problem lies not in the fact that the recommendation has been made, but in the way Member States deal with the recommendations.

For example, a Member State introduces a higher tax rebate for persons in work in order to increase the desired difference between the net incomes for persons in work and beneficiaries, thus making work more attractive. Suppose that the government claims that it has to do this in order to satisfy a recommendation of the EU. This makes it more difficult for the national parliament concerned, as it is not presented with alternative ways of satisfying the recommendation. It could also be that the Government does not explain that this measure is taken in order to satisfy a recommendation. In this case, the exercise of power lacks transparency and the democratic process is infringed. Although the problem lies at the national level, the effect is not irrelevant. A possible solution to counter this lack of transparency could be that Member States have to account for how they present the recommendations and their response to the national parliament and social partners.

A second aspect is whether stakeholders have access to Court if they disagree with the recommendation. At first sight, the discussion on whether cases can be brought before the Court of Justice may seem somewhat theoretical – why discuss starting court procedures if only a recommendation is involved? After all, recommendations seem only to be of soft law and there are no direct consequences if they are not followed. Indeed, there are no official sanctions for disobeying them, with the effectiveness of the OMC based more on 'peer pressure' by the other members of the Council.

However, suppose that a Member State is very much opposed to a particular recommendation, since it infringes on a particular fundamental characteristic of its system. An example could be that there is a recommendation to limit considerably employment protection laws or to lower or abolish minimum wages. If a Member State wants to go to Court in order to have the recommendation quashed, first of all, it has to be decided whether the Member State is admissible. To meet this requirement, a particular act or regulation must have legal effect. In the case of a recommendation it is not impossible for the Court to find that it can cause legal effect and that the Member State concerned is admissible, but this is far from certain. For others than Member States, direct access to the Court is not available since they are not addressed directly.

If the admissibility requirement is fulfilled, the next problem is that Article 148 TFEU does not give specific criteria for the possible contents of recommendations – in other words, it does not set limits of recommendations; Article 148(4) merely mentions that a guideline can be made by the Council 'if it considers it appropriate'. This gives a very broad discretionary power. Therefore the Court of Justice does not have much room to decide that a recommendation is contrary to this Provision. Of course, the Court could, in its considerations, also take other provisions or principles into account. An interesting source of such provisions could be the Charter of Fundamental Rights of the European Union (see also Article 6 TFEU), in which fundamental rights are laid down. However, the character and the broad wording of the recommendations would make such a test very difficult. Therefore, the protection by the Court against recommendations is very weak, event though they may exert a considerable influence.

6. THE FUNCTION OF THE LEGALITY PRINCIPLE VIS-À-VIS THE OMC LIGHT

As we saw in the previous section, the OMC in employment has a legal basis in Article 128. There is no such legal basis in the Treaty for the other OMCs. The OMC in social inclusion, the OMC pensions, the OMC in healthcare and the OMC in education have their legal basis in the so-called Presidential Conclusions of the European Council. The procedures and requirements are mentioned in the Presidency Conclusions of the Lisbon Summit of 23 March 2000.[9]

The status of these Conclusions is not undisputed, since the Treaty does not give explicit powers to the Council to take decisions on 'Presidential Conclusions'. On the website of the Council, maybe as a reaction to this discussion on the legal basis, the Presidential Conclusions are preceded by a reference to Article 4 TFEU: the European Council shall provide the Union with the necessary impetus for its development and shall define the general political guidelines thereof. However, general political guidelines for the development of the Union are not exactly the same as guidelines addressed at individual Member State level. This reference does not necessarily solve the dispute. Another argument is that the European Council does not need specific powers to adopt Conclusions; this does not seem too far-fetched.[10]

The OMCs in these areas (i.e., other than the OMCs in employment) are of a more limited character than the OMC in employment. On the one hand, a 'hard law' legal basis for these are missing, such as Article 148 for the OMC in employment, but on the other, these OMCs are limited to obtaining information from Member States, analysing this information, and benchmarking it. The role of the European Commission and Council in this procedure is therefore basically a monitoring one, since in these procedures no guidelines are given by the Council.

Consequently, with respect to the products of OMC light itself, no instruments are used which require a legal basis. Nor are specific guidelines or recommendations given to the Member States as a whole or to individual Member States. The legality principle is not infringed upon from a formal point of view – that is, that measures are taken for which the Treaty does not provide any powers. After all, it is a form of law that is even softer than the OMC in employment, as no guidelines and recommendations are given. However, while monitoring and discussing the benchmarks, the European Commission has ample opportunity to promote particular policies and to persuade reluctant Member States to implement agreed policies. As in the case of the OMC in employment, the European Parliament and the Court of Justice play a very small role or no role in this process. In this respect, the same problems with the regulatory and legitimation functions apply as with the OMC in employment, although the problems are less urgent since the instruments used in this OMC are weaker.

---

9. <http://europa.eu/european-council/index_en.htm> contains the Presidency Conclusions; para. 37 of the summit of March 2000 gives the requirements mentioned in the main text.
10. L. Senden, *Soft Law in European Community Law* (Oxford: Hart Publishing, 2004), 190 ff.

7. CONCLUSIONS: THE OPEN METHOD OF COORDINATION, THE FUNCTIONS OF LEGALITY AND THE MULTIPLE LEGAL ORDER

In this contribution I discussed the OMCs in relation to the functions of the legality principle. Are these functions still guaranteed, if not by legality itself, then by other, compensating rules? In the nation-state context the legality principle means that public authority is to be exercised on the basis of an Act. The use of an Act serves several functions, discussed in section 1, which are mainly meant to protect citizens.

In the EU context the legality principle mainly means that the Member States are protected against an excessive exercise of powers by EU institutions. Indirectly, legality here is also meant to protect citizens, to the extent that EU institutions cannot deprive Member States of their rights to protect citizens.

The national and EU legal orders are multiple legal orders. They are distinct, *inter alia*, to the extent that national orders have their exclusive domains, that some powers are attributed to EU institutions and others to national institutions, and that there are also separate spheres for courts and social partners to function.

Although the requirement of a legal basis for EU instruments is thus an important element of the EU legal order and is meant to provide protection to Member States and citizens, the lack of powers at the EU level to achieve some of the objectives mentioned in the Treaty is also a serious problem. This problem has to do with the fact that although Member States wished include these objectives in the Treaty, they did and do not wish to share any of their powers in such areas. Since the objectives are mentioned in the Treaty, the European Commission can feel obliged to take measures in these areas.

In view of this division of tasks between the Member States and the EU institutions, and in view of the need to take measures in order to meet objectives for which there is no competence, the OMC is an interesting instrument: it allows measures to be taken even if there is no legal power for such actions. At first sight a confrontation with the legality principle seems a fatal one, but in view of the way the OMC is elaborated – a recommendation is made and the Member State decides on its response to the recommendation – it can be seen as a way to reconcile the lack of powers with the need to take action.

So, within the framework of the multiple legal order, bearing in mind that actions have to be taken in order to meet particular objectives of the Treaty for which insufficient powers were given, the OMC has an important function, which is also in the interest of the citizens, since they aim to meet social objectives set by the Treaty.

Given the important role of the legal basis for the division of powers within the EU framework, and since all stakeholders are very well aware of the need of such a legal basis, it is not surprising that from a formal point of view the legality principle is not infringed upon by the OMCs. There is a legal basis for the employment OMC, and in the case of the light OMCs, where such a legal basis does not exist, the actions taken do not extend to the information and consultation phase.

The next question is whether there are sufficient checks and balances in the OMC procedures. The analysis of the OMC in light of the functions of the legality principle and the comparison with the safeguards given in provisions on 'hard' rules on social policy issues showed that clarity and protection are lacking. For this reason, the study of the function of legality principle is a very useful approach, also for multilevel legal orders.

The deficiencies of the OMC are the following. First, the stakeholders who have to be involved in consultation and legislative procedures on issues of social policy (Article 153 TFEU) do not have a role in the OMC process. Second, OMC recommendations can exert considerable pressure on the Member States in areas where they have exclusive rights. Setting more precise limits to the recommendations which could be issued and legal protection is therefore desirable.

Thus, the OMC has some problematic elements, because of the lack of checks and balances that exist in the hard law procedures. The stakeholders which play a role in hard law procedures on social policy should also be given a formal place in the OMC procedure.

To conclude, in a multiple order, the OMC is a useful instrument to reconcile the gap between objectives mentioned in the Treaty and the lack of sufficient competences where Member States wish to remain (exclusively) competent. The analysis from the point of view of the legality principle also shows the weak elements of the OMC. Insufficient checks and balances are guaranteed in the procedure, in any case in respect of the OMC in employment, since not all stakeholders are involved. If these stakeholders were involved, the at times far-reaching recommendations that touch on the limits set by the Treaty would sit better in the multi-level legal order.

Chapter 10

The Principle of Legality and the 'Soft Law' Regulation and Supervision of Financial Markets

Ton Duijkersloot

1. INTRODUCTION

This essay is about the principle of legality and the regulation and supervision of financial markets. More specifically, it is about soft law instruments that regulatory authorities have developed in order to achieve the policy goals that are behind this regulation of financial markets. Soft law instruments are developed on various levels. This essay deals with the instruments that have been developed at a global level, at a European Union (EU) level and at a national level, that is, the case of the Netherlands. The main question that will be addressed is how the use of these soft law instruments in this field matches with the legality principle. Firstly, some theoretical questions will be addressed: what do we mean by soft law? What is the essence of the legality principle? Why are financial markets the subject of supervision and regulation by hard law as well as soft law (section 2)? In section 3, soft law instruments developed at the various levels will be mapped out. Most of these instruments will be discussed in general, with one exception: last year's Memorandum of Understanding (MoU) on Cooperation between the Financial Supervisory Authorities, Central Banks and Finance Ministries of the EU on cross-border financial stability will be discussed in more detail, in order to make

Leonard Besselink, Frans Pennings & Sacha Prechal (eds), *The Eclipse of the Legality Principle in the European Union*, pp. 169–186.

analysis form a legality point a view a fruitful one. Finally, section 4 will provide this analysis and will deal with aspects concerning the relationship between this soft law regulation and the legality principle.

2. SOME THEORETICAL QUESTIONS: RATIONALES FOR REGULATION OF FINANCIAL MARKETS, SOFT LAW AND THE LEGALITY PRINCIPLE

2.1. The Rationales behind Regulation of Financial Markets

An essay about the legality principle and the relationship with soft law, and the regulation and supervision of financial markets raises a few basic but important questions.

The first question is why regulate financial markets? In other words, what are the objectives of financial market regulation? The basic economic rationale for regulating financial markets is quite straightforward. There can be externalities generated by financial market activity, which are not easily capable of being addressed by private sector actors.[1] In policy terms, the objectives of financial regulation can be regrouped under three core objectives[2]:

(1) the objective of systemic stability;
(2) the prudential objective;
(3) the objective of insuring appropriate business conduct.

The first objective aims to ensure the overall safety of the financial system, including the reliability of the payments system; this is traditionally the role of the central bank. The second objective aims at maintaining the safety and soundness of the individual supervised firms in order to protect customers and investors from the consequences of a firm's insolvency. This is the primary objective of the traditional banking and insurance supervisors. The 'conduct of business' objective aims at protecting individual investors dealing with supervised firms of supervised products against the dangers of market misconduct, information asymmetries and unfairness in contractual relations. Here the securities supervisor comes first in line, but *ex ante* rules regarding individual customer protection are also found in insurance regulation and banking regulation.

A second question with regard to financial market regulation has to do with the use of the concept of 'regulation' on the one hand, and 'supervision' on the other. Although the terminology is often mixed and confused, there are good reasons for distinguishing regulation from supervision. The former relates to the formulation of rules and behind these, the setting of the policies on which these

1. H. Davies & D. Green, *Global Financial Regulation* (Cambridge: Polity Press, 2008), 12–13.
2. E. Wymeersch, Cooperation between Authorities in the Community; The Case of Banking, Insurance and Securities Supervision, <www.law.yale.edu/documents/pdf/cbl/2-6Panel2-WYMEERSCH.pdf>, 1 Feb. 2010.

rules are based.[3] The second relates to the implementation of the rules and of the general principles underlying the rules. Regulation and supervision consist of different levels of abstraction: while the central rulemaking takes place by bodies that do not directly deal with individual cases and therefore formulate rules in abstract terms, the second level essentially deals with the actual implementation of the rules *vis à vis* regulated firms and transactions. When talking about the legality principle in section 2.3, the relevance of this distinction will be further elaborated upon.

Finally, it is of importance to introduce the much-debated difference between rules-based and principles-based regulation or supervision. First, there is the much-debated trend towards so-called 'principles-based supervison'.[4] In general terms, principles-based supervision can be described as moving away from relying on detailed, prescriptive rules, and relying more on high-level, broadly stated rules or principles to set the standards by which regulated firms must conduct business.[5] Various countries have, in recent years, embraced this concept. The reason for this acceptance is described by the British supervisory authority – the Financial Services Authority (FSA) – as follows:

> Past experience suggests to us that prescriptive standards have been unable to prevent misconduct. The ever-expanding rule books of our predecessor bodies and our consolidated Handbook, designed to prevent misdemeanour, have not stopped further misselling, market misconduct or other detriment. Instead we believe that detailed rules have become an increasing burden on our own and the industry's resources. Financial markets are constantly changing. Continuous innovation and new product development are important ways in which the financial services industry generates benefits for consumers and markets. It is important that regulation can respond rapidly to the pace of change in markets and so allow them to continue to develop for the benefit of their users. We believe regulation that focuses on outcomes rather than prescription is more likely to support this development and innovation. Any set of prescriptive rules is unable to address changing market circumstances and practices at all times, and it inevitably delays, and in some instances prevents, innovation. In a quickly changing marketplace, principles are far more durable. The complexity of a very prescriptive regime with thousands of detailed rules is also likely to make it inaccessible to many firms' senior management. Particularly for smaller firms, who do not generally have access to deep compliance or legal expertise, the amount of detailed rules can be bewildering.

3. See Wymeersch, 'Cooperation between Authorities in the Community', 2.
4. See J. Black, M. Hopper & C. Band, 'Making a Success of Principles-based Regulation', *Law and Financial Markets Review* 5 (2007): 191–206; J. Black, *Forms and Paradoxes of Principles Based Regulation*, LSE Law, Society and Economy Working Papers 13/2008; L.H. Hoogduin, V.N.G. van Leeuwen & E.J. Weller, 'Minder en Europeser is beter: naar een ander toezicht', *Tijdschrift voor Compliance* (2008): 245–253.
5. J. Black, M. Hopper & C. Band, 'Making a success of Principles-based regulation', 191.

> Finally, a large volume of detailed, prescriptive and highly complex rules can divert attention towards adhering to the letter, rather than the purpose of our regulatory standards. This would make it less likely that we will achieve our regulatory goals. For these reasons, we believe that further enhancing our risk-based and evidence-based approach to regulation with an increased emphasis on principles and outcomes is not only the right but also the only way to progress our regulatory regime. We have already made some important steps in this direction. Progressively over the next few years we intend to do more.

The EC Commission was also trumpeting the benefits of a principles-based approach. In the words of EC commissioner McCreevy:

> As European commissioner in this area, my approach is simple: We should not and cannot prescribe rules for every conceivable situation. There is a difference between accountancy and rocket science. The latter is science; the former is not and shouldn't be. Regulation must allow and encourage new ideas and innovation. As an accountant by profession, I might be expected to empathise with the urge some regulators seem to have to control every detail. But I think that box-ticking alone doesn't work. We need responsible judgment and disclosure.
>
> This is why I strongly favour a principles-based over a rules-based approach. Eliminating all risk is an illusion and will lead to unwanted consequences: less innovation and growth, a false sense of security, and reduced pressure to behave responsibly. That is, why I reject the siren calls for tougher regulation of hedge funds in Europe and why I strongly agree with the recent report of the President's Working Group on this issue. We must not endanger the benefits hedge funds and private equity have brought. They have increased efficiency and liquidity in our capital markets while keeping company managers on their toes. Are the regulatory hawks perhaps trying to protect weak management from shareholder activism? What the EU and U.S. both need is top-class regulation based on best practice – sound investor protection, balanced with a good dose of freedom for market participants. But if we want to have competitive and open capital markets in the U.S. and EU, we need to do something else: cooperate. We need to build on the regulatory pillars of the U.S., EU and other mature economies, based on equivalent but not identical standards that work for our investors and our markets.

These statements proclaiming the values and advantages of principles-based supervision have their origin only two or three years ago. With the recent developments in financial markets and the role of supervisors in mind, they are quite remarkable, and it seems very clear that these market developments will have a severe impact on this trend towards this principles-based supervision.[6]

6. See J. Black, 'Forms and Paradoxes of Principles Based Regulation', 1–7.

2.2. Soft Law

In the process of regulation and supervision of financial markets, soft law plays an important role. In section 3, the most important soft law instruments at a global, EU and state level will be mapped out.

An important question that has to be answered in advance is: what is meant by 'soft law'? In a very general sense, soft law is a phenomenon that is, especially common in international law. It is undisputed that historically, there are two main sources of international law: treaties and customary law. Soft law is a third source of international law that has developed rapidly in recent decades, especially to deal with sensitive matters such as human rights, the protection of the environment, bioethical issues and also financial market regulation. The category of soft law includes a great variety of instruments: declarations, recommendations, charters, resolutions, et al. Soft law agreements are often defined, as opposed to treaties, as non-binding instruments.[7] This non-binding character has often raised the question as to whether soft law is, in fact, non-law.[8] On the other hand, one can argue that soft law does establish quasi-legal rules that can affect state behaviour. As Senden has pointed out with respect to the use of the term 'soft law' in Community law, this concept of 'soft law' is used in many contexts, and for a huge variety of instruments.[9] She makes clear that in the context of the EC, legal writing points to three core elements of soft law.[10] The first element is that it is concerned with 'rules of conduct' or 'commitments'. Secondly, there is agreement on the fact that these rules or commitments are laid down in instruments that are not legally binding as such, but are, however, not devoid of all legal effect. Thirdly, they aim at, or may lead to, some practical effect or impact on behaviour. On the basis of these elements, Senden proposes the following definition of soft law: Rules of conduct that are laid down in instruments which have not been attributed legally binding force as such, but nevertheless may have certain – indirect – legal effects, and that are aimed at and may produce practical effects.[11] In this study this definition of soft law will be used.

7. See R. Adorno, 'The Invaluable Role of Soft Law in the Development of Universal Norms in Bioethics', <www.unesco.de/1507.html>, 1 Feb. 2010.
8. A. D'Amato, 'International Soft Law, Hard Law, and Coherence', <http://ssrn.com/abstract=1103915>, 1 Feb. 2010. See also T. Meyer, 'Soft Law as Delegation', <http://ssrn.com/abstract=1214422>, 1 Feb. 2010.
9. See L. Senden, 'Soft law, Self-regulation and Co-regulation in European Law: Where do they meet?', *Electronic Journal of Comparative Law* 9, no. 1 (2005): 22.
10. Ch.-A. Morand, 'Les recommandations, les résolutions et les avis du droit communautaire', *Cahiers Droit Européen* 6 (1970): 623; D. Thürer, 'The Role of Soft Law in the Actual Process of European Integration', in: *L'avenir du libre-échange en Europe. Vers un espace économique européen?*, ed. O. Jacot-Guillarmod & P. Pescatore (Zürich Schultess Polygraphischer Verlag, 1990), 131; G. Borchardt & K. Wellens, 'Soft Law in European Community Law', *European Law Review* 5 (1989): 267; F. Snyder, 'Soft Law and Institutional Practice in the European Community', in: *The Construction of Europe: Essays in Honour of Emile Noël*, ed. S. Martin (Dordrecht: Kluwer Academic Publishers, 1994), 197.
11. See in more detail, L. Senden, *Soft Law in European Community Law* (Oxford: Hart Publishing, 2004), 111–113.

2.3. The Legality Principle and Financial Supervisory Authorities

The view that is, traditionally held in the Netherlands with regard to the legality principle is that the formulation of rules is ideally dealt with by organs of the state that are part of the legislative power. Other authorities, for instance supervisory authorities, only have the power to formulate rules if the legislative authorities have specifically empowered them to do so. The reason behind this is, as is quite generally accepted, the fact that supervisory authorities have very limited democratic legitimacy. They are only indirectly controlled by parliament.[12] This is reflected in the 'Directions for legislation' – important rules formulated by the Prime Minister that should be taken into account during the process of making legislation. Direction 124f makes clear that the power to formulate general rules (legislation) should be attributed to so-called independent agencies (e.g., supervisory authorities dealing with financial markets) only as far as organizational and technical matters are concerned, or in exceptional cases and only if a ministerial power to approve these rules is provided for. More generally, independent agencies, supervisory authorities included, should, according to the Dutch government, only have limited discretionary power. Policy frameworks and legal norms have to be formulated by the legislator and have to be sufficiently explicit.[13] Recent developments in the Netherlands show that supervisory authorities have a tendency to test the limits of their (restricted) legislative powers. This will be further dealt with in section 3.3. It illustrates very clearly that supervisory authorities would like to have the power themselves to formulate rules. Although from a theoretical point of view those powers are, or at least should be, limited, one has to say that there are reasons for defending the argument that legislating by the supervisory authorities should be less restricted. It is of paramount importance that rulemaking remains directly linked to actual supervisory practice, by being undertaken by the practitioners responsible for supervision, and directly confronted with the experiences of the supervision of the regulated firms or practices.

This concept of legality is specific to the Dutch context.[14] In the introductory chapter of this book some important issues regarding the legality principle were dealt with in a more general way. Three typical functions of the legality principle are discerned: legitimation of public authority, attribution of public authority to designed public authorities, and regulation of the manner in which public authority is to be exercised. In more general terms, not typically dealing with the Dutch situation, we might describe the legality principle as follows. As is well known, the essence of a state – or any other entity vested with the exercise of government power based on the

12. See L.F.M. Verhey & N. Verheij, 'De macht van de marktmeesters', paper for the NJV 2005-1, 202 and S. Zijlstra, *Zelfstandige bestuursorganen in een democratische rechtsstaat* (The Hague: VUGA, 1997), 124–125 and 128–129.
13. Kaderstellende visie op toezicht, Dutch Ministry of Internal Affairs, 2005, 12.
14. See J. Schwarze, *European Administrative Law*, revised 1st ed. (London: Sweet & Maxwell, 2006), 227 et seq.

rule of law – is that government action is bound by the law. This can be said to require, on the one hand, governing *sub lege* and, on the other, governing *per legem*.[15] Governing *sub lege* does not only mean governing on the basis of the law, that is, that there is a competence-conferring legal basis, but it also means governing within the boundaries of the law – that is, in conformity with certain principles on which a constitutional state is based and which indicate the limits to the powers to be exercised, with a view to ensuring the freedom and liberty of citizens. Governing *per legem* means that power should be exercised through the adoption of laws, *inter alia*, with a view to ensuring legal certainty and equality. In section 4, how the use of various soft law instruments in financial market regulation and supervision on a global, EU and national level relates to this concept of legality will be analysed.

3. SOFT LAW INSTRUMENTS AND FINANCIAL MARKETS

3.1. Global

The most important 'soft law' instruments with regard to financial market regulation are the so-called Basel Accords.[16] The Basel Accords are the product of the Basel Committee on Banking Supervision, an institution created in 1974 by the central bank governors of the world's ten most financially developed nations after the famous Herstatt affair. This collapse of the West German Bankhaus Herstatt uncovered uncertainty about which supervisory authority, if any, was responsible for the foreign operations of a bank, and what that responsibility entailed. This was the main reason for introducing this formally arranged Basel Committee. This Committee set out to close some gaps in the supervisory network and agreed upon the so-called Basel 'Concordat' in 1975. In the 1980s the Basel I Accord was agreed upon. This contained a set of capital adequacy standards that govern how national regulators do their jobs. Because competition for financial resources is fierce between countries, there is enormous domestic pressure on governments to loosen regulatory restrictions on their financial institutions. In order to combat this 'race to the bottom', this set of capital adequacy standards was deemed necessary. In other words, international regulatory standards circumscribe the freedom of national regulators in national markets. Since 1988, this framework has been progressively introduced in member countries of G-10, currently comprising thirteen countries, namely, Belgium, Canada, France, Germany, Italy, Japan, Luxemburg, Netherlands, Spain, Sweden, Switzerland, United

15. See L. Senden, 'Soft law, Self-regulation and Co-regulation in European Law: Where do they meet?', *Electronic Journal of Comparative Law* 9, no. 1 (2005), referring to H. Gribnau, 'Legaliteit en legitimiteit. Fiscale rechtsvorming in de democratische rechtsstaat', *Nederlands Tijdschrift voor Bestuursrecht* 1, no. 1 (2001): 16.
16. See S. Emmenegger, 'The Basle Committee on Banking Supervision: A Secretive Club of Giants?', in: *The Regulation of International Financial Markets*, ed. R. Grote & T. Marauhn (Cambridge University Press, 2006), 224 et seq.

Kingdom and the United States of America.[17] Since the Basel I Accord was agreed upon, there has been a process of continuing periodic amendment to take account of the evolution of the markets. In 1998 the Basel Committee decided to reform earlier arrangements. Finally, in 2004 this resulted in the Basel II Accord. The objective of the Basel II Accord was to strengthen the soundness and stability of the international banking system, while maintaining sufficient consistency in order that capital adequacy regulation will not be a significant source of competitive inequality among internationally active banks. They rest on three pillars:

(1) minimum capital requirements;
(2) supervisory review, which includes an assessment of the quality of a bank's systems, controls and risk management; and
(3) market discipline, with rules on disclosure and transparency.

At least one hundred countries intend to implement Basel II, at varying dates.[18] The status of the Basel Accords as soft law is undisputed.[19] Of course, it is important to note the fact that the Accords acquire binding force and become 'hard law' in the process of their implementation into national law. As we will see in the next section, as far as the EU countries are concerned, this process takes place through the adoption of EU Directives implementing the Basel Accords in the EU.

3.2. European Union

In the EU, financial market regulation has been dealt with since the 1970s. The main instrument that has been used is the EC Directive. If we want to have any grip on the *mer a boire* of Directives and other legal instruments that have been developed over the last twenty years, a distinction should be made between, on the one hand, the prudential projects in banking, insurance and conglomerates – especially the banking Capital Requirements Directive, the insurance Solvency II project and the Financial Groups Directive for mixed conglomerates – and those aimed at the conduct of business in capital markets and investment services – that is, the MIFID Directive and the Transparancy Directive.[20]

As far as soft law is concerned, first it can be remarked that there has been a development of particular interest with regard to EC Directives. As mentioned before, soft law norms can 'harden'. Market practices can be given judicial

17. Meyer, 'Soft Law as Delegation', 5.
18. Davies & Green, *Global Financial Regulation*, 45. See also about Basel I and II, Bryan J. Balin, 'Basel I, Basel II, and Emerging Markets: A Nontechnical Analysis', <https://jscholarship.library.jhu.edu>.
19. See A.O. Lawrence L.C. Lee, 'The Basle Accords as Soft Law: Strengthening International Banking Supervision', *Virginia Journal of International Law* 39 (1998): 1 et seq.; Franz-Christoph Zeitler, 'Internationale Entwicklungslinien der Bankenaufsicht', *Zeitschrift für Wirtschafts- und Bankrecht* (2001): 1397 et seq., both cited by Emmenegger, 'The Basle Committee on Banking Supervision: A Secretive Club of Giants?', 233–234.
20. See Davies & Green, *Global Financial Regulation*, 133–135.

recognition, or can be incorporated into national legal systems. In this respect, it is important to take note of the fact that the EC Capital Adequacy Directive is the 'hardening' of the Basel II Capital Accord by the EU.[21] Where Dutch law is concerned, the so-called 'Besluit Basel 2' subsequently transformed those rules into 'hard' Dutch law.[22]

A second remark is related to soft law norms at the EU level itself. We can make a distinction between different categories. First, we have soft law norms agreed upon by various *public authorities*, an example being the use of so-called MoUs – Memoranda of Understanding between supervisory authorities. One example of an approach based on voluntary cooperation and soft law is the important upgraded MoUon Cooperation between the Financial Supervisory Authorities, Central Banks and Finance Ministries of the European Union on Cross-Border Financial Stability (published 20 June 2008).[23] This memorandum updates a 2005 MoU, and it is based on the realization that financial integration increases the scope for cross-border and cross-sector contagion and thus the likelihood of a systemic crisis affecting more than one Member State. Financial stability is, therefore, a common concern for all Member States and the EU as a whole, and must be safeguarded on the basis of close cooperation between all parties. The objective of the MoU is to ensure cooperation in financial crises between financial supervisory authorities, central banks and finance ministries, through appropriate procedures for the sharing of information and assessments, in order to facilitate the pursuance of their respective policy functions and to preserve stability of the financial system of individual Member States and of the EU as a whole. The legal status of this MoU is, according to the MoU itself, clear. Article 10.1 reads that 'as the provisions of this Memorandum are not legally binding on the parties, they may not give rise to any legal claim on behalf of any party or third parties in the course of their practical implementation'. Nevertheless, a closer look at the MoU may cast some doubt on this 'informal' character. The parties to this MoU agree upon various obligations. They agree to follow a set of common principles in the management of any cross-border financial crisis which involves at least one banking group that: (i) has substantial cross-border activities; and (ii) is facing severe problems which are expected to trigger systemic effects in at least one Member State; and (iii) is assessed to be at risk of becoming insolvent (Article 2). These principles contain among others:

- that the objective of crisis management is to protect the stability of the financial system in all countries involved and in the EU as a whole and to minimize potential harmful economic impacts at the lowest overall collective cost;
- that in a crisis situation, primacy will always be given to private sector solutions which, as far as possible, will build on the financial situation of a banking group as a whole;

---

21. See. J. Black & D. Rouch, 'The Development of the Global Markets as Rule-makers: Engagement and Legitimacy', *Law and Financial Markets Review* (May 2008): 224.
22. Stb. 2006, 662.
23. <www.ecb.europa.eu/pub/pdf/other/mou-financialstability2008en.pdf>.

- that the use of public money to resolve a crisis can never be taken for granted and will only be considered to remedy a serious disturbance in the economy and when overall social benefits are assessed to exceed the cost of recapitalization at public expense. Strict and uniform conditions shall be applied to any use of public money;
- that managing a cross-border financial crisis is a matter of common interest for all Member States affected. Where a bank group has significant cross-border activities in different Member States, authorities in these countries will carefully cooperate and prepare in normal times as much as possible for sharing a potential fiscal burden; and
- that arrangements and tools for cross-border crisis management will be designed flexibly to allow for adapting to the specific features of a financial crisis, individual institutions, balance sheet items and markets.

Various cooperation arrangements have also been agreed upon (Article 3). Rules with regard to the activation of procedures and responsibility for coordination in a cross-border crisis are laid down (Article 4). The party who becomes aware of the emergence of a potentially serious financial disturbance will inform, as soon as is practicable, the National Coordinator or the Cross-Border Coordinator. The National Coordinator or the Cross-Border Coordinator will ensure that information will be shared among the relevant parties. Similarly, a request for information or assessment from one relevant party to another will be promptly considered and fulfilled to the maximum extent possible without delay (Article 4.1). Also, as a rule, the National Coordinator of the home country assumes the task of Cross-Border Coordinator in the management of a cross-border financial crisis. The Cross-Border Coordinator may delegate tasks to authorities in a host country (Article 4.4). Rules concerning the exchange of information (Article 5) and public communication (Article 6) have been agreed upon. Also, the parties will endeavour to conduct, as part of contingency arrangements for managing crisis situations, stress-testing and simulation exercises (Article 7). Arrangements about confidentiality have also been made (Article 8).

All these commitments on coordination, secrecy and so on, raise the question of how such an MoU should be considered from a legality point of view. This question will be dealt with further in section 4.

It is interesting to see that within the EU, occasionally MoUs are agreed upon by only some of the Member States. Recently, for instance, the Dutch supervisory authorities (DNB and AFM), together with the British supervisor (FSA), signed an MoU on cooperation for the supervision of so-called clearing service providers.[24] This MoU came into force on 24 April 2009. Its purpose is to facilitate cooperation between the Dutch Authorities and the FSA in order to promote effective supervision by those authorities of clearing service providers regulated principally in either the Netherlands or the UK and operating in each other's jurisdiction, and to reduce any regulatory overlap. It is stated expressly that it does not modify or

24. <www.afm.nl/marktpartijen/upl_documents/mou_centrale_tegenpartijen.pdf>.

supersede any law or regulatory requirements in force in the Netherlands and the UK, and that it is not intended to create any binding legal obligations or to fetter the discretion of the authorities in any way in the discharge of their functions. MoUs are also agreed upon by some of the EU Member States and non-member countries. An interesting example is last year's MoU between the Netherlands and Iceland that had the purpose of limiting the damage suffered by Dutch savers due to the Icesave bankruptcy.[25]

Another category of soft law is soft law norms accorded by *private parties*. An example is the European Code of Conduct on Clearing and Settlement 2006.[26] This Code had been agreed upon by exchanges, clearing houses and central securities depositories, represented by the Federation of European Securities Exchanges (FESE), the European Association of Central Counterparty Clearing Houses (EACH) and the European Central Securities Depositories Association (ECSDA), who share the objective of achieving greater efficiency and further integration of European capital markets. The objective of the Code of Conduct – in line with the objectives of the European Commission – is therefore to allow investors to trade European securities within a consistent, coherent and cost-efficient European framework. It covers areas such as price transparency (to help customers understand and compare prices and services), standard unilateral access between organizations and interoperability (to enhance the ability of organizations to interconnect and ultimately increase freedom of choice for market participants), and service unbundling and accounting separation (to facilitate competition, increase customer choice and provide relevant information on the services provided).

The third category of soft law is what I might call the *institutional* category. This has to do with all kinds of norms, recommendations, guidelines et al., stipulated by European organizations which were created at the EU level after the famous Lamfalussy report.[27] Historically, banking supervisors in the EU have been meeting informally since the 1970s (the so-called 'Groupe de Contact'). This informal contact has now been formalized and extended to securities and insurance supervisors, and has led to a quite complicated web of committees with various tasks. There is the Committee of European Securities Supervisors (CESR), the Committee of European Insurance and Occupational Pension Supervisors (CEIOPS) and the Committee of European Banking Supervisors (CEBS). CEBS and CEIOPS have jointly constructed an Interim Working Committee on Financial Conglomerates (IWCFC) and a European Group of Audit Oversight Bodies (EGAOB) has also been set up. The fact that, for instance, in mid-2007 the CESR had no fewer than nine subgroups, makes it easy to understand that there has been growing pressure form market parties for simplification.[28]

25. MoU of 11 Oct. 2008. See about this MoU the *Icesave* judgment of the Council of State of 22 Apr. 2009, JB 2009/144.
26. Agreed on 7 Nov. 2006.
27. Final Report of the Committee of Wise Men on the Regulation of European Securities Markets, European Commission, 2001.
28. Davies & Green, *Global Financial Regulation*, 148.

3.3. The Netherlands

Let us conclude this overview of soft law norms in the financial market area at global, EU and state level, with some remarks about soft law norms at state level in the Netherlands. Of course, especially at this level, many norms have been laid down in 'hard law' like primary legislation (the Financial Supervision Act; Wet op het financieel toezicht (Wft)) and secondary legislation (amvb's and ministerial regulations) based upon this act. The supervisory authorities themselves (AFM and DNB), according to the Wft, also have the power to issue formal rules that market parties should obey. An example is the 'Nadere regeling gedragstoezicht financiële ondernemingen Wft'.[29] In this regulation, the AFM lays down many detailed rules with respect to the conduct of financial market parties, for instance, with regard to advertising, the financial information leaflet (financiele bijsluiter), and prospectuses *etc.*

One could question whether these rules are in line with the starting point discussed in section 2.3 – only as far as organizational and technical matters are concerned, or in exceptional cases, and only if a ministerial power to approve these rules is provided for – and one could also discern a tendency by supervisory authorities to extend their competences. This is illustrated by a recent discussion about restricting financial companies from offering certain hazardous mortgage contracts (tophypotheken). The Dutch supervisor (AFM) had the intention of doing so – its chairman Hoogervorst mentioned this during the presentation of the AFM annual report on 21 April 2009[30] – but in my point of view it was, and is, very questionable as to whether there is a legal basis for such a measure in Dutch law, especially the Wft. According to the Dutch government also, such a legal basis is lacking. Only a prohibition in individual cases falls within the competence of the AFM.[31]

One has to say though, that it is not only the supervisory authorities themselves who are to blame in exploring the limits of their competences. This is clearly illustrated by the example of the recent legislation issued by the Dutch government in reaction to the financial crisis that dramatically deepened with the fall of Lehman Brothers in September 2008. Within a period of ten days, from a proposal of 1 October 2008 to the coming into force on 10 October 2008, an amendment of Article 1:28 Wft was implemented, according to which, the supervisory authorities AFM and DNB were entrusted with new regulatory powers for 'special circumstances'.[32] Even more questionable is the fact that this amendment was applied retroactively, from January 2008 and even partly from January 2007. The main purpose of this amendment was to provide a legal base for the measure taken by the

29. Most recent version 1 Apr. 2009, Stcrt. 2009, 25.
30. <www.fd.nl/artikel/11451432/afm-maak-einde-tophypotheek>.
31. <www.nrc.nl/economie/article2221949.ece/De_Jager_AFM_kan_tophypotheken_niet_verbieden>.
32. Act of 9 Oct. 2008, Stb. 2008, 394. See D. Doornbos, 'Crisiswetgeving: blanco cheques voor toezichthouders', *Nederlands Juristenblad* (2008): 2360–2361.

AFM in September 2008 to prohibit so called naked short selling.[33] The tension with the legality principle in general, and the specific implementation thereof in the Dutch context, especially Directive 124f, is undeniable.

Besides the formal rules (legislation), rules of conduct are laid down in instruments that have not been attributed legally binding force as such, but nevertheless may have certain (indirect) legal effects, and are aimed at and may produce practical effects. An important category is the so-called policy rules. These are somewhere in between hard law and soft law. They are not legislation as such, but contain some elements that have a resemblance to legislation. The non-legislative character becomes clear even from the definition of a 'policy rule' in Article 1:3, fourth indent, of the General Administrative Law Act (GALA): a policy rule means an order, *not being a generally binding regulation*, which lays down a general rule for weighing interests, determining facts or interpreting statutory regulations in the exercise of a power of an administrative authority. The similarities to legislation are also clearly present. According to Article 4:84 of the GALA, the administrative authority shall, in principle, act in accordance with the policy rule. This might only be different if, due to special circumstances, the consequences for one or more interested parties would be out of proportion with the purposes of the policy rule. Further, according to Article 4:82 GALA, for authorities who want to explain the reasons for an order, it is sufficient to refer to a fixed practice, in so far as this practice is contained in a policy rule. One might also keep in mind that some decades ago, the first examples of policy rules were called 'pseudo-legislation'. The aforementioned definition of policy rules also makes clear that there are various types of policy rules: rules with regard to: (i) weighing interests; (ii) determining facts; and (iii) interpreting legislation. They are frequently used by the Dutch supervisory authorities.[34] Sometimes they are explicitly called 'policy rules' (beleidsregels). Important examples are the 'Policy rule on integrity testing' and the 'Policy rule on the expertise requirements for company directors.'[35]

Because of the fact that the labelling of a certain recommendation, guideline, et al. as a policy rule is not decisive for the policy rule character of that instrument (this character has to be established according to the aforementioned definition in Article 1:3 GALA), it is interesting to point at the various recommendations, guidelines et al. that Dutch supervisory authorities have issued. An interesting example of such an instrument can be found in the practice of the so called 'interpretations'. The AFM regularly publishes its views about the interpretation of laws and regulations on the AFM website. By doing so, market parties are provided with an insight into the vision of the AFM as far as those subjects are concerned. The AFM, through its contacts with the market parties, lawyers, et al., establishes which subjects need interpretation. As the AFM puts it, those interpretations do not provide any rights and are not binding. One might ask though, whether these

33. See Annual Report DNB (2008): 208.
34. See *Besluit tot vaststelling beleidsregels in het kader van de Wet op het financieel toezicht*, Stcrt. 2006, 251,42.
35. Stcrt. 2004, 74 and 2008, 69.

'interpretations' should not be regarded as the aforementioned third category of policy rules: policy rules with regard to the interpretation of legislation. That would have as a consequence that, according to Article 4:82 and 4:84 GALA, they would have, at least, some binding aspects.

Finally, an example of the use of soft law is the AFM Recommendation transparency investment institutions ('Aanbeveling transparantie beleggingsinstellingen').[36] With this recommendation, the AFM asks all investment institutions to verify that websites, prospects and financial information leaflets comply with legislation and, if necessary, to adapt these as soon as possible. The AFM will monitor this in the future, so the recommendation concludes.

4. FINANCIAL MARKET REGULATION, SOFT LAW INSTRUMENTS AND THE LEGALITY PRINCIPLE: A FURTHER ANALYSIS

The main question that is, at the heart of the relationship between the use of soft law and the legality principle in financial market regulation is whether this use of soft law matches with the legality principle, or whether there are tensions between both. As made clear already (section 2.3), three typical functions of the legality principle can be discerned: legitimation of public authority, attribution of public authority to designed public authorities, and regulation of the manner in which public authority is to be exercised.

First, some remarks about 'hard law' regulation of financial markets and the legality principle. In section 2.1 it was indicated that in the last five years there has been a tendency towards a principles-based regulation and supervision of financial markets. From a legality point of view, this trend is somewhat problematic. These problems are on the one hand connected to the aspect of the attribution of public authority (competences), and also to the aspect of regulation of those competences. Open norms with vague terms leave much discretion to the supervisory authorities to interfere in the market. This approach has the advantage of having the ability to adapt quickly to changes in market processes, but the disadvantage from a legality point of view is quite clearly the lack of a clear-cut competence for the supervisory authorities. Legality problems arise especially with regard to the sanctioning of market parties who do not obey these 'open norms'. Very often the competences to apply sanctions are connected to the question of whether a certain legal rule has been infringed. Because of the vague and open character of this legal rule in a system of principles-based supervision, the answer to this question is not always very clear and straightforward. This leads to a situation in which supervisory authorities are attributed with rather undefined competences to sanction market parties. This results in the risk of these competences being used in an arbitrary way. And, as we all know, it was precisely this arbitrary use of powers that the legality principle was meant to protect against. Fortunately, at least from the legality point

36. <www.afm.nl/marktpartijen/default.ashx?DocumentId=10349>.

of view, market events during the last two years have uncovered the risks of this principles-based regulation and have moderated the trend towards this regulation and supervision to a certain extent.

Now some remarks about soft law, the legality principle and financial market regulation. How do these elements match? It has become clear that various soft law instruments are used in financial market regulation and supervision: on an international level, agreements like the Basel Accords and MoUs between supervisory authorities, and on a national (Dutch) level, instruments like policy rules and recommendations. The Basel Accords have been transformed into 'hard' law by EU directives (especially the Capital Adequacy Directive) and national (Dutch) legislation (The 'Besluit Basel II'). From a legality point of view, there is no problem. Legitimation of public authority, attribution of public authority to designed public authorities and regulation of the manner in which public authority is to be exercised have been taken care of by these hard law rules.

On a national (Dutch) level I have indicated that there are various soft law instruments used by the supervisory authorities. Questions might be raised about their non-binding character. We have focused attention on the instrument of policy rules that is, frequently used. We have made clear that this instrument has certain important binding aspects. Instruments that do not have the policy rule label also might be policy rules according to the definition in Article 1:3 GALA. This might be the case with certain 'interpretations' issued by the AFM and DNB. These 'interpretations' are said to be non-binding. Because of the fact that they might be seen as policy rules with regard to the interpretation of legislation – one of the various types of policy rules according to Article 1:3 GALA – this non-binding character might be questioned. We have also witnessed a tendency by legislator and supervisory authorities to stretch the limits of their competences. Of course, in many cases these practices are triggered by market events and are deemed necessary 'in the general interest'. A key element of the legality principle, especially as it is understood in Dutch law, is that rules and decisions have a specific basis in legislation. Especially as far as the regulatory capacity of the AFM and DNB is concerned, a general consensus laid down in the 'Directives for drafting legislation' (Article 124f), is that only technical rules fall within their competences. The new, very broad Article 1:28 Wft does not conform with this Directive. Of course, the major crisis in the financial markets was the impetus for this law, but, it is questionable whether this is a legitimate reason to set aside the legality principle.

As far as the frequently used MoUs are concerned, some questions concerning legality can also be raised. One point of view could be that, although these instruments have no binding force as such, they might very well be of relevance for supervisory authorities in developing policies and even taking decisions. One has to say though, that it is difficult to pinpoint this influence more specifically. One of the features of MoUs is that, in contrast to treaties, they do not have to be published and ratified. Democratic control and influence of elected bodies is difficult. Confidentiality is sometimes even a reason to opt for using the MoU instrument. From a legality point of view, this causes doubts: if it is correctly assumed that, at least de facto, these soft law rules influence the behaviour of public authorities but the precise impact of the rules is not fully clear, this calls into question important legality aspects. One could say that certain aspects of the exercise of public authority by supervisory authorities in financial markets are being 'regulated' or at least influenced by MoU soft law. According to the principle of legality, such regulation should be done by law itself because of the demands of legal certainty and the *ex ante* influence of parliament. Even if the assumption is not correct, or only partly so, the sheer existence of these instruments and their assumed influence on supervisory behaviour puts this legal certainty into question. Of course, another point of view could be that in the end the acts and decisions of supervisory authorities are based on hard law as such. These hard law rules are published, and thus legitimate, foreseeable and in accordance with the notion of legal certainty. Anyhow, if not de jure, de facto the soft law instruments have a certain 'power' that is, not clearly retraceable. When we take a closer look at the MoU on Cooperation between the Financial Supervisory Authorities, Central Banks and Finance Ministries of the European Union on Cross-Border Financial Stability, we might conclude that very important policy choices on how to deal with cross-border financial crises have been agreed upon. Of course, these policies have to be implemented with the use of the various hard law instruments that are laid down in the various EC Directives, as well as in national law. This might lead to a situation that, technically speaking, the acting of the various authorities is in accordance with the legality principle: they act *sub* and *per lege*. So, an important rationale of the legality principle – that binding rules should be issued by the legislator and therefore also the parliament, and indirectly, the people – has still been met. Important policy choices have been made on another level though, a level that is, less democratic and less accountable. Although these choices are supposed to be non-binding, their importance and influence in practice is undeniable.

So, as far as the use of soft law in financial market regulation and supervision is concerned, the general conclusion might be that, from a legality point of view, there are some tensions and problems. Of course, at the end of the day, soft law in its various presences in regulation and supervision remains *de iure* non-binding, and for it to become binding it has to be transformed in hard law, and in many cases it is. In this process of transformation, parliament plays its role, so in essence one of the main features of the legality principle – that binding rules are formulated by organs of the state that are part of the legislative power – is upheld. On the other hand, this non-binding character is, in fact, somewhat questionable. Important policy choices are made when enacting these soft law agreements and these choices have a lasting impact. One of the essential elements of the legality principle, that is, that policy frameworks and legal norms have to be formulated by the legislator, might be de facto set aside or, at least, suggested to be compromised.

In this regard, one has to point at the fact that the legality principle, and especially the various functions it is supposed to comprise (legitimation, attribution and regulation of public authority), can, and maybe should, not only be guaranteed by the influence of democratically elected bodies in rule and policymaking *ex ante*. Another mechanism is, of course, democratic control *ex post*. Parliament in some way or the other has various means of controlling rulemaking and policy-making by the executive, and especially by supervisory authorities. In the Dutch example, this is dealt with by the concept of ministerial responsibility: the minister responsible for the actions of the AFM and DNB is responsible to parliament and has to answer questions raised in parliament. The scope of this ministerial responsibility is limited though, and depends, to a large extent, on the powers of the ministry towards the supervisory authorities. Similar indirect control mechanisms exist in other countries, sometimes with more, sometimes with (even) less influence. Sometimes even, like in the United States, this control towards supervisory agencies even has a direct character.[37] Whether this *ex post* control mechanism can play its role as far as (especially) MoUs between supervisory authorities are concerned, seems to be questionable at least.

Finally, we turn our attention to the role of the judiciary. As already has been elaborated on in other contributions to this monograph, the judiciary might fill possible legality gaps as part of its function to control the exercise of public authority. This might also be true as far as the use of soft law instruments – such as MoUs – in financial market supervision is concerned. A recent example of this might be found in the aforementioned Dutch Icesave judgment of the Council of State of 22 April 2009.[38] This case was about the spontaneous annulment by the Dutch Crown[39] of the decision of various Dutch lower authorities (holders of Icesave deposits) to start proceeding against the State of Iceland after the Icesave bankruptcy. The reason for this was the fact that those proceedings were contrary to the general interest, one of the legal grounds for quashing such a decision. According to the Dutch Crown, the Dutch government had agreed upon a MoU with the government of Iceland, in which was declared that Dutch savers (including some public authorities like those lower authorities) would qualify for compensation according to the Icelandic deposit guarantee scheme. Negotiations about a more specific MoU that would elaborate on the more general one, were pending. The decision of the lower authorities to start proceedings themselves would harm these negotiations and would harm the parity of creditors. It is very interesting to take note of the way the Dutch court reviewed this decision of the Crown: in its review, the Council of State paid specific attention to the MoU that was agreed upon between Iceland and the Netherlands. The reasoning by the Dutch Crown relating to this MoU was not reviewed in a restrained way. The Council of State considered that the decision of the Crown mentioned the fact that an MoU was agreed upon, according to which the parity of creditors was a leading principle.

37. See Aalt Willem Heringa and Luc Verhey, 'Independent Agencies and Political Control', in: *Agencies in European and Comparative Law*. ed. Tom Zwart & Luc Verhey (Antwerp-Oxford-New York: Intersentia, 2003), 155 et seq., esp. 160–161.
38. See n. 25. The Council of State is one of the administrative courts in the Netherlands adjudicating in last instance.
39. Article 132(4) of the Dutch Constitution. A decision by the Crown means a decision signed by both a Minister In this case the Minister of Finance: And the Queen. In fact, one can say that it was the decision of the Minister of Finance.

According to the Council, it was by no means clear why the Crown attributed importance to this principle in its decision to annul the decisions of the lower authorities. This reasoning, according to the Council of State, was incomprehensible. Although this judgment deals with a quite particular type of competence under Dutch law (spontaneous annulment), it could be regarded as an illustration of the fact that some exercise of public authority – in this case, by the Dutch Minister of Finance (*de iure* the Crown) – based upon a soft law instrument like an MoU, is controlled by the court by way of full review.

5. CONCLUSION

The main question that has been addressed in this essay is how the use of soft law instruments in the field of financial market regulation matches with the legality principle. We have indicated that, from a legality point of view, most of the time there are no severe problems as far the most important functions of the legality principle – legitimation, attribution and regulation of public authority – are concerned. This mainly has to do with the fact that *de iure* soft law in this field is also non-binding. *De iure*, public authority is exercised based upon hard law, be it EU Directives or national legislation. There is the risk of possible mismatches though. They have to do with the fact that the influence of various soft law instruments in this field, like the frequently used instrument of MoUs, might de facto lead to a situation where important policy decisions in the regulation of financial markets have already been made on this soft law level. Because of this, one of the essential elements of the legality principle – that is, that policy frameworks have to be formulated by the democratically legitimized legislator – might be de facto set aside, or at least suggested to be compromised. However, we have also indicated that other mechanisms might serve as a means to mitigate this problem: the judiciary and democratic control *ex post* might play their gap-filling role in this respect.

Chapter 11

The Quasi-legislative Powers of the European Social Dialogue: Imperfect Delegation of Powers or Ambivalent Recognition of Contractual Autonomy?

Albertine Veldman

1. INTRODUCTION

1.1. THE START OF THE EUROPEAN SOCIAL DIALOGUE

This contribution seeks to study some aspects of public decision-making, more specifically the setting of legislative standards, in the field of European social policy. The decision-making process has for long been troublesome in this area. Despite political aspirations to raise the legitimacy of European Union (EU) by recognizing the need of a 'social face' to redress some of the perceived downsides of the internal market project, social integration has not kept up with economic integration. The institutional framework for decision-making in the social policy field was considered to be one of its reasons.[1] Throughout the 1980s, the complexity of

1. See B. Keller and B. Sörries, 'The New European Social Dialogue: Old Wine in New Bottles?', *Journal of European Social Policy* 9/2 (1999): 111–125 at 111.

Leonard Besselink, Frans Pennings & Sacha Prechal (eds), *The Eclipse of the Legality Principle in the European Union*, pp. 187–209.

the Council's bargaining process, which required in most cases unanimous decisions, created blockages to further social integration. To overcome the deadlock some major changes were agreed on in the early 1990s, as defined in the Social Policy Agreement (SPA), binding the eleven Member States. The SPA was *verbatim* inserted in the EC Treaty by the Amsterdam Treaty, ending the 'opt-out' of the UK.

Especially Articles 3 and 4 of the SPA (now Articles 154 and 155 Treaty on the Functioning of the European Union (TFEU))[2] were 'revolutionary' from a public law view of establishing legal procedures for decision-making.[3] The said provisions render private agents (management and labour organized at the European level) competences to make social policy by enabling them to reach European collective agreements (ECAs),[4] which, through a Council decision, can be enacted as European Directives.

The procedure, commonly referred to as the European Social Dialogue (ESD),[5] was welcomed as a 'new mode of governance'.[6] In contrast to the traditional Union law instruments, the ESD is based on 'contractual governance' rather than top-down legislative precepts. It was expected to allow for more flexibility and to enhance 'participatory democracy'. The latter was in fact taken a considerable step further. The procedure of, now, Articles 154 and 155 TFEU *prioritize* agreements concluded by the social partners over traditional legislation, in that it offers these private actors the opportunity to replace proposed legislation by the European Commission (hereafter: the Commission) by a bargained solution. In this respect, the prerogatives of the European social partners could be regarded as an articulation of 'horizontal subsidiarity', perhaps best described in this context as a functional attribution of powers to those actors that are deemed to be closest to the societal problem to be remedied and most affected by the solutions found. Compared to other conceived new modes of governance, such as the OMC, the results of the procedures of the ESD are not restricted to instruments of a policy nature only. Quite to the contrary, the procedures can result in the ESD producing substantive law obligations that are generally binding in the Union's legal order. The institutionalization of the ESD has, therefore, puzzled public law scholars and labour law scholars alike.

1.2. Legality of the Social Dialogue: Key Issues

The corporatist mode of decision-making in the social policy field, resulting from Articles 154–155 TFEU, has raised numerous questions after its introduction.

2. Ex Arts 138–139 TEC. The Lisbon Treaty has not altered the respective social provisions, except for the stipulation that the European Parliament will be informed of a Commission's proposal for implementation of a social partner agreement.
3. C. Barnard, *EC Employment Law* (Oxford: Oxford University Press, 2006), 19.
4. The agreements are also referred to as Social Partner Agreements or Framework Agreements.
5. In a broader sense the social dialogue at European level encompasses the bilateral relations between employers' and trade union organizations as well as tripartite consultation of the European social partners by the European institutions. Here, the term is reserved to bilateral relations only.
6. COM (93) 600, 10.

Where does it derive its legitimacy from, to start with? When an ECA is transposed into a Directive without the involvement of the European Parliament (hereafter: EP), are the European social partners to be conceived of as representative institutions? If the procedures of the ESD would imply a distribution of powers according to horizontal subsidiarity, another legitimate question would be whether the European social partners are attributed well defined powers in terms of their scope. The latter question probably has to be preceded by ones probing the autonomy of the social partners vis-à-vis the traditional EU institutions. Could the Commission and the Council, for instance, deny a European collective agreement acquiring the status of Union law? Are the powers of the European social partners safeguarded in anyway and who bears the responsibility for the sound application of the outcomes of the ESD? Also in regard to the regulatory products of the ESD a set of questions may come forward. The general qualities required of sound legislation, more specifically the ones relating to legal certainty, can be at odds with the contractual nature of the instrument of the ECA. Contracts can expire or, at the will of the signatories, be renegotiated or terminated. In that case, what will be the result once such a contract has become an integral part of a statutory instrument? Will the implementing Directive instantaneously follow the fate of the collective agreement, or will it continue to apply in its own right, although dispossessed of its objective?

The issues raised all refer back to the 'legality' concept, including its ascribed functions, underlying the research reflected in this book. This chapter will seek to analyse some of the questions that the formal procedures of the ESD seem to provoke against this theoretical backdrop. The subject of the social dialogue shall be restricted to its capabilities to set social standards by contract, envisaged in Article 155(2) TFEU.[7] Put shortly, the said provision prescribes that social partner agreements are implemented, either by national collective bargaining procedures and practices (so-called autonomous agreement) or by Council decision (in practise a directive).

In the following, first of all the powers of the ESD will be set out in some more detail (section 2). It will turn out that qualifying the nature of the procedures that apply, complicates matters immediately. Scholars disagree profoundly about how to behold the true nature of the powers attributed to the ESD. The dispute boils down to the question whether the social dialogue must be regarded as an assist for public law-making in social policy matters, or, alternatively, European law-making must be seen as an assist for private autonomous, collective bargaining. The way in which one perceives the nature of the institutionalized social dialogue may have consequences for the conditions of legality that apply to it. This will be further discussed in the third section, addressing the aspects of the legitimacy of the social dialogue. Following that, an analysis will be made of the practice of the ESD. In what ways have the social partners exercised their powers and what were the regulatory implications of governance 'by contract' in respect of *inter alia* legal

7. Other aspects of the social dialogue, to be found in the various EC Directives on workers' involvement within transnational enterprises, is addressed in Ch. 8 (Meyers & Jaspers).

certainty (section 4)? In the concluding section the findings will be evaluated, not only from the theoretical view whether the procedures of the ESD live up to the legality principle as such, and the appropriateness of this concept, but also from a more practical perspective whether the ESD could possibly warrant legality in its own right.

2. THE POWERS ATRRIBUTED TO THE EUROPEAN SOCIAL DIALOGUE

2.1. The Origins of the European Social Dialogue

To properly understand the nature of the institutional framework of the ESD under the Treaty, and, hence, the powers that are attributed to management and labour within this context, one needs to reflect shortly on the origins of the social dialogue.

The Commission had long aspired to develop European level-collective bargaining. Since the 1960s joint committees were established with the Commission's assistance, especially in EC relevant sectors like agriculture, fisheries and transport. Nevertheless, genuine industrial relations did not start off.[8] New impetus was gained at the time of the Single European Act (1986). According to Jacques Delors, the incoming President of the Commission, the creation of the single market was 'inconceivable without some harmonization of social legislation'.[9] To break the deadlock in this respect, this was particularly to be arrived at by social dialogue. It was the Commission's view that there should be a twin-track approach to European social policy-making.[10]

In 1985, following the idea of social dialogue as vehicle for social policy, Delors launched regular meetings between ETUC, UNICE (now BUSINESSEUROPE) and CEEP.[11] It was against this background of, what became known as, the Val Duchesse talks, that Article 118b was introduced by the SEA. The provision instructed the Commission 'to develop the dialogue between management and labour at the European level, which could, if the two sides consider it desirable, lead to relations based on agreement'. Despite these wordings, the Val Duchesse talks did not result in any agreement.[12] Article 118b did, however, pave the way for a prominent role of social dialogue in the Community Charter,[13] and, with assistance of the Commission, for a joint text of the three social partner organizations on

8. Barnard 2006 n. 4, 760–761.
9. *EC Bulletin* 2/86, 12.
10. *Social Europe 1/* 88, 67.
11. European Trade Union Confederation (ETUC), Union of Industrial and Employers' Confederations of Europe (UNICE, now BUSINESSEUROPE) and European Centre of Public Enterprises (now Enterprises with Public Participation and Enterprises of General Economic Interest – CEEP).
12. B. Keller & M. Bansbach, 'Social Dialogues: An Interim Report on Recent Results and Prospects', *Industrial Relations Journal* 31/4 (2000): 291–307.
13. Article 12(2) of the Community Charter on the Fundamental Social Rights of Workers (1989).

social dialogue, to be presented to the Maastricht IGC.[14] This text was with few modifications transposed into Article 3 and 4 of the SPA.

It can be drawn from the above, that the European social dialogue appears more to be constructed than institutionalized after the fact. Its introduction does not resemble in anyway the *genesis* of independent collective bargaining, rooted in the traditions and practises of the Member States.[15] Historically, collective bargaining at Member State level developed in a spontaneous and autonomous (industrial) order. It presupposes a labour movement organizing itself bottom-up in the defence of worker's interests. From this collective autonomy the right to bargain collectively on labour contracts was vindicated and, basically, enforced by the threat of industrial action. The autonomous phenomenon was recognized by the nation state in the twentieth century, acknowledging the fundamental freedoms of association, collective bargaining and collective action. The binding nature of the collective labour agreement per se was accepted, and supported by elaborating national legal frameworks.

The ESD, to the contrary, is not founded on a pre-existing and spontaneous labour movement at the European level. Its bargaining process lacks the threat of EU-wide industrial action. Some scholars have, for these reasons, questioned whether the ECA can be construed as an outcome of collective autonomy, and whether the ESD is truly intended to promote independent collective bargaining. The political aspirations to break the deadlock on Community social regulation at the time and the 'neo-corporatist' cloak of European industrial relations conducted under the auspices of the Commission, might refute that.

2.2. Competences and Procedures (Articles 154–155 TFEU)

The assumption to be drawn, would be that the ESD was mainly institutionalized to introduce a twin-track approach to European social policy-making. Hence, social partner agreements were to be given some kind of a legally binding effect. How this was exactly done can be deferred from the Treaty procedures. We will take a closer look at the exact powers and competences of management and labour in the context of the social dialogue and, especially, try to examine whether, and to what extent, they show evidence of absorption of the law-making capabilities of the traditional EU institutions.

Decision-making in the social policy field, according to Article 154 TFEU, is subjected to a mandatory two-step consultation procedure. In the first stage the Commission is obliged, before submitting proposals in the social policy field, to consult management and labour on the possible direction of EU action. In the second stage the Commission shall consult management and labour on the content

14. According to the summary given by the Commission, COM (1993) final 600.
15. See F. Dorssemont, 'Some Reflections on the Origin, Problems and Perspectives of the Social Dialogue', in: *A Decade Beyond Maastricht: The European Social Dialogue revisited*, ed. M. de Vos (The Hague: Kluwer Law International, 2003), 3–32, at 12.

of the envisaged proposal. At this instance the social partners can decide to enter a process of negotiation. Article 154(4) indicates, more precisely, that management and labour may inform the Commission of their wish to initiate a process of social dialogue as provide for in Article 155. From Article 155(1) it can be attained that, should management and labour so desire, the dialogue between them may lead to 'contractual relations, including agreements'. The terminology used, seems confusing. Are there other contractual relations besides agreements feasible?[16] Article 155(2), finally, specifies that agreements concluded at European level 'shall be implemented either in accordance with the procedures and practices specific to management and labour and the Member States or, in matters covered by Article 153, at the joint request of the signatory parties, by a Council decision on a proposal from the Commission'.[17]

The most remarkable, and most debated, consequences of the procedures explained, would be the suspension,[18] and, if the social partners succeed to reach an agreement, even the substitution of the institutional powers of the Union in the field of social policy. The relevant provisions, however, are obscure in regard of these legal effects, and, hence, are source of much speculation.

2.2.1. Suspension of the Traditional Decision-Making Powers in Social Policy?

Some have argued that the ESD can never take precedence over the institutional powers of the EU.[19] This standpoint must imply a perception of the social dialogue as either a non-binding consultation procedure, or a procedure to enhance *private* collective bargaining that has to be fully distinguished from public decision-making. Still, in respect of the issue of *suspension* during the bargaining process of the powers of the Commission to initiate social policy regulation, the limit to the duration of the said process under Article 154(4) TEC would be meaningless if suspension would not be implied.[20] In a series of communications the Commission elaborated some ground rules for the application of the ESD.[21] This frame of references clearly shows that the Commission acknowledges the suspension of the legislative process it initiated. The Commission, however, draws from that

16. See on the possible origins of terminology used, Barnard 2006 n. 4, 89, 158.
17. 'Decision' does not refer to the term used in Art. 288 TFEU (Ex Art. 249 TEC). On this: B. Hepple, *European Social Dialogue: Alibi or Opportunity?* (London: Institute of Employment Rights, 1993), 31.
18. Article 155(4) TFEU indicates a period of or nine months, which can be extended by mutual decision of the social partners and the Commission.
19. See F. Dorssemont, referring to Guery & Langlois, 'Contractual Governance by Management and Labour in EC Labour Law', in: *Multilevel Governance in Enforcement and Adjudication*, ed. A. Van Hoek et al. (Antwerp: Intersentia, 2006), 291.
20. L. Betten, 'The Role of Social Partners in the Community s Social Policy Law-making: Participatory Democracy or furthering the Interests of Small Elites?', in: *Labour Law and Industrial Relations at the turn of the Century*, ed. C. Engels & M. Weiss (The Hague: Kluwer Law International, 1998), 250–251.
21. COM (93) 600 final; COM (98) 322 final; COM (2002) 341 final; COM (2004) 557 final.

a special responsibility to take on an *ex-ante* assessment of the agreement before submitting a proposal to the Council, as well as *ex-posteriori* assessment of autonomous agreements, following an Article 154-consultation, in regard of their contribution to the European Union's objectives.[22]

2.2.2. Substitution of the Traditional Decision-Making Powers in Social Policy?

Whether the procedures of the ESD can possibly *replace* some of the decision-making prerogatives of the EU institutions, will, amongst other factors, depend on the degree of autonomy of the European social partners to render their agreements generally binding effect. Article 155 provides two routes for implementation, the 'autonomous' one by the national social partners' structures, and the 'institutional' one by Council decision.

Whether the autonomous route may indeed lead to a generally binding effect of the ECA concluded, is highly uncertain. It will depend on the national collective bargaining structures in place – including possibilities for third party effects – the initial coverage of sectors and professions by the members of the European social partners, the extent to which these national members actually take part in bilateral negotiations processes and, last but not least, if they are in anyway obliged to transpose ECAs.[23] From a declaration originally annexed to the SPA it can, furthermore, be attained that the Member States have no responsibilities to apply ECAs directly, to transpose them or to facilitate their implementation.[24] The Commission seems aware of the difficulties of implementation by the autonomous route, where its states that in case 'fundamental rights or important political options are at stake, or in situations where the rules must be applied in a uniform fashion in all Member States and coverage must be complete, preference should be given to implementation by Council decision'.[25]

This concerns the institutional route. In respect of the autonomous powers of the European social partners to render their agreements generally binding effect, the questions, however, arise whether the Commission and the Council are *obliged* to implement ECAs, if so requested, and to implement it as such. Article 155(2) states that agreements concluded at European level shall be implemented, expressing an obligation on the part of the Commission and the Council. Nevertheless, as far as the 'decision' of the Council is concerned, the provision also indicates in which subject matters this will require, respectively, qualified majority voting or unanimity. The requirement of sufficient political support clearly leaves open the possibility of a refusal to transpose the agreement.

---

22. COM (2004) 557 final, 10.
23. Binding obligations between the European associations and their affiliates would have to be inferred from applicable national laws, posing several legal difficulties (i.e., do national laws acknowledge European trade unions? Can there be a private law obligation, not only to engage in bargaining but to *conclude* agreements?).
24. Declaration 26 SPA, included as Declaration 27 in the Treaty of Amsterdam.
25. COM (2004) 557 final, 9–10.

Alternatively, the said provision can be interpreted as compelling the Commission to submit a proposal for the transposition of the agreement to the Council, if so requested. However, in the framework of references mentioned earlier, the Commission allows itself some discretion.[26] Before putting an ECA to the Council, the Commission tends to examine, on a case-to-case basis, the appropriateness of EU action.[27] This includes the monitoring of the representative status of the signatory parties, the lawfulness of the clauses and compliance with the Treaty provisions concerning small and medium-sized enterprises.[28] Finally, in respect of an obligation on the part of the Commission and the Council to implement agreements as such, the Commission holds the opinion that no amendments can be made without unduly interfering with the autonomous status of the social dialogue. In practice this seems to have been acknowledged by the Council.

2.3. The Ambiguous Nature of the Europe Social Dialogue

It seems the institutional framework of the ESD provided by the Treaty does not surpass an embryonic state. It is not only silent on who 'management and labour' exactly is, but, moreover, lacks clear demarcation of the powers of the social partners vis-à-vis those of the Commission and the Council. The Commission's framework of references has not been entirely helpful in this respect. Accordingly, the appropriateness of the 'collective route' to social policy legislation shall be assessed on a case-to-case basis, depending on the content of the agreement. As these ground rules, moreover, flow from non-binding instruments, they do not seem a suitable remedy for the 'legality deficit' of the ESD.

Nevertheless, the Court of First Instance did sanction some aspects of these informal rules in its UEAPME-case.[29] Being the only case law on the ESD its implications will be addressed more extensively below. Here, it may suffice to note that the Court found that the Commission and the Council are under the obligation to act in conformity with the (democratic) principles governing their actions in the field of social policy.[30] More particular, this imposes a duty on the Commission, when resuming control of the procedure, to examine the representativity of the signatories of an agreement and to refuse its implementation when this is lacking.[31] One could possibly also detect the acknowledgment by the Court of the temporary suspension of the powers of the Commission to initiate legislative proposals, where it states that the Commission '*resumes* control of the procedure' (emphasis added).[32]

26. This was contested by the EESC on the grounds that the Commission was obliged to put the agreement to the Council (Opinion, OJ 1994, C 397/40).
27. E. Franssen, *Legal Aspects of the European Social Dialogue* (Antwerp: Intersentia, 2002), 207–208.
28. COM (2002) 341, 19.
29. Case No. T-135/96 [1998] ECR II-2335.
30. Paragraph 85.
31. Paragraph 90.
32. Paragraph 84.

Still, the ESD, even when the ground rules of the Commission were to be included, continues to be too ambiguous to be conclusive of its precise objective. If the ESD-procedure is to attribute the European social partners the powers to substitute for the traditional mode of governance in the social policy area, competences and responsibilities are not clearly distributed accordingly. The spheres of responsibilities of the EU institutions and the European social partners overlap one another, making it difficult to discern where responsibilities begin or end. According to the Commission, 'it is for the social players to make the first move to arrive at appropriate solutions coming within their area of responsibility; the EU institutions intervene, at the Commission's initiative, only where negotiations fail'.[33] At the same time the Commission infers from its own prerogatives the responsibility to (*ex ante*) assess the appropriateness of EU action by social dialogue. Moreover, it flows from the Treaty itself that intervention by agents other than the European social partners themselves, is a prerequisite to render their 'solutions' any effect. Despite the prioritized position of the social partners, one has, therefore, to conclude that if the 'collective route' to EU legislation implies a 'horizontal' delegation of powers, this delegation is, at most, of an ad hoc and conditional nature.

In the alternative, if the procedure is not about public decision-making, but merely intents to support autonomous collective bargaining at European level, this seems again rebutted by the various interventions of EU institutions, compromising true self-governance by the private agents concerned. Admittedly, in respect of the implementation of ECAs by Council decision, the necessary intervention by the Council may resemble national procedures for the extension of collective labour agreements (CLAs) to non-signatory parties in some of the Member States. But there are also some significant differences. Such procedures at national level mostly require an administrative decision in order to have the applicability of the CLA extended, not a political vote in order to transpose the CLA into a formal legislative act. Furthermore, in the majority of cases, such national collective bargaining laws recognize the (normative) binding effect of CLAs between, at least, the members of the signatory parties, that is to say without the need of ad hoc political intervention.

3. THE (DEMOCRATIC) LEGITIMACY OF THE SOCIAL DIALOGUE

Another troublesome aspect of the ESD involves its legitimacy. From the very start it was under attack from several sides, including the EP, the European Economic and Social Committee (EESC) and even some European trade unions and employers' associations themselves. When an ECA is *verbatim* transposed into a EU Directive without the involvement of the EP, must the European social partners be conceived of as representative institutions? The procedure of Articles 154–155 TFEU is silent as to the identification of 'management and labour'. It stipulates

33. COM (2002) 341 final, 8.

no requirements in respect of whether this encompasses individuals, associations or perhaps an institutional joint committee, let alone the need for a representative status of these entities.

3.1. Notions of Representativity Developed at European Level

Soon after the entry into force of the Maastricht Treaty the Commission determined its own representativity criteria for the consultation procedure of, now, Article 154 TFEU.[34] These criteria are as follows:

(1) the organization should be cross-industry or relate to specific sectors or categories and be organized at European level;
(2) consist of organizations which are themselves an integral and recognized part of Member State social partners structures and with the capacity to negotiate agreements, and which are representative of all Member States, as far as possible;
(3) to have adequate structures to ensure their effective participation in the consultative process.[35]

Despite much criticism,[36] the criteria still prevail today. The number of recognized, representative social partner organizations consulted under Article 154 has gradually grown to over sixty organizations. In respect of the representative partners that can enter the negotiation stage, the Commission holds the opinion that 'this is entirely in the hands of the different organizations'.[37] In fact a Social Dialogue Committee (SDC) was set up in 1992. The SDC succeeded the former Steering Group on Social Dialogue, which was composed of the established social partners of Val Duchesse. Recognizing that there is 'a substantial body of experience behind the social dialogue between UNICE, CEEP and ETUC',[38] these organizations were again represented in the SDC. Since than, only two of the organizations criticizing the privileged position of the established social partners acquired (indirect) access to the negotiating table by concluding a cooperation agreement with these partners.[39] Judicial review proceedings had failed to do so.

This concerned the UEAPME-case.[40] UEAPME, a cross-industry association of Crafts and SMEs, was denied access to the negotiations on the Parental Leave

34. Doc. No. V/6141/93/E.
35. COM (93) 600 final, point 24.
36. See for the responses, Commission's Communication, 'The Development of the Social Dialogue at Community level', COM (96) 448 final.
37. COM (93) 600 final, point 31.
38. *Ibid.*, final, point 25.
39. At the employees' side two professional and managerial organizations (EUROCADRES and CEC) signed an agreement in 2000 establishing a 'liaison committee' with the ETUC. UEAPME takes part in the cross-industry social dialogue at the employers' site after reaching a cooperation agreement with BUSINESSEUROPE in December 1998.
40. Case No. T-135/96 [1998] ECR II-2335.

Agreement. In order to get access, it had to resort to an annulment action, under Article 230 TEC (now Article 263 TFEU), of the Directive implementing the Agreement.[41] Consequently, UEAPME had to demonstrate to be 'individually concerned'. It claimed in this respect to be representative because it was consulted by the Commission. Furthermore, it represented more SMEs than UNICE. The CFI, however, denied a general right for those consulted to take part in negotiations, the latter constituting a voluntary process.[42] Still, the Court did find that the Commission and the Council were under a duty to examine the representativity of the signatories to the agreement. The CFI stressed the importance of this: 'The principle of democracy on which the Union is founded requires – in the absence of the participation of the EP in the legislative process – that the participation of the people be otherwise assured, in this instance through the parties representative of management and labour who concluded the agreement.'[43] From this, the Court concluded that the social partner organizations that were initially consulted by the Commission but were no parties to the agreement, and whose representation is necessary to raise the collective representativity of the signatories to the required level, have the right to prevent the implementation of the agreement by legislative instrument.[44] After noting that the Parental Leave Agreement applies to all employment relationships, the Courts considered the original signatories to be sufficiently representative, since they are cross-industry organizations with a general mandate, thereby representing all categories of workers and undertakings.[45] UEAPME's participation was, therefore, not required.

One can say the Court condoned the 'established' social partners of the Val Duchesse talks by taking a collective as well as a qualitative approach to the concept of representativity. Doing otherwise would have been the end of the ESD, given the number of national trade union affiliation in Europe. Whether the concept of representativity applied to the European social partners actually renders legitimacy to the procedure, will, again, partly depend on whether the social dialogue is initially perceived of as a public or a private law route to decision-making.

3.2. Legitimacy Perceived Form a Public Law Model

Proceeding from a public law model, in which ECAs must be construed as a source of law, the legality principle requires formal legislation to be adopted in a way that

41. Council Directive 96/43/EC.
42. Paragraph 78.
43. Paragraph 89.
44. Paragraph 90.
45. It can be remarked though, that ETUC, according to its internal rules, can be mandated to negotiate and conclude agreements by a two-third majority, leaving the possibility of exclusion of some categories of workers. BUSINESSEUROPE requires an unanimous vote to be mandated, but has only national umbrella organizations as members without the capacity to negotiate at national level. Public employers, with the exception of the public enterprises, are not represented.

guarantees its democratic legitimacy. The CFI seems to adopt such a constitutional law paradigm by stating that the participation of the people in the exercise of power must be assured in case collective agreements are endowed with a legislative foundation. Due to the absence of the EP, the role of the people has to be fulfilled by the social partners. Taken the model of *representative democracy* underlying this all, the qualitative and flexible concept of representativity applied by the Court, seems rather incompatible with this. When one seeks representative democracy, one would expect the social partner organizations to represent a (qualified) majority of workers and undertakings in the Union. The EESC, for instance, argued that an agreement, in the context of the legislative procedure, should be concluded by organizations that represent a sufficient quantity of employers and employees. According to the EESC, this should, however, not be addressed by figures, but allowing every representative social partner organization to be admitted to the negotiation stage.[46] It may be remarked that with over sixty recognized organizations today, one can wonder whether this creates a very practical solution for any negotiation process.

It appears that the contractual and voluntary nature of the social dialogue is difficult to reconcile with democratic public decision-making. Moreover, from the perspective of constitutional law it should be pointed out that the procedure of the ESD lacks a clearly defined notion of representativity or any formal requirement enacted by law in this respect. Admittedly, the Court created a faculty of legal control *a posteriori* on the democratic legitimacy of the legislative act incorporating an agreement,[47] but this seems seriously hampered by the limited *locus standi* of the European social partners.[48]

Given these problems, is has been argued that the legitimacy of the ESD must be sought in a *participatory* model of democracy.[49] Such an approach would better correspond with the notion of representativity applied by the CFI, which seems to take account of interests rather than numbers. Nevertheless, one may doubt if participatory democracy is meant to supplant, rather than supplement, representative democracy.[50] The procedure of the ESD seems to go beyond the participatory model endorsed by the EU institutions. According to the Interinstitutional Agreement on Better Law-Making, its most far-reaching alternative of

46. Opinion of the Economic and Social Committee on the Commission communication concerning the development of the social dialogue at Community level, OJ 1997, C 89/27, points 1.8 and 1.9. Concurring: A. Lyon-Caen, 'Les négociation collective dans ses dimensions internationales', *Droit Social* no. 4 (1997): 352–367.
47. Critical: M. Moreau and M. Blas López, Trade unions in the EU facing global companies: legal obstacles and innovations, *EUI Working papers*, LAW 2007/27, 6.
48. An ETUC-resolution of 15–16 Jun. 2000 to provide the social partners a comparable status as the EP under Art. 230 TEC, was denied at the Nice IGC, see R. Blanpain (ed.), *Labour Law, Human Rights and Social Justice* (The Hague: Kluwer Law International, 2001), 147.
49. See C. Barnard 2006 n. 4, 101
50. See D. Obradovic, 'Accountability of Interest Groups in the Union Lawmaking Process', in: *Law Making in the EU*, ed. Craig & Harlow (London: Kluwer, 1998), 354–385; L. Betten, 'The Democratic Deficit of Participatory Democracy in Community Social Policy', ELRev. 23 (1998): 20–36.

'co-regulation' by civil actors entails 'the mechanism whereby a Community legislative act entrusts the attainment of the objective defined by the legislative authority to civil parties that are recognized in the field'.[51] As argued by Branch, the ESD does not fit the description.[52] An ECA, implemented by Council Directive, actually determines the content of the legislative act, and the details are instead fleshed out at the national level by Member States. The ETUC in the past, indeed, stressed the unique position of the European social partners under the Treaty, cautioning the Commission to avoid any confusion with regular consultation of private actors.[53]

Based on the foregoing, it seems unsatisfactory to interpret the legitimacy of the social dialogue to result from participatory democracy only. This seems also the position of the EP that has kept an ambiguous attitude towards the social dialogue. Whilst the EP sees the collective approach to legislation as a step towards greater involvement of citizens in policy-making, it criticizes its 'democratic deficit', claiming the EP should be granted power of approval or refusal.[54]

3.3. Legitimacy Perceived from a Private (Industrial) Law Model

As already addressed, scholarly views differ strongly on the nature of the ESD. Labour law scholars, like Bercusson, have doubted the validity of viewing the ESD through a public law lens. With its roots in private law and industrial relations, ESD should not been seen as a legislative process at all.[55] Perceived from such an industrial law model, the representativity of trade unions and employers' organizations is not a matter of electoral concepts, but is derived from membership. All (inter)professional associations are representative of the interests of their members.[56] Consequently, the legitimacy of the social dialogue is not at stake when agreements would bind the members of the signatory parties. Representativity could be of relevance, nevertheless, if the personal scope of a binding

51. European Parliament, Council, Commission, Inter-institutional agreement on better lawmaking, OJ 2003, C 321/01.
52. A. Branch, 'The Evolution of the European Social Dialogue Towards Greater Autonomy: Challenges and Potential Benefit', *International Journal of Comparative Labour Law and Industrial relations* 21/2 (2005): 323.
53. ETUC, 'Position paper on the Communication from the Commission concerning the re-examination of Directive 93/104/ EC concerning certain aspects of the organization of working time (Working Time Directive)', Brussels, 17–18 Mar. 2004, <www.etuc.org>.
54. *Inter alia*, EP Resolution on the new social dimension of the Treaty on European Union, OJ 1994, C 77/30; EP Resolution on the Commission communication concerning the development of the social dialogue at Community level, OJ 1997, C 286/338. In practice the Commission informs the EP when it passes a proposal to this effect to the Council. This is made official by the Lisbon Treaty, see n. 3.
55. B. Bercusson, 'Democratic Legitimacy and European Labour law', *Industrial law Journal*, 28/2 (1999): 153–170.
56. *Ibid.*, 159; Dorssemont 2003 n. 16, 22.

collective agreement would be extended beyond the original parties, which is the case when an ECA is implemented by means of a Council Directive. Requirements of representativity are indeed part of most collective bargaining procedures, allowing for the extension of CLAs at Member State level. Due to the private and autonomous nature of collective bargaining, however, suitable criteria of representativity may differ from those accepted in the public sphere.

Public authorities, to start, should not unduly interfere with the recognized fundamental freedoms of association and collective bargaining,[57] when setting such requirements. According to ILO standards in this respect, the determination of representative organizations should be based on objective and pre-established criteria and not impede the creation of new or alternative unions.[58] Some Member States recognize for this purpose 'the most representative' organizations of workers and employers.[59] It is undisputed that the three established social partners organizations fit such a requirement at European level. But, when reasoning from an industrial relations model, the rationale of extending the applicability of a CLA to third parties must be kept in focus too. It is generally understood this flows foremost from the protection of autonomous collective bargaining, by preventing non-members to undercut the terms of employment within the industrial or territorial scope of the CLA. Public checks tend to take account of whether the CLA qualifies for protection because it resulted from an independent and balanced bargaining process. Representativity in the context of industrial relations can, therefore, not be dissociated from checks on the independency and (equal) bargaining powers of the social partners. The latter requires trade unions at least to have the ability to threaten social peace.

When applied to the European social partners, it is clear the position of, especially, the trade unions is far weaker than at the domestic level due to the absence of any economic pressure, such as industrial action. Especially the possible inequality of bargaining powers weakens the representative status of the European social dialogue and, hence, the legitimacy of extending the applicability of the social agreements reached on the basis thereof.[60]

In respect of its legitimacy as well as its attributed powers, the quintessence, so far, seems to be that the ambiguity of the ESD prevents its legality to be fully satisfactorily explained, either from constitutional law or industrial law principles.

57. ILO-conventions no. 87 and 98; Art. 8 ICESCR; Art. 11 ECHR; Art. 6 ESC; Art. 12(1) and Art. 28 EU Charter of Fundamental Rights.
58. The Commission's ground rules on assessing representative status on a case-to-case basis hardly fulfil these criteria.
59. For example, France and Belgium, featuring more 'corporatist-like' collective bargaining structures. However, in the case of the extension of CLAs in, for instance, Germany and the Netherlands, besides independency from the employer, also quantitative criteria apply in respect of workers covered (by adding the numbers of unionized and non-unionized workers employed by undertakings bound to the CLA).
60. Barnard 2006 n. 4, 101 referring to S. Fredman, Social Law in the EU: The Impact of the Law-making Process, in: *Law Making in the EU*, ed. Craig & Harlow (London: Kluwer, 1998), 410.

This being so, it does not yet answer the question whether this has hampered the proper functioning of the social dialogue in practice. In other words, how academic is the 'legality-deficit' of the ESD? Did it further European social policy regulation and what were the regulatory implications of 'contractual governance' so far, in terms of transparency, legal certainty or effectiveness? These questions will be addressed in the following section.

4. THE PRACTICE OF THE EUROPEAN SOCIAL DIALOGUE

4.1. Quantitative Results of the ESD

4.1.1. Cross-Industry Agreements

During the 1990s, which can be labelled as the first stage of the ESD, the Commission was the prime mover. Against the backdrop of a large number of legislative proposals in the social field on which no consensus was reached in the pre-Maastricht structures, the Commission explored the new collective route regularly. Despite the Commission's opinion that the social dialogue provisions 'now makes the social partners the central players in the European social arena',[61] the results of the cross-industry dialogue were not overwhelming. Three framework agreements were concluded on, respectively, parental leave (1995), part-time work (1997) and fixed-term work (1999).[62] In respect of major issues in the realm of the social partners, such as the information and consultation of workers, voluntary negotiations either failed or were not initiated. In its second stage (2000–2008) the dialogue came almost to a complete standstill in respect of cross-industry agreements to be implemented by Directive. It failed on, *inter alia*, subjects as temporary agency work (revision of social regulation on) collective redundancy, employers' insolvency, transfer of undertakings, the European works council and pregnancy leave. Only recently, again a cross-industry agreement was concluded on parental leave (2009), which involved the revision by the partners of their own former agreement (see section 4.2.2 *infra*).

The Commission repeatedly urged the European partners to seize the opportunities afforded by the Treaty, but the reasons for the disappointing results seem of a more fundamental nature. According to Keller and Bansbach, both sides of industry opted for opposing strategies. The ETUC has always been interested in far-reaching European social policy, preferably implemented by legislative instruments. BUSINESSEUROPE, however, is definitely not interested in binding directives because the status quo serves the interests of the vast majority of its national

61. European Commission, 'Industrial Relations in Europe', COM (2000) 113 final, 8.
62. Implemented by EC Directive 96/43 (parental leave); EC Directive 97/81 (part-time work) and EC Directive 99/ 70 (fixed-term work).

members best.[63] The employers' association, in the past, frankly expressed that their acceptance of European level-bargaining was primarily instigated by diluting the Commission's social policy initiatives, once the Maastricht Treaty broadened qualified majority voting in the field.[64] Consequently, they keep a 'wait-and-see' position, which is strengthened by the absence of the weapon of European industrial action at workers' site. Negotiations on framework agreements, as is generally understood, are only embarked on in case of a (serious) threat of legislative action by the Commission, in which the trade unions have little option but to follow suit due to a weaker bargaining position.[65]

The lack of any legislative results over the last ten years, with the exception of the recent revision of the Parental Leave Agreement, coincides with a shift in approach of the social dialogue from a reactive one to a more independent attitude.[66] In the context of the parallel EU debate on subsidiarity and better governance,[67] the cross-industry social partners indicated in 2001 their desire to pursue a more autonomous social dialogue.[68] The voluntary framework agreements on telework (2002), work-related stress (2004) and harassment and violence at work (2007), concluded in the second stage, all resulted, nevertheless, from Commission's proposals. However, due to the refusal by the employers to request implementation by Council decision, the social partners for the first time opted for the autonomous route to implementation.

The voluntary agreements, and other types of joint texts adopted after 2000,[69] manifested also greater autonomy, in that they belong to, so-called, new generation texts. These differ from the earlier joint opinions aimed at influencing European policy and legislation, by being directed instead at their members. In these texts the social partners make certain commitments or recommendations to their members, which they then seek to implement and follow up themselves at the national level.[70] The new generation texts and the 'voluntary' route to their implementation, however, have also brought confusion, or even disagreement, about their regulatory intentions. In the case of the first autonomous agreement on telework, for example, the ETUC held the opinion the agreement contains legal minimum standards, while UNICE stressed its process-oriented nature, arguing that telework is a way of working, not a legal status. Furthermore, the employers' association understands 'voluntary framework agreements' to be non-legally binding. According to

63. B. Keller & M. Bansbach 2000, n. 13, 294.
64. Cited in R. Blanpain, *European Labour Law* 11th edn (The Hague: Kluwer Law International, 2008), 189.
65. Branch 2005 n. 53, 335; Keller and Bansbach 2000 n. 13, 294. Also Dorssemont 2003 n. 16 and Barnard 2006 n. 4.
66. Branch 2005 n. 53, 324.
67. European Commission, 'European Governance: A White Paper', COM (2001) 428 final.
68. ETUC/UNICE/CEEP, 'Joint contribution by the social partners to the Laeken European Council', 7 Dec. 2001.
69. Notably, 'Framework of Actions on the Lifelong Development of Competencies and Qualifications' (February 2002); 'Framework of Actions on Gender Equality' (March 2005).
70. COM (2004) 557 final.

the ETUC, initially opposed to autonomous implementation, 'voluntary' refers merely to the fact that the agreement is not implemented by directive. In practise, the autonomous agreements were implemented in various forms at national level, including non-binding guidelines and recommendations.[71]

4.1.2. Sectoral Agreements

At the end of the 1990s, in order to enhance social dialogue, the Commission decided to revitalize dialogue at sectoral level.[72] It abolished the old structures of the joint committees (see section 2.1, *supra*). Instead, the social partners had to make a joint request in order to establish a sectoral social dialogue committee and to fulfil the criteria of representativity (see section 3.1, *supra*). In respect of their legitimacy and the clear demarcation of their area of competences, these sectoral committees pose even greater problems than at interprofessional level. Defining 'sectors' proofs to be complicated, which leads to overlap and gaps.[73] In addition, the necessary organizational substructure at sectoral level, especially on the employers' side, is more fragmented and comparatively underdeveloped, making it hard to establish representative status. By flexible application of the criteria at least thirty sectoral committees have been installed so far. The restructuring led Keller to remark that the social partners from sectors with 'old' structures managed to conserve their privileged status.[74]

Sectoral dialogues produced a large, but uneven distributed, number of joint texts over the last decades. Qualitative evaluation, however, causes De Boer *e.a.* to conclude that the dialogue does not constitute a system of industrial relations, but serves as an alternative lobbying channel for the social partners involved.[75] The majority of joint texts still encompass recommendations directed at the EU institutions or national governments. Still, some sectors also turned to new generation texts (guidelines, codes of conduct) directed at the national affiliates. Agreements, or any texts with binding obligations, however, are rare, the exception being the sectoral agreements, implemented by Council decision, on aspects of

---

71. European Foundation for the Improvement of Living and Working Conditions and European Commission/DG V, 'Industrial Relations Developments in Europe 2004' (Luxembourg: Office for Official Publications of the European Communities, 2005). On the experiences with the Framework Agreement on Telework, see Branch 2005, n. 53, 332–334.
72. Commission's Communication, 'Adapting and Promoting the Social Dialogue at Community level', COM (1998) 322 final.
73. For example, there are six committees on transport. Furthermore, committees range from very broad defined sectors as 'commerce' to very small ones like 'hairdressing'.
74. B. Keller, 'Social Dialogue: The Specific Case of the European Union', *International Journal of Comparative Labour Law and Industrial Relations* 24/2 (2008), 216. Being included in a Sectoral Dialogue Committee (with up to 54 representatives) ensures logistical and financial support provided by the Commission (*inter alia* simultaneous translation facilities, coverage of travel expenses, secretarial services).
75. R. de Boer, H. Benedictus & M. van der Meer, 'Broadening without Intensification: The Added Value of European Social and Sectoral Dialogue', *European Journal of Industrial Relations* 11/1 (2005): 51–70.

working time in the transport sectors.[76] These agreements were again triggered by the threat of European legislation. In 2000 the Council and the EP revised their Working Time Directive 1993, including transport sectors previously left out.[77] The revised Directive excludes seafarers, on which a framework agreement was reached in 1998, but covers the other transport sectors.[78] The sectoral agreements on mobile workers reached later on in civil aviation and railways supplement the Directive, making use of certain provisions that allow for more specific standards. It was not until 2008 before another sectoral agreement was concluded, again in maritime transport, which, however, concerns a singular case (see section 4.2.2 *infra*).

4.2. Qualitative Results of the ESD: Accessibility, Implementation and Modification

When viewing the regulatory function of the ESD from a qualitative perspective, the question arises whether it produced 'sound regulation'. In case of binding obligations, it seems fair to say that legal certainty is furthered by standards that are accessible to the addressees, transparent, generally applied and effective. In practice, the ESD experiences major challenges in this respect.

4.2.1. Accessibility and Implementation

In regard to accessibility, the over 300 social partner texts produced are hardly disseminated at national level. In regard to transparency, their significance and (legal) status is difficult to grasp because of the diverse range of titles and formats employed and loose use of terminology (i.e., agreements, recommendations, declarations, policy orientations, guidelines, codes, framework of actions).[79] To address the problems, the Commission developed a typology, that is, urging the social partners to reserve the term 'agreement' to texts to be implemented according to Article 155(2) TFEU, and a drafting checklist, pointing to basic aspects as the need for clear terms, indication of purpose and status and addressees, relevant dates and deadlines, reference to original language, etcetera. The Commission now publishes autonomous agreements and undertakes an ex-ante assessment as it does for institutional agreements. It is not clear, however, what should be the consequence when an autonomous agreement would not pass such an assessment.

Inprecise terminology as well as failure to clarify the follow-up of texts in negotiations, result in difficulties when it comes to implementing them in

76. Directive 99/63 (European agreement on the organization of working time of seafarers, 1998); Directive 2000/79 (European agreement on the organization of working time of mobile staff in civil aviation, 2000); Directive 2005/47 (Agreement on certain aspects of the working conditions of railway mobile workers assigned to interoperable cross-border services, 2004).
77. Directive 2000/34 revising Directive 93/104 (now consolidated by Directive 2003/88).
78. The social partners in the Joint Committee on Rail Transport simply agreed in 1998 to include railway workers under Directive 93/34. In the route transport sector no agreement was reached.
79. Also according to the Commission: COM (2002) 341 final; COM (2004) 557 final.

practice.[80] Effective implementation of, especially, autonomous agreements, or next generation texts that turn to OMC-like methods, will depend on setting clear goals and benchmarks, followed up by (on-the-spot) monitoring and periodical reporting. These mechanisms, however, are insufficiently provided in the majority of European social partners' texts.

Even greater problems to autonomous implementation by national affiliates flow from the absence of the necessary preconditions for bilateral bargaining in some Member States. The problem substantially increased with the enlargement of the EU. In many sectors members at the employers' side are general business organizations and not specific employers' associations involved in bilateral collective bargaining. In the 'new' Member States, more generally, social partners' structures are often restricted to national, tripartite consultation, social partner organizations at sectoral level hardly exist, existing associations have rather weak capacities and density rates are low.[81] Therefore, coverage by autonomous ECAs will be far from complete and vary strongly among the Member States as well as the industrial sectors. Furthermore, as already discussed above, due to conflicting interpretations whether 'voluntary framework agreements' are to be implemented by binding instruments at national level, the social standards concerned, if implemented, may differ in regard of their binding character.

4.2.2. Modifications of Agreements incorporated in Directives

Finally in regard to agreements incorporated in legislative acts, the contractual nature of the agreement may raise questions in regard of regulatory qualities such as transparency and legal certainty. Contracts can expire or at will be renegotiated. What will in the case of modifications of ECAs be the status of public laws of which these contracts are an integral part? Additionally, modification can raise questions in regard of competing powers and responsibilities. Can social partners' contracts, when implemented by Council Directive, modify directives adopted by the 'traditional' legislative route, thereby 'overruling' the EP? The Commission, in fact, has consulted the partners frequently on the revision of 'traditional' social legislation, as it is obliged to do under Article 154, but up till now the social partners never managed to reach agreement on the subjects involved. Just recently, the social partners, on the initiative of the Commission, did revise two of their own agreements that are incorporated in a Directive.

In June 2009 the European social partners revised the Parental Leave Agreement of 1995.[82] One has to assume the revised agreement to be valid as from this date (no other date of entry is specified). This can have unexpected consequences.

80. COM (2004) 557 final, 7.
81. Communication from the Commission, 'Partnership for change in an enlarged Europe: Enhancing the contribution of European social dialogue', COM (2004) 557 final, 3. See also Keller 2008, n. 75, 212; Branch 2005, n. 53, 330–331.
82. BUSINESSEUROPE, UEAPME, CEEP and ETUC, Framework Agreement on Parental Leave (Revised), 18 Jun. 2009.

Strictly arguing, Directive 96/43 could have been deprived of its objective since June 2009, as it no longer implements a valid agreement. The matter may appear rather academic, but could lead to an impasse if, subsequently, the Council were to refuse the implementation of the revised agreement. The Commission did not address the issue, but simply put forward a proposal for a new Council Directive,[83] implementing the revised agreement. Interestingly, Directive 96/43 is not to be revised but to be repealed, which may possibly effect the validity of the case law of the ECJ developed hereupon.

In the case of the revision of the (sectoral) European Agreement on the Organization of Working Time of Seafarers (1998), implemented by Directive 99/63, the transparency of the EU decision-making process is challenged even more. On initiative of the Commission, the EC Ship-owners' Associations and the European Transport Workers' Federation concluded in May 2008 the 'Agreement on the ILO Maritime Labour Convention 2006', and requested its implementation by Council decision. Council Directive 2009/13, adopted in February 2009, 'will help bring about the simultaneous entry into force and uniform transposition in all Member States of the standards of Maritime Labour Convention 2006, to which it refers'.[84] The Directive, rather surprisingly, overrides the national sovereignty of the Member States under international law, which would have allowed them not to ratify this particular ILO Convention. The point to be made here, however, is that by way of an annex to the Agreement on the Maritime Labour Convention also necessary amendments were made to another social partner agreement, that is the European Agreement on Working Time of Seafarers (1998), implemented by Directive 99/63. Hence, straightforward implementation of the Agreement on the Maritime Labour Convention by Council Directive could possibly have as its byproduct the amendment of the annex to Directive 99/63. Modification of one directive by way of an annex to a social partner agreement that itself is annexed to another directive, does not appear to contribute to better law-making. Still, the Commission and the Council took another course when adopting Directive 2009/13 on the Maritime Labour Convention. The annex to the social partner agreement to be incorporated in the Directive was left out and the necessary amendments to Directive 99/63 on Working Time were instead included in the body of Directive 2009/13 itself. But this again, might imply that the amendments made to Directive 99/63 do not flow directly from a social partner agreement that is implemented according to, now, Article 155(2). The latter provokes the question whether the amendments constitute a 'traditional' change of legislation on the basis of Article 153 TFEU that would have required co-decision by the EP.[85]

83. COM (2009) 410 final.

84. 'Proposal for a Council Directive implementing the Agreement concluded by the ECSA and the ETF on the Maritime Labour Convention, 2006 and amending Directive 1999/63/EC', COM (2008) 422 final, 8.

85. Perhaps particularly interesting because the actual amendments made included *reformatio in peius*.

5. CONCLUSIONS

Viewed purely through a public law lens, the ESD hardly fits the legality requirements as defined in the research context of this book. To the extent that the ESD can result in generally binding law obligations, it lacks clearly defined powers that are enacted by law. Its application flows from non-binding Commission's communications. Public interventions in the 'autonomous' social dialogue causes the spheres of responsibilities of the EU institutions and the European social partners to overlap, blurring the concept of accountability (section 2 *supra*). Furthermore, the ambiguity of the notions of representativity applied to the ESD prevents the legitimacy of its generally binding outcomes to be satisfactorily explained, either on the basis of constitutional law principles or industrial law ones (section 3 *supra*). Contractual self-governance, finally, poses difficulties in regard of transparency, legal certainty or effective application in the cases of autonomous implementation and modification of ECAs (section 4 *supra*).

But how appropriate or exhaustive is this legality concept in respect of European law-making, and, more specifically, in respect of the ESD? One might argue the multi-layered context of legal orders concerned and increasing internationalization and complexity of society in general, require different, and new, checks and balances in case of EU decision-making. This question, however, demands a subtle approach in my opinion.

On the one hand, the concept of legality, as understood in this research context, should not too easily be abandoned because it is conceived to refer to national concepts only. It cannot be ignored that the legality-deficit of the ESD could amount to serious constitutional problems in respect of European social policy-making. Standoffs are to be expected once the implementation of an ECA is refused by the Council; implementation is requested of mutual opposing ECAs because of the overlap of competences between the Sectoral Social Dialogue Committees or between the Sectoral and Cross-Industry Committees; a Social Policy Directive adopted by the Council and the EP is amended (*in pejus*) by an ECA implemented by Council Directive or an autonomous ECA would pursue social objectives considered to fall outside the powers conferred upon the Union, et cetera. The ESD could be a legal 'minefield' in this respect. No accidents occurred yet, but this seems basically due to the strong guidance by the Commission – anticipating such problems, but compromising autonomy –[86] and the rather low success-rate of the dialogue in general.

On the other hand, it must be admitted that the multi-layered nature of the Union's legal order also introduced new and different aspects to required checks

86. For instance in the case of the Agreement on the Maritime Labour Convention, the Commission instructed the social partners that certain matters covered by the ILO Convention as well as the Agreement fell outside the scope of Art. 137 TEC, while others would necessitate political unanimity in the Council according to Art. 139 TEC. The Commission 'invited' the social partners 'to delete' all of these provisions, which was done so (Minutes of the working group meeting of the Sectoral Social Dialogue Committee 'Maritime transport', held on 23 Apr. 2008, Social Dialogue texts database at <http://ec.europa.eu/social>, 6 Jun. 2009).

and balances in case of public decision-making. Specific 'European' concepts were developed, such as the conferral of power doctrine, requiring a legal basis for EU actions. To tackle the complexity as well as legitimacy of multi-level governance, more recently, new modes of European governance were introduced, allowing for flexibility and subsidiarity. Should the legality of the ESD not (also) be assessed from this more 'European' perspective?

Indeed, the ESD has its legal basis in the Treaty. Nevertheless, the embryonic stage of its institutional design is troublesome. In 2002 the Commission remarked that 'the ESD raises the question of ECAs as sources of law, which should be taken into consideration on the forthcoming reform of the Treaty'.[87] In the wake of the debate on better governance the Commission, later on, shifted its focus to the qualities of the ESD as 'a pioneering example of improved consultation and the application of subsidiarity'.[88] In respect of its consultative function this seems undisputed, but, as discussed above (section 3.2, *supra*), are the decision-making powers of the ESD, capable of resulting in binding Union law, that have been questioned?

European collective agreements are potentially a powerful means in the field of social regulation. They can contribute significantly to flexibility according to cross-border industrial sectors as well as national practices. The ESD, however, did not fulfil these expectations in practice. Besides other factors, it appears its ambiguous nature prevented this. No choice was made between a constitutional or an industrial law model, resulting in imperfect delegation of powers, as well as ambivalent recognition of contractual autonomy. In case of the institutional route, it seems the advantages of flexibility and subsidiarity are largely diminished. If a bargaining process is embarked on, the mould of the future legislative act seems to produce the same kind of top-down precepts as otherwise would have been proposed, albeit watered down due to the weaker bargaining position of the trade unions. The autonomous route, a much more promising way in regard of subsidiarity, lacks the necessary institutional requirements in order to be effective. OMC-methods, on which the social partners increasingly relied themselves, do not seem well-suited for core issues of industrial relations. As pointed out by Keller, the OMC encompasses strict cooperation of public authorities with common interests and shared goals, while collective bargaining indicates the pursuit of, often, opposing self-interests.[89] The autonomous agreements concluded so far are indeed restricted to consensual topics, such as heath and safety.

Based on the foregoing, raising the legality of the social dialogue would require clear-cut choices. In the end, I would say, better social governance at European level could profit most in case legislative social acts are not supplanted, but supplemented by genuine CLAs. This implies a reform of the quasi-legislative procedure of the ESD into a European legal framework supporting collective bargaining, including recognition of the binding nature of the CLA, procedures

87. COM (2002) 341 final, 19.
88. COM (2004) 557 final, 5–6.
89. Keller 2008 n. 75.

(and legal redress) to establish independent, representative status and mechanisms for third-party effects. Of course, it should be realized that even than cross-border industrial relations will not emerge any time soon, due to need of sufficient self-organization of workers and employers at grassroots level. Still, introducing the necessary structures to promote and support collective bargaining at European level could be an impetus, and would be a recognition of the international law standards in this respect.

The likelihood of political action in the near future, however, seems small, especially when taking into account that, despite several Treaty-reforms, the procedure has never been altered in face of criticism in the past. Perhaps, one would almost hope one of the legal 'mines' in the field, as referred to above, to explode in order to put the ESD back on the political agenda.

Part V

Legality and Concealed Mechanisms behind Extension of EU Powers

Chapter 12

The Principle of Attributed Powers and the 'Scope of EU Law'

Sacha Prechal, Sybe de Vries & Hanneke van Eijken

1. INTRODUCTION

Under the principle of attributed powers, the European Union (EU) and formerly the EC only enjoy powers that have been granted by the Treaties. The principle is laid down in two closely linked Treaty provisions: Article 5(1) Treaty on European Union (TEU) provides that '[t]he limits of Union competences are governed by the principle of conferral'. Article 5(2) TEU elaborates: 'Under the principle of conferral, the Union shall act only within the limits of the competences conferred upon it by the Member States in the Treaties *to attain* the objectives set out therein. *Competences not conferred upon the Union in the Treaties remain with the Member States.*' Article 13(2) TEU prescribes that each institution must act 'within the limits of the powers conferred upon it by [the] Treaties, *and in conformity with the procedures, conditions and objectives set out in them*'. Note that both Article 5 and 13 contain a number of amendments to their counterparts in the EC Treaty. We have marked the most important ones in italics. It is not difficult to imagine that the main purpose of these additions reflects a new endeavour to stop competence creep.

Although Article 5 relates to the division of competences between the EU and the Member States and Article 13 rather to the 'separation' of powers between

Leonard Besselink, Frans Pennings & Sacha Prechal (eds), *The Eclipse of the Legality Principle in the European Union*, pp. 213–247.

institutions, the so-called institutional balance – the relationship between the provisions – comes particularly to the fore when we consider the legal basis requirement, one of the most important expressions of the principle of attributed powers. What the EU and the institutions are required or entitled to do is laid down in the Treaties in a series of separate provisions, generally referred to as the 'legal basis'. The legal basis in European law defines the EU competence *ratione materiae* and specifies the means of exercise of competence (instruments to be used and decision-making procedures to be followed; the latter implies, *inter alia*, the institution competent to act and the degree of EP involvement et al.). All these aspects reflect the complex and delicate balance of powers between the Member States, the EU and the institutions.

The principle of attributed powers and its 'derivative', the legal basis requirement, have, as a primary function, to uphold the institutional balance and the division of powers between the EU and its Member States. Nevertheless, we submit that they can also be considered, in the EU context, as the equivalent of the principle of legality, to be understood as the requirement that any act of government that imposes unilateral obligations on citizens must have a basis in law, that is, must have a statutory basis. Thus, for instance, the European Court of Justice (ECJ) will not accept instruments which confer rights or impose obligations on individuals or Member States if they do not have a proper legal basis in primary or secondary law.[1] The rudimentary outline of the principle of attributed powers here above reflects the various functions legality has in a legal system. It is supposed to attribute specified powers in order to realize a certain division and separation of powers; by setting limits, it aims to regulate the exercise of the powers, and in the procedures it implies, it legitimates the exercise of public authority.

However, Articles 5 and 13 TEU (or their predecessors), as well as the legal basis requirement are apparently unable to stop the creeping expansion of the EU competences. One of the most important reasons behind this so-called 'competence creep' is the liberal interpretation of the legal basis provisions by both the EU institutions and, in particular, the ECJ, in combination with the rather vague and open wording of the legal basis provisions themselves.

The problem of 'competence creep', in particular in relation to the legal basis case law of the ECJ and practice of the institutions, has generated considerable scholarly (and political) discussion and writing.[2] The competence creep we are talking about here concerns, primarily, *positive intervention* by the EU institutions, that is, notably the exercise of legislative powers, although other methods of intervention by the EU may be included as well.[3] However, there also operates

1. T. von Danwitz, *Europäisches Verwaltungsrecht* (Berlin: Springer, 2008), 346 e.v.,
2. See *inter alia* S. Weatherill, 'Competence and Legitimacy', in: *The Outer Limits of European Union Law*, ed. Barnard & Odudu (Oxford: Hart Publishing, 2009), 17 and Wyatt, 'Community Competence to Regulate the Internal Market', in: *50 Years of the European treaties*, ed. Dougan & Currie (Oxford: Hart Publishing, 2009), 93, both with many further references.
3. Such as the use of soft law instruments or OMC, financial incentives, coordination, development of policies et al.

another 'mechanism' that is often perceived as a matter of 'competence creep'. This occurs as soon as the – usually – Member State action[4] can be situated within the scope of the Treaty or EU law. When this is the case, various limits imposed by EU law have to be observed, even if the subject matter at issue falls outside the scope of EU competence to act and the Member States are in principle free to regulate on the matter. Although this is, in our opinion, not a matter of competence creep in a proper, or perhaps narrow, sense, it is often considered a form of competence creep. Member States, and in particular various actors within the Member States, often make no subtle distinctions between the scope of application of EU law on the one hand, and the matter of competence to act (often legislate) on the other.

Indeed, part of the problem here is that the distinction between the 'scope of the Treaty' and the 'competence of the EU institutions' is often blurred, or both notions are – erroneously – conflated. Although there is an overlap, the former is broader than the latter. Matters within the scope of the Treaty are not per se matters on which the EU may act. In this chapter we will, in the first place, explore the question of how the ECJ decides whether a matter is within the scope of the Treaty. The second aim of the present contribution is to analyse the relationship between the principle of attributed powers and the doctrine of 'the scope of EU law/the Treaty'. Here, we focus on the question of what are, viewed through the prism of the principle of attributed powers, the consequences of declaring an action to be within the scope of EU law.

These questions are explored in four subject areas of EU law: The first concerns the application of fundamental rights and, in particular, general principles of EU law.[5] The second area is the application of Article 12 of the former EC Treaty (now 18 Treaty on the Functioning of the European Union (TFEU)) – the general prohibition of discrimination on grounds of nationality. This prohibition applies only 'within the scope of application of this Treaty'. There exists extensive (but overall relatively poorly analysed) case law on this issue, including the very dynamic case law on EU citizenship. The third area deals with the 'Treaty freedoms' and their interpretations by the ECJ, in particular with regard to the notion of discrimination/restrictions and the scope left for justification. The last area is that of Treaty provisions on competition, where broad interpretation of notions such as 'undertaking' and 'economic activity' cause EU competition law to apply. We wind up with a brief assessment of our findings, in particular from the perspective of the principle of legality.

4. Sometimes more neutral terms are used, such as whether 'a situation' is within the scope of EU law.
5. For a more detailed discussion see S. Prechal, 'Competence Creep and General Principles of Law', *Review of European Administrative Law* 1 (2010).

2. WHEN IS MEMBER STATE ACTION WITHIN THE SCOPE OF EU LAW?

2.1. FUNDAMENTAL RIGHTS, GENERAL PRINCIPLES OF LAW AND MEMBER STATE ACTION

There is an intimate link between fundamental rights and general principles of law. For want of a Community list of fundamental rights, the latter were protected in the EU as 'general principles of Community law'. This has remained the case after the entry into force of the Lisbon Treaty reforms. Although it raises the Charter of Fundamental Rights to the level of treaty law, Article 6(3) TEU retains the provision that '[f]undamental rights, as guaranteed by the European Convention for the Protection of Human Rights and Fundamental Freedoms and as they result from the constitutional traditions common to the Member States, shall constitute general principles of the Union's law'.

Obviously, the notion of fundamental rights as general legal principles poses problems – for instance, the distinction between fundamental rights and 'ordinary' general principles is not always clear-cut. It will sometimes be clear that we are dealing with a 'true' fundamental right, such as the freedom of expression; in other cases, such as the prohibition of discrimination, the classification is less self-evident.[6] However, the very fact that fundamental rights are treated as a category of principles of law implies that various features from the case law on fundamental rights also apply to principles (and *vice versa*). This is, *inter alia*, the case with regard to the question of when fundamental rights and general principles of law bind the Member States.

In the EU legal system, fundamental rights and general principles of EU law do not operate in a self-standing fashion or in the abstract. As far as the measures taken by the Member States are concerned, the latter must comply with fundamental rights and general principles only if the measures fall within the scope of the law of the Union. Three categories of situation can be distinguished here: the measures at issue implement EU law; the Member State relies on some permitted derogation under EU law; measures fall otherwise within the scope of the law of the Union – for example, some specific substantive rule of EU law is applicable.[7]

The first category is relatively well-defined and the least contested. The Member States act as 'agents' of the EU. The activities involved include the implementation of directives,[8] the application or so-called operationalisation of regulations,[9] and

6. The discussion is further also complicated because, in Community law, some fundamental principles are actually enshrined in the Treaty, for example, Art. 18 TFEU – see below.
7. See Opinion of AG Sharpston in Case C-427/06, *Bartsch* [2008] ECR I-7245, in particular point 69.
8. Joined Cases C-20/00 and C-46/00, *Booker Aquaculture* [2003] ECR I-7411; Case C-144/04, *Mangold* [2005] ECR I-9981; C-442/00, *Caballero* [2002] ECR I-11915.
9. Case C-345/06 *Heinrich*, Judgment of 10 Mar. 2009, n.y.r.; Case C-349/07 *Sopropé*, Judgment of 18 Dec. 2008, n.y.r.

the enforcement of EU law.[10] It also relates to the interpretation of national law implementing a framework decision[11] et al. The fact that the Member State enjoys discretion and the degree of that discretion is irrelevant.[12] Also, where a Member State amends national legislation within the discretion granted by a directive or anticipates an amending directive, the obligation to observe general principles applies.[13]

The *locus classicus* of the second – a slightly more contested – category is the *ERT* case[14] – the Greek television monopoly case. One of the issues in this case was the scope of the freedom to provide services. The disputed State restriction on broadcasting was, at first sight, incompatible with the freedom to provide services, and therefore it had to be justified. In this process of justification, Article 10 of the European Convention for the Protection of Human Rights (ECHR) – the freedom of expression – had to be taken into account. The ECJ found that the public policy, public security and public health derogation must be interpreted and applied in such a way as to respect Article 10 ECHR. Ever since *ERT*, there have been cases in which the ECJ either imposed additional – general principles or fundamental rights based – requirements upon the Member States,[15] or it has accepted that the fundamental rights may themselves be relied upon as derogation from a Treaty freedom.[16]

The third category is the most difficult to grasp. A case that seems to fall within this last category is *Karner*.[17] It concerned an Austrian restriction on commercial advertisement. However, the Austrian provision at issue was not covered by Article 28 EC Treaty (now 34 TFEU) since it was considered a selling arrangement within the meaning of *Keck*. This implied that there was no need to review whether the restriction was justified under the EC Treaty or the rule of reason. Nevertheless, the ECJ proceeded with an independent test under Article 10 ECHR. Apparently (the 'why' was not substantiated by the ECJ) the national rules were believed to be 'within the field[18] of application of Community law'. A possible explanation could lie in the fact that the *potential qualification* of a measure as a restriction prohibited under Article 28 suffices to consider the matter to be within the scope of Community law. In another case, the exercise of a Member State's autonomous powers in relation to VAT (retention of tax credit

10. Case C-28/05, *Dokter* [2006] ECR I-5431.
11. Case C-105/03, *Pupino* [2005] ECR I-5285.
12. Joined Cases C-378-380/07, *Angelidaki*, Judgment of 23 Apr. 2009, n.y.r. (point 85).
13. Case C-376/02, *Stichting Goed Wonen* [2005] ECR I-3445; Case C-81/05, *Alonso* [2006] ECR I-7569.
14. Case C-260/89 *ERT* [1991] ECR I-2925.
15. Case C-60/00, *Carpenter* [2002] ECR I-6279; Case C-109/01, *Akrich* [2003] ECR I-9607; C-368/95, *Familia Press* [1997] ECR I-3689; Joined Cases C-482/01 and C-493/01, *Orfanopoulos and Oliveri* [2004] ECR I-5257, C-441/02, *Commission v. Germany* [2006] ECR I-3449; C-370/05, *Festersen* [2007] ECR I-1129.
16. Case C-112/00, *Schmidberger* [2003] ECR I-5659; Case C-438/05, *Viking* [2007] ECR I-10779.
17. Case C-71/02, *Karner* [2004] ECR I-3025.
18. In our view there is essentially no difference between the scope and the field of EU law/the Treaty.

by the tax authorities, *inter alia*, in cases where there are grounds for presumption of tax evasion) was not, as such, governed by the 6th VAT Directive. Nevertheless, the Court pointed out that the Member States must observe the principle of proportionality and must employ such means that are the least detrimental to the objectives and the principles laid down by the relevant Community legislation.[19] Some specific substantive rule of EC law happened to be applicable to the situation. Unfortunately, these cases do not provide much guidance as to the question of when a situation, within this third category, falls within the scope of EU law. Moreover, one may wonder whether there exist other connecting factors with EU law on the basis of which the Member States can be said to act within the scope of EU law, and can therefore be bound by the general principles. In *Bartsch*,[20] the Commission relied on the judgment in *Saldahna*, where an empowering Treaty provision brought the case within the scope of the Treaty for the purposes of then Article 12 TEC.[21]

The case of Ms. Bartsch concerned a refusal to pay her a widow's pension on basis of a 'age-gap clause' in an occupational pension scheme, which provided that payments would not be made if the widow/widower was more than fifteen years younger than the former employee. The national court wondered whether such a clause was compatible with the general principle prohibiting age discrimination, as identified by the ECJ in *Mangold*.[22] The transposition period of the relevant Directive, Directive 2000/78 on equal treatment in employment and occupation, was at the material time still running. In contrast to Commission's submission, neither the AG nor the ECJ found a connecting factor to be present. This is remarkable in so far as the matter of occupational pensions is rather extensively dealt with in Directives 86/378, 96/97 and 2006/54 (all concerning equal treatment of men and women in occupational pension schemes) and, in fact, also in Article 157 TFEU (ex 141 TEC).[23] Moreover, the treatment of Ms Bartsch could have qualified as indirect sex discrimination. Either this point escaped the parties and the ECJ in the case, or the connecting factor was too remote. Yet it is dangerous to speculate on basis of arguments that have been ignored. In any case, *Bartsch* would suggest that there is no general rule that national provisions that happen to fall within the scope of a new Directive[24] must be compatible with general principles of law. This also seems to imply that the 'competence-approach', discussed in the next section in relation to the former Article 12 TEC, does not work when fundamental rights or general principles of law are at stake.[25]

---

19. Joined Cases C-286/94, C-340/95, C-401/95 and C-47/96, *Garage Molenheide et al.* [1997] ECR I-7281.
20. Case C-427/06, *Bartsch* [2008] ECR I-7245.
21. Case C-122/96, *Saldanha* [1997] ECR I-5325, for a discussion see below, s. 2.2.
22. Case C-144/04, *Mangold* [2005] ECR I-9981.
23. Case 80-70, *Defrenne I* [1971] ECR 445; Case C-262/88, *Barber* [1990] ECR I-1889.
24. That is, Directive (EC) 2000/78 of the Council of 27 Nov. 2000 establishing a general framework for equal treatment in employment and occupation, OJ 2000, L303/16.
25. See also the rather straight forward case law like Case C-328/04, *Vajnai* [2005] ECR I-8577.

2.2. Article 18 TFEU in general

As was observed above, according to Article 18 TFEU, the general prohibition of discrimination based on nationality is only applicable 'within the scope of application of [the EC] Treaty'. Thus, in order to rely on Article 18 TFEU, a certain situation has to be within the scope of the Treaty itself or covered by secondary EU law respectively.[26] Moreover, the prohibition is applicable 'without prejudice to any special provisions'. In particular, since the Treaty freedoms include prohibition of discrimination on grounds of nationality, Article 18 TFEU does not apply in any of the situations where a specific Treaty freedom provision can be invoked.[27]

Article 18 TFEU does not specify who may rely on the prohibition or which situations are within the scope of the Treaty. Yet, in the case law of the ECJ we can discern certain elements which are used by the Court in order to decide whether a situation falls within the scope of Community law or not. First, only interstate situations are within the scope of Community law, at least in the case of free movement in conjunction with Article 18 TFEU. So, reverse discrimination is not 'caught' by the Article 18 TFEU. A Union citizen cannot claim equal treatment from his own Member State in order to claim benefits granted to nationals of other Member States. The fact that a tax system is more generous to workers of other Member States than for its own nationals cannot be solved by Article 18 TFEU. For the latter category of individuals the interstate link is missing.[28] Furthermore, there are basically two approaches to determining the scope of Community law in the sense of Article 18 TFEU: a 'competence approach' and an 'internal market approach'.[29]

In *Forcheri,*[30] the ECJ held that although the Community has no competence to legislate on educational and vocational training policy, this does not mean that this area falls outside the scope of Community law. The ECJ referred to Article 128 Treaty on the European Economic Community (TEEC) in its reasoning (now Article 166 (and 6) TFEU), which provides the complementary competence to contribute to the improvement of vocational training, with the explicit exclusion of harmonization by the Community. The same reasoning was followed in the case of *Gravier*[31] on the payment of fees for vocational training. The Court concluded

---

26. In two recent cases the ECJ made clear that the principle laid down in Art. 12 also applies within the scope of the Euratom Treaty (Case C-115/08 *Land Oberösterreich*, Judgment of 27 Oct. 2009, n.y.r.) and when the Member States give effect to a Third Pillar framework decision (Case C-123/08 *Wolzenburg,* Judgment of 6 Oct. 2009, n.y.r.).
27. See for example, Case 186/87, *Cowan* [1989] ECR 195, para. 17.
28. Case 44/84, *Hurd* [1986] ECR 29.
29. See also T. Ackermann, Case C-43/95, *Data Delecta Aktiebolag and Ronny Forsberg v. MSL Dynamics Limited* (Sixth Chamber) Judgment of 26 Sep. 1996 [1996] ECR I-4661; Case C-323/95, *David Charles Hayes and Jeanette Karen Hayes v. Kronenberger GmbH,* in liquidation (Sixth Chamber) Judgment of 20 Mar. 1997 [1997] ECR I-1711; Case C-122/96, *Saldanha* (Sixth Chamber) Judgment of 2 Oct. 1997, n.y.r., *Common Market Law Review* 3 (1998): 790.
30. Case 152/82, *Forcheri* [1983] ECR 2323.
31. Case 293/83, *Gravier* [1985] ECR 593.

that due to the same Article and Regulation 1612/69,[32] the requirements for access to vocational training fall within the scope of Community law. In the case of *Lair*,[33] the Court made a distinction between access to education (and the directly related conditions) and the grant of allowances for the maintenance of those students. The ECJ found that study grants fell 'in the present stage of development of Community law' outside the material scope, because those funds were a '*matter of educational policy, which is not as such included in the spheres entrusted to the Community institutions*' (referring to then Article 128 TEEC). Moreover, the Court added, such assistance to students was also '*a matter of social policy, which falls within the competence of the Member States in so far as it is not covered by specific provisions of the EEC Treaty*'.[34]

So far the Court of Justice seems to refer to the existence of a competence in the Treaties. However, three other cases reveal a different approach by the ECJ. In these cases a national provision of civil law was at stake, which required foreign plaintiffs to secure a sum for the costs of legal proceedings before bringing a case before the national court.[35] Such a provision is obviously discriminatory, but the crucial question was whether the civil procedure requirements fell within the (material) scope of Community law. In the cases of *Data Delecta* and *Hayes*, the Court found that the national provision was within the scope of Community law and thus was caught by the prohibition of discrimination on grounds of nationality, because the requirement was liable to have an (indirect) effect on the trade in goods and services between the Member States. In addition, the ECJ stressed that it is not necessary to connect the national measure with the specific Treaty provisions on free movement. Also, in the case of *Phil Collins*, the Court pointed out that copyright and related rights were included within the Community law scope of application, because of their potential effect on the internal market (free movement of goods and services and competition distortions).[36]

In the case of *Saldanha*, the same kind of national requirement was at stake as in *Data Delecta* and *Hayes*, but the ECJ followed a slightly different reasoning. It concluded that the situation fell within the scope of Article 18 TFEU on basis of Article 50(2)(g) TFEU, and not for reasons of indirect effect on the internal market. Because Article 50(2)(g) confers the competence on the Council and the Commission to coordinate safeguards in the field of company law, the protection of stakeholders fell within the material scope of Community law. The difference

32. Regulation (EEC) 1612/68 of the Council of 15 Oct. 1968 on freedom of movement for workers within the Community, OJ 1968, L 257/2, provided for the right to education for family of workers. Note that as a student, *Gravier* did not fall under the personal scope of this regulation.
33. Case 39/86, *Lair* [1988] ECR 3161.
34. Case 39/86, *Lair* [1988] ECR 3161, para. 15.
35. Case C-43/95, *Data Delecta* [1996] ECR I-4661; Case C-323/95, *Hayes* [1997] ECR I-1711; Case C-122/96, *Saldanha* [1997] ECR I-5325.
36. Joined cases C-92/92 and C-326/92, *Phil Collins* [1993] ECR I-5145, paras 22–28 and also Case C-398/92, *Mund & Fester* [1994] ECR I-467, para. 11, where the Court argued that a national provision on civil procedure fell within the scope of Community law on the basis of Art. 293 EC and the Brussels Convention. According to the Court, the purpose of the possibility of negotiations on civil procedures is to facilitate the internal market.

between the first two cases and *Saldanha* is that Mr Saldanha, as a shareholder, brought a case to the national court to prevent the company from selling shares without the approval of shareholders, whereas in *Hayes* and *Data Delecta*, the foreign plaintiffs were parties in a commercial agreement. The connection with the interstate trade was therefore more obvious. However, in *Saldanha* the Court pointed out that such connection is not necessary in order to consider a matter to be within the scope of application of the Treaty.[37]

Summing up, the scope of Union law is triggered for the purposes of the application of Article 18 TFEU by two different approaches: when the interstate trade is affected in some way (even indirectly),[38] or when there is some competence within the Treaty to act on a certain issue. In that last situation it does not matter whether the competence to regulate an area is used in the specific situation, or what kind of competence it is (even empowering Treaty provisions and provisions on the encouragement of certain policies are sufficient in this respect). As Jacobs rightly pointed out in his conclusion in the case of Phil Collins:

> The application of the principle of non-discrimination is not dependent on the harmonization of national law; on the contrary, it is precisely in areas where harmonization has not been achieved that the principle of national treatment assumes special importance.[39]

2.3. Article 18 TFEU Married to European Citizenship

The introduction of EU citizenship in the EC Treaty by the Treaty of Maastricht gave an important impetus to the case law on Article 18 TFEU. In its case law, the Court used the EU citizenship in conjunction with Article 18 in order to 'put flesh on the bones'[40] of European citizenship. In order to qualify a situation as being 'within the scope of application', two major questions emerged: when or how do persons or situations fall within the personal and material scope of Community law, so as to trigger the application of Article 18 TFEU? As we discuss below, the economic free movement has been subject to a broad interpretation by the Court of Justice. Union citizenship contributed to that case law in different ways. The case of *Bickel and Franz*[41] about a discriminatory regulation on the language to be used in criminal proceedings shows the sometimes fluid relationship between economic free movement (in this case the free movement of recipients of services) and the

37. See the comment of T. Ackermann on these cases in *Common Market Law Review* 3 (1998): 783–799.
38. See also the case of *Cowan* as an example of the broad interpretation of the effect on the internal market as a receiver of services, Case 186/87, *Cowan* [1989] ECR 195 and Case C-172/98, *Commission of the European Communities v. Kingdom of Belgium* [1999] ECR I-3999, para. 12.
39. Opinion of Mr Advocate General Jacobs delivered on 30 Jun. 1993, *Phil Collins* [1993] ECR I-5145, para. 23.
40. Terms are from S. O'Leary, 'Putting Flesh on the Bones of European Citizenship', *European Law Review* 24 (1999): 68–79.
41. C-274/96, *Bickel & Franz* [1998] ECR I-07637.

free movement of persons in their capacity as European citizens.[42] The case was finally decided under Article 56 TFEU, but the Court of Justice also referred to Article 21 TFEU as an alternative provision to grant equal treatment in criminal law proceedings.

2.3.1. Personal Scope

It is generally accepted[43] that persons qualified as European citizens under 20(1) TFEU fall within the scope *ratione personae* of Article 18 TFEU. Until the case of *Vatsouras*,[44] there was some speculation as to whether third country nationals could also invoke Article 18 TFEU. In the preliminary procedure of *Vatsouras*, the opposite question was at stake, namely whether Article 18 TFEU demands that social benefits granted to third country nationals also have to be granted to Union citizens that used their right to move and reside in another Member State. The ECJ held that the prohibition of discrimination 'concerns situations coming within the scope of Community law in which a national of one Member State suffers discriminatory treatment in relation to nationals of another Member State solely on the basis of his nationality and is not intended to apply to cases of a possible difference in treatment between nationals of Member States and nationals of non-member countries'.[45]

In the case law on European citizenship the Court of Justice is quite consistent in its approach to the personal scope. The case of *Martinez Sala* is the starting point of the line of case law we discuss here. Sala was a Spanish national who had been living in Germany for more than twenty years. The child-raising allowance she requested was refused because she did not have German nationality or a residence permit (but was a lawful resident), which constitutes discrimination based on nationality. The next question was whether she could rely on Article 18 TFEU. According to the Court, Sala fell within the personal scope of this provision because she was '*a national of a Member State lawfully residing in the territory of another Member State*'.[46] The same test was performed in the cases of *Grzelzyk,*[47] *Trojani,*[48] *Avello,*[49] *Bidar*[50] *and Förster.*[51] Especially in the case of

42. Niamh Nic Shuibhne, 'The Outer Limits of EU Citizenship', in: Barnard & Odudu (eds), *supra* n. 2, 171.
43. C. de Keersmaeker and T Pauweis, in: *On the law of the European Union 2005*, ed. Smit & Herzog, LexisNexis Matthew Bender, Ch. 89 on Art. 12 TEC.
44. Joined cases 22/08 and C-23/08, *Vatsouras*, Judgment of 4 Jun. 2009, n.y.r.
45. Third country nationals sometimes also profit indirectly from the rights granted to Union citizens' free movement. *Metock* is an example, where the ECJ declared that extra requirements put on TCN married to Union citizens may infringe Community law because it could hinder a Union citizen in moving to another Member State.
46. Case C-85/96, *Martinez Sala* [1998] ECR I-2691, para. 61.
47. Case C-184/99, *Grzelczyk* [2001] ECR I-6193, para. 32.
48. Case C-456/02, *Trojani* [2004] ECR I-7573, para. 43.
49. Case C-148/02, *Carlos Garcia Avello* [2003] ECR I-1161, para. 27.
50. Case C-209/03, *Bidar* [2005] ECR I-2119, para. 32.
51. Case C-158/07, *Förster* [2008] ECR I-8507, para. 43.

Förster the Court emphasized that the intentions of migration were not important. The fact that the student was legally residing in the host Member State seemed to be crucial. Legal residence is thus a key element, but does that mean that migration is a precondition to coming within the personal scope of the Treaty?

The question is whether one may consider the 'lawful residence' as an extra criterion to coming within the personal scope of Article 18 TFEU.[52] Or is it enough for someone to have the nationality of a Member State and therefore also the *destined fundamental status*[53] of a European citizen?

The abovementioned cases have in common that the citizens at stake claimed equal treatment from their host State, rather than from the Member State of origin. This explains why the ECJ used the lawful residence as criterion. The criterion 'lawful residence' seems to be a way of avoiding the question of whether Article 21 TFEU grants the right of access to a Member State. Thus, when a Union citizen is granted access to and resides lawfully in another Member State – either on basis of Community law or national law – he or she should be treated equally in comparison with the nationals of that Member State.[54] In another category of cases on Union citizenship it is clearer that the personal scope is solely based on the status of EU citizenship. These cases deal with Union citizens claiming equal treatment against their own State.

In the case of *D'Hoop*,[55] for example, Nathalie D'Hoop claimed equal treatment with regard to a tide-over allowance – a social benefit for persons who completed their education in Belgium. Because she studied in France, this allowance was refused. In this case the ECJ found that since Ms D'Hoop was a Union citizen (due to her Belgium nationality), she fell within the personal scope of Community law and could claim equal treatment.[56] In the case of *Schempp*, the ECJ was quite clear on the migration element, concluding that:

> Article 17(2) EC attaches to the status of citizen of the Union the rights and duties laid down by the Treaty, including the right to rely on Article 12 EC in all situations falling within the material scope of Community law.[57]

Union citizens can claim equal treatment grounded on their status as Union citizens. The migration element is thus not crucial, at least not in order to come within the personal scope of Article 18 TFEU.

---

52. This has to be distinguished form the question of whether Art. 18 applies – see above (2.2) on the 'interstate requirement'.
53. Case C-184/99, *Grzelczyk* [2001] ECR I-6193, para. 31; Case C-224/98, *D'Hoop* [2002] ECR I-6191, para. 28; Case C-148/02, *Avello* [2003] ECR I-1161, para. 22; Case C-403/03, *Schempp* [2005] ECR I-6421, para. 15.
54. An example is Case C-456/02, *Trojani* [2004] ECR I-7573. He lived and worked in a Salvation Army hostel and did not satisfy the conditions for lawful residence based on Community law. The fact that he was granted a residence permit by national law was sufficient to trigger the application of Art. 18, together with 21 TFEU.
55. Case C-224/98, *D'Hoop* [2002] ECR I-6191.
56. Paragraph 27–28.
57. Case C-403/03, *Schempp* [2005] ECR I-6421, para. 17.

In brief, in order to come within the personal scope of Article 18 TFEU, one must have the nationality of one of the Member States, and consequently the status of a European citizen by virtue of Article 20(1) TFEU. Note however, that the national rules governing nationality remain a matter of Member States' competence, with the case of *Chen*[58] as an extreme example. This means that the personal scope of Article 18 TFEU, when combined with EU citizenship, is dependent on the choice of the Member States. This implies that one of the elements that makes the situation 'enter into the scope of the Treaty', with all the potential consequences discussed below, derives directly from the Member State rules on nationality of persons.[59]

2.3.2. Material Scope

A more complex question than the personal scope of citizenship provisions is when or how the material scope in the application of Article 18 TFEU is triggered by certain claims of European citizens.[60] Is it enough that the situation of the person concerned has a cross-border element, and therefore falls within the scope of Article 21 TFEU? Or should, in addition to Article 21, the specific claim (mostly social benefits, but also the registration of a surname) also be covered by another provision in Community law? Or should the specific benefit be directly related to movement and residence (e.g., social benefits, rented housing) and therefore derive directly from Article 21 TFEU?[61]

From the case law of the ECJ it is clear that the right to free movement and residence laid down in Article 21 TFEU as such is the core element to bring a situation within the scope of Union law. The ECJ concludes in many cases that the material scope 'include[s] those [situations] involving the exercise of the fundamental freedoms guaranteed by the Treaty and those involving the exercise of the right to move and reside within the territory of the Member States'.[62]

A close look at the case law on citizenship in conjunction with Article 18 shows that the ECJ, at least initially, did not rely solely on Article 21 TFEU to fulfil the material scope. It seemed also to require that the benefit (or other claim) at stake fell within the material scope of Union law as well. For instance, in *Sala* the ECJ concluded that a child-raising allowance (as social benefit provided for in

58. Case C-200/02, *Chen* [2004] ECR I-9925.
59. Recently the Court of Justice decided that rules on nationality may be subject to review on compatibility with Union law. Although the Court concluded that the withdrawal of nationality in certain circumstances is allowed by Union law, the Member States have to comply with the principles of proportionality. Case C-135/08, *Rottmann,* Judgment of 2 Mar. 2010, n.y.r.
60. Y. Borgmann-Prebil, 'The Rule of Reason in European Citizenship', *European Law Journal* 3 (2008): 328.
61. G. Davies, European Internal Market Law, 2nd ed. (London: Cavendish Publishing, 2003), 119.
62. See Case C-209/03, *Bidar* [2005] ECR I-2119, para. 33, the same phrase is found in Case C-184/99, *Grzelczyk* [2001] ECR I-6193, para. 33; Case C-148/02, *Avello* [2003] ECR I-1161, para. 24; Case C-224/98, *D'Hoop* [2002] ECR I-6191, para. 29; Case C-224/02, *Pusa* [2004] ECR I-5763, para. 17; Case C-520/04, *Turpeinen* [2006] ECR I-10685, para. 19; Case C-76/05, *Schwarz* [2007] ECR I-6849, para. 87; Case C-158/07, *Förster* [2008] ECR I-8507, para. 37.

Regulations 1408/71 and 1612/68) fell within the material scope. In *Grzelczyk*, a student of French nationality requested a '*minimex*' (a minimum social allowance) in Belgium after three years of studying. In the first three years of his education *Grzelczyk* was able to work and to provide for his own cost of living. The *minimex* was refused and he therefore turned to Article 18 TFEU. The ECJ found first of all that the *minimex* was a social benefit which fell within the material scope of Community law on the basis of Regulation 1612/68.[63] The same reasoning can be found in *Trojani*.[64] In *D'Hoop*, the material scope was triggered by Article 21 TFEU, and furthermore by Article 3 TEC that mentioned contribution to education as an objective of the Community (repealed) and by Article 149 TEC (165 TFEU).[65] Article 165 TFEU was also used as a supporting argument in *Bidar*.[66] In that case, the Court also had to explain why study grants fall under the material scope, because in earlier case law those maintenance grants where excluded. The Court reasoned in a quite creative fashion: since Directive 2004/38 gives the possibility to limit such benefits to certain groups of citizens, those grants are governed by Community law, and thus fall within the scope *ratione materiae*.

However, other cases indicate that in order to come within the material scope in the sense of Article 18 TFEU, the sole exercise of the rights laid down in Article 21 TFEU is sufficient to bring a given situation within the material scope. The Court seems to examine whether there is some competence in the Treaty in the particular area as a supportive argument of its decision.[67] Such competence provisions are not, however, crucial. This is illustrated by the case of *Avello*,[68] a judgment handed down between *Sala* and *Bidar*. In *Avello* the Court had to decide whether the national rules on surnames fell within the scope of Community law. This case was rather sensitive because of the consequences for the civil code governing the conferral of names. From the *Konstantinidis*[69] case it was already clear that the spelling of names may be contrary to Article 49 TFEU, but in that case the conclusion of the Court was strongly related to the exercise of a profession. The case of *Avello* was, however, not related to economic free movement, nor did the ECJ use a supporting provision to bring the situation within the material scope of Community law, as it did in the earlier case law on non-economic free movement. The ECJ concluded straightforwardly that the 'freedom to move and reside within the territory of the Member States, as conferred by Article 18 EC'[70] falls within the material scope of Community law. That means that although 'the rules governing a person's surname are matters coming within the competence of the Member States, the latter must none the less when exercising that

63. Regulation (EEC) 1612/68 of the Council of 15 Oct. 1968 on freedom of movement for workers within the Community, OJ 1968, L 257/2, para. 27.
64. Case C-456/02, *Trojani* [2004] ECR I-7573, para. 42.
65. Case C-224/98, *D'Hoop* [2002] ECR I-6191, paras 29–32.
66. Case C-209/03, *Bidar* [2005] ECR I-2119, para. 33.
67. See also 'some competence' argument in discussed in 2.2.
68. Case C-148/02, *Avello* [2003] ECR I-1161.
69. Case C-168/91, *Konstantinidis* [1993] ECR I-1191.
70. Case C-148/02, *Avello* [2003] ECR I-1161, para. 24.

competence, comply with Community law'.[71] This case illustrates the far-reaching consequences of Article 21 TFEU, *inter alia*, in terms of 'drawing' within the scope of Community law certain aspects that are, as such, left to the Member States.

Summing up, the key element of all these cases is the sole exercise of free movement (or legal residence) of Article 21 TFEU. It is not necessary that there is an empowering competence in the Treaty in order to come within the material scope of the Treaty. Whenever the Court can find extra and supporting arguments, it will take those Treaty provisions into account. However, such provisions are not necessary to determine that the matter is within the scope of Community law.

2.4. Free Movement

2.4.1. Four Freedoms in General: The 'Economic Connotation'

Although in the field of the free movement of EU citizens the economic connotation as shown above has become increasingly irrelevant, it remains significant for the 'economic freedoms' on goods, services, persons[72] and capital. Goods, for examples, are defined as 'products which can be valued in money and which are capable, as such, of forming the subject of commercial transactions',[73] including cultural goods such as paintings or other works of art, narcotic drugs,[74] and waste products (whether recyclable or not).

Services are provided for remuneration and, for the purposes of Article 56 TFEU, even include activities of a particularly sensitive character, such as lotteries.[75] There is also by now well-established case law[76] under which medical activities, including medical termination of pregnancy, are generally considered to be services within the meaning of Articles 56 and 57 TFEU. The special nature of

71. Case C-148/02, *Avello* [2003] ECR I-1161, para. 25. See also the more recent Case C-353/06, *Grunkin* [2008] I-7639, para. 16–18. In this case the ECJ found no discriminatory effect of the regulation at stake. However, the national competence of regulation surnames is nevertheless subject to the prohibition on discrimination on nationality.
72. Traditionally to be understood as free movement of workers and the freedom of establishment.
73. Case 7/68, *Commission v. Italy (Italian Arts Treasures)* [1968] ECR 423, also published in other special editions of the European Court Reports; see also Case C-2/90, *Commission v. Belgium* [1992] ECR I-4431.
74. Case C-324/93, *Evans Medical* [1995] ECR I-563.
75. Case C-275/92, *Schindler* [1994] ECR I-1039, para. 34. The ECJ stated that: 'like amateur sport, a lottery may provide entertainment for the players who participate. However, that recreational aspect of the lottery does not take it out of the realm of the provision of services. Not only does it give the players, if not always a win, at least the hope of a win, it also yields a gain for the operator [. . .]'.
76. Joined cases 286/82 and 26/83, *Luisi & Carbone* [1984] ECR 377; C-159/90, *Grogan* [1991] ECR I-4685 and, in particular, Case C-158/96, *Kohll* [1998] ECR I-1931; Case C-157/99, *Smits & Peerbooms* [2001] ECR I-5473; Case C-385/99, *Müller-Fauré* [2003] ECR I-4509; Case C-372/04, *Watts* [2006] ECR I-4325.

certain services does not remove them from the ambit of the fundamental principle of free movement. In the same vein, the fact that the Treaty excludes a certain area from the Community's competence is no reason in itself to exclude the application of the free movement rules. After all, the Treaty does not place particular sectors of the economy outside the scope of the fundamental freedoms. According to the ECJ in the *Laval* judgment, where Member States are competent, they must exercise that competence consistently with Community law: 'Therefore, the fact that Article 137 EC (now Article 153 TFEU) does not apply to the right to strike or to the right to impose lock-outs is not such as to exclude collective action such as that at issue in the main proceedings from the domain of freedom to provide services.'[77] Or, in other words, the fact that, for example, provisions on health care and education leave the financing and organization of educational and health care systems to the Member States has not stopped the Court from reviewing the systems under the provisions on the Treaty freedoms.

Where there is no gainful activity involved, or where certain goods are not subject to commercial transactions, the Treaty provisions on free movement will not be applicable. But the distinction between economic and non-economic is not always easy to draw. The case law shows that in some situations education, for example, falls outside the scope of the EC Treaty provisions on free movement and sometimes within it, depending on how it is funded.[78]

2.4.2. The Restriction Approach in Free Movement Cases: Market Access as Leading Criterion

The apparently broad interpretation of the concept of economic activity implies that this notion can only play a minor role in delimiting the scope of Community law. The same also holds true for the interpretation of the Treaty prohibitions.[79] What is prohibited on the basis of the rules on free movement are not only discriminatory measures – although the principle of non-discrimination on grounds of nationality remains the cornerstone of the four freedoms[80] – but also all measures restricting free movement.

Ever since the *Dassonville* case,[81] subsequent cases – and in particular *Cassis de Dijon*[82] – have entailed that not only discriminatory or distinctly applicable measures, but also indistinctly applicable product requirements are caught by the prohibition on restricting trade in goods as contained in Article 28 EC

77. Case C-341/05, *Laval* [2007] ECR I-11767, para. 88; see with respect to competition law, below, s. 2.5.
78. See Case 263/86, *Humbel* [1988] ECR 5365; Case C-109/92, *Wirth* [1993] ECR I-6447.
79. See O. Odudu, 'Economic Activity as a Limit to Community Law', in: Barnard & Odudu (eds), *supra* n. 2, 243.
80. C. Barnard, *The Substantive Law of the EU: The Four Freedoms* (Oxford: Oxford University Press, 2007), 17.
81. Case 8/74, *Dassonville* [1974] ECR 837.
82. Case 120/78, *REWE-Zentral v. Bundesmonopolverwaltung* [1979] ECR 649.

(now Article 34 TFEU).[83] In the context of the provisions on services and persons, the Court made clear that these provisions also apply to indistinctly applicable measures. Rather than extending the concept of selling arrangement, which was introduced in the *Keck* case in respect of the free movement of goods, the Court has always preferred to adopt a 'market access based test' in the context of the free movement of persons and services.[84] This entails that also in more 'sensitive' areas such as healthcare or culture, Member States have no unlimited powers, but have to respect the requirements of primary Community law; the market access based test implies that national measures readily fall within the scope of the prohibitions.[85] Hence, market access appears to be the criterion for adjudicating national laws under the prohibitive rules on free movement, but what does it actually mean? When are national measures deemed to restrict market access? The Court does not employ an 'economic test' under the free movement rules similar to the one it does under the competition rules (see hereafter, section 2.5). A *de minimis* test, for example, as used within the context of Article 81(1) EC (now Article 101(1) TFEU) has never been explicitly employed by the Court.[86] But in the case *Commission v. Italy* regarding an Italian prohibition on the use of trailers for motorcycles, the Court referred to the 'considerable influence on the consumers' as the indicator for whether the national rule impeded market access.[87] What considerable influence on the consumers actually means was not, however, clarified by the Court in its judgment either. Does the Court and, if so, to what extent, by introducing such a criterion intend to delimit the scope of Community law?

In any case, a number of attempts have been made by the ECJ itself to set boundaries for the Treaty freedoms. In the first place, the Court has used the 'criterion of remoteness', or hypothetical situations, which implies that where national rules have too uncertain or indirect an effect on trade, they will not fall

83. Barnard, *supra* n. 80, 83; P. Oliver, *Free Movement of Goods in the European Community* (assisted by Malcolm Jarvis) (London: Sweet & Maxwell, 2003), 115–118.

84. Barnard, *supra* n. 80, 262–273; see also H. Luijendijk, *Nederlandse gemeenten en het Europese personenverkeer* (Deventer: Kluwer, 2005), 166. In Case C-405/98, *Gourmet International* [2001] ECR I-1795, the Court had the possibility to extend its *Keck* (Joined cases C-267/91 and C-268/91, *Keck* [1993] ECR I-6097) approach to the free movement of services, but did not do so.

85. Recently: Case C-169/07, *Hartlauer*, Judgment of 10 Mar. 2009, n.y.r.

86. Case C-67/97, *Bluhme* [1998] ECR I-8033; Ch. Denys, 'European Court of Justice: Case Report', *European Enviromental Law Review* (1999): 87; see also P. Oliver, Some further reflections on the scope of Arts 28–30 (ex 30–36) EC, *Common Market Law Review* 4 (1999): 790.

87. Case C-110/05, *Commission v. Italy*, Judgment of 10 Feb. 2009, n.y.r., para. 56; AG Kokott in Case C-142/05, *Mickelsson*, Judgment of 4 Jun. 2009, n.y.r., held that: 'it is possibly not actually necessary, for the purposes of assessing the present case, to examine whether there are domestic products which are in competition with personal watercraft and whether those comparable products are less affected by the Swedish rules. In this respect it is not only rules which result in complete exclusion, such as a general prohibition on using a certain product, that are to be regarded as preventing access to the market. A situation where only a marginal possibility for using a product remains because of a particularly restrictive rule on use is to be regarded as preventing access to the market' (paras 64 and 67).

within the scope of the free movement rules.[88] In several cases the ECJ has endorsed this doctrine, but the case law is not consistent on this matter.[89]

In the second place, from the case law in the field of sports and Community law, it appears that certain rules laid down by sporting associations will not be considered a restriction within the meaning of Article 56 TFEU if they are inherent in the conduct of a sports event.[90] How far this can be generalized beyond sports is far from clear. Furthermore, the inherent restriction approach seems to be borrowed from EC competition law, where, contrary to the free movement regime, little or no grounds for public interest exceptions exist (see hereafter).[91]

Last but not least, the much-debated *Keck* case introduced a turning point in the case law on the free movement of goods at the time. National rules on selling arrangements were placed outside the scope of Article 34 TFEU, provided that these rules apply to all affected traders operating within the national territory and provided that they affect in the same manner, in law and in fact, the marketing of domestic products and those from other Member States. The outcome of *Keck* is that, if a measure is classified as a product requirement, it will be presumed to impede market access (per se illegal); if on the other hand, the measure is classified as a selling arrangement, the presumption will be that it does not restrict market access (per se legal). This presumption can be rebutted if it is shown that the national law in question discriminates, or even merely hinders, market access.[92]

The importance of *Keck* should nevertheless be put into perspective.[93] First, a clear distinction between product requirements on the one hand and selling arrangements on the other is difficult to make in practice.[94] Second, it is not self-evident that rules regulating selling arrangements do not restrict trade in goods at all.[95] Similarly, in the context of exportation, national rules regulating selling arrangements may have a negative impact on the export of goods. This is illustrated by the *Gysbrechts* case, in which the ECJ not only made clear that Article 29 EC (now Article 35 TFEU) on exports should, from now on, be

---

88. E. Spaventa, 'The Outer Limit of the Treaty Free Movement Provisions: Some Refections on de Significance of *Keck*, Remoteness and *Deliège*', in: Barnard & Odudu (eds), *supra* n. 2, 250–254. For example, Case C-20/03, *Burmanjer* [2005] ECR I-4133.
89. See also K.J.M. Mortelmans, 'The Functioning of the Internal Market: The Freedoms', in: *The Law of the European Union and the European Communities*, ed. Kapteyn & VerLoren van Themaat (Alphen a/d Rijn: Kluwer Law International, 2008), 632–633. In other literature the significance has been questioned (Spaventa, *supra* n. 88, 266).
90. Joined Cases C-51/96 and C-191/97, *Deliège* [2000] ECR I-2549. According to Spaventa (270), there is a conceptual difference between the *Keck* approach and the inherent restriction approach. The latter presumes that, provided there is a legitimate interest at stake, the restriction of free movement stemming from the rules at issue coincides with the purpose to be achieved and should therefore not be scrutinized under the free movement rules.
91. S. de Vries, *Tensions on the Internal Market* (Groningen: Europa Law Publishing, 2006), 45.
92. See also Barnard, *supra* n. 80, 160.
93. See Spaventa, *supra* n. 88, 271.
94. Case C-368/95, *Familiapress* [1997] ECR I-3689; Case C-67/97 *Bluhme* [1998] ECR I-8033.
95. Particular rules on advertising have a great impact on the marketing of goods and hence on trade in goods; Case C-458/06, *Gourmet* [2008] ECR I-4207; Joined cases C-34/95, C-35/95 and C-36/95, *De Agostini* [1997] ECR I-3843.

interpreted broadly including indistinctly applicable export restrictions, but also that *Keck* is difficult to apply in the context of exportation of goods.[96] Third, in recent case law concerning national rules regulating the use of goods such as the *Commission v. Italy* case on national rules prohibiting the use of motorcycles towing a trailer,[97] the Court has not been willing to extend *Keck* to these types of rules. And finally, the *Keck* case has not, so far, found a counterpart in the fields of services, persons or capital, where the Court has continued to apply a market access test instead.

2.4.3. Broad Conception of What Constitutes An Obstacle or Restriction

The second factor that is liable to extend the scope of the free movement rules is that the ECJ also has a broad view of what actually constitutes an obstacle or restriction. Although the jurisprudence of the ECJ is not entirely consistent on the matter,[98] there is a line emerging in the case law, according to which, the question of whether there is an obstacle to free movement or a discriminatory act contrary to the Treaty is separated from the question of whether the actor at the origin of the restriction is a person bound by the relevant Treaty prohibitions. In other words, there seems to be an independent test in which it is first of all of importance to determine what exactly the restriction consists of – does it consist of legislation, binding decisions or also of actual practice – and related to this, who causes the restriction. Is it the legislature, the central or local government, a civil servant, a public organization, is it a sporting federation or a trade union or even individuals holding demonstrations? In the *Laval* case, trade union action and right of unions to take collective action were considered to be a restriction within the meaning of Article 56 TFEU.[99] In *AGM COS-MET*, the statements made by the Finnish civil servant, Lehtinen, were considered to constitute a measure having equivalent effect within the meaning of Article 34 TFEU.[100] In the *Spanish Strawberries* and *Schmidberger* cases it was private action by angry farmers and an environmental organization respectively which constituted the obstacle to free movement.[101]

---

96. As counterpart of the market access test, AG Trstenjak therefore suggested the introduction of a 'market leaving' criterion for national measures restricting the export of goods, which the ECJ, however, has not – at least not explicitly – followed.
97. Case C-110/05, *Commission v. Italy*, Judgment of 10 Feb. 2009, n.y.r.; see also in Case C-142/05, *Mickelsson*, Judgment of 4 Jun. 2009, n.y.r., on the use of personal watercraft in Swedish waters.
98. There are cases in which the very fact that the measure at issue is not a measure taken by the Member States is sufficient to keep them out of the free movement rules. See Case 311/85, *Vlaamse Reisbureaus* [1987] ECR 3801;Case 65/86, *Sullhofer* [1988] ECR 5249. See also the somewhat unclear reasoning in Case C-341/05, *Laval* [2007] ECR I-11767, paras 98 and 99.
99. Case C-341/05, *Laval* [2007] ECR I-11767.
100. Case C-470/03, *AGM COS-MET* [2007] ECR I-2749; see also 'Annotation S. de Vries', *Common Market Law Review* 2 (2008): 569.
101. Case C-265/95, *Commission v. France* [1997] ECR I-6959; Case C-112/00, *Schmidberger* [2003] ECR I-5659.

2.4.4. Justification: A Trompe-L'œil Escape?

As national measures impeding trade between Member States fall under the prohibitions, the justification for such obstacles is crucial. The scope of Member States' exercise of competences is thus largely determined by the justification grounds and, as a consequence, by the application of the proportionality principle. As the Treaty itself is silent on how the justification grounds and the proportionality test should be applied, the ECJ, while struggling to shape the justifications further, is induced and even forced to develop a substantive policy on the justification test. However, in doing so, proportionality is used by the ECJ not only as a device to take account of particular features of national policies and domestic preferences, but may also serve as an instrument to impose certain substantive and procedural requirements on the Member States relating to the choice of the legislative instrument, transparency and good governance principles. We will come back to this below, in section 3.2. Perhaps even more importantly, at the point when the issue of justification is raised, it is clear that the Member States act within the scope of EU law and the Treaty freedoms in particular, with all the possible consequences discussed below.

2.4.5. The Fifth Freedom? towards a Restriction Approach in Citizenship Cases

Recently a new line emerged in the Court's citizenship jurisprudence. The ECJ applied Article 21 TFEU here as an independent source of rights, instead of using Article 18 TFEU in conjunction with Articles 20(1) and 21 TFEU as the foundation of its decisions. The judgments in the cases of *Tas-Hagen & Tas,*[102] *Schwarz,*[103] *Morgan*[104] and *Nerkowska*[105] are exemplary in this respect. The terms used by the ECJ in these cases were 'disadvantage' and 'restriction of the free movement' rather than being limited to 'discrimination' or 'equality'. The application of Article 21 FTEU is moving in the direction of the other 'classical' Treaty freedoms. According to this case law, the right to move and reside freely in the territory of the Member States is nowadays no longer necessarily combined with the prohibition of discrimination on nationality. National measures are instead examined through the prism of a 'restriction assessment'. This is to say, the scope of application of Article 21 TFEU has been extended to situations that are beyond discrimination on grounds of nationality. This has the ultimate consequence that even more national rules are brought within the scope of Community law and have to comply

102. On a benefit to civilian war victims ECJ C-192/05, *Tas-Hagen* [2006] ECR I-10451, para. 31.
103. On tax relief for the costs of private schools, ECJ C-76/05, *Schwarz* [2007] ECR I-6849, para. 93.
104. On a training grant to students, Joined Cases C-11/06 and C-12/06, *Morgan* ECR [2007] I-9161, para. 25.
105. On disability pensions granted to civilian victims of war or repression, Case C-499/06, *Nerkowska* ECR [2008] I-3993, para. 32.

with it, as well as – where appropriate – with general principles of law and fundamental rights.

2.5. The Competition Rules

2.5.1. The Scope of the Competition Rules and the Concept of Economic Activity

Of central importance to the assessment of the scope of the application of the competition rules is the concept of 'undertaking'. For the purposes of this contribution, this question is particularly pertinent in situations where the State allows organizations discretion in setting their own market strategy and pursuing public interests at the same time. One can think of the fields of health care, housing or professional services – for example, the legal profession – where semi-public/semi-private organizations or even private companies have, to a greater or lesser extent, been granted certain regulatory powers.[106] The government itself, be it local, regional or national, may also be engaged in activities in the market place, while pursuing public interest goals.

According to the definition provided by the Court in *Höfner* and subsequent cases, the concept of 'undertaking' encompasses 'every entity engaged in an economic activity, regardless of the legal status of the entity and the way it is financed'.[107] This definition raises two questions. First, what is to be understood by 'economic activity'? Second, how broadly should this definition be interpreted?[108] The functional character of the concept of 'undertaking', which implies that the type of activity performed rather than the characteristics of the actors which perform it is relevant, the social objectives associated with it, or the regulatory or funding arrangements to which it is subject in a particular Member State,[109] entail that all sorts of activities can be brought within the ambit of the competition rules. This broad definition also implies that even governmental bodies can sometimes be seen as undertakings, or that public organizations, like universities, may sometimes be seen as undertakings whenever they are engaged in economic activities.

106. See also S. Lavrijssen & S. de Vries, 'Netherlands', in: *The Changing Legal Framework for Services of General Economic Interest – Between Competition and Solidarity* (The Hague: Asser Press 2009), 383–421.

107. Case C-41/90, *Höfner and Elser* [1991] ECR I-1979, para. 21; Joined Cases C-159/91 and C-160/91, *Poucet* [1993] I-637, para. 17; see more generally Bellamy & Child (Edited by P.M. Roth QC), *European Community Law of Competition* (London: Sweet & Maxwell, 2001), 45; A. Jones & B. Sufrin, *EC Competition Law* (Oxford: Oxford University Press, 2004), 107–127.

108. A. Winterstein, 'Nailing the Jellyfish: Social Security and Competition Law', *European Competition Law Review* 6 (1999): 325; V. Louri, 'Undertaking as a Jurisdictional Element for the Application of the EC Competition Rules', *Legal Issues of Economic Integration* 2 (2002): 146.

109. Opinion of AG Jacobs of 22 May 2003 in Joined Cases C-264/01, C-306/01, C-354/01 and C-355/01, *AOK Bundesverband* [2004] ECR I-2493, para. 25.

But the personal scope of the competition rules is not infinite. In two ways the ECJ has set limits to the broad concept of an undertaking:

(1) activities which are connected with the exercise of the powers of a public authority; or
(2) activities which by their nature, aim and the rules to which they are subject do not belong to the sphere of economic activity fall outside the scope of application of the competition rules.[110]

The boundary between economic and non-economic is, however, not always easy to draw and it depends on the factual circumstances whether certain 'social bodies' qualify for this 'exception'.[111]

Considering this view of the Court, the relevance of the competition rules, also in areas where public interests are pursued by private companies, semi-private/semi-public organizations, or even the State itself, becomes apparent. But we also see that the Court is more reticent in assessing whether certain activities are economic for the purposes of competition law than for the purposes of free movement law. The concept of 'undertaking' is therefore more of a key jurisdictional tool to determine whether an entity and its activity fall within the ambit of the competition rules[112] than the concept of 'economic activity' under the free movement regime, which is eroding as a result of citizenship. At the same time, the potential of the competition rules to absorb national regulatory powers is considerable. The problem then arises as to at what stage Member State interests in exercising their competences within a reasonable degree of autonomy can be taken into account under the application of the competition rules, either under the prohibitive provisions, or under the exceptions, which makes recourse to a justification ground pertinent (see hereafter).

2.5.2. The Restriction/Justification Approach in Competition Cases

Particularly under Article 101 TFEU, the Commission and the Community Courts employ various devices to assess whether an agreement has an 'appreciable impact on competition,' and thereby delimit the scope of the cartel prohibition. Examples are the '*de minimis*' rule, where, *inter alia*, market shares determine the

110. Case C-309/99, *Wouters* [2002] ECR I-1577, para. 57.
111. Furthermore, in the *MOTOE* case (MOTOE is a non-profit association governed by private law whose object is the organization of motorcycling competitions in Greece), the Court held that the fact that a legal person is, for the exercise of part of its activities, vested with public powers, does not, in itself prevent it from being classified as an undertaking for the purposes of competition law. According to the Court 'the classification as an activity falling within the exercise of public powers or as an economic activity must be carried out separately for each activity exercised by a given entity'. Case C-49/07, *MOTOE* [2008] ECR I-4863, para. 25.
112. V. Louri, 'Undertaking as a Jurisdictional Element for the Application of EC Competition Rules', *Legal Issues of Economic Integration* 2 (2002): 143–176.

appreciability of the restrictive effects of the agreement,[113] or the 'inherent restriction approach', which is particularly relevant for certain public interests. The initial impetus for this doctrine was given in sports cases.[114] Later on this technique was also used in the *Wouters* case, which concerned rules set up by the Netherlands Bar Association, although this case can also be seen as an example of the application of the rule of reason.[115] So far, the inherent restriction approach has only been used in cases of sports and professional services. Nonetheless, it allows the Member State, or the semi-private/semi-public organization in these areas where the Community is not competent to take action, certain opportunities to exercise their powers.

Generally, though, the competition rules are broadly applicable, which brings the exceptions to the fore. Although, as stated before, recourse to a public interest exception in the field of competition law is most contentious, this is not true for Article 86(2) EC (now Article 106(2) TFEU), which offers an explicit exception ground for undertakings entrusted with services of general economic interest. Here, the Court appears to apply a flexible approach towards proportionality, which may nevertheless require an assessment of whether a less restrictive measure was available or not.[116] But generally Member States have a large margin of discretion in defining and entrusting public service tasks to undertakings, in the review of which the particular features of a certain sector are taken into account by the Court. In addition, Article 106(2) TFEU plays a key role in the field of State aid granted to public service undertakings. Here we see that the European Commission appears to assess more carefully whether the requirements under Article 106(2) TFEU and the proportionality principle are complied with than the European Courts do (see also below, section 3).[117] But compared to the free movement rules, the question as to the personal scope of the competition rules is even more crucial here, as public interest justification grounds remain, apart from Article 106(2) TFEU, largely absent.

3. THE EFFECTS OF BRINGING MEMBER STATE ACTION WITHIN THE SCOPE OF EU LAW AND THE PRINCIPLE OF ATTRIBUTED POWERS

Whenever Member States action or, more generally, when a certain situation is said to be within the scope of EU law or the Treaty, this has various consequences for

113. Commission notice on agreements of minor importance (*de minimis* notice), OJ 2001, C 368/13.
114. See for example, Case T-313/02, *Meca Medina* [2004] ECR II-3291; Case C-176/96, *Lehtonen* [2000] ECR I-2681; Joined Cases C-51/96 and C-191/97, *Deliège* [2000] ECR I-2549.
115. Case C-309/99, *Wouters* [2002] ECR I-1577.
116. Case C-203/96, *Dusseldorp* [1998] ECR I-4075; Case C-209/98, *Sydhavnens FFAD* [2000] ECR I-3743; Case C-475/99, *Ambulanz Glöckner* [2001] ECR I-8089; Case T-289/03, *BUPA* [2005] ECR II-741.
117. Case T-289/03, *BUPA* [2005] ECR II-741; Joined Cases T-309/04, T-317/04, T-329/04 and T-336/04, *TV2/Danmark* [2008] ECR II-2935.

both Member States and EU institutions. For the purposes of this contribution we consider these consequences in relation to the principle of attributed powers. In this respect, three different scenarios can be distinguished, which, though, do not necessarily correspond with the four areas discussed above.

The first scenario concerns the very fact that declaring a matter to be within the scope of the Treaty may trigger the (exercise) of EU competence. In other terms, the finding – often perceived as extension of the scope of the Treaty – may 'activate' a legal basis provision, sometimes also the one which was until then believed to be unsuitable or as not providing the necessary basis for acts of the EU institutions.

While in the first scenario one may properly speak of 'competence creep', in the second, the mechanism that operates is more subtle. At first sight and indeed most importantly, at the very moment when a matter is within the scope of the Treaty, the Member States competences to act are limited by the relevant Treaty provisions, general principles of law or fundamental rights. Yet, this form of what is primarily considered a negative intervention may imply, upon second analysis, positive obligations – that is to say, obligations for the Member States to act. This, however, is often believed to be primarily a matter of implementation of EU legislation. Unsurprisingly, this shift from negative to positive obligations raises questions in relation to the principle of attributed powers.[118]

Finally, as was already indicated in the introduction, the mere fact that a matter is declared to be within the scope of EU law, and hence imposing limits on Member States action, is often also perceived as 'competence creep', since the ECJ, through its judgments, seems to extend the scope of application of EU law. From the perspective of the principle of attributed powers, this situation touches on the limits of the powers of the ECJ itself.

3.1. Triggering a Legal Basis

The most explicit examples of how the extension of the scope of application of EU law may activate legal basis provisions are indeed found in the area of free movement. The Monti Regulation is a particularly nice example of 'trigger and creep,' as it shows how an extensive interpretation of primary law, in this case Article 28 TEC (now 34 TFEU), may lead to the adoption of secondary legislation.[119] As a direct consequence of the *Spanish Strawberries* case,[120] Commissioner Monti proposed putting pressure on the Member States through the adoption of a Council Regulation to remove obstacles to the free movement of goods, including those caused by private individuals. The evolving case law, introducing a independent test on what constitutes an obstacle to trade and providing for a broad conception of

118. See also the contribution of Woltjer to this volume (Ch. 6).
119. Regulation (EC) 2679/98 of the Council of 7 Dec. 1998 on the functioning of the internal market in relation to the free movement of goods among the Member States. OJ 1998, L 337/8.
120. Case C-265/95, *Commission v. France* [1997] ECR I-6959.

obstacle or restriction, has thus induced the Community legislature to use Article 308 TEC (now 352 TFEU) as a legal basis obliging the Member States to implement the Court's case law further.

Another recent example of such a spill-over effect is the proposal of the European Commission for a Directive on patients' rights in cross-border healthcare based on Article 95 TEC (now 114 TFEU), considering that health care is an area that primarily belongs to the competence of the Member States.[121] After all, Article 152 TEC (now 168 TFEU) explicitly excludes harmonization of national laws in the field of health care. Considering the case law of the Court on medical services as economic activities, the Commission stresses in the preamble of the proposal that 'it is necessary to improve clarity to ensure a more general and effective application of freedoms to receive and provide health services'.[122]

Although it is assumed that the patients' mobility Directive must not detract from Member States the power to organize and finance their health systems according to Article 168(7) TFEU, it does involve obligations for Member States to protect patients' rights and to address common values and principles of health care, which were previously matters for each Member State only.[123]

There are, of course, quite a number of other examples in the field of free movement, like, for instance, the Television without Frontiers Directive (now called the Audiovisual Media Services Directive).[124] This Directive could be validly adopted on the basis of Articles 47(2) TEC and 55 TEC (now Articles 53 and 62 TFEU) on services, as the Court in *Sacchi* held that television signals should be regarded as a service.[125] Apart from the fact that *at the time* television was seen as something more cultural and informative than economic, it is striking to see that the Directive also contains a quota-provision pushing the Member States to broadcast mainly European programmes (Article 4). As, according to the European Commission, the quota-provision ensures minimum representation of national and European cultures on European screens,[126] it can certainly be seen as part of a cultural policy, which, according to Article 151 TEC (now Article 167 TFEU), belongs to the primary competence of the Member States. Hence, in the slipstream of the free movement of media services, the Community legislature managed to include aspects of a cultural policy, like the highly contentious quota-provision, which actually belongs to the domain the Member States.

121. COM (2008) 414 final. Although no political agreement was reached (yet) in the Council.
122. M. Dougan, 'The Spatial Restructuring of National Welfare States within the European Union: The Contribution of Union Citizenship and the Relevance of the Treaty of Lisbon', in: *Integrating Welfare Functions into EU Law*, ed. U. Neergaard (Copenhagen: Djøf Publishing, 2009), 175–176.
123. See also W. Sauter, 'The Proposed Patient Mobility Directive and the Reform of Cross-Border Health Care in the EU', (TILEC Discussion Paper, September 2008), 43–45.
124. Directive (EEC) 89/552 of the Council of 3 Oct. 1989 on the coordination of certain provisions laid down by Law, Regulation or Administrative Action in Member States concerning the pursuit of television broadcasting activities, OJ 1989, L298/23 as amended.
125. Case 155/73, *Sacchi* [1974] ECR 409.
126. European Commission, First Report on the Consideration of Cultural Aspects in European Community Action, COM (96) 160 final (Part III – Audiovisual Policy).

In the field of competition law the situation is somewhat different due to the dominant role of the European Commission in the decision-making process. An attempt, though, was made by the Socialist Group in the European Parliament (ESP) to draft a European framework directive on services of general economic interest, which was accordingly discussed by several academics. In anticipation of the Treaty of Lisbon, which offers an explicit legal basis for such an instrument, this framework directive would have to be based, *inter alia*, on Article 95 TEC (now Article 114 TFEU), and would, apart from certain safeguards, also contain clear obligations for Member States in the form of, *inter alia*, setting quality standards which must be controlled by a competent authority.[127] Hence, a broad conception of undertaking yet entrusted with public service tasks may indeed trigger the application of a legal basis to push for a positive integration approach. But, so far the Commission has not seized the opportunity to take over the initiative of the ESP.

So, where on the one hand a broad conception of economic activity and restriction leads to spill-over effects, it is questionable whether a more restrictive approach to free movement (or competition), as the Court exposed in the *Keck* case, will lead to exactly the opposite. The judgment in *Keck* rightly raises the question of whether recourse to Article 114 TFEU must be more limited. The 'Tobacco cases'[128] indeed make it clear that not 'everything' can be harmonized just like that on the basis of Article 114 TFEU.[129] According to the ECJ, in these cases a measure based on Article 114 TFEU must genuinely have as its object the improvement of the conditions for the functioning of the internal market.[130] In case of the emergence of future obstacles, these obstacles are likely to occur and the measure has the aim and is designed to prevent them.[131] The competences of the Community have thus been placed under more stringent judicial review, although, the ECJ does not seem to apply the criteria very strictly.[132] But the difference between *Keck* and the 'Tobacco cases' is that the ECJ in the latter case law has not opted for a formalistic approach. The recent case law on free movement with more emphasis on market access therefore seems to fit in with this approach and confirms the view that the Community legislature may even regulate some selling arrangements. An example is the proposal for a Directive on consumer rights, which replaces four directives in the field of consumer policy and also contains rules on selling arrangements, although the rules on distance selling

127. Reference: A new impetus for public services in Europe – Ensuring legal certainty, local autonomy and citizens' rights, to be found at <www.socialistgroup.eu/gpes/media3/documents/1917_EN_public_services_en_november_2006.pdf>.
128. Case C-376/98, *Germany v. European Parliament and Council* [2000] ECR I-8419; Case C-491/01, *BAT* [2002] ECR I-11453.
129. K. Mortelmans, 'The Relationship between the Treaty Rules and Community Measures for the Establishment and Functioning of the Internal Market – Towards a Concordance Rule', *Common Market Law Review* 6 (2002): 1326.
130. Case C-376/98, *Germany v. European Parliament and Council* [2000] ECR I-8419, para. 83.
131. *Ibid.*, para. 86.
132. Case C-301/06, *Ireland v. European Parliament & Council,* Judgment of 10 Feb. 2009, n.y.r.

stemming from the four directives on distance selling would, according to *Keck*, have to be placed outside the internal market context.[133]

The area of EU citizenship and Article 18 TFEU is also illustrative of the sort of competence creep at issue in the present section, in various respects. First, the case law on Article 18 TFEU triggered the Community legislature to act in the field of free movement of students. Thus, the 'old student directive,'[134] which was adopted as a result of Court's early case law on access to vocational training for students of the Union, aimed to facilitate equal access to vocational training.

Second, both the combination of EU citizenship with Article 18 TFEU and the autonomous application of Article 21 TFEU in the more recent case law may result in the exercise of legislative competence. Article 21(2) TFEU provides that the Council may adopt Community provisions when Community action would be necessary to facilitate the exercise of free movement of Union citizens and the Treaty does not provide the necessary competence to take Community measures. One does not need much imagination to see the potential spill-over effect in the area of European citizenship. While a considerable quantity of the domestic regulations and legislation are potentially restricted by the free movement of Union citizens, it is likely that legislative gaps will increase, because national measures that discriminate against Union citizens must be set aside. From this perspective Advocate-general Sharpston emphasized in her recent opinion in the case of *Bressol*[135] the need for legislation in the field of the free movement of students. The fact that in recent case law any unjustified restriction of free movement is also 'caught' by Article 18 TEC affects the national regulatory autonomy even more.[136] It means that Member States have to explain why a certain measure is objectively justified, which shifts 'the burden of proof' to the Member States.

Although the Lisbon Treaty did not change the provisions on European citizenship much, in the context of the present discussion it should be noted that it extended Article 21 TFEU even further, enhancing the potential 'spill-overs'. While the old Article 18(3) EC explicitly excluded measures in the area of social security or social protection, Article 21(3) may now serve as legal basis for measures concerning social security or social protection in order to facilitate the right of EU citizens to move and reside freely within the territory of the Member States.

In relation to general principles of law and, in particular, fundamental rights, the situation is more complex and, to an extent, also speculative in nature. In so far as certain principles or fundamental rights are provided for in the Treaty, the mechanism discussed here above – that is, the extension of the scope followed

133. COM (2008) 614 final.
134. Directive (EEC) 93/96 of the Council of 29 Oct. 1993 on the right of residence for students, OJ 1993, L 317/59.
135. Case C-73/08, *Bressol*, Opinion of AG Sharpston of 25 Jun. 2009, n.y.r.
136. In general on the restriction-approach: Barnard, 19.

by legislative action – may operate as well. Prohibition of discrimination on grounds of nationality is the best example.[137]

However, this is not the end of the story. As is well documented elsewhere,[138] the potential extension of fundamental rights protection and, in the wake of that, EU law, was, for the Member States, a reason to make various efforts during the drafting of the Charter of Fundamental Rights and the Constitutional Treaty to set clear limits to any possible expansion. This has, *inter alia*, resulted in Article 51, which calls upon the institutions, bodies, offices and agencies of the Union and the Member States 'only when they are implementing Union law' to '. . . respect the rights, observe the principles and promote the application thereof in accordance with their respective powers and respecting the limits of the powers of the Union as conferred on it in the Treaties.' The second paragraph adds: 'The Charter does not extend the field of application of Union law beyond the powers of the Union or establish any new power or task for the Union, or modify powers and tasks as defined in the Treaties'. The intentions of the drafters are clear. However, apart from being considered as judicially enforceable standards,[139] in contemporary understanding fundamental rights are also tasks and mandates for the legislature, policymakers and the administration. Often they call for proactive measures that are necessary to realize fundamental rights, such as the right to a clean environment, the right to social protection, or adequate protection in criminal proceedings. In other terms, there is some intrinsic dynamism in these rights that puts limitations such as those in Article 51 of the Charter under pressure. Arguably, the 'flexible' scope of EU law will play a pivotal role in this respect.

3.2. Shift from Negative to Positive Intervention

The second scenario concerns the situation where Member States action is within the scope of EU law and is, for that reason, also limited by its provisions. Such limitations – notably the prohibitions of restriction in the context of the Treaty freedoms and the prohibition of discrimination – are perceived as a form of negative intervention. However, there are instances where this negative intervention seems to imply positive obligations as well. The most clear-cut example of this

137. Note that initially the same process took place in relation to sex discrimination: the old Art. 119 TEEC provided for equal pay only. Further legislation, going beyond pay, was based on 308 TEC (then Art. 235 TEEC), partly due to the case law of the ECJ. See also A. Dashwood, 'Article 308 EC as the Outer Limit of Expressly Conferred Community Competence', in: Barnard & Odudu (eds), *supra* n. 2, 35–45.

138. See for instance, I. Pernice, 'The Treaty of Lisbon and Fundamental Rights', in: *The Lisbon Treaty: Constitutionalism without an Constitutional Treaty?*, ed. S. Griller & J. Ziller (Wien: Springer, 2008) and J. Dutheil de la Rochère, 'The Protection of Fundamental Rights in the EU: Community of Values with Opt-Out?', in: *Ceci n'est pas une Constitution – Constitutionalisation without a Constitution?*, ed. I. Pernice & E. Tanchev (Baden-Baden: Nomos Verlag, 2009).

139. Which is not, however, true for all fundamental rights.

transformation can be found in areas where the non-discrimination principle operates, either as a general principle of law, or in its written 'expression' laid down in the Treaty.[140] A case in point is *Coname* and its progeny.[141]

Coname concerned the award of concession contracts that are governed by the Treaty provisions on the free movement of services and establishment. The ECJ found that the principle of equal treatment enshrined in these provisions implies an obligation of transparency. What matters here is the *creation* of equality of opportunity, thus, to place all potential bidders on an equal footing. According to the ECJ, transparency affords all interested parties equality of opportunity in formulating the terms of the applications for, and participation in, the tenders. The absence of any transparency may amount to indirect discrimination on the ground of nationality which is prohibited by the Treaty, in particular under Articles 43 and 39. The obligation of transparency involves a whole list of more specific requirements to be satisfied, including the obligation of publicity: There must be at least a certain a degree of publicity or advertising in order to enable the market in question to be opened up to competition.

At first sight, such a positive obligation flowing from the (negative) prohibition of discrimination may seem rather surprising. However, by now extensive literature on equality and non-discrimination makes clear that upon a substantive understanding of equality, a prohibition of discrimination is not sufficient, but has to be complemented with proactive -policies and the so-called positive duties.[142] Similarly, the ECJ case law confirms this in many instances of a substantive understanding of equality, by accepting that 'equal' treatment can in fact lead to discrimination. While, according to well-established case law, both the principle of equality and the prohibition of discrimination require that, save where there is an objective justification, comparable situations must not be treated differently and that different situations must not be treated in the same way, there may be situations which are so different that treating them equally may amount to discrimination. The device is then to treat those cases differently – in other words, differentiation. In brief, the prohibition of discrimination, which is an expression of the principle of equality, may involve positive obligations.

Against this background, the *Coname* judgment is less surprising. At the same time, such an understanding of what non-discrimination is about may have potentially far-reaching consequences for Member States action in all the areas where non-discrimination and equality apply.

Our second example draws upon the application of the principle of proportionality in the context of the Treaty freedoms. We have already alluded to the fact that, in this area, proportionality is used by the ECJ as an instrument to impose

140. Thus in particular Arts 18, 45, 49 and 57 TFEU (ex 12, 39, 43 and 50 TEC).
141. Case C-231/03 *Coname* [2005] ECR I-7287.
142. See C. McCrudden & S. Prechal, The Concepts of Equality and Non-discrimination in Europe: A Practical Approach, Brussels 2009, available at <http://ec.europa.eu/social/main.jsp?catId=641&langId=en>.

certain substantive and procedural requirements on the Member States.[143] Cases in the field of consumer protection, for instance, show how the ECJ imposes substantive requirements on Member States by in fact requiring the States to replace prohibitive product standards by appropriate labelling, which is more proportionate to the aim of consumer protection. In *Familiapress*, the ECJ required the national court to first conduct a market analysis to determine whether an Austrian law prohibiting prize competitions truly served the aim of maintaining press diversity.

As far as procedural requirements are concerned, an example can be drawn from the area of prior authorization procedures. Here the following specific requirements can be discerned in the case law:

(a) the procedure in question must be readily accessible and concluded within reasonable time;
(b) the relevant rules and conditions must be set out clearly and made known in advance;
(c) the criteria used in the procedures must be objective and non-discriminatory;
(d) decisions must be backed by a statement of reasons;
(e) any negative decision, in particular refusing an authorization, must be open to challenge before the courts.[144]

All these matters that impose positive obligations in the Member States are considered by the ECJ primarily as a matter of the proportionality test, and therefore the application of the principle of proportionality.

The problem with the principle of attributed powers here is twofold: The Member States are obliged to act without EU legislative measures to that effect having been adopted first; this implies that similar obligations are imposed on the Member States as in the case of such measures, however without the (procedural) guarantees that are inherent to a legal basis.

Although within this framework Member States maintain a (certain) degree of autonomy,[145] it is also clear that in areas, which do not, or hardly, belong to the competence of the Community, such as health care or culture, Member States are prevented from acting in the absence of justification. In the field of cross-border health care, for example, the balancing exercise by the ECJ of, on the one hand, the right of patients to get the costs of medical treatment abroad reimbursed and, on the other hand, the safeguarding of a national health care system, has had repercussions on the way in which health care is to be organized; a matter, which, according to

143. See above, s. 2.4.

144. See for instance, Case C-205/99, *Analir* [2001] ECR I-1271; C-372/04, *Watts* [2006] ECR I-4325; Case C-169/07, *Hartlauer*, Judgment of 10 Mar. 2009, n.y.r. See also the golden shares cases, for example, Case C-503/99, *Commission v. Belgium* [2002] ECR I-4809; Joined Cases C-282/04 and C-283/04, *Commission v. The Netherlands* [2006] ECR I-9141. For a more detailed discussion and analysis *see* S. Prechal, 'Free Movement and Procedural Requirements: Proportionality Reconsidered', *Legal Issues of Economic Integration* 3 (2008): 201–216.

145. See Weatherill, *supra* n. 2, 24.

Article 168(5) TFEU, is the primary responsibility and within the competence of the Member State.[146]

A third and last example draws upon the application of Article 106(2) TFEU to public service undertakings. As stated before, the Commission appears to assess State aid to public service broadcasters cautiously. This led to the adoption of a revised Broadcasting Communication in 2009, wherein the Commission introduced the requirement for Member States to conduct an *ex ante* market impact assessment for public service broadcasting,[147] which, in a number of Member States, aroused strong criticism, as this would severely impinge upon the principle of subsidiarity and hence Member States' competence in the field of media and cultural policies.

3.3. ECJ: Extending the Reach of EU Law

The third scenario differs from the previous two in the sense that there is no trigger of or no spill-over to EU based (positive) regulation. In that sense, there is no 'competence creep' proper. However, as we have pointed out, competence creep can also be understood – and is certainly perceived as such – in a broader sense, including the extension of the scope of the application of EU law. The key issue here is that it is the ECJ itself who extends its own jurisdiction in the first place. Once the matter is within the scope of EU law, the Court may seek to limit the exercise of Member States' powers.

Just to mention a few examples, in the recent judgment of the Court in case *3F*, which concerned tax relief measures for seafarers employed on board vessels registered in the Danish International Register, the ECJ accepted trade unions as a party under the State aid rules seeking annulment of a Commission Decision approving the tax measures.[148] Irrespective of an earlier judgment of the Court in which it held that collective agreements are not caught by Article 81 EC (the *Albany* case), the Court of Justice ruled in this case that this does not mean that collective negotiations or the parties involved in them are likewise excluded from the scope of the Treaty rules on State aid, contrary to the opinion of the Court of First Instance.[149] Hence, the fact that the competitive position of trade unions in this case was affected by the positive decision of the Commission brought the social field directly within the scope of the State aid rules. The judgment fits in with the previous judgments in *Laval* and *Viking*.[150] The issue of collective labour agreements, which was previously thought to fall outside the scope of competition

146. C-372/04, *Watts* [2006] ECR I-4325, S.A. de Vries, 'Patiëntenzorg in Europa na Watts: wiens zorg?', SEW 4 (2007): 132–140.
147. See <http://ec.europa.eu/competition/state_aid/legislation/broadcasting_communication_en.pdf>; State aid E 3/2005 – Financing of public service broadcasters in Germany, COM (2007) 1761 final, para. 328.
148. Case C-319/07 P, *3F*, Judgment of 9 Jul. 2009, n.y.r.
149. Case T-30/03, *SID* [2007] ECR II-34, para. 32.
150. Case C-341/05, *Laval* [2007] ECR I-11767; Case C-438/05, *Viking* [2007] ECR I-10779.

law and, by some labour lawyers, of EU law altogether, is now to some extent being brought under the jurisdiction of the Court.

An illustration of how Treaty freedoms, general principles and fundamental rights can get entangled is provided by the Carpenter case.[151] According to the ECJ, the decision to deport Mrs Carpenter did not strike a fair balance between the competing interests – that is, on the one hand, the right of Mr Carpenter to respect of his family life, and, on the other hand, the maintenance of public order and public safety. The justification based on public order and safety had to be considered in the light of Article 8 ECHR and interpreted and applied in such a way that it respected the right to family life. As it did not, the deportation was believed to be disproportionate.

As we have seen above, whenever a situation is brought into the scope of Article 18 TFEU, national authorities are limited by the principle of non-discrimination, even in sensitive areas in which the Union has no, or only a 'complementary,' competence, or even where the competence to harmonize is explicitly excluded, such as in education[152] or direct taxation.[153] Considering the case law, Community law restricts a huge quantity of national measures. This expansion of the scope of EU law at the expense of national 'sacred cows' is reinforced by the recent development of a restriction approach instead of a discrimination model when citizenship comes to the fore.

Perhaps even more remarkable are the cases in which the extension of the scope of certain provisions of EU law result in imposing limits upon the competence left to the EU institutions – and in that context, indirectly, also to the Member States – by the empowering provisions of the Treaty. Famous, in this respect, is the case of *Dany Bidar.* As mentioned, the ECJ found that student assistance fell within the material scope of the Treaty, because Directive 2004/38 – at that date not in force – provides for an exception to the equal treatment with regard to such study grants.[154] Although the 'old student directive' excluded assistance for maintenance costs for students, the case of *Bidar* was finally decided on Article 18 in combination with Article 21 TFEU and the Directive on residence of persons with independent means.[155] Thus, the question remained as to how the ECJ would deal with further cases under the new Directive 2004/38, in which that assistance is also excluded for students that not have acquired the right of permanent residence (Article 24 (2) and 16 of Directive 2004/38). In the case of *Förster*, the ECJ, however, conformed to the limitation the Union legislature has set, and held that the Dutch five-year residence requirement for assistance for the costs of maintenance was in accordance with Community law.

151. Case C-60/00, *Carpenter* [2002] ECR I-6279. See also Case C-109/01, *Akrich* [2003] ECR I-9607, where the ECJ emphasized again that the Member States have to take into account the effects of their action – a decision to deport the person concerned – on the right to family life.
152. See the case law on the free movement of Union citizens as analysed under s. 2.3.
153. In the field of national tax law the case of Turpeinen is an example, C-520/04, *Turpeinen* [2006] ECR I-10685.
154. Case C-209/03, *Bidar* [2005] ECR I-2119, para. 43
155. Council Directive 90/364/EEC of 28 Jun. 1990 on the right of residence (so called Directive on independent means).

On the edge of European citizenship and general principles of law we find the case of *Eman and Sevinger*[156] – two Dutch nationals and therefore, according to the ECJ, also EU citizens, who lived, however, on Aruba, which is outside the territorial scope of the EC and EU Treaties. In this case, the ECJ held, first, that the definition of the persons entitled to vote and to stand for election for the European Parliament falls within the competence of each Member State. Second, it confirmed that the Netherlands are not required to hold elections to the European Parliament on Aruba and the Dutch Antilles, which are subject to the special association arrangements in Part Four of the Treaty and the general provisions of the Treaty, and also that those provisions related to EP elections do not apply here. So *prima facie,* the matter seemed outside the territorial scope of the Treaty. Nevertheless, since the Member State's competence has to comply with general principles of law and therefore also the principle of equal treatment, the ECJ de facto reviewed the applicable Dutch rules against this principle and found that the principle of equal treatment prevented the application of the criterion of residence as applied under the Dutch rules.

Another striking example of judicial competence creep is the judgment in *Mangold,*[157] which is often understood as ignoring the discretion left by the legal basis at stake – Article 19 TFEU (ex 13 TEC). In this case, the ECJ found that the principle of non-discrimination on grounds of age is a general principle of the Community, which the Member States have to observe when they act within the scope of Community law. For that same reason, the observance of the principle could not be made conditional upon the expiry of the transposition date of Directive 2000/78.[158] The national court had to set aside any provision of national law that may have conflicted with the principle. Yet, the authors of the Amsterdam Treaty – that is, when that Article was inserted into the EC Treaty – made a conscious choice not to impose a directly effective prohibition of non-discrimination, as in the case of Article 18 TFEU. Rather, they preferred to leave further elaboration of the various non-discrimination principles to the Community legislature. The latter made a number of choices, translated in, *inter alia*, more precise provisions of the 2000/78 Directive. The Directive leaves, certainly as far as disability and age discrimination are concerned, broad discretion to the Member States in relation to the implementation and, in particular, the balancing of the interests at stake. An intervention such as the one by the ECJ in *Mangold* seems to take place on the verge of the division of powers between the Community and the Member States, and may be questioned from the point of view of unnecessarily interfering with the powers left to the Community legislature and the Member States themselves.[159]

---

156. Case C-300/04, *Eman & Sevinger* [2006] ECR I-8055.
157. Case C-144/04, *Mangold* [2005] ECR I-9981.
158. Directive (EC) 2000/78 of the Council of 27 Nov. 2000 establishing a general framework for equal treatment in employment and occupation, OJ 2000, L303/16.
159. See for this type of critique, for example, AG Geelhoed in his Opinion in Case C-13/05, *Chacón Navas* [2006] ECR I-6467, point 54. In the same sense AG Mazák in his Opinion in Case C-411/05, *Palacios* [2007] I-8531, point 138.

How then, can the type of developments briefly described in section 3 be assessed from the perspective of the principle of attributed powers? In relation to the Treaty freedoms, Azoulai has observed that it must be assumed that in conferring on the Community the competence to implement the objectives of integration by using the market freedoms as a means, the Member States also agreed that the exercise of this Community competence should result in constraints on the pursuit of all national policies. Similarly, by giving the ECJ the jurisdiction to identify such constraints, the ECJ was made master of the limits of the scope of Community rules. The ECJ cannot, as such, determine which fields fall within Community competence. However, it can decide which situations fall within the Community framework and what the content is of this framework.[160]

In our opinion, this observation seems to hold true for a broader area than the Treaty freedoms. It also makes clear that, at the end of the day, this is about the mandate of the ECJ itself to interpret EU law, which is only very generally underpinned by Article 19 TEU (ex 220 TEC), and, indeed, a matter of limits of judicial interpretation. We come back to this in the next section.

4. A BRIEF ASSESSMENT

In a nutshell, the ECJ uses a number of techniques to decide whether Member State action is within the scope of EU law. Some of the criteria and their application are well-established, such as the exercise of free movement under Article 21 TFEU, the existence of a restriction to free movement, or the notion of 'undertaking'. Other criteria seem less predictable. This is true in particular for the 'connecting factors' that bind Member States to general principles of law, and sometimes also for the application of Article 18 TFEU. Overall, however, the tests are relatively easily satisfied: Member State action is more often 'inside' than 'outside' the scope of EU law.

This first step – that is, defining the reach of EU law – is quintessential for the second issue, namely, what are the consequences for Member State powers? We have distinguished three scenarios. First, a situation being within the scope of EU law may trigger the use of a legal basis for – often legislative – intervention. The area of Treaty freedoms and the activation of Article 114 TFEU are notorious in this respect. Second, positive obligations are read into provisions that are meant to pose limits to Member State action. This may result in discrete harmonization by the back door, instead of intervention by the EU legislature. The prohibition of discrimination on grounds of nationality and the application of the Treaty freedoms provide a good example here. Finally, we have identified a sort of 'judicial creep'. The ECJ defines the reach of EU law and, in doing so, it decides the margins for the exercise of Member States' powers, in particular, those of the domestic legislature.

160. L. Azoulai, 'The Court of Justice and the Social Market Economy: The Emergence of an Ideal and the Conditions for its Realization', *Common Market Law Review* 5 (2008): 1335.

The principle of attributed powers is apparently unable to stop this expansion of EU law. Viewed from the perspective of the principle of legality, legality is leaking here. That is to say, the guarantees the principle aims at – division and separation of powers, regulation of and legitimating the exercise of public authority – are safeguarded in a rather loose and flexible legal context which is perceived by the Member States and, ultimately, by the individuals in the Member States, as facilitating an unpredictable and uncontrollable competence creep.

As we have set out in the previous sections, the key player in the extension of the scope of EU law is the ECJ. In the case law there are intriguing instances of bootstrapping. This is in particular the case where competences laid down in the Treaty serve as arguments for bringing a matter within the scope of EU law[161] and *vice versa*: bringing a matter within the reach of the Treaty may trigger the use of certain competences. Equally fascinating are the processes in which provisions aimed at the regulation of powers of the Member States – the 'negative' rules like Treaty freedoms of general principles of law – turn into power creating norms, in the sense that they are used to create new, positive obligations for the Member States.

Although the ECJ is also bound by Articles 5(1 and 2) and 13(2) TEU, the principle of attributed powers does not play an appreciable role in imposing limits. Are there then, alternative mechanisms that can stand in for or complement the operation of the principle of attributed powers? Without embarking upon the eternal debate on the limits of judicial interpretation, we briefly point at the most important internal limit, which is 'judicial wisdom' and a degree of self-restraint on the part of the ECJ. In some instances the Court has made attempts to limit the scope of the Treaty provisions, like in *Keck*. The gambling cases are also evidence of a more restrained approach.[162] Overall, however, these attempts have not been very successful, last but not least because the former EC Treaty itself, with the functionally-driven provisions, is probably the main culprit in encouraging expansion and competence creep. Despite a number of efforts to limit competence creep, the new Treaties – TEU and TFEU – are not really much different in this respect. Another striking and relatively new factor in the case law is the use of general principles of law, in particular the principle of equality, which often sweep into areas of domestic law that the Member States had considered as being 'safe' from EU intervention.

Are there perhaps external limits that are more effective? We indentify three of them. First, there is the 'legislature' that may intervene, in the sense that she corrects or approves what the Court is doing. The 'Barber protocol,' annexed to the Maastricht Treaty, may be used as an example, 'explaining' the consequences of the Barber judgment of the ECJ.[163] Directive 2004/38 (free movement and residence rights of EU citizens) codifies and clarifies, for an important part, ECJ case law, but also sets certain limits that have been accepted in the meantime by the

161. See above, s. 2.2 where the so-called 'competence approach' has been briefly discussed.
162. See recently Case C-42/07, *Liga Portugesa*, Judgment of 8 Sep. 2009, n.y.r.
163. Case C-262/88, *Barber* [1990] ECR I-1889.

ECJ. Sometimes even the Commission – under pressure from the EP – may consider acting by means of, for instance, a communication.[164]

Another crucial external factor is national – constitutional – courts. The well-known 'red light signals' in the direction of the ECJ concern the interpretation of the legal basis provisions and the use of bridging clauses or emergency brakes – all topics the present contribution is not concerned with, at least not directly.[165] However, also with respect to other subject matters, the national courts may draw lines. A case in point is the interpretation by the ECJ of non-discrimination provisions or the equality principle,[166] the protection of fundamental rights – in particular in criminal matters[167] – and the effects that the various instruments may produce.[168]

Finally, there is a role for legal scholars. Critical, well-substantiated comments on the case law and its tendencies may serve as a mirror for the Luxembourg courts and provide them with academic feedback.[169] Yet, one might go a step further here: most European lawyers tend to argue from the logic of the case law and, indeed, the logic of the Treaty. In doing so, they contribute to the expansion of the EU law – that is, a sort of 'doctrinal creep' is taking place.[170] Perhaps the time has come to critically reflect upon this logic itself and to contribute to the articulation of some more bright line rules that should compensate for the weaknesses of the principle of attributed powers.

---

164. The Commission then organized a forum on 9 Oct. 2008 on the rights of employees and economic freedoms to discuss the implications of the judgments of the Court of Justice of the European Communities on the posting of workers (*Laval*, *Viking*, *Rüffert* and *Commission v. Luxembourg* judgments). Initially, it also announced the possibility of adopting new interpretation guidelines but this did not happen. More recently, Commissioner Andor announced a legislative proposal aiming at the amendment of the Posted Workers Directive. See the Commissioner's speech at the 'Conference on Posting of Workers and Labour Rights', Oviedo, 17 and 18 Mar. 2010.
165. The most evident and relatively recent example is the Lisbon judgment of the BverG of 30 Jun. 2009, available at <www.bverfg.de>, where the German constitutional court clearly postulated a number of national constitutional limits for European competences.
166. See the pending constitutional complaint 2 BvR 2661/06 (Honeywell), colloquially called the 'German Mangold-case'.
167. See the judgments of the BverfG (18 Jul. 2005, available at <www.bverfg.de>) and the Polish Constitutional Tribunal (of 27 Apr. 2005, available at <www.trybunal.gov.pl>) both concerning the European Arrest Warrant.
168. See the discussion in some distant past on the effects of directives. In its judgment of 16 Jul. 1981 (EuR (1981): 442), the *Bundesfinanzh of* held that there could be no reasonable doubt that a directive was incapable of creating legal rules directly applicable in a Member State. Some years later it was however overruled by the BverfG (judgment of 8 Apr. 1987, EuR (1987): 333). See on this 'Kloppenburg-saga', M. Hilf, 'Der Justizkonflikt um EG-Richtlinien: gelöst', EuR (1988): 1.
169. See U. Everling, *Reflections on the Reasoning in the Judgments of the Court of Justice of the European Communitites, in Festskrift til Ole Due* (København: Gads Forlag, 1994), 69.
170. With thanks to S. Weatherill who drew our attention to this aspect.

Chapter 13

Eurojust II: Un tiens vaut mieux que deux tu l'auras?*

Tony Marguery

1. INTRODUCTION

Eurojust is a European agency with legal personality created in 2002 by Council Decision 2002/187/JHA (hereafter, the Decision).[1] Its objective is to coordinate the prosecution of serious crimes between Member States, to improve cooperation in criminal matters and to support Member States in order to render the fight against crime more effective.[2] Eurojust was not created as a supranational prosecution agency. The agency is composed of national members who are 'prosecutors, judges

* A bird in the hand is worth two in the bush.

1. The setting up of Eurojust was one of the main points decided during the Tampere European Council. A provisional Eurojust Unit was established upon the initiative of Germany, Portugal, France, Belgium and Sweden by the Council Decision of 14 Dec. 2000 on setting up a Provisional Judicial Cooperation Unit, OJ 2000, L 324/2. It was soon replaced by the Council Decision of 28 Feb. 2002 setting up Eurojust with a view to reinforcing the fight against crime, OJ 2002, L 63/1; the financial provisions of the Decision have been amended by the Council Decision of 18 Jun. 2003, OJ 2003, L 245/44.
2. The jurisdiction of Eurojust *ratione materiae* is limited to organized crime, terrorism and other serious crimes for which Europol is competent. These crimes are listed in Art. 4 of the Council Decision of 6 Apr. 2009 establishing the European Police Office (Europol), OJ 2009, L 121/37 (e.g., unlawful drug trafficking, trafficking in human beings, motor vehicle crime, murder or grievous bodily injury).

Leonard Besselink, Frans Pennings & Sacha Prechal (eds), *The Eclipse of the Legality Principle in the European Union*, pp. 249–272.

or police officers of equivalent competence'.[3] Together the national members form the College, which is headed by a President and two Vice-Presidents elected from amongst the national members. The College decides, in principle, by majority vote (qualified two-thirds majority or simple majority), each member having one vote. Decisions taken by Eurojust are never binding. The enforcement of its requests depends partially on the status and powers conferred by the Member States upon their national members. The Member States remain, in principle, entirely free to organize their public prosecution services. Therefore, the European concept of 'prosecutor, judge or police officer of equivalent competence' seems empty. The Decision, nonetheless, obliges the Member States to adapt their legislation in order to 'allow Eurojust to operate properly'.[4] The Eurojust national members should at least have access to information contained in criminal records, should be able to contact directly a national competent authority, and should be able to exchange information. The 2002 Decision does not mention any other powers.[5]

In December 2008, the Council adopted a decision revising the Eurojust decision and strengthening the agency (hereafter, the amended Decision).[6] The competences, objectives and tasks of Eurojust remain mainly untouched, but important changes were made to the Eurojust institutional framework.[7] In particular, the amended Decision established in greater detail the status and powers of national members.[8] However, the basis and conditions of these powers continue to be established by national law and national members carry out their powers within a national jurisdiction. They contribute to the exercise of a right to punish (*ius puniendi*), which is one of the sovereign rights of the States. Governments exercise this right in order to assert their legitimacy and establish their

3. The majority of the national members are public prosecutors. However, the power to prosecute a case is not the exclusive right of public prosecutors in all the Member States. In this respect, important differences exist. Therefore, it was important to give large discretion to the Member States for the appointment of an authority competent in criminal proceedings. In Anglo-Saxon countries the Crown Prosecution Service does not enjoy the same power to prosecute as generally understood in civil law systems for public prosecutors. They share this power with police officers. In certain Member States, such as France, examining judges may be involved in a decision to prosecute a case.
4. Article 9 (1) of the Council Decision of 28 Feb. 2002 setting up Eurojust with a view to reinforcing the fight against crime, OJ 2002, L 63/1.
5. For complete study over Eurojust, see for example, J. Costa, 'Eurojust vis-à-vis the European Public Prosecutor', in: *Justice and Home Affairs in the EU: Liberty and Security Issues after Enlargement*, ed. J. Apap (Cheltenham: Edward Elgar, 2004); N. Thwaites, 'Eurojust, une autre brique dans l'édifice de la cooperation judiciaire en matière pénale ou solide mortier?' *Revue de Sciences Criminelles* 1 (2003): 45–61.
6. Council Decision of 16 Dec 2008 on the strengthening of Eurojust and amending Decision 2002/187/JHA setting up Eurojust with a view to reinforcing the fight against serious crime, OJ 2009 L 138/14. The Decision entered into force on 4 Jun. 2009.
7. For a complete overview of the key issues see S. Peers, 'Revising the Eurojust Decision: *Effectiveness v. Accountability*', *Journal of European Criminal Law* 2 (2008): 5–18.
8. The amended Decision aims also at clarifying the relationship between Eurojust and the European Judicial Network, but the present contribution will not cover this aspect of the new act.

political power within the territorial limit of a State. Criminal justice traditionally has two functions. On the one hand, it is an instrument of public safety. States have an obligation to protect individuals against crime within their territory.[9] Public prosecutors enjoy important powers of decision in criminal proceedings. A prosecutor can decide whether or not to bring a case to court. In several Member States, prosecutors also enjoy the power to settle certain types of cases out of court and to impose a penalty.[10] On the other hand, States must prevent any breach of the fundamental rights of those who are suspected to have committed a crime. As a result, criminal justice may have a strong impact on citizens' lives and freedom. If penal law is weak or ineffective, basic human rights may be at stake. States must therefore safeguard the equilibrium between the 'sword' and the 'shield' functions of *Justitia*.[11] The exercise of public authority must be constrained by enacted laws to safeguard this equilibrium. In a mere national context, the members' status and functions are attributed in such a way as to comply with the principle of legality at national level.

From a purely intergovernmental perspective, one may consider that Eurojust does not raise any question of legality in the European Union's (EUs) multi-levelled legal order. Indeed, the acts setting up and reforming Eurojust were adopted unanimously and could not entail direct effect. The Member States determine, in theory, the status and legal effects of these acts according to their rules on the effect of public international law. However, one cannot ignore the influence of Eurojust on national legislation concerning national prosecutors, in particular, Eurojust prosecutors.[12] The status and powers of these prosecutors are partly designed at the European level. This may hold true especially for the recent amendment of the Decision. The legal position of citizens can be significantly affected by a prosecutor's decision. It is, therefore, paramount to ensure that the acts attributing the status and powers of prosecutors are also legitimate and provide protection against uncertainty and abuse at the European level. The aim of this contribution is to analyse whether the Eurojust Decision – and in particular its amended version – fulfils the functions of the principle of legality as understood for the purpose of the present project. The public prosecutors' authority to take decisions must be

9. Article 2(1) of the ECHR implies a duty for the states to secure the right to life by putting in place effective criminal law provisions to deter the commission of offences. It also implies a positive obligation on the authorities to take preventive operational measures to protect an individual whose life is at risk from the criminal acts of another individual, see ECtHR, *Osman v. United Kingdom* [1998] ECHR-VIII, at para. 115.
10. For example, in the Netherlands, a public prosecutor may sentence an accused with a criminal order (*strafbeschikking*). Such an order may carry a penalty such as a fine or community service of up to 180 hours. A comparable power exists in France (*comparution sur reconnaissance préalable de culpabilité*).
11. See on the concept of sword and shield of justice, J. Vervaele, 'Régulation et répression au sein de l'Etat providence : la fonction "bouclier" et la fonction "épée" du droit pénal en déséquilibre', *Déviance et Société* 2 (1997): 121–122.
12. In this contribution, the term 'Eurojust prosecutors' will be used where the Decision and the amended Decision apply to the national member, to his/her assistant(s) and now to his/her deputy(ies).

exercised on the basis of, and in accordance with, 'enacted laws'. The analysis will neither cover the discussions on the prosecutors' discretion to prosecute a case (e.g., opportunity to prosecute versus legality) nor the legality of crimes (*nullum crimen, sine lege*) for which Eurojust has competence. Rather, the question will be whether or not the Eurojust Decision grants prosecutors with formal powers to take decisions (i.e., the power to institute or discontinue criminal proceedings) that may influence the legal position of citizens. Does the Eurojust Decision have an influence on the exercise of prosecutors' powers? If so, may the Eurojust Decision be considered as 'enacted law'? Does it offer safeguards and live up to the functions of legality in such a way that the equilibrium between the sword and the shield of *Justitia* is ensured at the European level?

Before going on with the analysis, it seems important to demonstrate whether Eurojust actually has (and will have) any influence on the organization of national prosecution services. Therefore, I will identify the provisions concerning the status and powers of Eurojust national members and investigate to what extent national legislation has been changed (and will be changed) in this respect.[13] Secondly, I will scrutinize the requirements of legality with regard to Council decisions. How were the functions of legality safeguarded in the case of Eurojust? The contribution will address aspects concerning the legitimation and the regulation functions of legality.[14] It should be mentioned that the Council decisions concerning Eurojust were adopted before the entry in force of the Treaty of Lisbon and within the so-called third pillar of the EU. Nevertheless, these acts will remain in force unless they are amended, repealed or annulled. Lastly, some implications of the Treaty of Lisbon for Eurojust will be assessed.

2. THE STATUS AND POWERS OF PUBLIC PROSECUTORS THROUGH EUROJUST

The Agency may act through its national members or as a College (Articles 6 and 7 of the Decision). In other words, a national member may receive a request from another national member, or from Eurojust acting as a College. The content of this decision may be similar, the wording of Articles 6 and 7 being almost identical, however in the first situation the decision is taken by an individual, whereas in the second, it is taken by a collective body. Firstly, this section will analyse the status and powers of national members since the entry into force of the Decision setting

13. The comparative research on the implementation of the Decision in the Member States is based on Commission's reports and communications and Eurojust annual reports, as well as other Council reports. Specifically, figures concerning powers and status of national members may be found in the Eurojust report of 6 Sep. 2005 on judicial powers of the national members of Eurojust, Council doc.11943/05, and in the Commission Communication of 23 Oct. 2007 on the role of Eurojust and the European Judicial Network in the fight against organized crime and terrorism in the European Union, COM (2007) 644 final.
14. For reasons relating to focus constraint, the scope of this contribution will not address aspects concerning the attribution function of the principle of legality.

up the Agency. Secondly, it will focus on the modifications required by the amended Decision.

2.1. Status and Powers of National Members in the Eurojust Decision

2.1.1. National Members' Status in the Eurojust Decision

At the creation of Eurojust, each Member State appointed a public prosecutor, judge or police officer of equivalent competence as a national member to Eurojust, and could appoint one or more assistants. The assistant(s) were to replace the national member if necessary. A large margin of discretion was given to each Member State to choose the status of their members. All Member States have now appointed at least one public prosecutor or a member of the public services responsible for public prosecutions.[15] According to each domestic system, the appointed members could keep their permanent places of work in their home countries. In 2005, out of twenty-five national members, more than thirteen retained previous prosecutorial powers in their Member States, and in 2007, out of twenty-seven national members, fifteen retained such powers. The national members' terms of office also varied from one State to another (from one year renewable to open-ended). Eventually, national members could be removed of his or her function at any time.

With regard to the Eurojust prosecutors' responsibilities, the Decision provides an obligation of confidentiality without prejudice to any obligations and duties resulting from the law of their home countries. National members are accountable in their home countries and according to the law of their countries for unauthorized or incorrect processing of data.[16] The Member States are free to decide how and to what extent their national members are able to use the data collected in national registers and to what extend they are accountable in their home countries. A Member State may be held liable for damage caused by its national member or deputy who processes data illegally or without authorization.

2.1.2. National Members' Powers in the Eurojust Decision

The Member States had to ensure that their national members could have access to the information contained in the national criminal records or any other register of their Member States,[17] could contact the competent authority of their Member States directly,[18] and could exchange any information necessary for the

15. Certain Member States have appointed a prosecutor as national member and an examining judge or police officer as assistant, see COM (2007) 644 final.
16. Article 24 of the Decision.
17. Article 9(4) of the Decision.
18. Article 9(5) of the Decision.

performance of Eurojust's tasks without prior authorization.[19] More than thirteen national members enjoyed direct access to national criminal records in 2005 and 17 in 2007; more than thirteen national members could directly contact or exchange information with a competent national authority in 2005; in 2007, respectively, twenty-five and twenty-seven members were granted such powers.

The Decision did not request that any other specific powers should be granted to Eurojust prosecutors. Nevertheless, when one considers Eurojust's tasks,[20] further powers were obviously necessary. In order to fulfil these tasks, it was expected that national members were at least able to ask a competent national authority to act in criminal proceedings.[21] In 2005, more than thirteen national members could ask their national authorities to open an investigation in their own Member States. In 2007, twenty-seven national members enjoyed this power. More than thirteen national members could suggest the setting up of Joint Investigation Teams (JIT) in 2005, whereas in 2007, twenty-two members could request (and intervene in) such teams to be set up.[22] Finally, a few Member States – 3 to 5 in 2005, and 8 in 2007 – granted their members the power to act directly in criminal proceedings and, for example, to institute proceedings.

These figures show a trend, although very limited, towards approximation of the status and powers of national members. However, the important diversity between the national members' status and powers remained the source of several problems. In fact, Eurojust could not always function efficiently, if at all. Problems in the functioning of Eurojust, such as a limited recourse to Eurojust from national authorities or the absence of a quorum for the College to record any formal decision, were often mentioned.[23] Two important sets of reasons seemed to be the source of the diversity and hence, of the problems. Firstly, the Member States failed to implement the Decision. According to the Commission in 2007, only ten Member States had implemented the Decision.[24] Secondly, the Decision did not provide a clear status and well-defined powers that should be granted equally to all members.[25] One of the purposes of the revision of the Eurojust Decision was to

19. Article 13(2) of the Decision.
20. Article 6 and 7 of the Decision.
21. For example, request to undertake a prosecution or investigation, accept that one authority is in a better position than another authority to prosecute specific acts or set up a joint investigation team.
22. A Joint Investigation Team consists of judicial and police authorities from at least two Member States. It is responsible for carrying out criminal investigations into specific matters for a limited period; see Council Framework Decision of 13 Jun. 2002 on joint investigation teams, OJ 2002, L 162/1.
23. Concerning the national members' status and powers shortcomings, see for example, the Draft Council Conclusions of 22 Sep. 2005 on the third Eurojust Annual Report (calendar year 2004), Council doc. 12527/05 and COM (2007) 644 final.
24. COM (2007) 644 final.
25. See on this, for example, Communication from the European Commission of 20 Nov. 2000 on the Establishment of Eurojust, Com(2000) 746 final; 2001 Pro-Eurojust Report of 20 Dec. 2001, Council doc. 15545/01; Report from the European Commission of 6 Jul. 2004 on the Legal Transposition of the Council Decision of 28 Feb. 2002 setting up Eurojust with a View to

create such a common basis of equivalent judicial powers and status for national members.[26]

2.2. Status and Powers of National Members in the Amended Eurojust Decision

2.2.1. National Members' Status in the Amended Eurojust Decision

The Member States' margin of discretion to attribute status to Eurojust prosecutors was considerably reduced in the revised Decision. First, the national members must now have their regular place of work at The Hague and must be appointed for at least four years.[27] This change should be welcomed as giving more stability to Eurojust. It is also important because an 'on-call coordination' is established, which implies that at least one Eurojust prosecutor *per* Member State is able to act 'on a 24 hour/7day basis'.[28] Secondly, a Member State cannot remove his national member from their position before the end of the term without informing the Council of the reasons for this removal.

Thirdly, the Member States must now appoint one deputy and 'another person as an assistant'. More deputies and assistants may be appointed with the agreement of the College. A difference in status in the hierarchy between a national member, a deputy and an assistant is possible. A deputy 'shall', while an assistant 'may', be able to 'act on behalf of or to substitute the national member'. The deputy and the assistant may have their regular place of work at The Hague. The amended Decision remains, however, is silent as to the length of their appointment. Ideally, the length of deputies' and assistants' terms of office should have been mentioned. The amended Decision goes further than the Decision, which mentioned that the

reinforcing the Fight against Serious Crime, COM (2004) 457 final; Eurojust report of 6 Sep. 2005 on judicial powers of the national members of Eurojust, Council doc. 11943/05; Annual Report of 17 Mar. 2006 of Eurojust 2005, Council doc. 7318/06; Report of 19 Oct. 2006 of the Seminar: 'A Seminar with 2020 Vision: The Future of Eurojust and the European Judicial Network', Council doc. 14123/06; Eurojust Report 21 Mar. 2007 of Eurojust 2006, Council doc. 7550/07.

26. Recital 5 and page 6 of the Explanatory memorandum to Council Decision on the European Judicial Network and to Council Decision on the strengthening of Eurojust amending Council Decision 2002/187/JHA of 28 Feb. 2002, as amended by Council Decision 2003/659/JHA setting up Eurojust with a view to reinforcing the fight against serious crime, Council doc. 5038/08.
27. The amended Decision provides that where a national member is President or Vice-President, his term of office should be at least equivalent to the President or Vice-President term of office. Art. 3 (6) of the Rules of Procedure of Eurojust provides, in its current redaction, for a three years term of office of the President or Vice-President. It would seem logical to amend the Rules of Procedure as to give the President or Vice-President a term of office at least equivalent to those of other national members.
28. Article 5a of the amended Decision.

Member States could appoint an assistant (the concept of a deputy was not yet introduced) who was only required to be able to replace the national member. In short, each Member State must now appoint at least two prosecutors or a competent authority equivalent to a prosecutor at Eurojust for at least four years. The national members cannot retain previous prosecutorial powers in their State of origin. Ideally, this could be applicable to deputies and assistants.

Lastly, one should mention the provision on the liability of Eurojust other than liability for unauthorized or incorrect processing of data.[29] According to this provision, Eurojust shall make good any damage caused through the fault of a national member, a deputy or an assistant in the performance of his duties. If the fault is committed pursuant to the powers granted to them in the amended Decision, their State of origin must reimburse Eurojust. Such a provision may imply a higher degree of approximation in the practice of the Member States with regard to Eurojust prosecutors' responsibility. Indeed, one may regret the absence in the amended Decision of any common standard of public prosecutors' professional accountability.[30]

2.2.2. National Members' Powers in the Amended Eurojust Decision

The amended Decision obliges Member States to ensure that their national members have the powers that would be available to them as prosecutors in their domestic systems.[31] It does not oblige the Member States to create powers that would not be normally available to national prosecutors. As the explanatory memorandum to the amended Decision indicates, 'because of constitutional requirements in a majority of Members States and possibilities offered by Article 31 EU, these powers of national members must be understood as powers used by the national member acting as a national authority of its Members State of origin. Therefore, conferring such powers to national members do not in any way make Eurojust a supranational body'.[32] On the one hand, there are powers that the national members must have. This may be considered as a codification of the current situation. On the other hand, there are powers that can be granted to national members unless it would be contrary

29. Article 27c of the amended Decision.
30. There is no code of ethics adopted by Eurojust and binding on Eurojust prosecutors. The guidelines for deciding which jurisdiction should prosecute (annex IV to the Annual Report 2004) provide some guidance for national members in order to respect principles such as *ne bis in idem*, the protection of witnesses, delay, and the interests of victims. These guidelines are not binding.
31. Article 9a (2) of the amended Decision.
32. Page 14 of the Explanatory memorandum to Council Decision on the European Judicial Network and to Council Decision on the strengthening of Eurojust amending Council Decision 2002/187/JHA of 28 Feb. 2002, as amended by Council Decision 2003/659/JHA setting up Eurojust with a view to reinforcing the fight against serious crime, Council doc. 5038/08.

to the Member States' constitutional rules, the fundamental aspects of their criminal justice system.[33]

First, the national members must have 'at least equivalent access to, or at least be able to obtain the information' contained at national level in criminal records, registers of arrested persons, investigation registers, DNA registers, and any other registers which would be useful for them to fulfil their tasks.[34] The list of databanks that should be available to national members is greater than in the original Decision. However, not all the Member States have established all the required databanks. This provision may call for further approximation of databanks available to judicial authorities and of rules concerning judicial accountability for processing these data. Secondly, Member States must also grant their national members sufficient powers in order to 'receive, transmit, facilitate, follow up and provide supplementary information' in relation to the execution of requests for judicial cooperation.[35] National members must also be able to participate in or set up JIT.[36] However, the Member States may make this right subject to an agreement with the competent national authority who may be a local prosecutor. The necessity for such an agreement may be detrimental to the efficiency of Eurojust. A national member may waste precious time while obtaining such an agreement. A direct power for the national member to set up a JIT would probably be adequate. One may regret that the amended Decision does not go further and does not provide national members with a right to act directly at national level. This would definitely have increased efficiency, allowing all members to take a decision without referring to their superiors or asking permission from the competent authority.

Instead of such a right to act directly, the Council amended Decision provides two other types of powers. Firstly, Member States must ensure that their national members, in agreement with a competent national authority or at its request, may issue, complete or execute a request for judicial cooperation. This means, for example, that if Eurojust proceeds with a file where a letter rogatory[37] is necessary, a national member may issue the letter in his or her capacity, but under supervision of the competent national authority. Such a request includes instruments giving effect to the principle of mutual recognition, such as a European arrest warrant. Member States' criminal procedure will likely have to be amended in order to organize relations between national competent authorities and Eurojust

33. The Decision mentions the following aspects: the division of powers between the police, prosecutors and judges, the functional division of tasks between prosecution authorities or the federal structure of the Member State concerned (Art. 9e of the amended Decision). This provision aims at lifting one of the obstacles to increase the powers of the national members. In certain countries (in particular, Anglo-Saxon countries) it is not possible to give a national member who is a prosecutor powers which belong to the police or to a judge, see General report of 21 Nov. 2007 on the seminar 'Eurojust: navigating the way forward', Lisbon, 29 and 30 Oct. 2007, Council doc. 15542/07.
34. Article 9 (3) of the amended Decision.
35. Article 9b of the amended Decision. See also n. 23.
36. Article 9f of the amended Decision.
37. A letter rogatory is a request whereby a judicial authority calls upon another judicial authority in another country for judicial assistance, such as the taking of evidence in a particular case.

prosecutors. The amended Decision grants large discretion to Member States in this respect. Secondly, it is in urgent cases only, and 'in so far as it is not possible for them to identify or to contact the competent national authority in a timely manner' that a national member may execute a request for judicial cooperation directly. A national member may authorize and coordinate controlled deliveries in their Member State.[38] As soon as it is identified, the competent national authority must be informed of the case. Nonetheless, one may wonder if it is possible that a Eurojust prosecutor cannot identify the authority competent to act in their home State. National members are supposed to be experts in their home country. They should be able to contact directly anyone who can indicate who is a competent authority. This power to act directly (without referring to local authorities), exercised in all circumstances, would make Eurojust more efficient.

The amended Eurojust Decision will actually oblige Member States to approximate their legislation concerning the status and powers of Eurojust prosecutors to an important extent. It will influence national legislation and regulation concerning the organization and the functioning of public prosecution services and all national authorities competent in criminal proceedings. On the organizational side, national provisions concerning the appointment and the place in the hierarchy of Eurojust prosecutors will have to be adapted. On the functional side, national provisions concerning the powers of Eurojust prosecutors within their domestic jurisdictions, and the relations between Eurojust and the domestic institutions involved in criminal proceedings (e.g., police or public prosecution services) will need adaptation. This, in particular, will be true as regards the important power to act directly in urgent cases. Therefore, criminal codes of procedure will likely have to be amended.

3. ANALYSIS OF LEGALITY IN THE AMENDED EUROJUST DECISION

Firstly, this section will analyse the competence of the EU to strengthen Eurojust before the Treaty of Lisbon. Secondly, the discussion will concern the extent to which the legitimation and regulatory functions of legality have been safeguarded within the exercise of this competence.

3.1. The Legal Basis and the Choice for the Instrument to Strengthen Eurojust

Article 31 TEU (repealed)[39] is the legal basis of the amended Decision. It should be read in combination with Article 29 TEU (repealed),[40] which set the objectives of

38. Article 9d of the amended Decision.
39. Article 31 TEU has been replaced by Arts 82, 83 and 85 TFEU.
40. Article 29 TEU has been replaced by Art. 67 TFEU.

the Union in Police and Judicial Cooperation in Criminal matters (PJCC). According to these provisions, the Union shall 'provide citizens with a high level of safety within an area of freedom, security and justice'. In order to attain this objective, preventing and combating crime should be ensured through closer police cooperation, 'closer cooperation between judicial and other competent authorities of the Member States including cooperation' through Eurojust and 'approximation, where necessary, of rules on criminal matters in the Member States'.[41] The Council could enable Eurojust to 'facilitate proper coordination between Member States' national prosecuting authorities,' promote 'support by Eurojust for criminal investigations in cases of serious cross-border crime' and facilitate 'close cooperation between Eurojust and the European Judicial Network'. The Treaty did not mention the relevant instrument for the action of the Council in order to strengthen Eurojust. Consequently, the Council enjoyed a large margin of appreciation in determining the correct instrument.

Before the entry in force of the Treaty of Lisbon, PJCC could be regulated through specific instruments that were common positions, framework decisions, decisions and conventions. Determining which instrument to use depended on its envisaged purpose. The Court of Justice ruled that 'the Council may have a choice between several instruments in order to regulate the same subject-matter, subject to the limits imposed by the nature of the instrument selected'.[42] In the case of strengthening Eurojust, a common position would not have been appropriate because its object was only to define the 'approach of the Union to a particular matter' (common positions were especially relevant in the field of the Common Foreign and Security Policy).[43] It is, moreover, questionable whether common positions are binding.[44] Conventions were not efficient in comparison with other instruments. The necessity to ratify conventions limits the efficiency of such an instrument, as ratification procedures are long and their outcomes are uncertain. This may explain why they have been phased out since the entry into force of the Treaty of Amsterdam.[45] The Council could either use a framework decision or a decision. The Treaty did not establish a hierarchy between the two instruments.[46] However, they differed from each other in their purpose.

According to Article 34(2)(c) TEU (repealed), the Council could adopt decisions binding on Member States 'for any purpose consistent with the objectives' of

41. Initially the Treaty on the European Union as amended by the Treaty of Maastricht and the Treaty of Amsterdam did not make any reference to such an agency as Eurojust. It established the possibility of achieving the objectives of the Treaty by means, amongst others, of 'closer judicial cooperation'. The Treaty of Nice discretely added a second paragraph to Art. 29 EU mentioning Eurojust and modified consequently Art. 31 EU. The Treaty of Nice, which entered in force in 2003, four years after Tampere, provides for a clearer legal basis to Eurojust.
42. Case C-305/05, *Adocaten voor de Wereld* [2007] ECR I-03633, para. 37.
43. See for example, the Common Position of the Council of 27 Dec. 2001 on combating terrorism, OJ 2001, L 344/90.
44. S. Peers, *EU Justice and Home Affairs Law*, 2nd ed. (Oxford: Oxford University Press, 2006), 33.
45. *Ibid.*, 33–34.
46. See on this issue, P.Y. Monjal, 'Le droit dérivé de l'Union Européenne en quête d'identité', *Revue Trimestrielle de Droit Européen* 2 (2001): 335–369.

the PJCC, but 'excluding any approximation of the laws and regulations of the Member States'. Alternatively, framework decisions could only be adopted 'for the purpose of approximation of the laws and regulations of the Member States'. The third point of the amended Decision's Preamble reads: 'The time has come to ensure that Eurojust becomes more operational and that the status of national members is approximated.' We may raise the question of whether this could happen on the basis of a decision. The Council could probably have abrogated the Eurojust Decision and replaced it by a 'Eurojust Framework Decision'.[47] However, it decided to revisit the initial text by way of another decision. This question may be relevant for the present contribution only if the use of a framework decision rather than a decision would have ensured that the functions of legality are fulfilled successfully.

3.2. Safeguarding the Legitimation Function in the Amended Eurojust Decision

The function of legitimation served by the principle of legality would be fulfilled, for example, if the decision-making procedure applied in order to strengthen Eurojust was democratic. Did this procedure involve representative institutions, for example, in particular, the European Parliament? If so, to what extent was it involved? The function of legitimation may equally be effectively safeguarded if, for example, the decision to strengthen Eurojust involved independent actors.

3.2.1. Role of Representative Institutions in the Decision to Strengthen Eurojust

The reform of Eurojust was envisioned in the Hague programme that was approved during the Brussels European Council of 4 and 5 November 2004.[48] The Council adopted the amended Decision following an initiative of fourteen Member States.[49] The initiative was first discussed by experts in meetings of working parties, before passing to a conciliating committee. The Committee prepared the work for the COREPER and the Council. The text was adopted at a unanimity vote during a Council meeting after the Parliament was consulted. This procedure was specific to the third pillar and applied equally to framework decisions and decisions. The role of the European and national Parliaments seemed weak at two levels: firstly, with regard to their role in the control exercised on the right of

47. See for example, the Framework Decision of 26 Feb. 2009 on the organization and content of the exchange of information extracted from the criminal record between Member States, OJ 2009 L 93/23, which repealed and replaced the Council Decision 2005/876/JHA of 21 Nov. 2005 on the exchange of information extracted from the criminal record, OJ 2005, L 322/33.
48. See the Hague Programme, OJ 2005, C 53/1 and the Presidency Conclusions, paras 14 to 20, Council doc. 14292/04.
49. The initiative of the Belgium, the Czech Republic, Estonia, Spain, France, Italy, Luxembourg, the Netherlands, Austria, Poland, Portugal, Slovenia, Slovakia and Sweden was issued on 7 Jan. 2008, Council doc. 11769/08.

legislative initiative, and secondly, with regard to their participation in the decision-making process itself.

Firstly, the existence of a right to initiate the legislative process in the hands of any Member State or the Commission – which was not repealed at Lisbon[50] – called for questions in terms of legitimation of public authority. The Commission is subject to more direct control by the European Parliament than the Member States.[51] An impact assessment accompanies all major legislative initiatives taken by the Commission.[52] Such an impact assessment identifies the potential positive and negative impacts of proposed policy actions, for example, on the economy, on society or on the environment. Reports are published and they contribute to the transparency of the decision-making process.[53] The Member States, contrary to the Commission, had no obligation to inform the European Parliament and national parliaments about their initiative,[54] and no impact assessment was carried out. Doubt has been cast on the timing of the Member States' initiative to strengthen Eurojust by revising the Decision. The Commission and the European Parliament recommended strengthening the Eurojust's powers after the entry into force of the Treaty of Lisbon, in which the role of representative institutions and independent actors in the decision-making process at European and national level was enhanced.[55] The Member States' motivation to act before the entry into force of the new Treaty thus remains unclear.

Secondly, the European Parliament only had the right to be consulted on initiatives concerning PJCC.[56] In the case of Eurojust, the Parliament fully used

---

50. Nevertheless, Art. 76 TFEU (introduced by Lisbon) provides that *a quarter* of the Member States have the right of initiative in PJCC.
51. The Parliament approves the appointment of the Commission's President and Commission's members (Art. 214 EC now as amended Art. 17 (3) and (7) TEU) and can adopt a motion of censure on the activities of the Commission (Art. 201 EC now as amended Art. 234 TFEU.)
52. According to the Commission Guidelines, an impact assessment is necessary 'for the most important Commission initiatives and those which will have the most far-reaching impacts. This will be the case for all legislative proposals of the Commission's Legislative and Work Programme (CLWP) and for all non-CLWP legislative proposals which have clearly identifiable economic, social and environmental impacts (with the exception of routine implementing legislation) and for non-legislative initiatives (such as white papers, action plans, expenditure programmes, negotiating guidelines for international agreements) which define future policies'. See Impact Assessment Guidelines of 15 Jan. 2009, s. (2009) 92 and Communication of 5 Jun. 2002 from the Commission on Impact Assessment, COM (2002) 276 final.
53. For an example in PJCC, *see* the impact assessment concerning the Proposal for a Regulation establishing an Agency for the operational management of large-scale IT systems in the area of freedom, security and justice a Framework Decision on procedural rights in criminal proceedings. s. (2009) 837.
54. Alternatively, Art. 69 TFEU (introduced by Lisbon) enhances the role of national parliaments with regard to all initiatives notable adopted in the field of PJCC. Proposals submitted by the Member States must be forwarded to national parliaments; *see* the Protocol on the Role of National Parliaments in the European Union, OJ 2007, C 306/148 and the Protocol on the Application of the Principles of Subsidiarity and Proportionality, OJ 2007, C 306/150.
55. COM (2007) 644 final and European Parliament report on the strengthening of Eurojust, A6-0293/2008.
56. Article 39 TEU (repealed).

its right to adopt recommendations. The European Parliament delivered a recommendation to the Council and the European Council on 14 October 2004 concerning the draft of the Hague Programme.[57] It then published a report on 7 July 2008 on the Member States' initiative to strengthen Eurojust.[58] Nevertheless, in terms of democratic accountability, this picture cannot remain without comment. Indeed, the Council had no obligation to consider recommendations and amendments to third pillar initiatives fully. This is regrettable, since in its reports the Parliament drew the Council's attention to several shortcomings, such as the absence of clear definitions for certain concepts (e.g., the power to 'take special investigative measures' provided in Article 6(a)(vi) of the amended Decision) or the necessity to take account of the rights of defendant and victims when Eurojust exercises its tasks. Specifically, the Parliament proposed several amendments to ensure that the Member States would safeguard the suspects' rights to fair trial and to judicial remedy.[59] Moreover, the involvement of national parliaments in the establishment of a national position to be represented in the pre-Lisbon EU decision-making procedures differed significantly between the Member States.[60] The parliamentary involvement varied from ad hoc simple consultation to systematic and obligatory assessment, and a not only politically but also legally binding mandate. If no act of parliament is adopted to give effect to the amended Decision, national representatives may never be consulted.

3.2.2. Independent Actors' Involvement in the Decision to Strengthen Eurojust

The proposal to revise the Eurojust Decision was the conclusion of detailed discussions. Representatives of all EU institutions, Eurojust, Europol and many practitioners from all relevant sectors took part in these discussions. The process started with a seminar organized on 25–26 September 2006 by the Presidency (the former Austrian and the Finnish Presidency), the Commission, the General Secretariat of the Council and the European Criminal Law Academic Network (ECLAN) in Vienna.[61] The seminar was followed by a Communication of the Commission

57. European Parliament recommendation of 14 Oct. 2004 on the future of the area of freedom, security and justice, P6_TA(2004)0022.
58. See the European Parliament report on the strengthening of Eurojust, A6-0293/2008. With regard to the Decision setting up Eurojust, the Council has consulted the Parliament twice; see Gebhardt report approved by committee, A5-0398/2001.
59. The Parliament proposed to introduce several recitals in the Eurojust Decision. One recital would ensure that the rights of the defendants and victims be taken into account in determining which Member States is best placed to prosecute. Another recital would focus on the necessity to make adequate procedural safeguards a necessary condition for the execution of mutual recognition of judicial decisions.
60. See on this T. Takács, *Participation in EU Decision Making, Implications on the National Level* (The Hague: T.M.C. Asser Press, 2009): 218–233.
61. Report of 19 Oct. 2006 of the seminar 'A Seminar with 2020 Vision: The Future of Eurojust and the European Judicial Network', Council doc. 14123/06.

to the Parliament and the Council on 23 October 2007,[62] a questionnaire prepared by Eurojust and the Member States' replies[63] and, finally, a general report from the General Secretariat of the Council to Delegations.[64]

The Eurojust Joint Supervisory Body (EJSB) has commented on the proposal.[65] The main activity of the EJSB is to ensure that Eurojust acts in line with the rules set up by the Decision when it processes data. The EJSB did not have any function in the decision-making process concerning the strengthening of Eurojust. Nevertheless, in its 2007 activity report, the EJSB mentioned that a future review of the Eurojust Decision should take into account the need for a greater flexibility in the rules concerning the restrictions on the processing of personal data. Article 15 of the Decision held, amongst others, that Eurojust may process only certain types of personal data (e.g., nationality, sex or bank accounts) on certain persons (e.g., those subject to a criminal investigation or prosecution for one or more of the offences for which Eurojust is competent). Although the recommendations of the EJSB are neither binding on the Member States nor on the Council, the Council considered the EJSB's recommendations and consequently modified Article 15.[66]

Finally, the decision to strengthen Eurojust has been the subject of an opinion of the European Data Protection Supervisor (EDPS.)[67] The task of the EDPS is to monitor the application of data protection by Community institutions and agencies. The scope of its advisory duties could cover legislative proposals in the third pillar, although it was established in the first pillar.[68] Regrettably, there was no obligation for a Member State or a group of Member States to ask the EDPS for advice when conceiving draft legislation. In its opinion, the EDPS, highlighting the absence of an impact assessment, pointed out the lack of transparency and the questionable quality of the legislative process attached to the amended Decision. The EDPS also emphasized that it might have been better to wait until the entry into force of the Lisbon Treaty to reform Eurojust.

The role of representative institutions and independent actors in the decision-making process with regard to the strengthening of Eurojust has been rather weak. Even though the issue received much attention from all European institutions and

---

62. COM (2007) 644 final.
63. Questionnaire of 2 Jul. 2007 on the implementation of the Council Decision of 28 Feb. 2002 setting up Eurojust with a view to reinforcing the fight against serious crime, Council doc. 11143/07.
64. General report of 21 Nov. 2007 on the seminar 'Eurojust: Navigating the Way Forward', Lisbon, 29 and 30 Oct. 2007, Council doc. 15542/07.
65. The EJSB consists of an independent judge appointed by each Member State.
66. Explanatory memorandum to Council Decision on the European Judicial Network and to Council Decision on the strengthening of Eurojust amending Council Decision 2002/187/JHA of 28 Feb. 2002, as amended by Council Decision 2003/659/JHA setting up Eurojust with a view to reinforcing the fight against serious crime, Council doc. 5038/08.
67. Opinion of the EDPS of 25 Apr. 2008, OJ 2008, C 310/1.
68. See for a complete analysis of the EDPS, G.G. Fuster & P. Paepe, 'Reflexive Governance and the EU Third Pillar: Analysis of Data Protection and Criminal Law Aspects', in: *Security versus Justice*, ed. E. Guild & F. Geyer (Aldershot: Ashgate, 2008), 129–150.

other relevant independent actors, the final decision was mainly taken at the level of the Member States' executives. Moreover, one may question the democratic value of the involvement of these independent actors in the decision-making process.[69] The legitimation of Eurojust is, therefore, debatable. The Eurojust reform will have an influence on the criminal justice systems of the Member States and may affect the legal position of citizens. Important recommendations made during the decision-making process were not taken into account. This 'eclipse' of legitimation may well be prejudicial to the regulatory function that the legality principle seeks to safeguard.

3.3. Safeguarding the Regulatory Function in the Amended Eurojust Decision

Eurojust has the potential to influence the legal position of citizens. Therefore, the provisions of the amended Eurojust Decision should be clear and precise. They should provide safeguards against abuse of power or arbitrariness. The provisions must ensure that the fight against crime is effective without undermining the interest of the suspects and the victims of crimes. This is particularly desirable because currently Member States enjoy a large margin of discretion when implementing third pillar decisions. At the same time, however, this discretion may be detrimental to the actual regulatory effect of the Decision and consequently to the powers of Eurojust towards Member States.

3.3.1. Appraisal of the Quality of the Amended Decision

In addition to the deficiencies already discussed (see above), the amended Decision may not meet the requirements of a successful regulation in other respects. For example, the amended Decision introduces a provision on Eurojust liability.[70] Disputes relating to Eurojust liability, and, indirectly, to Eurojust prosecutors, shall be brought before the competent court as determined in the Council Regulation 44/2001.[71] The competent court will not necessarily be established in the country of origin of the person whose liability is being challenged. Could a case involving a Eurojust prosecutor be tried by a court in another Member State than the prosecutor's State of origin, such as the State in which a victim has his or her home? It is also regrettable that the concept of 'urgent cases' is not defined. It will be up to a Eurojust prosecutor on duty to decide when a case is urgent. What criteria should be retained to decide that a case is urgent? To whom is the prosecutor accountable? How will

69. See the Judgment of the German Constitutional Court of 30 Jun. 2009 on the compatibility of the act approving the Treaty of Lisbon to the German basic law. According to the Court, only the peoples of the Member States are the holders of the constituent power; BVerfG 30 Jun. 2009, 2 BvE 2/08, 2 BvE 5/08, 2 BvR 1010/08, 2 BvR 1022/08, 2 BvR 1259/08, 2 BvR 182/09.
70. Article 27c of the amended Decision.
71. Council Regulation (EC) No. 44/2001 of 22 Dec. 2000 on jurisdiction and the recognition and enforcement of judgments in civil and commercial matters, OJ 2001, L 12/1.

such a decision in an urgent case be taken and supervised in order to avoid abuse of powers?[72] In this respect, common binding standards would be useful.

The amended Decision does not provide any common standard regarding the accountability of national members for the use of data collected in national registers. On the side of Eurojust, a protection is ensured. Only certain personal data may be processed in specific circumstances and under the supervision of the independent data protection officer and the EJSB.[73] Nevertheless, the rules of procedure on the processing and protection of personal data at Eurojust do not cover information transmitted to a national member exercising their powers.[74] This seems rather unfortunate. A significant improvement has been made recently with the adoption of the framework decision on the protection of personal data, which covers cross-border exchanges of personal data within the framework of police and judicial cooperation.[75] However, the protection neither covers the processing of data within a domestic system (outside a PJCC context) nor the Eurojust processed data.

Moreover, the Decision as amended remains silent with regard to the rules that Eurojust should apply when resolving a conflict of jurisdiction. No mechanism of control over Eurojust as a body has been established. Eurojust may recommend that a prosecution should take place in a certain Member State rather than in another. In addition to the support that Eurojust offers to national members for request of mutual assistance in criminal proceedings, it may recommend one or more Member States to take certain actions in criminal proceedings and resolve conflicts of jurisdiction.[76] The Eurojust Decision does not explain the rules that should be applied to reach a recommendation. It does not provide remedies to individuals affected by such a recommendation. This is regrettable, because a recent proposal for a framework decision on conflicts of jurisdiction obliges the Member States to ensure that their authorities refer cases to Eurojust when no consensus to resolve conflicts of jurisdiction can be reached.[77] These weaknesses raise concerns about the respect of the right to a fair trial and to legality in criminal matters (*nullum crimen sine lege*) that could be undermined by the possibility of a prosecutorial 'forum shopping'.[78]

---

72. Similar concerns have been pointed out in the reporter's position following the Parliament consultation, A6-0293/2008.
73. Articles 15, 17 and 23 of the amended Decision.
74. Article 2 (3) of the Rules of Procedure on the Processing and Protection of Personal Data at Eurojust, OJ 2005, C 68/1.
75. Council Framework Decision of 27 Nov. 2008 on the protection of personal data processed in the framework of police and judicial cooperation in criminal matters, OJ 2008, L 350/60.
76. For example, Eurojust may ask one Member State to accept that another Member State is better situated to prosecute a case for which both states have jurisdiction. Such a situation implies that one prosecutor accepts waiving his/her jurisdiction in a particular case in favour of a prosecutor established in another Member State.
77. See Art. 12 (2) of the Proposal of 6 Apr. 2009 for a Council Framework Decision on prevention and settlement of conflicts of exercise of jurisdiction in criminal proceedings, Council doc. 8338/09.
78. V. Mitsilegas, 'The Third Wave of Third Pillar Law: Which Direction for EU Criminal Justice?', *European Law Review* 4 (2009): 523–550.

These shortcomings affecting the amended Decision impair the quality of the legislation at the EU level. This is probably not successfully living up to the requirements of the regulatory functions of the principle of legality.

3.3.2. Effects of the Decision in the Member States

Member States enjoy a large margin of discretion when they implement third pillar decisions.[79] Decisions are binding on them, but shall not entail direct effect. In order to discover the effects of such acts on the national legal systems, certain authors have compared third pillar decisions to first pillar decisions *sui generis*.[80] Others compared them to regulations because they were 'mainly used to legislate in matters which concern the EU itself or its institutions necessitating no direct action from the Member States'.[81] Nevertheless, regulations are never transposed.[82] Third pillar decisions could also be compared to framework decisions. They, as is the case for Eurojust, de facto approximate the laws and regulations of the Member States. Moreover, the Member States must, where necessary, conform their national law with third pillar decisions 'at the earliest opportunity and in any case no later than' the date provided in the decisions.[83] There are, however, differences between decisions and framework decisions. The obligation to implement framework decisions is comparable with that of directives. The Member States have, in general, a positive obligation to implement framework decisions.[84] They must adopt the measures necessary to give effect to framework decisions. The Commission construes this obligation in the same terms as it does for directives. The Member States must comply with the case law of the Court of Justice

79. As I recall, this type of decision has been repealed by the Treaty of Lisbon, nevertheless those adopted before the 1 Dec. 2009 must be implemented.
80. Dashwood compares third pillar decision with decisions *sui generis* or 'innominate' decisions. See A. Dashwood, 'Issues of Decision-Making in the European Union after Nice', in: *Accountability and Legitimacy in the European Union*, ed. A. Arnull & D. Wincott (Oxford: Oxford University Press, 2003).
81. M. Fletcher, R. Lööf & B. Gilmore, *EU Criminal Law and Justice* (Cheltenham: Edward Elgar, 2008), 35.
82. None the less, it almost always happens that execution measures are adopted to ensure that regulations correctly function.
83. Member States should have implemented the Decision no later than 6 Sep. 2003 and will have to implement the amended Decision no later than 4 Jun. 2011.
84. In very exceptional cases, the ECJ decided that the implementation of a directive did not imply the adoption of national measures. However, the Court imposes very strict conditions to the Member States pretending that no act of transposition is necessary. These conditions guarantee the principle of legal certainty. A 'copy/paste' of the directive's provisions in the national legislation is, in principle, not sufficient to fulfil the obligation to implement; see for example, Case C-221/94, *Commission v. Luxemburg* [1996] ECR I-5669 and Case C-96/95, *Commission v. Germany* [1997] ECR I-1653; see for example, on the implementation of framework decisions and comparison with directives, M. Borgers, 'Implementing Framework Decisions', CMLRev. 5 (2007): 1361–1386; S. Prechal & T. Marguery, 'La mise en œuvre des décisions-cadres', in: *L'exécution du droit de l'Union, entre mécanismes communautaires et droits nationaux*, ed. J. Dutheil de la Rochère (Brussels: Bruylant, 2009).

developed for the transposition of directives.[85] This case law aims at ensuring that directives are equally transposed in the Member States. Contrary to what happens with directives and framework decisions, Member States are not always obliged to adopt a national measure in order to adapt their laws and regulations to a decision. A Member State will pass a law or adopt a regulation only if it deems it necessary. Therefore, the implementation of third pillar decisions may be, first of all, a political decision. The Member States enjoy a large discretion in justifying their compliance with their obligation. For example, the mere fact of relying on actual legislation is enough for a Member State to fulfil its obligation of implementation.[86] The Member States' large margin of discretion to implement third pillar decisions is certainly in line with the subsidiarity principle and the third pillar's intergovernmental character. In the present case, it respects the existing diversity between Member States in the way their public prosecution services or national authorities of equivalent competence are regulated.[87] Certain Member States gave effect to the Eurojust Decision by way of an act of parliament,[88] others by an administrative decision.[89] Certain Member States did not consider it necessary to modify their laws and regulations. The same will probably happen for the amended Decision.

In the absence of a general positive obligation to implement decisions, it will be difficult to prevent or lessen Member States' hesitation to give effect to the amended Decision, and it is doubtful that it will be equally implemented in the Member States. The Council, nevertheless, improved the supervisory role of the Commission in the amended Decision.[90] The Commission will have to examine the implementation of the Decision 'at regular intervals' and 'submit a report thereon to the European Parliament and to the Council'. The Commission will also be able to submit 'necessary proposals to improve judicial cooperation and the functioning of Eurojust'. This improvement is certainly welcome, but will probably remain more political than legal. Indeed, one may wonder what exactly the Commission will examine. As the Commission already mentioned in its Report on the Legal Transposition of the Eurojust Decision, the evaluation can mainly be based on the will of the Member States to reply on questionnaire sent to the Commission.[91] In this respect, the choice of a framework decision would have obliged the Member States to adopt binding national provisions that the

85. For example, Case C-48/75, *Royer* [1976] ECR 00497; Case C-236/85, *Commission v. the Netherlands* [1987] ECR 3989.
86. This is not allowed in the case of directives. See for example, Case C-96/95, *Commission v. Germany* [1997] ECR I-1653.
87. See for example, P. Tak, *Tasks and Powers of the Prosecution Services in the EU Member States* (Nijmegen: Wolf Legal Publisher, 2005); T. Marguery, *Unity and Diversity of the Public Prosecution Services in Europe* (Groningen: University of Groningen, 2008).
88. For example, Belgium, France or Portugal.
89. For example, Cyprus or Hungary.
90. See Art. 2 of the Decision amending the Eurojust Decision.
91. Report from the European Commission of 6 Jul. 2004 on the Legal Transposition of the Council Decision of 28 Feb. 2002 setting up Eurojust with a View to reinforcing the Fight against Serious Crime, COM (2004) 457 final.

Commission would successfully be able to monitor. However, the Commission has no power to bring an infringement procedure against the Member States that do not correctly – if at all – implement third pillar law. The choice of a framework decision could legally have been more efficient and add more legal certainty, but in fact would probably have made no difference. The large discretion enjoyed by the Member States will probably not ensure that the amended Decision is efficiently and equally implemented in all legal systems. The amended Decision seeks the elimination of differences between criminal justice systems that undermine the successful functioning of Eurojust. However, considering the effects that third pillar decisions have in the Member States it is not certain that the regulatory effect of Eurojust will be equally satisfactory at all.

Nonetheless, one may wonder whether there are limits to the discretion of Member States and whether such limits would ensure that Eurojust functions equally and efficiently towards all Member States. One of the limits to that discretion could be found in the principle of loyal cooperation. The principle, now provided in Article 4(3) TEU,[92] has applied to third pillar law since the judgment *Pupino*.[93] The principle obliges the Member States to 'take any appropriate measures, general or particular, to ensure the fulfilment of the obligations arising out of the Treaties or resulting from the acts of the institutions of the Union'. Besides, they must 'facilitate the achievement of the Union's tasks and abstain from any measure which could jeopardise the attainment of the Union's objectives'. All national public authorities are bound by this principle. As an emanation of the State, public prosecutors fall within the scope of the principle. Therefore, all public prosecutors in the Member States – not only Eurojust prosecutors – must ensure that the Eurojust Decision as amended is further implemented and that no national measure impedes its implementation. As a consequence of this, where the amended Eurojust Decision provides for clear and precise powers that must be granted to national members, Eurojust prosecutors should enjoy such powers even if no national measures have transposed this act. On a more general note, public prosecutors should have recourse to Eurojust whenever this is necessary in order to provide citizens with a high level of safety and to make sure that cooperation between prosecution services is not impeded. Whether individuals could rely on the Eurojust Decision is more uncertain. Indeed, it does not really provide citizens with rights. Rather, it provides prosecutors with powers. It may not be *a priori* in the interest of a citizen to argue, for example, that a clear provision of criminal procedure should entitle a national member in The Hague to the power to act directly in the place of a local prosecutor or to order the police to take investigative measures. Nevertheless, it is in the interest of any citizen involved in criminal

92. Originally the ECJ referred to Art. 10 EC (repealed) as the base of the principle; see on this principle, for example, J. Temple Lang, 'Article 10 EC – The most important "General Principle" of Community Law, Swedish Network for European Legal Studies Stockholm Conference', in: *General Principles of EC Law in a Process of Development Number 62 in the series European Monographs*, ed. U. Bernitz, J. Nergelius & C. Cardner (The Hague: Kluwer Law International, 2008).

93. Case C-105/03, *Pupino* [2005] ECR I-5285, para. 42.

proceedings, for example, to know what decisions a national member can take and what remedy against such decisions are available. This will have to be clearly provided in the criminal procedure if a national member happens to have the power to decide. It may also be in the interest of the victim of a crime to rely on an efficient prosecution service fully enjoying the support provided by Eurojust.[94] This would not be the case if the criminal procedure were not in line with the amended Decision. The victim's interest may be raised in several proceedings concerning crimes such as motor vehicle crime, murder or grievous bodily injury, for which Eurojust is competent. However, it should be noted that national courts are obliged to interpret provisions of substantive law in conformity with European law. This does not hold true for criminal procedure unless a breach of the right to fair trial is involved.[95] The amended Decision probably will only affect national provisions on criminal procedure and regulations on the prosecution service. Therefore, an individual seeking an interpretation of national law in the light of the Decision will have to prove a breach of his right to fair trial in order to rely on that Decision. This is very unlikely to happen since the rights to fair trial are mainly granted to suspects rather than victims. It is, therefore, doubtful whether individuals will be able to invoke the Eurojust Decision before a court.

The regulation of the manner in which public authority of Eurojust is to be exercised has so far proven unsatisfactory in several respects. As regards provisions on national members' accountability and rules on conflict of jurisdiction, the amended Decision is ill- defined. Clear and precise provisions would have ensured a higher degree of legal certainty. Moreover, the implementation and effects of the amended Decision in all the Member States will probably be weak. This may result in an unequal implementation of the act, which will undermine the regulatory function that the Eurojust Decision should ensure. This could eventually impede the judicial protection for all EU citizens, whether victim or suspected of a crime.

4. STRENGTHENING EUROJUST AFTER LISBON

The following section will give a short overview of the modifications that the Lisbon Treaty may imply for Eurojust. As the European Parliament and the EDPS indicated,[96] reforming Eurojust under the Lisbon framework would probably have been a better option in terms of democratic accountability of decision-making. The Treaty of Lisbon puts an end to the pillar structure of the Union. It provides a new legal basis for Eurojust in Article 85 Treaty on the Functioning of

94. Since the Framework Decision of 15 Mar. 2001 on the standing of victims in criminal proceedings, OJ 2001 L 82/1, the Member States must provide victims with a real role in criminal proceedings. Arts 2, 3 and 4 grant victims with minimum rights in the course of criminal proceedings. Accordingly, Member States may provide the victim of a crime with the right to participate in the decision-making on the evidence of the guilt and on the sentence.
95. Case C-105/03, *Pupino* [2005] ECR I-5285, paras 44, 47 and 59.
96. A6-0293/2008 and Opinion of the EDPS of 25 Apr. 2008, OJ 2008, C 310/1.

the European Union (TFEU). A new framework for Eurojust adopted in application of this article will involve all important EU institutions and national parliaments in a transparent and legitimate manner. This implies a stronger supervision from the Parliament and the conducting of an impact assessment. The consultation of the EDPS will also be made compulsory. The European Parliament will be strongly involved in the decision-making process. Indeed, 'Eurojust's structure, operation, field of action and tasks' will be determined by means of regulations. Such acts will be adopted pursuant to the ordinary legislative procedure (ex co-decision procedure) provided in Article 294 TFEU, where the Parliament and the Council exercise legislative functions jointly. Moreover, national parliaments will be implicated in this process. Any legislative proposal will have to be sent to all parliaments (and to other EU institutions) at the same time.[97] A national parliament would be able, within eight weeks (from the moment it receives a proposal), to send a reasoned opinion to the Presidents of the Commission, the European Parliament and the Council explaining why the project does not comply with the subsidiarity principle.[98]

In application of the Protocol on transitional provisions annexed to the Treaty of Lisbon, the amended Eurojust Decision will remain in force unless it is amended, repealed or annulled.[99] Member States must have implemented this Decision by no later than 4 June 2011. The same Protocol provides for a period of five years after the entry into force of the Treaty of Lisbon (with an exception for the United Kingdom) before the Commission will be able to bring an infringement procedure against a Member State who has failed to implement the amended Decision.[100] If the amended Eurojust Decision remains in force, the Treaty of Lisbon will not immediately improve the level and quality of the Decision's implementation. However, the Stockholm Programme adopted in 2009 clearly invites the Commission to consider a reform of Eurojust 'including giving further powers to the Eurojust national member, reinforcement of the powers of the Eurojust College or the setting-up of a European Public Prosecutor'.[101] This may happen on the basis of an assessment of the implementation of the amended Decision. According to Article 85 TFEU, the Parliament and the Council could give Eurojust the power to institute criminal proceedings and resolve conflicts of jurisdiction. The Commission may propose a draft legislation repealing the amended Decision and providing Eurojust with an efficient operational function. Future reform of Eurojust would provide an opportunity to ensure that supervision mechanisms guarantee a thorough accountability of Eurojust for its activities. Clear provisions on the suspect's right to a fair trial and judicial remedy against decisions made by

97. Protocol on the Role of National Parliaments in the European Union, OJ 2007, C 306/148.
98. Article 6 of the Protocol on the Application of the Principles of Subsidiarity and Proportionality, OJ 2007, C 306/150.
99. Article 9 of Title VII of the Protocol on Transitional Provisions, OJ 2007, C 306/159.
100. Article 10 of Title VII of the Protocol on Transitional Provisions, OJ 2007, C 306/159.
101. See draft of the Stockholm Programme submitted on 2 Dec. 2009 by the Presidency for approval and publication, Council doc. 17024/09 24.

national authorities towards Eurojust, and by Eurojust towards Member States, should also be established.

5. CONCLUSION

This contribution has demonstrated that the amended Eurojust Decision will have an effect on the legislation of the Member States. First, this effect will be on the status and powers of public prosecutors, judges or police officers appointed as national members, deputies or assistants to Eurojust. Second, national criminal procedures may have to integrate national members as competent authorities to decide directly in criminal proceedings. The Council adopted a decision aimed at setting up an agency, but in fact it will approximate criminal procedures. Third pillar decisions offer flexibility to the Member States when adapting their legislation. The reform of Eurojust may enhance the efficiency of the prosecution of serious crimes. The quest for efficiency was probably the main motivation of Member States who proposed to strengthen Eurojust. In an area of freedom, security and justice, citizens should be able to rely on efficient public prosecution services operating with equal powers in all Member States. The Member States must exercise public authority in order to protect the citizens against crime. The new Decision goes in that direction, but the Member States must thoroughly implement the amended Decision.

However, the analysis of this Council Decision shows several shortcomings in terms of legality. This is especially true with regard to the legitimation and regulatory functions that the principle of legality seeks to ensure. If it is fully implemented, the Decision's potential to affect the citizen's legal position should not be underestimated. However, the Decision does not always provide Eurojust with clear and precise rules that it should apply when acting. The individual's protection against the agency is weak or non-existent. This is worrying because provisions on the agency's accountability are missing in the Decision. If the European Parliament's role in the decision-making process had been stronger, Eurojust would certainly have been more legitimate. More legitimation of Eurojust could have ensured a more successful regulatory effect of Eurojust. As a consequence of this, the Decision as amended does not offer the adequate mechanisms and provisions that would guarantee that the agency exercises its powers in such a manner in which the rights of the individuals are effectively protected. Citizens should also be protected against a deficient, ill-defined or unequal implementation of national members' status and powers between the Member States. Public prosecutors are certainly bound to implement the Decision in application of the principle of loyal cooperation; nevertheless a strong monitoring from the Commission will be missing for the next five years.

The institutional framework laid down in the Treaty of Lisbon could remedy these shortcomings. Besides the involvement of representatives of national and European parliaments, the Commission would extend its monitoring role to ensure successful implementation. Nevertheless, new legislation clarifying the role of

Eurojust in resolving conflicts of jurisdiction will be necessary. The rules concerning the accountability of the agency will also need further development. This is essential in order to preserve the right to a fair trial. Not only would the citizens' interests be safeguarded through parliamentarians, but the overall 'European interest' would be protected by the Commission. The 'eclipse of legality' affecting the strengthening of Eurojust today requires an adequate balance between the sword and the shield in the Eurojust of tomorrow.

Chapter 14

Legality and Data Protection Law: The Forgotten Purpose of Purpose Limitation

Evelien Brouwer

1. INTRODUCTION

Data protection law regulates the various stages involved in the processing of data or information on individual, physical persons (and sometimes groups and organizations of such persons).[1] One of the core principles of data protection law is purpose limitation. This principle provides that personal data must be collected for specified, explicit and legitimate purposes and must not be further used in a way incompatible with those purposes. Purpose limitation implies different standards data processors should take into account, including time limits for the storage of data and limitations with regard to the quality and relevance of the information being collected or stored. Both at the European union (EU) as at the national level, the principle of purpose limitation seems to be undermined by current developments in the field of data collection and data sharing. Laws establishing new databases or prescribing the exchange of personal data (e.g., PNR data) often

1. L.A. Bygrave & J.P. Berg, 'Reflections on the Rationale for Data Protection Laws, in: *25 Years Anniversary Anthology*, ed. J. Bing & O. Torvund (Tano: Norwegian Research Center For Computers and Law, 1995), 3 ff. See also L.A. Bygrave, *Data Protection Law: Approaching its Rationale, Logic and Limits* (The Hague: Kluwer Law International, 2003).

Leonard Besselink, Frans Pennings & Sacha Prechal (eds), *The Eclipse of the Legality Principle in the European Union*, pp. 273–294.

include vague and open criteria on the use of these systems, time limits, and on the authorities having access to these data.

This blurring of purpose limitation, also referred to as 'function creep' seems to be based on the idea that this principle is only a rule of 'soft law'. In this view, purpose limitation should only be dealt with as a guideline for data processing, allowing data owners or data users to derogate when considered necessary.[2] The aim of this contribution is to restate the meaning of purpose limitation by emphasizing its close relation with the principle of legality. In fact, the data protection principle of 'purpose limitation' can be considered an important case study of the meaning of legality within the multilayered legal order of the EU.

In order to clarify the very sense and aim of purpose limitation, the three functions of legality as discussed by others in this volume – legitimation, attribution, and regulation – will be applied to data processing. It will be held that the aim of purpose limitation is comparable to the general aim of the principle of legality: limiting the powers of government. We will see that in dealing with the collection and use of personal information, the legitimation of public powers is not self-evident: what is the legal basis of current measures? What is the role of the European Parliament and national parliaments with regard to the adoption of the EU legislation at stake? With regard to the function of attribution of public authorities, one has to consider the definition of powers and actors in the new rules dealing with data processing and data exchange. Are the powers and actors sufficiently defined? What rules apply to the use of personal information or international databases with regard to the accountability and responsibility of national authorities? Finally, considering the function of regulation of powers, one has to ask whether the rules involved protect individuals from misuse of powers or arbitrariness. What mechanisms are available to control the powers of authorities?

2. SHORT INTRODUCTION TO DATA PROTECTION LAW

2.1. Development of Data Protection Law

Generally, the basic principles of data protection were formulated in the period between 1970 and 1981. During this period, the 'pioneer states' of data protection, including Germany and Sweden, introduced laws including mechanisms of prior control of databases such as prior registration or licensing systems. The second period, between 1981 and 1988, marked the end of an isolated national legislation process. Concerns about data protection on the one hand, and the free flow of information on the other, resulted in the adoption of the Organisation for Economic

2. An example is the report of Commissie Brouwer with the title '*Gewoon doen*' ['Just do it', EB] on the use of data for security purposes. One of its central recommendations is that 'if necessary for the security, authorities should share personal information' without further taking into account data protection law or the right to privacy. Report to the Netherlands Minister of the Interior, January 2009, <www.minbzk.nl>, 1 Jan. 2010.

Co-operation and Development (OECD) Guidelines in 1980 and of the Data Protection Convention of the Council of Europe in 1981. Now, almost thirty years after their adoption, the standards formulated in these instruments have 'stood the test of time' and still can be considered as guiding principles for data protection laws.[3] An important development for the data protection laws of EU Member States was the adoption of the EC Directive 95/46 on the protection of personal data. This Directive was aimed at preventing diverging national data protection laws from hampering the free flow of information between the EU Member States. By offering harmonized rules and emphasizing and developing further the data protection principles of the aforementioned Data Protection Convention, its implications reached much further. Since its adoption, data protection and the protection of individual rights to privacy could no longer be neglected by the EU and national legislatures. The period since 2000–2001 has provided a new era in data protection history. On the one hand, we have seen the introduction of new information technologies, including the use of biometrics, large-scale databases, 'machine-readable documents', and the efforts of national legislatures to respond to these developments. On the other hand, this period has been marked by the recognition of data protection as an independent human right under Article 8 of the Charter on the Fundamental Rights of the EU.[4]

2.2. Objectives and Principles of Data Protection Law

Too often data protection is marginalized to an individual, private interest which, especially in the context of public order and security, must be weighed against more general and public rights and interests. However, when discussing the meaning of data protection law, it is necessary to understand its different objectives, because this clarifies the close relationship of data protection rules with the principle of legality. In my view, one could distinguish three objectives of data protection.[5] The first is the protection of individual rights, and, more specifically, the protection of the right to privacy. This right, protected under Article 8 European Convention on Human Rights (ECHR) and Article 7 of the EU Charter, includes the right to be let alone, the right to liberty and the right to informational self-determination. The second objective of data protection, also referred to in the

---

3. Richard Thomas, 'Information Commissioner of the United Kingdom', Annual Report 2006–2007.
4. Article 8 of the Charter states:

   1. Everyone has the right to the protection of personal data concerning him or her.
   2. Such data must be processed fairly for specified purposes and on the basis of the consent of the person concerned or some other legitimate basis laid down by law. Everyone has the right of access to data which has been collected concerning him or her, and the right to have it rectified.
   3. Compliance with these rules shall be subject to control by an independent authority.

5. See also my dissertation, *Digital Borders and Real Rights: Effective Remedies for Third-Country Nationals in the Schengen Information System* (Leiden/Boston: Martinus Nijhoff Publishers, 2008), 194 ff.

preamble to the Data Protection Convention, is the protection of the rule of law. For this purpose, the concept of the 'rule of law' should be interpreted widely, similar to the German and Dutch concepts of *Rechtsstaat*. In this meaning, the 'rule of law' refers to a legal order in which the powers of the state (and possibly of civil actors) are constrained for the protection of rights and liberties and the equality and legal certainty of individuals.[6] This concept of the rule of law includes the principle of division or balancing of powers, the protection of human rights, and a democratic legal order.[7] By emphasizing this objective separately, it becomes clear that data protection law not only protects the individual, but also the community of individuals as a whole: this has been described as 'the social function' of data protection.[8] A third objective of data protection law concerns the protection of 'good governance' or 'good administration'. This objective protects the interests of both the data subject and the data controller, by guaranteeing the integrity and accuracy of the information being held, and by safeguarding the security of information systems and time limits with regard to the storage of data.

There is no absolute or definitive set of data protection principles. In the relatively young history of data protection law, varying lists have been defined as to what should be considered basic rules of data protection.[9] In general, one could say that the core of data protection law includes the following principles: purpose limitation, purpose specification, data quality, use limitation, security safeguards, openness, individual participation, and accountability.[10]

3. THE PRINCIPLE OF PURPOSE LIMITATION

3.1. General

One of the central principles of data protection is the principle of purpose limitation, or the principle of 'finality'.[11] It not only implies the prior limitation or

6. Ph. Kunig, *Das Rechtsstaatsprinzip: Überlegungen zu seiner Bedeutung für das Verfassungsrecht der Bundesrepublik Deutschland* (Tübingen: Mohr (Siebeck), 1989); M. Burkens et al. *Beginselen van de democratische rechtsstaat* (Alphen aan den Rijn: Kluwer, 2006) and D.J. Elzinga, 'De democratische rechtsstaat als ontwikkelingsperspectief. Over machtsregulering als ontwikkelingslijn', in: *De rechtsstaat herdacht*, ed. J.W.M. Engels & E.M. Middel (Zwolle: W.E.J. Tjeenk Willink, 1989).
7. The explanatory memorandum to this Convention explicitly refers to 'the necessity of data protection as a tool of balancing powers'.
8. Arthur J. Cockfield, 'Protecting the Social Value of Privacy in the Context of State Investigations Using New Technologies', *U.B.C. Law Review* 40, no. 1 (May 2007), 41, available at <http://ssrn.com/abstract=1031964>, 1 Jan. 2010.
9. Bennett refers to the six 'core fair information principles': principles of openness, individual access and correction, collection limitation, use limitation, disclosure limitation and security, Bennett (1992), 101 ff.
10. See for example, the European Data Protection Supervisor (EDPS) in his Opinion of 28 Feb. 2006, Brussels: <www.edps.europa.eu>, 1 Jan. 2010.
11. In the German and Dutch language, this principle is referred to as 'Zweckbindung', respectively 'doelbinding'.

definition of the objective of data processing, but also refers to the subsequent use of data. The meaning of purpose limitation may be clarified considering an important provision of one of the oldest legal sources of data protection law: Article 5 of the Council of Europe Data Protection Convention. Under the heading of 'Quality of data', this provides that personal data automatically processed shall be:

(a) obtained and processed fairly and lawfully;
(b) stored for specified and legitimate purposes and not used in a way incompatible with those purposes;
(c) adequate, relevant and not excessive in relation to the purposes for which they are stored;
(d) accurate and, where necessary, kept up to date;
(e) preserved in a form which permits identification of the data subjects for no longer than is required for the purpose for which those data are stored.

The purpose limitation has been included in Article 6(1)(b) of EC Directive 95/46, providing that personal data must be collected for specified, explicit and legitimate purposes, and may not be further processed in a way incompatible with those purposes.

Considering these provisions in Article 5 DPC and the EC Directive, one can see that purpose limitation includes different layers of protection. Firstly, it prohibits the collection of personal data for unknown or unspecified purposes, referred to as the 'ban on aimless data collection'. Secondly, it implies that the goals of data processing should be legitimate, meaning in accordance with the law and not infringing these laws. Thirdly, it says that the goals must be specified prior to the data collection: purpose specification. Fourthly, any use or disclosure of personal data for goals incompatible to the (specified) goals of the data processing must be considered as unlawful. Finally, purpose limitation implies that data may not be retained longer than necessary for the purposes for which the data are stored: in other words, the data controller should be bound by time limits. These different layers of protection will be explained further in the following sections.

3.2. Ban on Aimless Data Collection

The 'ban on aimless data collection', also described by German scholars as '*Verbot pragmatikloser Datensammlung*', refers to the principle that personal data should not be collected or stored without the prior specification of the objective of this data processing.[12] According to this principle, it is prohibited to collect or gather information just to keep these data 'in stock' for future unspecified purposes. In the Council of Europe Recommendation R (87) on police files, this principle is explicitly included with regard to data processing for criminal investigation procedures. According to principle 2.1 of the Recommendation on police files, the collection of

12. A. Podlech, 'Gesellschaftspolitische Grundlagen des Datenschutzes', in: *Datenschutz und Datensicherung*, ed. Dierstein, Fiedler & Schulz (Köln, 1976), 311. Cited by H.P. Bull (1985), 13.

personal data for police purposes should be limited to such as is necessary 'for the prevention of a real danger or the suppression of a specific criminal offence'. The Recommendation therefore prohibits the general collection of data, unrelated to any specific criminal investigation. The importance of the principle of 'if there is no crime, there is no investigation', was confirmed in the second evaluation of Recommendation R (87) in 1998.[13] This evaluation describes the matching of police data gathered in the course of criminal investigations based on vast numbers of persons, completely unrelated to any crime. According to the conclusions of this evaluation, these general data surveillance checks should be limited to specific cases described in national criminal law *and* be granted on the basis of a specific mandate from the judiciary.

3.3. Legitimacy

The principle of purpose limitation not only requires the availability of a specific purpose for data processing, but also implies the legitimacy of this purpose. This principle of a legitimate purpose is included in Article 5 of the Data Protection Convention. EC Directive 95/46 goes further, with the inclusion of a limitative enumeration of purposes for which personal data may be processed. According to Article 7 of the EC Directive, data processing is legitimate if:

- the data subject has given his consent;
- the data processing is necessary for a contract to which the data subject is a party;
- the processing is necessary for compliance with a legal obligation to which the controller is subject;
- it is necessary in order to protect the vital interests of the data subject; or
- for the performance of a task in the public interest or in the exercise of an official authority vested in the controller or in a third party to which the data are disclosed and, finally;
- when processing is necessary for the legitimate interests of the controller or the third party to whom the data are disclosed, except where such interests are overridden by the fundamental rights and interests of the data subject.

According to these criteria of the EC Directive, it is not always necessary for data processing by public authorities to be explicitly provided for by law. For example, a legal basis is not required if the data subject has given his or her consent, if the data processing is necessary to protect the vital interests of the data subject, or if this is necessary in the public interest or in the exercise of an official authority vested in the controller or in a third party to whom the data are disclosed. The general provision in Article 6(1)(a) of the EC Directive only requires that

13. Report by A. Patijn, CJ-PD expert from the Netherlands, *Data protection and the police. Evaluation of Recommendation* R (87)15, 1998, available at <www.coe.int/T/E/Legal_affairs/Legal_co-operation/Data_protection/Documents>, 1 Jan. 2010.

data must be processed fairly and lawfully. This does not mean that data processing must always have a legal basis, but only that it should not be unfair and not be in breach of the applicable law.

3.4. Purpose Specification: Transparency of Data Processing

Purpose limitation is closely related to the principle of 'purpose specification'. This principle secures the transparency of data processing, obliging data owners to inform data subjects on the purposes for which the data may be collected, stored, used or transmitted to other organizations. As we have seen, it is included in Article 5b Data Protection Convention and Article 6(1)(b) of EC Directive 95/46, on the basis of which automatically processed personal data must be stored or collected for specified purposes. According to consideration no. 42 of the explanatory report to the Convention, the reference to 'purposes' in Article 5 indicates that data should not be stored for undefined purposes, however, the way in which the legitimate purpose is specified may vary in accordance with national legislation. Article 10 and 11 of the Directive 95/46 includes the obligations for data controllers to inform the data subjects on the purposes of data processing, the identity of the controllers, and further, on the recipients or categories of recipients and on the existence of the rights of data subjects.

Purpose limitation, in the sense of purpose specification, reflects the idea that data processing should be foreseeable for the data subject and should not go beyond the reasonable expectations of the person concerned.[14] This condition of 'foreseeability' of data processing is closely related to legitimacy as a function of legality. As we will see below, in its case law on the protection of the right to a private life, the ECtHR explicitly emphasized the importance of 'foreseeability' with regard to the processing of personal data by governmental authorities.

3.5. Use or Disclosure Limitation: Informational Division of Powers

The principle of 'use or disclosure limitation' implies that personal data should not be used or transmitted for purposes other than the initial purpose defined at the time of data collection or storage. In general, this purpose limitation principle is not very strictly defined. As we have seen, Article 5(b) of the Data Protection Convention states that data processing must be stored for specified and legitimate purposes and 'not used in a way incompatible with those purposes'. Article 6(1)(b) EC Directive 95/46 allows for the use or disclosure of information for purposes 'which are not incompatible' with the initial purposes. Of course, this criterion can be applied in

14. See D. Elgesem, 'The Structure of Rights in Directive 95/46 on the Protection of Individuals with Regard to the Processing of Personal Data and the Free Movement of such Data', *Ethics and Information Technology* 1 (1999): 283–293.

various ways. It allows data holders to define very broadly the purposes of their databases or the authorities or users who have access to them. In practice, it will often be difficult for individuals and data protection authorities to enforce or verify the observance of this principle. For example, it is not always easy to establish which use of the information at stake is 'incompatible' with the original purposes.

The old adage 'information is power' relates to an important objective of purpose limitation. In the same way as we expect the functional powers of public authorities to be described in legislative rules, it is also necessary to have rules on which authority may collect or use which information.[15] Closely related to the idea of division of powers within the administration is the concept of informational division of powers or '*Informationelle Gewaltenteilung*'. As predicted by Westin in 1967, new information technologies caused radical changes to the governmental organization: 'All the government agencies concerned with a problem, such as health, employment, education, etc. whatever their level of government, will be part of an integrated information system and will coordinate their information to make decisions'.[16] Therefore, the concept of the informational division of powers was in the first place rooted in the concerns of administrative organizations about the consequences of information technology for their mutual relations. German scholars advocated a more general theory of prohibition to exercise control through the use of information beyond organizational borders.[17] This principle would protect citizens against a concentration of power by the government, by preventing one authority having access to information from other authorities, regardless of organizational boundaries or the purposes for which the information was gathered.[18]

In the *Census* case or *Volkszählungsurteil* of 1983, the German Constitutional Court acknowledged the importance of an informational division of powers.[19] The Court held in this judgment that the public administration does not constitute 'one informational unit' (*Informationseinheit*) in which personal data can be freely exchanged. According to the Court, it is the task of the legislator to provide guarantees against 'alienation of purpose' or *Zweckentfremdung*.[20]

Elsewhere, I have argued that this principle of use or disclosure limitation is closely linked to the prohibition of *détournement de pouvoir* in administrative law.[21] Considering 'good administration' as one of the goals of data protection described above, individuals should have the assurance that in their relations with

15. See on the subject of division of powers within the administration: B. Schlink, *Die Amtshilfe. Ein Beitrag zu einer Lehre von der Gewaltenteilung in der Verwaltung.* (Berlin: Duncker & Humblot, 1982).
16. Westin (1967), 325.
17. A. Podlech, *Gesellschaftspolitischen Grundlagen des Datenschutzes* (1976), cited in Bull (1985), 13.
18. See among others, H.P. Bull, *Datenschutz oder die Angst vor dem Computer* (München-Zürich: Piper, 1984), 113, and A. Roßnagel, *Datenschutz und Datensicherheit (DuD)*, 10/95, 584.
19. BVerfgE 65, 1, paras 46 and 69.
20. S. Simitis (ed.) *Bundesdatenschutzgesetz* (Baden-Baden: Nomos, 2006), 75.
21. See further, Evelien Brouwer, *Digital Borders and Real Rights: Effective Remedies for Third-Country Nationals in the Schengen Information System* (Leiden/Boston: Martinus Nijhoff Publishers, 2008), 201–202.

governments, information given to one authority is not automatically available to other authorities as well. In other words, this principle should, to a certain extent, safeguard the informational division of powers. I deal further with this subject in section 6.2, below.

3.6. Time Limits

Finally, the principle of purpose limitation prescribes that personal data be retained no longer than necessary for the purpose for which the data are stored or processed. This principle is laid down in the different European instruments of data protection, although these instruments do not include explicit time limits. For example, according to Article 5e of the Data Protection Convention, automatically processed data may not be stored in a form which permits identification of the data subjects for longer than is required for the purpose for which those data are stored. The content of this wording is similar to the (much shorter) wording of Article 6.1 (e) of the EC Directive: 'no longer than is necessary for the purposes for which the data were collected or for which they are further processed'.

More specific criteria have been included in Principle 7 of the Recommendation No. R (87) 15 on police files. According to this provision, the states should ensure that personal data kept for police purposes are deleted if they are no longer necessary for the purposes for which they were stored. Regarding the decision on whether longer storage is necessary, the following criteria should be taken into account: the need to retain data in the light of the conclusion of an inquiry into a particular case; a final judicial decision, in particular, an acquittal; rehabilitation; spent convictions; amnesties; the age of the data subject; and particular categories of data. Furthermore, the Recommendation explicitly requires the adoption of rules aimed at fixing storage periods for the different categories of personal data, and that regular checks on their quality should be established in agreement with the supervisory authority or in accordance with domestic law.

4. MULTIPLE LEGAL ORDERS WITHIN THE EU: STRENGTHENING PURPOSE LIMITATION OR ENCOURAGING FUNCTION CREEP?

It is very difficult on the basis of the different decisions which have been adopted, to get an overall picture of the EU architecture for the collection and sharing of personal information. EU decision makers gradually extended the use, the functions, and the content of existing and planned databases. In 2004, the European Commission launched the principle of availability and the necessity of interoperability of different EU databases.[22] These principles, together with the creation of

22. This communication was followed by a Commission proposal for a framework decision on the exchange of information under the principle of availability, COM (2005) 490, October 2005. Due to a lack of support by the Member States, it meanwhile has been withdrawn.

large-scale, multipurpose databases such as the Visa Information System (VIS) and SIS II, seem difficult to reconcile with the principle of purpose limitation, including limits on the use and disclosure of personal information. Other developments, such as, for example, the adopted Decision on the access of law enforcement authorities and Europol to VIS,[23] are clear examples of deviation of the original, limited purposes of the databases. This problem has also been addressed by the European Parliament and the European Data Protection Supervisor (EDPS) Mr Hustinx.[24]

A further development eroding the principle of purpose limitation is the adoption of numerous instruments providing for the exchange of personal information between Member States. between Member States and third states, and between Member States and private organizations (e.g., SIS, Prüm, and different agreements on transfer of passenger data to EU Member States and to third countries).[25] Also, the introduction of biometrics in passports and travel documents issued by EU Member States on the basis of Regulation 2205/2004 can lead to unexpected and unforeseen purposes.[26] Once biometrical data and corresponding information are available, the risk of their use for purposes other than the ones they were collected for will undeniably remain present. On the one hand, the use of biometrics enables national governments to secure identity documents against theft or fraud. On the other, it enables national authorities to use different databases, primarily set up for limited and specified purposes, as investigation or intelligence files. The possibility that the data subject will never be aware of such uses and processing of data is realistic as well.[27]

A very clear example of 'function creep' is the proposal of the European Commission to give law enforcement authorities and Europol access to Eurodac, a EU database containing fingerprints of asylum seekers, under certain circumstances.[28] This database became operational in 2003, with the sole purpose of establishing the EU Member State responsible for the asylum application, and to prevent multiple asylum applications within the EU. The proposal to extend the

23. Decision 2008/633 of 23 Jun. 2008 on the access of designated national authorities and Europol to the Visa Information system for the purpose of prevention, detection, and investigation of terrorist offences and other serious criminal offences OJ L 218, 13 Aug. 2008.
24. European Data Protection Supervisor, Opinion of 20 Jan. 2006 on the Proposal for a Council Decision concerning access for consultation of the Visa Information System (VIS) by the authorities of Member States responsible for internal security and by Europol for the purposes of the prevention, detection and investigation of terrorist offences and of other serious criminal offences (COM (2005) 600 final), <www.edps.eu.int>, 1 Jan. 2010.
25. The meaning (or remains) of purpose limitation in the third pillar has been described by Els de Busser in: Purpose Limitation in the EU-US Data Exchange in Criminal Matters; the Remains of the Day, in: Marc Cools (e.a.) *Readings on Criminal Justice, Criminal Law and Policing. Governance of Security* Research paper series (GofS) vol. 2 (Antwerpen: Apeldoorn: Maklu, 2009), 163–193.
26. Council Regulation of 13 Dec. 2004, OJ L 385, 29 Dec. 2004.
27. See also the reaction of the Art. 29 Data Protection Working Party, *Opinion on Implementing the Council Regulation (EC) No 2252/2004*, 9.
28. COM (2009) 342 and 344. 10.09.09.

current function of Eurodac was criticized by the EDPS in his opinion of 7 October 2009, expressing his serious doubts on the legitimacy of the proposal and the fact that the necessity of the proposal has not been proven.[29] The national data protection authorities, represented in the Working Party on Police and Justice (WPPJ), also stated that the proposal runs counter to fundamental data protection principles such as proportionality of data processing and respect for purpose limitation.[30]

The Data Retention Directive 2006/24 obliges internet providers to store data on their clients for a minimum of six months and a maximum of two years to allow further access and use by national law enforcement authorities.[31] On the basis of Directive 2004/82 on the obligation of carriers to communicate, passenger data carriers can be fined with a maximum of EUR 5,000 and a minimum of EUR 3,000 when they fail to transmit information concerning the passengers at the request of the authorities responsible for border checks. Shortly before the final adoption of this Directive, the strict purpose limitation within the original draft was extended by the Council. In the first place, Member States may derogate from the general rule that data transferred to border authorities must be deleted within twenty-four hours: the data may be stored for a longer period if they are needed later 'for the purposes of exercising the statutory functions of the authorities responsible for the external border checks'. Secondly, a provision has been included on the basis of which Member States also may use the passenger data for law enforcement purposes.

Finally, I refer to the development and adoption of the EU Framework Decision 2008/977 of 27 November 2008 on the protection of personal data in the field of police and judicial cooperation in criminal matters. Its final text establishes the result of continuous and persistent lobbying of European data protection authorities and the EDPS and must be considered as a compromise between the negotiating partners. With regard to principles of lawfulness, proportionality, and purpose limitation, Article 3 provides that personal data may only be collected by the competent authorities for specified, explicit and legitimate purposes in the framework of their tasks, and may be processed only for the same purpose for which the data were collected. Furthermore, processing of the data must be lawful and adequate, relevant and not excessive in relation to the purposes for which they are collected. Article 3(2) however permits 'further processing for another purpose' in so far as: 'it is not incompatible with the purposes for which the data were collected; the competent authorities are authorized to process such data for such other purpose in accordance with the applicable legal provisions, and processing is necessary and proportionate to that other purpose. Here, the Framework Directive links the criterion 'compatibility', also referred to in the EC Directive 95/46, to the principle of necessity and proportionality. This leaves the question open as to what is compatible use, and what is necessary and

29. Published on <www.edps.europa.eu>, 1 Jan. 2010.
30. Published on the website of the Dutch Data Protection Authority, CBP, <www.cbpweb.nl>, 1 Jan. 2010.
31. OJ L 105, 13 Apr. 2006.

proportionate. On this question, as we will see in the next session, the case law of the European Court for Human Rights (ECtHR) and the EC Court of Justice provides us with some clues.

5. SETTING STANDARDS: THE CASE LAW OF THE ECtHR AND THE ECJ[32]

5.1. ECtHR and Article 8 ECHR

In its case law, the ECtHR emphasized repeatedly the close relationship between the protection of personal data and the right of privacy: 'the protection of personal data is of fundamental importance to a person's enjoyment of his or her right to respect for private and family life, as guaranteed by Article 8 of the Convention'. For our purpose, this case law is especially important, because on the basis of Article 8 (2) ECHR, the ECtHR developed specific criteria underlining the meaning of purpose limitation. According to Article 8 (2) each interference to the right to private life must be in accordance with the law and necessary in a democratic society in the interests of national security, public safety or the economic well-being of the country, for the prevention of disorder or crime, for the protection of health or morals, or for the protection of the rights and freedoms of others. The criteria as developed by the ECtHR relate to the specification of purpose or transparency of the data processing at stake, limitation of powers, and the necessity of time limits.

5.1.1. Purpose Specification or Transparency of Data Processing

In the *Leander* case on the practice of secret police files, the ECtHR found that it is not sufficient for the interference to have some basis in domestic law: the law in question must be accessible to the individual concerned and its consequences must be predictable. The ECtHR acknowledged that the requirement of predictability in the special context of secret controls of staff in sectors affecting national security cannot be the same as in many other fields. 'Thus, it cannot mean that an individual should be enabled to foresee precisely what checks will be made in his regard by the Swedish special police service in its efforts to protect national security.' Nevertheless, the ECtHR added that in a system applicable to citizens generally, as under the Personnel Control Ordinance, 'the law has to be sufficiently clear in its terms to give them an adequate indication as to the circumstances in which, and the conditions on which, the public authorities are empowered to resort to this kind of secret and potentially dangerous interference with private life'.[33]

32. See also the contribution of Aleidus Woltjer in this volume on the jurisprudence of these courts with regard to the principle of legality.
33. Leander case, 26 Mar. 1987, §§ 50–51.

In *Malone v. UK*, dealing with secret telephone tapping, the ECtHR stated that 'in accordance with the law' refers not only to the availability of domestic law, but also to the 'quality of the law'. Here, the Court explicitly referred to the necessity of the measures being compatible with the rule of law.[34] The requirement of quality of law was further specified in *Huvig and Kruslin v. France*.[35] These cases concerned the claims based on Article 8 ECHR of Mr and Mrs Huvig and Mr Kruslin, whose phones were tapped during criminal proceedings by the French authorities. The question in these cases was not so much whether this telephone tapping constituted an interference with the applicant's right to a private life, but whether the applicable French law was clear and foreseeable. The ECtHR held that, where tapping and other forms of telephone conversation represent a serious interference with private life and correspondence, this must be based accordingly on a law that is, particularly precise. According to the ECtHR, clear, detailed rules on the subject are essential, especially since the technology available for use is continually becoming more sophisticated, as in the case in question. Since the French law at stake, written and unwritten, did not indicate with reasonable clarity the scope and manner of exercise of the relevant discretion conferred on the public authorities, the ECtHR found a breach of Article 8 of the Convention.[36]

5.1.2. Limitation of Powers and Time Limits

In the *Huvig and Kruslin* judgments, the ECtHR further defined a set of criteria for lawful telephone tapping that should have been provided for in French law. These criteria included the categories of persons liable to have their telephones tapped by judicial order and the nature of the offences which may give rise to such an order; the lack of an obligation to set a limit on the duration of telephone tapping; the circumstances under which recordings may or must be erased or the tapes destroyed, in particular, when an accused party has been discharged by an investigating judge or acquitted by a court.[37] Interestingly, a comparable list of criteria was given in *Rotaru v. Romania* with regard to the law regulating the collection, recording and the archiving of information in secret files. Assessing the 'quality' of the Romanian law involved, the ECtHR concluded that this law did not include any limits on the exercise of the powers on the storage and use of the information by the Romanian Intelligence Services. Furthermore, Romanian law did not specify which information could be collected or stored, and against which categories of people or under which circumstances these surveillance measures were allowed. Also, there were no limits on the length of time for which the information could be stored.[38] In the view of the ECtHR, the criteria of 'in accordance with the law'

34. Malone case, 2 Aug. 1984, no. 8691/79, *Series A* 82.
35. Both cases of 24 Apr. 1990, no. 11801/95, *Series A* 176A (Kruslin) and no. 11105/84, *Series A* 176B (Huvig).
36. See Kruslin, § 36, and Huvig, § 35.
37. Kruslin § 35, Huvig § 34.
38. *Rotaru v. Romania*, § 41.

and 'quality of law' require supervision procedures and adequate and effective safeguards against abuse of the rule of law.[39] Since the Romanian system did not provide such safeguards or a supervisory mechanism, the ECtHR ruled that the refuted storage and use of information by the intelligence service was not 'in accordance with the law'.

The objective of purpose limitation of protecting individuals against arbitrary interference by national authorities was implicitly underlined by the ECtHR in the judgment *Segerstedt-Wiberg v. Sweden.*[40] In this case, the ECtHR dealt with the storage of personal information in files of the Swedish Security Service on the basis of the Swedish Police Data Act. Assessing whether the interference of the right to a private life was 'in accordance with the law', the ECtHR focussed on the question of whether the Swedish criterion 'special reasons' included 'unfettered powers' for the security agencies. The ECtHR stated that the scope of discretion conferred upon the competent authorities and the manner of its exercise must indicate with 'sufficient clarity, having regard to the legitimate aim of the measure in question, to give the individual adequate protection against arbitrary interference'.[41]

Also relevant in this context is the judgment in the case *S. and Marper v. the UK*, in which the ECtHR dealt with UK law permitting long-term, systematic storage of fingerprints and DNA samples of individuals, including minors, suspected of having committed criminal offences. The ECtHR found that the applicable UK law violated Article 8 ECHR, particularly on the grounds that these data were stored for indefinite periods and also related to unconvicted persons.[42] In this regard, paragraph 119 is important, in which the ECtHR remarked upon 'the blanket and indiscriminate nature of the power of retention in England and Wales' and the fact that 'the material may be retained irrespective of the nature of gravity of the offence with which the individual was originally suspected or of the age of the suspected offender'. According to the ECtHR, there were only limited ways for the individual to have the data removed from the nationwide database or to have the materials destroyed. Finally, the ECtHR criticized the absence of provisions for independent review of the justification for the retention of data, and the possibility to assess factors such as the seriousness of the offence, previous arrests, the strength of the suspicion against the person and any other special circumstances.

39. *Rotaru v. Romania*, § 43.
40. *Segerstedt-Wiberg and others v. Sweden*, 6 Jun. 2006, appl. no. 62332/00. Published in *EHRC* (2006): 89 with annotation of Jan Peter Loof.
41. *Segerstedt-Wiberg*, § 79. In this case, the ECtHR found that the Swedish law was sufficiently clear and that the interference was in accordance with the law. Nevertheless, with regard to four of the five applicants, the ECtHR concluded that the continued storage of the information (in one case up to thirty years) constituted a disproportional interference of their right to private life.
42. *S.& Marper v. the UK*, 4 Dec. 2008, appl.no. 30562/04 and 30566/04.

5.2. ECJ and EC Directive 95/46

5.2.1. *Rechnungshof v. Österreichischer Rundfunk*: Broad Interpretation of Data Protection

The *Rechnungshof v. Österreichischer Rundfunk* judgment was the first decision of the ECJ dealing with the interpretation of EC Directive 95/46.[43] It concerned the question of whether the rules of the Austrian Court of Auditors (*Rechnungshof*), on the basis of which organizations and holdings had to disclose information about their employees and pensioners, including names, positions, salaries and their pensions, were in accordance with the provisions of the EC Directive and the Community principles on the protection of privacy. In this judgment, the ECJ confirmed that the scope of the applicability of this Directive has to be interpreted broadly. According to the ECJ, the scope of applicability of the Directive would not be limited to data processing directly linked to the freedoms of free movement as protected in the EC Treaty.[44] The ECJ made it clear that every other interpretation would run the risk of making the boundaries of the Directive's application too uncertain and too vague. Furthermore, it considered that the principles and criteria for legitimate data processing, as laid down in Articles 6 and 7 of the Directive, so including the purpose limitation, have direct effect in the sense that an individual may seek access to a national court in order to prevent the application of national rules contrary to these principles.[45]

In the same judgment, the ECJ explicitly stated that EC Directive 95/46 must be interpreted in accordance with the right to a private life as protected under Article 8 ECHR. According to the ECJ, if national courts were to conclude that the national legislation with regard to the processing of personal data is incompatible with Article 8 of the Convention, that legislation would also be 'incapable of satisfying the requirement of proportionality in Articles 6(1)(c) and 7(c) or (e) of Directive 95/46'.[46] Therefore, exceptions included in Article 13 of that Directive must comply with the requirement of proportionality with respect to the public interest objective being pursued. In the words of the ECJ: 'that provision cannot be interpreted as conferring legitimacy on an interference with the right to respect for private life contrary to Article 8 of the Convention'. This means, that even if the EC Directive 95/46 allows exceptions to a strict purpose limitation, or leaves questions with regard to the interpretation of 'compatible use of data', data processing and the further use of personal information must always meet the criteria of Article 8 (2) ECHR, mentioned above in section 5.2.

---

43. *Rechnungshof v. Österreichischer Rundfunk and Others*, 20 May 2003, Joint Affairs C-465/00, C-138/01 and C-139/01.
44. Paragraph 39–47.
45. Paragraph 100.
46. C-465/00, para. 91.

5.2.2. *Huber v. Germany*: Linking Purpose Limitation to Non-Discrimination

In the judgment *Huber v. Germany*, the ECJ indirectly linked the principle of purpose limitation to the non-discrimination principle of Article 12 EC, and developed further in. This case dealt with the registration of an Austrian citizen, Mr Huber, in the German central aliens administration or AZR.[47] During the procedure before the German courts, Huber argued that his registration as an EU citizen in the AZR constituted an infringement of EC law, in particular, Article 12 EC prohibiting discrimination between EU citizens and EC Directive 2004/38 on the free movement of EU citizens and their family members. The German administrative court (Oberverwaltungsgericht Nordrhein Westfalen) issued preliminary questions on this case to the ECJ. In this case, the ECJ had to assess three different uses of the registered data on aliens: firstly, the use for administrative purposes by the authorities responsible for border and immigration control. Secondly, the ECJ was asked to rule on the lawfulness of the use of the German aliens administration for statistical purposes. Finally, the ECJ was asked whether the use of the data on EU citizens for law enforcement purposes was compatible with EC law.

In its decision, the ECJ firstly concluded that a system for processing personal data relating to Union citizens who are not nationals of the Member State at stake, such as that put in place by German law (*Gesetz über das Ausländerzentralregister*), and having as its object the provision of support to the national authorities responsible for the application of the law relating to the right of residence can be considered to satisfy the requirement of necessity laid down by Article 7(e) of EC Directive 95/46, interpreted in the light of the prohibition on any discrimination on grounds of nationality, as long as:

- it contains only the data which are necessary for the application by those authorities of the legislation on the right to residence, and;
- its centralized nature enables the legislation relating to the right of residence to be more effectively applied as regards Union citizens who are not nationals of that Member State.

In general, the ECJ found that it must be possible for the authorities of Member States to have 'relevant particulars and documents available to it in order to ascertain, within the framework laid down under the applicable Community legislation, whether a right of residence in its territory exists in relation to a national of another Member State and to establish that there are no grounds which would justify a restriction on that right'. It follows that the use of a register such as the AZR for the purpose of providing support to the authorities responsible for the application of the legislation relating to the right of residence is, in principle, legitimate and, having regard to its nature, compatible with the prohibition of discrimination on grounds of nationality laid down by Article 12(1) EC. For this purpose, however, the ECJ concluded that it must be assessed whether the AZR includes no other data

47. C-524/06, 16 Dec. 2008.

than contained in the documents referred to in Articles 8(3) and 27(1) of the Directive 2004/38. Furthermore, the ECJ explicitly referred to the duty of the national authorities of Member States to guarantee the accuracy and relevance of the data being stored 'since a change in the personal situation of a party entitled to a right of residence may have an impact on his status in relation to that right, it is incumbent on the authority responsible for a register such as the AZR to ensure that the data which are stored are, where appropriate, brought up to date so that, first, they reflect the actual situation of the data subjects and, secondly, irrelevant data are removed from that register' (paragraph 60).

Considering the storage and processing of personal data containing *individualised personal information* in a register such as the AZR for statistical purposes, the ECJ found that this cannot, on any basis, be considered to be necessary within the meaning of Article 7(e) of Directive 95/46 (para 68). According the ECJ, the German authorities could use anonymous data for this purpose.

Finally, with regard to the use of the AZR for law enforcement purposes, the ECJ held that this was not compatible with the prohibition of discrimination as included in Article 12 EC. According to the ECJ, '12(1) EC must be interpreted as meaning that it precludes the putting in place by a Member State, for the purpose of fighting crime, of a system for processing personal data specific to Union citizens who are not nationals of that Member State' (para 52). As in the aforementioned judgment in the case *Rechnungshof v. Österreichischer Rundfunk*, the ECJ in *Huber v. Germany* underlined the necessity of a maximal interpretation of the level of data protection based on the EC Directive. Referring to the eighth and tenth recital in the preamble of the EC Directive 95/46, the ECJ concluded that this Directive is intended to ensure that the level of protection of the rights and freedoms of individuals with regard to the processing of personal data is equivalent in all Member States, and that the approximation of the national laws applicable in this area must not result in any lessening of the protection they afford but must, on the contrary, seek to ensure a high level of protection in the Community.

Furthermore, referring to its conclusion in the earlier *Lindqvist* case, the ECJ emphasized that the harmonization of those national laws should not be limited to minimal harmonization, but 'amounts to harmonization which is generally complete'.[48] More interesting is the fact that in *Huber v. Germany*, the ECJ explicitly clarified that the aim of a harmonized and high level of data protection also applies to the principle of purpose limitation:

> having regard to the objective of ensuring an equivalent level of protection in all Member States, the concept of necessity laid down by Article 7(e) of Directive 95/46, the purpose of which is to delimit precisely one of the situations in which the processing of personal data is lawful, cannot have a meaning which varies between the Member States. It therefore follows that what is at issue is a concept which has its own independent meaning in Community law

48. Case C-101/01 *Lindqvist* [2003] ECR I-12971, para. 96. Referred to by the ECJ in para. 51 of the *Huber* case.

> and which must be interpreted in a manner which fully reflects the objective of that directive, as laid down in Article 1(1) thereof.[49]

This conclusion is important as it not only applies to the problem of this particular case: non-discrimination rights of EU citizens, but also to the general interpretation of the basic principles of data protection law within the laws of the EC Member States implementing EU law.

6. RESTORING THE PRINCIPLE OF PURPOSE LIMITATION: APPLYING THE FUNCTIONS OF LEGALITY

6.1. Legitimacy

An important function of legality is the legitimation of public authorities. It refers to a classic principle of constitutional law dealing with the relationship between state and citizens: the 'social contract' on the basis of which citizens accept the powers of their government in so far as these powers are considered legitimate and in so far as these powers are not misused. This principle also applies to the informational powers of the state. We accept legislation by which we have to transmit personal data to the government, as long as we are convinced that the government needs this information: tax law, population administration, law enforcement. We also accept the exchange of information between different organizations so long as we understand the connection between these organizations. This requirement of public acceptance of public powers is closely related to the criteria formulated by the ECtHR in its case law on Article 8 ECHR with regard to the 'foreseeability'of the law. For example, mentioned by the House of Commons in the report *A Surveillance Society?*, we may think of the exchange of information between tax authorities and social security as foreseeable for the citizen, however, between tax authorities and the police it is not.[50]

One could wonder whether transparency is not replacing *legitimacy* as the core value of data protection, considering the numerous grounds included in the EC Directive 95/46 and other instruments legitimising data processing, and the special emphasis on transparency and informing the data subject. Or, in the words of De Hert and Guthwirth, 'Legitimate is whatever processing that has been rendered transparent.'[51] However, it should be clear that legitimacy and transparency are not to be considered as alternatives, but as supplements to legality.

---

49. *Huber v. Germany*, para. 52.

50. Report House of Commons, Home Affairs Committee, 'A Surveillance Society?', Fifth Report of session 2007–08, published 8 Jun. 2008 (London: The Stationery Office Limited, 2008), 55, <www.parliament.the-stationery-office.co.uk/> 1 Jan. 2010.

51. P. de Hert, S. Guthwirth, Making sense of privacy and data protection: a prospective overview in the light of the future identity, location-based services and virtual residence, Annex 1 to the report *Security and Privacy for the Citizen in the Post-September 11 Digital Age: A Prospective Overview*, Technical Report Series, Institute for Prospective Technological studies, Brussels, July 2003, 146.

The restoration of legitimacy of the information policy is necessary for increasing the involvement of (national and European) parliaments, but especially of the public. This requires more discussion on the aims and objectives of the proposed systems, on the definitions of crimes for which data may be exchanged, on the use of biometric data, including DNA, and the access of governments to data communication of their citizens. An interesting example of public involvement with decisions on the use of personal information is the recent referendum in Switzerland with regard to the biometric passport. Joining EU's travel free zone in 2008, the Swiss government had to decide on the introduction of biometric data in the Swiss passport. The Swiss voters (turnout 38%) accepted by a narrow margin the biometric passport: 50.1% approved, 49.9% rejected the passport.[52] Although one may doubt whether this specific outcome of the referendum is sufficient to legitimize the measure at stake, the instrument as such, can be a useful tool of legitimacy, in the meaning of democratic accountability. That 'legitimacy' in this latter meaning is not synonymous with 'legitimate' meaning lawful or legal, was proven by the outcome of a more recent referendum in Switzerland on the so-called 'minaret ban'.[53] In this referendum of 29 November 2009, 59% of the Swiss voters supported the proposed ban on the further construction of minarets in Switzerland. However, as was held by different commentators (including the Swiss government), the implementation of this ban would be in violation of the Swiss Constitution and international human rights obligations.

Another tool in obtaining (or regaining) legitimacy for measures adopted in the legal framework of the EU could be the use of impact assessment studies by the Commission for important legislative and non-legislative proposals. In the Hague Programme of November 2004, the Member States agreed on the necessity of the 'assessment of added value of new EU databases'. According to this principle, the added value should be established before the setting up of new large scale EU data systems. However, the use of these extended impact assessment studies requires that they are based on transparent and independent research, in which human rights consequences are sufficiently taken into account and not overriden by economical and technical aspects.

6.2. Attribution

In the legal and political debate on data processing and the use of new databases or connection between existing databases, 'legality,' in the sense of strict rules on who receives which powers, receives little or no attention. As I have tried to develop in section 3.5 above, one of the important aims of purpose limitation is the restriction of powers by 'informational division of powers' and to protect individuals against misuse of powers or arbitrariness. Defining in advance the purposes for which personal information may be used prevents that personal

52. Source: <www.swissinfo.ch> visited 17 May 2009.
53. Source: <www.swissinfo.ch> visited 1 Jan. 2010.

information acquired in a specific context under specific conditions will be accessible by other authorities for other purposes or tasks. In this view, purpose limitation is, for example, difficult to reconcile with 'fishing expeditions'.[54] The UK House of Commons, in the aforementioned report of 2008 on surveillance and the use of personal data, emphasized the need of strict purpose limitation, and even advocated a principle of *data minimisation*. According to this report, the principle of restricting the amount of information collected to that what is needed to provide a service should guide the design of any system that involves the collection and storage of personal information.

Furthermore, attribution of powers, when applied to the collection and storage of personal information, requires strict rules on the time limits and the powers of authorities to retain personal information in their files. As we have seen, this has been emphasized by the ECtHR in *Segerstedt Wibergh*, dealing with the storage of information on Swedish citizens by the national security services. What is important to understand when dealing with the storage of personal information is that the longer information is retained, the more likely it is that the information will be out of date and inaccurate. It is precisely for this reason that the ECJ emphasized in the case of *Huber v. Germany* the duty of national authorities to guarantee the accuracy and relevance of data being stored. The need of time limits was also an important conclusion of the 2008 report of the House of Commons:

> Information should only be held as long it is necessary to fulfil the purpose for which it was collected and if information is to be retained for 'secondary purposes' rather than service delivery it should normally be anonymised and retained only for a previously specified purpose.[55]

In other words, not only must the powers to collect personal information be regulated sufficiently clearly, but also the powers of data storage and retention. This requirement of time limits is closely related to 'regularization' of data processing, dealt with in the following final section.

6.3. Regulation

Once powers have been attributed to governmental organizations, the use of these powers needs regulation. Here, I use 'regulation' in the meaning of rules making it possible to control and counterbalance public powers, for example, by offering citizens certain rights, by introducing independent control authorities, or by providing mechanisms by which unlawful use of powers may be sanctioned. This regulatory function has been underlined by the ECtHR in the aforementioned case law. Understanding 'regulation' as such, one may see the direct relation

54. See Colin J. Bennett, *Regulating Privacy. Data Protection and Public Policy in Europe and the United States* (Ithaca and London: Cornell University Press, 1992), 108.
55. Report House of Commons, Home Affairs Committee, 'A Surveillance Society?', Fifth Report of session 2007–08, published 8 Jun. 2008 (London: The Stationery Office Limited, 2008).

between purpose limitation and the other principles of data protection law, for example, individual rights on access, correction, or deletion, the establishment of independent supervisory authorities, or, as mentioned above, time limits on data retention.

One of the current problems of 'regulating' informational powers of governmental authorities is that, although there is a general acceptance of the substance and importance of data protection law, the applicable rules allow for many exceptions under various circumstances. This implies the risk that many provisions of data protection will continue to be considered 'soft law' instead of becoming 'hard law'. The EC Directive 95/46 permits, under certain conditions, limitations on data protection principles, including restriction of participation rights, of the ban on processing sensitive data, and of purpose limitation. If the purpose of data processing and the group of authorities having access to data are defined very widely, purpose limitation as such will not offer any extra safeguard for the persons concerned. The same problem arises with regard to the principle of restricting the storage of data over time. The obligation to apply time limits is only effective as long as these time limits are based on a fair balance between the different interests at stake.

In practice, an important problem remains the ignorance of individuals, not only with regard to their rights, but also with regard to what is happening with their personal information. This can be perceived as a problem of regulation, but also of the legitimacy of informational powers. It requires not only transparency, but also the education and encouragement of persons to use their rights.[56]

7. CONCLUSION

The function of legality is to restrict governmental powers in order to safeguard rights and liberties of citizens. In this contribution, I have tried to establish that the principle of purpose limitation has a similar function with regard to the restriction of informational powers. With regard to the effective meaning of purpose limitation, we saw that Europeanization of law has a double, not to say contradictory, impact. On the one hand European law, and in particular the case law of the ECtHR and the ECJ, reinforced the meaning and importance of purpose limitation, emphasizing its functions of legitimacy, attribution, and regulation. On the other hand, EU policies and legislation tend to undermine the meaning of purpose limitation, by providing vague definitions on the intended use of personal information, the establishment of multifunctional databases, and by extending the use of existing databases for other purposes ('function creep').

56. Richard Thomas, Information Commissioner in the UK, in: *A Surveillance Society?* Fifth Report of the House of Commons, Home Affairs Committee, 44. See also Birte Siemen, *Datenschutz als europaïsches Grundrecht* (Berlin: Duncker & Humblot, 2006), 331: *'Damit dieses Recht seine volle Geltung erlangt, muss es von den Bürgern allerdings auch wahrgenommen werden'.*

To regain the legality of the 'EU information network', improvements are to be made at both the level of 'legitimacy', 'attribution', and 'regulation'. This requires in the first place, a legislative process which involves both the European parliament and national parliaments, and which is transparent to the citizens and inhabitants of the EU. Secondly, the attribution of 'informational powers' of governments needs further regulation, including strict rules on the purpose of data processing and the authorities having access to these data, respecting the criteria of necessity and proportionality of such access. Thirdly, further guarantees are to be developed to counterbalance the use and possible misuse of personal information. These guarantees may include the extension of powers for data protection authorities, the strengthening of the individual rights (including the right to financial compensation), and the provision and application of sanctions to the misuse of data.

Chapter 15

Conclusion: The Eclipse of Legality: An Assessment

Leonard Besselink

1. INTRODUCTION

The previous chapters were written in the context of the question whether the principle of legality as a cherished foundation of the democratic State based on the rule of law has been eclipsed in the overlapping multiple legal orders in Europe. To what extent has legality as we knew it from within the State context, if at all, been obscured behind and within other legal orders, especially the European Union? What has been offered in return, and can that compensate for the functions and purposes that legality served? The rich materials offered in the previous chapters provide various clues as to possible answers to these questions.

2. WHO ATTRIBUTES AND REGULATES THE EXERCISE OF PUBLIC POWER OVER CITIZENS?

It is important to recognize that legality and the principle that the exercise of public authority ought to be based on parliamentary legislation serves a variety of purposes. Firstly, it legitimizes the exercise of public power, in as much as parliamentary legitimacy derives from periodic democratic elections. Hence, legality and democracy are closely linked.

Leonard Besselink, Frans Pennings & Sacha Prechal (eds), *The Eclipse of the Legality Principle in the European Union*, pp. 295–303.

In this context, the chapter by *Jurgens, Verhoeven and Willems* (Chapter 3) reasserts the prevalence of the idea that indeed parliamentary legislation serves as a necessary condition for imposing measures curtailing civil liberty both in Germany and in the UK. This is not to say, of course, that the state of affairs is quite the same in these countries. The starting point in English law remains that power inheres in the Executive and law is there not so much to create as to restrain government. The chapter shows how this ends up in a position that is, close to that of the German constitutional doctrine.

Clearly, the principle of legality does not have equal scope and meaning in each and every of the other EU Member States. Notwithstanding the fact that elsewhere in continental Europe the principle of legality is the pedigree of the French Revolution, the present-day French doctrinal position of State power seems closer to the British than to the German view. But although there is a considerable *pouvoir réglementaire* for the government independent from Parliament, and the scope of the principle is more restricted, even there, governmental action affecting fundamental liberties requires legislative action by Parliament.

There are countries like Italy, where at first sight there seems to be a strict adherence to a principle of legality, but this leads regularly to the parliamentary act being little more than an empty shell, because all substantive norm-setting power is delegated to or derives from executive decrees. (In the case of Italy there is the power for the government to provide temporary legislation with the power of statute law in cases of urgency, which needs confirmation by Parliament within three months, but which is effectively forced down the throat of it by making it a matter of political confidence in the government). Framework legislation with little more than a bare minimum of normative content in the act of parliament occurs elsewhere also. This clearly shows that legality does not always and necessarily fulfil all the functions it is meant to. The Welfare State requires relatively large discretionary powers for the Executive, and the social market economy needs independent regulatory agencies. So, democratic legitimacy inheres in parliamentary legality, but this legitimacy does not always extend quite as far as one would ideally think appropriate when it creates regulatory discretion.

As *Woltjer* points out (Chapter 6), in the multiplicity of legal orders in Europe the ECHR comes to the rescue to some extent and in a sense supplements some shortcomings. This is in the field of the restriction of the ECHR rights, which requires restrictions to be provided 'by law'. These restrictions cannot formally depend on the nature of the institution issuing the relevant legislation, because the powers of parliaments and executives to set legislative norms differ among the European States party to the ECHR, as we just indicated. The ECtHR has, however, set standards concerning the quality of restrictive legislation in terms of its foreseeability, accessibility, clarity and precision, thus providing legal certainty and contributing to the rule of law. Whether these requirements are met is up to the courts – ultimately the ECtHR – to decide, and remains independent from the question of the democratic legitimacy of the relevant rule-maker – an unelected executive body may also issue 'legislation' which meets the qualitative criteria of the ECtHR. This proves that democratic legitimacy does seem to have somehow receded into the background.

There is another side to the multiplicity of orders in Europe which may be taken as an erosion of legality at the national level, but which in turn is then supplemented at the EU level. This is a core element of the contribution of *Verhoeven* and *Widdershoven* in Chapter 4. EU law prescribes in certain cases Member State implementation or enforcement measures for which a basis in the national legal order is missing. The question is whether or not legal grounds for implementation or reparation, which are absent in the national legal order, can be supplied in (any kind of) secondary EU law, as long as it is specific enough. Strictly speaking, the case law that the contributors analyse does not unambiguously resolve this problem. From the point of view of the precision of the relevant EU norm, there may be no objection to seeking a basis of competence for a national authority at the EU level. In a sense, this is what already happened in the *Francovich* line of case law with regard to the competence of courts – the infamous 'European mandate' of the courts.

To conclude from the principle that law is binding and must be complied with that there exists an enforcement competence founded in EU law, even in the absence of a legal basis for the body exercising the coercive powers, would seem to indicate that somewhere there is a change in the function of a norm, from a regulative norm (aiming to regulate how Member States should go about using their autonomous powers for the purpose of enforcing EU law) into an attributive norm (a norm attributing new powers to national institutions which it did not possess under national law). Europe no longer merely indicates how Member State authorities (legislatures as well as executives) should make use of powers that they possess autonomously (i.e., European norms which are merely regulatory), but it also tells public authorities to act without them previously possessing the relevant powers within their autonomous legal order to do so. Regulative norms change into attributive norms.

A similar shift from a regulative to an attributive norm can be observed in criminal law matters. The ECJ case law has always stressed that criminal law is primarily a Member State competence. In the background of this there is no doubt a confluence of the idea of criminal law as emanation of sovereign power (the State monopoly over physical violence) with the very strict legality requirement in continental criminal law. However, secondary EC and EU law has addressed regulating norms to Member States to such an extent that it may end up attributing powers to them[1] – the amount of EU norms which regulate if and how the Member States may and must make use of their powers to punish can become so large and incisive that there is little room for the Member States to claim ultimate authority to impose criminal sanctions: the legal basis for those powers is found in EU law, and no longer in any meaningful sense in national law. This is not yet the case in the sphere of public prosecution. Nevertheless, Chapter 13 by *Tony Marguery* on Eurojust sketches in detail a similar movement affecting the powers of public prosecution services in the Member States under the influence of the 'third pillar' law, which has now become regular EU law. He raises the issue of democratic

1. A relevant line of case law is that leading to ECJ Environmental Criminal law; Ship source pollution.

legitimacy flaws of third pillar instruments, and points to the fact that the right of initiative and decision-making does not live up to similar guarantees as in the first pillar, though some improvement might be expected since the entry into force of the Lisbon Treaty.

The change from regulatory norms to attributive norms can be considered a form of 'function creep'. 'Function creep' is the central phenomenon in the contribution of *De Vries, Prechal and Van Eijken* (Chapter 12). Though conceptually clear, the dividing line between the competence to *regulate the exercise* of powers and the competence to *create new* powers can be quite thin in practice, as they demonstrate in a variety of contexts. However, first a matter must be drawn into the scope of EU law. This is the question when an autonomous action of Member State authorities comes within that remit. The ECJ case law shows that answering this question offers many opportunities for competence creep. The case law also shows that the issue of competence in EU law is not primarily concerned with providing the democratically legitimate basis to the exercise of authority over citizens, but much rather with the division of powers between Union and Member States. The issue of attribution of power is about the enumeration of powers pretty much in the manner in which this happens in federal systems: it is a manner of legitimating power by dividing it, rather than by creating it in a particular formal manner (as nationally in acts of parliament).

Another relevant issue raised in many of the chapters is what *Lavrijssen and Ottow* (Chapter 5) refer to as the 'institutional autonomy' of the Member States, which includes national conceptions of legality.[2] Part of the EU constitutional principles is that it is up to the Member States to determine their own internal constitutional arrangements. This also applies when it comes to authority, institutions and powers engaged in applying EU law. One of the elements of that autonomy is legality and the various definitions of the principle of legality, which requires a basis for public authority in an act of parliament.

Whereas in Chapter 4 this concerned the requirement of a legal basis for the exercise of enforcement powers in national law over and above a basis in EU law, in Chapter 5 this is discussed in terms of the influence of European law on the primacy of the legislature in relation to national regulatory authorities. The conclusion here is that EU law curtails the Member States' institutional and procedural autonomy considerably by enhancing the development of independent rule makers, separate from market parties as well as independent from the political system.

3. THE QUALITY OF LEGISLATION: WHAT QUALIFIES AS LEGISLATION?

A further complication arising in connection with the theme of legality is the question of what qualifies as legislation. In Chapter 10, *Duijkersloot* describes

2. This point was put forward by judge Arjen Meij in a discussion of the draft version of Ch. 4 by Verhoeven and Widdershoven at the international conference on legality at the University of Utrecht of 5 Nov. 2010, when a first draft of this book was discussed.

the crucial role of 'soft law' in the regulation and supervision of financial markets. The nature and peculiarities of these markets as well as the risks these entail in case of mishaps all contribute to the necessity of national and transnational regulation, coordination and cooperation with enough flexibility to respond to the necessities as they occur. Market supervision is exercised by regulatory agencies that are primarily national in origin and scope of competence. At the basis of their competence there is hard law – legislation based on an act of parliament. Both at the origin of this hard law and the action resulting from hard law, however, is soft law. Much of what is done by national regulators is decided by experts from the national financial authorities who meet in European or international settings, acting either of their own accord, or stimulated to do so by international and European organizations and their Member States as well as such unregulated informal political clubs as the G20. What they produce does not have the quality of legislation in a proper sense, yet comprises highly detailed arrangements, procedures and standards from which it is hard to deviate without consequence: for all intents and purposes it can be qualified as international or transnational quasi-legislation. Much of the output of national regulatory agencies within their jurisdictions is not hard law either, but remains soft law and also comprises statements, guidelines and 'interpretations' which they understand to be within their discretionary competence. The objective of these is indeed to regulate behaviour of persons legal and natural.

Similar phenomena are associated with the procedure known as the Open Method of Coordination (OMC) discussed by *Pennings* in Chapter 9. The lack of formal power – that is, to say a competence which has a basis in a democratically legitimated act in EU law – is conspicuous. The output is national action, which is not the product of European legislative action, but is coordinated on the basis of exchange of information, the setting of benchmarks and the definition of 'best practices'. It enables EU institutions, in particular the Commission and the European Council, to overcome the problem of the lack of competence to make rules, while at the same time allowing them to ask Member States to undertake policy measures in areas that may or may not be indicated as a European concern in the founding Treaties. In this respect it tends to contribute to competence creep, particularly if we consider the fact that it can trigger national law that binds citizens. What we are dealing with here is the soft law paradox: in the absence of a legal basis for hard law, soft law can be made precisely because it is not formally binding. To the extent that it produces factual consequences and not abiding by it may even be considered in conflict with principles of good faith and loyalty, it remains controversial from the perspective of the legitimating function of legality.

Several chapters discuss another aspect of the quality of EU legislation. Both the chapters by *Jaspers and Meijers* and by *Burri* point out the difficulties and shortcomings of legislation in areas of social law due to the incremental nature of decision-making on the relevant topics. Both with regard to information and the consultation of workers directives and the equality and anti-discrimination directives, progressive developments in the case law and in the legislative field necessitate codification, consolidation and improvement of the corpus of decision-making. The consistency and clarity which one is to expect from rules deserving the name of legislation is not always found when attempts at doing so are undertaken.

It is equally clear from the essays in this book, however, that many of the functions associated with legality have not diminished, much rather they have come to the fore in the context of a plurality of legal orders. This increased awareness of the quality of legislation when the multiplicity of orders meet and overlap may bring certain shortcomings (such as those just mentioned) in EU decision-making to the fore, although they are not absent in national decision-making either. Thus, *Brouwer* highlights in her conclusion to Chapter 14 the importance of transparency when traditional objectives of legality threaten to become obsolete. There is total consensus on transparency as a prime principle of governance in the EU, imperfect as its realization in practice may be. In fact, transparency as a condition of democratic governance has been fostered under EU influence in Member States in which it previously did not seem important. Indeed, when legality may no longer play the role it did in national contexts, some of its functions have certainly been reinforced.

4. DEMOCRACY AND ITS ALTERNATIVES; EXPERTISE AND SOCIETY

Legality is closely tied up with democracy. If legality's prime role is waning, this has consequences for democracy. These are indicated in several chapters in this book. No doubt, the prime addressees of an alternative form of governance such as OMC are the Member States. But as *Pennings* points out, the European Parliament like the national Parliaments are totally excluded from the process, and although sometimes stakeholders may be involved, in the policy area of employment even the social partners are excluded.

This should not make us forget that democracy need not be identified with the State. In this respect we are well beyond the framework of the French Revolution. Communication between citizens, parties whose interests are at stake, and brokers of power exist beyond and outside the classic political context of the State. This should alert us to alternative forms of democracy in the EU context, as they existed of old in some of the Member States. The social dialogue that we know in the EU context, as analysed and discussed by *Veldman* in Chapter 11, exists in some Member States as well. It is quite clear from the discussion by *Veldman* that democracy as it takes shape in the social dialogue shares some of the functional aspects attributed to legality.

Soft law may also be understood in the context of democracy: much of the substance of the output of regulatory agencies (and some of the forms of OMC) is soft law precisely because it shares some of the nature of participatory democracy, in particular the quasi-voluntary acceptance of the outcome of the relevant processes. Nevertheless, the legitimacy of bodies like the Basel Committee, which triggers much regulation, lies in their expertise and in their authority within the sector – it is not democratic in nature.

5. AN ASSESSMENT

The overall picture resulting from the chapters in this book confirm that the principle that the exercise of public power must ultimately rest on an act of parliament has in a variety of sectors receded into background due to the demands of European law and the integration of legal orders. Legality has waned, and one can say that at least the foundational function of legality has been eclipsed, just like one heavenly object can place another in its shade. To the extent that the basis of public power shifts from the national to the European legal order there is more than an eclipse. One not merely gets in the way of the other, but it replaces it. Does this matter?

We must be aware that the present state of affairs is no doubt a reflection of the state of European integration as well as of the national context of the State. It is not always quite clear where the ultimate source of legitimacy of governmental power over citizens should lie and which institution – part of the comprehensive European order – should represent that source. The democratically elected national parliaments have not given up the claim to be the expression of the popular will which is the foundation of the Member State polities and of the exercise of power over citizens in it, nor can they really be expected to do so. The role of the European Parliament has greatly increased within the EU institutional design. Still, its position is not quite like that of a national parliament, although it is directly elected. This may have to do with the fact that it has not articulated the claim to be representative of a sovereign popular will, overruling that of the Member State parliaments. This is only natural in a historical political enterprise aimed at overcoming the worst excesses of sovereignty. At the same time this makes for a significant difference between the European Parliament and (most) national parliaments.

Sovereignty apart, we should not forget that there are many institutions rightfully claiming democratic representativeness in the EU decisional institutions as well as in the Member States. Within the Member States, executives can lay claim to representativeness because national and local executives enjoy and need support in their parliaments and elected representative bodies in order to be able to function (or, as is the case for some heads of State with executive powers, they are directly elected). This locus of representation has become more important due to the generally diminished role of parliamentary legislatures to the benefit of executive power, which is a common feature in the Member States since the development of the Welfare State. In most Member States it is also the development of the Welfare State which has contributed to the gradual recognition of social partners, civil society organizations and stakeholder interests as politically relevant actors which need representation within public decision-making structures.

This is entirely the same in the EU decision-making structures. The Council and European Council can claim to be representative in as much as they are bearers of a political mandate derived from directly elected bodies; the European Parliament is itself directly elected and the Commission's mandate has developed in an increasingly political direction: witness the European Parliament's investiture since the nomination of the first Barroso Commission. The input of stakeholders within the EU decision-making process is in many cases prominent, thus increasing the legitimacy of decisions among those who are affected. All this has diminished the uniqueness of the claim which legality can lay to democratic legitimacy.

Executive dominance in the process of EU legislation is glaring and is here to stay, notwithstanding the increased input of the European Parliament, which was further enhanced after the entry into force of the Lisbon Treaty. National parliaments clearly cannot fulfil the same role with regard to EU decision-making as they can with regard to national policy and legislative decision-making.

On a positive note one may say that the exercise of powers as divided over various levels, institutions, and executives prevents power concentration as much as it has always done. This is the classic justification for the division of powers as a political good. That the number of *loci* of power has increased can hardly detract from that fact.

In the increased role of expertise and experts – as much in national as in European contexts – we noticed above, one can also notice something positive. It contributes to 'competent' governance in the substantive sense of this adjective. In a technologically advanced society, an amount of technocracy is necessary to avoid substantively incompetent governance.

There are also down sides to all this. The claims of executives, civil society, social partners and stakeholders to democratic representativeness are dispersed to such an extent that one may wonder whether in the eyes of the citizen this can make up for the waning of parliaments. Expertise driven governance (as with regulatory agencies) goes hand in hand with a certain amount of de-politicization. This does not only have a positive side to it; it also decreases civil involvement in government.

It may be true that the European mandate of national courts has been relatively easily accepted, at least among lawyers. Just as the national courts are European courts when applying European law, so the national parliaments when passing implementing legislation are also European parliaments, just as they are when they exercise parliamentary scrutiny of European decision-making. It is generally accepted that national executives, when members of the Council or European Council, and also the lesser bureaucrats when they operate within the comitology structure, act simultaneously as national and European executives. But are the European citizens in the Member States ready for a European mandate when executives enforce EU law without a national mandate and possibly against the preferences of the national representative organs?

The different meaning of the principle of attributed powers in EU law was explained by its quite different function from that of the attributive function legality in national contexts: in EU law it is not to create democratic legitimacy, but to demarcate EU competence from Member State competence.[3] This may account for the eclipse of legality as we know it in the national constitutional context. An amount of 'de-legalization' must necessarily follow from this (soft law, OMC, etc.). One of the most pressing questions with which the EU shall be grappling for the coming decades will be what this implies for democracy, and what democracy really should mean.

3. See Ch. 9 by *Pennings*, and the elaboration in Ch. 12 by *Prechal, De Vries and Eijken.*

Table of Cases

A

B

C

D

E

F

G

H

I

J

K

L

M

N

O

P

R

S

T

U

V

W

EUROPEAN MONOGRAPH SERIES

1. Lamm Betten (ed.), *The Future of European Social Policy*, 1991 (ISBN 90-654-4585-4).
2. Annemarie Loman, Kamiel Mortelmans, Harry H.G. Post & Stewart Watson, *Culture and Common Law: Before and After Maastricht*, 1992 (ISBN 90-654-4638-9).
3. John A.E. Vervaele, *Fraud against the Community: The Need for European Fraud Legislation*, 1994 (ISBN 90-654-4634-6).
4. Philip Raworth, *The Legislative Process in the European Community*, 1993 (ISBN 90-654-4690-7).
5. Jules Stuyck, *Financial and Monetary Integration in the European Economic Community*, 1993 (ISBN 90-654-4718-0).
6. Jules Stuyck & A.J. Vossestein (eds), *State Entrepreneurship, National Monopolies and European Community Law*, 1993 (ISBN 90-654-4773-3).
7. Jules Stuyck & A. Looijestijn-Clearie (eds), *The European Economic Area EC-EFTA*, 1994 (ISBN 90-654-4815-2).
8. Rosita B. Bouterse, *Competition and Integration: What Goals Count?*, 1995 (ISBN 90-654-4816-0).
9. René Barents, *The Agricultural Law of the EC: An Inquiry into the Administrative Law*, 1994 (ISBN 90-654-4867-5).
10. Nicholas Emiliou, *Principles of Proportionality in European Law: A Comparative Study*, 1996 (ISBN 90-411-0866-1).
11. Eivind Smith, *National Parliaments as Cornerstones of European Integration*, 1996 (ISBN 90-411-0898-X).
12. Jan H. Jans, *European Environmental Law*, 1996 (ISBN 90-411-0877-7).
13. Síofra O'Leary, *The Evolving Concept of Community Citizenship: From the Free Movement of Persons to Union Citizenship*, 1997 (ISBN 90-411-0878-5).
14. Laurence W. Gormley (ed.), *Current and Future Perspectives on EC Competition Law*, 1983 (ISBN 90-411-0691-X).
15. Simone White, *Protection of the Financial Interests of the European Communities: The Fight against Fraud and Corruption*, 1998 (ISBN 90-411-9647-1).
16. Morten P. Broberg, *The European Commission's Jurisdiction to Scrutinize Mergers*, 3rd Edition, 2006 (ISBN 978-90-411-2474-6).
17. Doris Hildebrand, *The Role of Economic Analysis in the EC Competition Rules: The European School*, 2nd Edition, 2002 (ISBN 90-411-1706-7).
18. Christof R.A. Swaak, *European Community Law and the Automobile Industry*, 1999 (ISBN 90-411-1140-9).
19. Dorthe Dahlgaard Dingel, *Public Procurement: A Harmonization of the National Judicial Review of the Application of European Community Law*, 1999 (ISBN 90-411-1161-1).
20. John A.E. Vervaele (ed.), *Compliance and Enforcement of European Community Law*, 1999 (ISBN 90-411-1151-4).

21. Martin Trybus, *European Defence Procurement Law: International and National Procurement Systems as Models for a Liberalized Defence Procurement Market in Europe*, 1999 (ISBN 90-411-1167-0).
22. Helen Staples, *The Legal Status of Third Country Nationals Resident in the European Union*, 1999 (ISBN 90-411-1277-4).
23. Damien Geradin (ed.), *The Liberalization of State Monopolies in the European Union and Beyond*, 1999 (ISBN 90-411-1264-2).
24. Katja Heede, *European Ombudsman: Redress and Control at Union Level*, 2000 (ISBN 90-411-1413-0).
25. Ulf Bernitz & Joakim Nergelius (eds), *General Principles of European Community Law*, 2000 (ISBN 90-411-1402-5).
26. Michaela Drahos, *Convergence of Competition Laws and Policies in the European Community*, 2002 (ISBN 90-411-1562-5).
27. Damien Geradin (ed.), *The Liberalization of Electricity and Natural Gas in the European Union*, 2001 (ISBN 90-411-1560-9).
28. Gisella Gori, *Towards an EU Right to Education*, 2001 (ISBN 90-411-1670-2).
29. Brendan P.G. Smith, *Constitution Building in the European Union*, 2001 (ISBN 90-411-1695-8).
30. Friedl Weiss & Frank Wooldridge, *Free Movement of Persons within the European Community*, 2nd Edition, 2007 (ISBN 978-90-411-2545-3).
31. Ingrid Boccardi, *Europe and Refugees: Towards an EU Asylum Policy*, 2002 (ISBN 90-411-1709-1).
32. John A.E. Vervaele & André Klip (eds), *European Cooperation Between Tax, Customs and Judicial Authorities*, 2001 (ISBN 90-411-1747-4).
33. Wouter P.J. Wils, *The Optimal Enforcement of EC Antitrust Law: Essays in Law and Economics*, 2002 (ISBN 90-411-1757-1).
34. Damien Geradin (ed.), *The Liberalization of Postal Services in the European Union*, 2002 (ISBN 90-411-1780-6).
35. Nick Bernard, *Multilevel Governance in the European Union*, 2002 (ISBN 90-411-1812-8).
36. Jill Wakefield, *Judicial Protection through the Use of Article 288(2) EC*, 2002 (ISBN 90-411-1823-3).
37. Sebastiaan Princen, *EU Regulation and Transatlantic Trade*, 2002 (ISBN 90-411-1871-3).
38. Amaryllis Verhoeven, *The European Union in Search of a Democratic and Constitutional Theory*, 2002 (ISBN 90-411-1872-1).
39. Paul L.C. Torremans, *Cross Border Insolvencies in EU, English and Belgian Law*, 2002 (ISBN 90-411-1888-8).
40. Malcolm Anderson & Joanna Apap (eds), *Police and Justice Cooperation and the New European Borders*, 2002 (ISBN 90-411-1893-4).
41. Christin M. Forstinger, *Takeover Law in EU and USA: A Comparative Analysis*, 2002 (ISBN 90-411-1919-1).

42. Antonio Bavasso, *Communications in EU Antitrust Law: Market Power and Public Interest*, 2003 (ISBN 90-411-1974-4).
43. Fiona G. Wishlade, *Regional State Aid and Competition Policy in the European Union*, 2003 (ISBN 90-411-1975-2).
44. Gareth Davies, *Nationality Discrimination in the European Internal Market*, 2003 (ISBN 90-411-1998-1).
45. René Barents, *The Autonomy of Community Law*, 2003 (ISBN 90-411-2251-6).
46. Gerhard Dannecker & Oswald Jansen (eds), *Competition Law Sanctioning in the European Union*, 2004 (ISBN 90-411-2100-5).
47. Nauta Dutilh (ed.), *Dealing with Dominance: The Experience of National Competition Authorities*, 2004 (ISBN 90-411-2211-7).
48. Stefaan van den Bogaert, *Practical Regulation of the Mobility of Sportsmen in the EU Post Bosman*, 2005 (ISBN 90-411-2327-X).
49. Katalin Judit Cseres, *Competition Law and Consumer Protection*, 2005 (ISBN 90-411-2380-6).
50. Philipp Kiiver, *The National Parliaments in the European Union: A Critical View on EU Constitution Building*, 2006 (ISBN 978-90-411-2452-4).
51. Alexander Turk, *The Concept of Legislation in European Community Law*, 2006 (ISBN 978-90-411-2472-2).
52. Dimitrios Sinaniotis, *The Interim Protection of Individuals before the European and National Courts*, 2006 (ISBN 978-90-411-2498-2).
53. M. Holoubek & D. Damjanovic, M. Traimer (eds), *Regulating Content: The European Regulatory Framework for the Media and Related Creative Sectors*, 2006 (ISBN 978-90-411-2597-2).
54. Anneli Albi & Jacques Ziller (eds), *The European Constitution and National Constitutions: Ratification and Beyond*, 2006 (ISBN 978-90-411-2524-8).
55. Gustavo E. Luengo, *Regulation of Subsidies and State Aids in WTO and EC Law: Conflicts in International Trade Law*, 2007 (ISBN 978-90-411-2547-7).
56. Eniko Horvath, *Mandating Identity: Citizenship, Kinship Laws and Plural Nationality in the European Union*, 2007 (ISBN 978-90-411-2662-7).
57. Rass Holdgaard, *External Relations Law of the European Community: Legal Reasoning and Legal Discourses*, 2007 (ISBN 978-90-411-2604-7).
58. Jill Wakefield, *The Right to Good Administration*, 2007 (ISBN 978-90-411-2697-9).
59. Dimitry Kochenov, *EU Enlargement and the Failure of Conditionality: Pre-accession Conditionality in the Fields of Democracy and the Rule of Law*, 2008 (ISBN 978-90-411-2696-2).
60. Despina Mavromati, *The Law of Payment Services in the EU: The EC Directive on Payment Services in the Internal Market*, 2008 (ISBN 978-90-411-2700-6).
61. Anne Meuwese, *Impact Assessment in EU Lawmaking*, 2008 (ISBN 978-90-411-2720-4).

62. Ulf Bernitz, Joakim Nergelius & Cecilia Cardner (eds), *General Principles of EC Law in a Process of Development*, 2008 (ISBN 978-90-411-2705-1).
63. Johan van de Gronden (ed.), *The EU and WTO Law on Services: Limits to the Realisation of General Interest Policies within the Services Markets?*, 2008 (ISBN 978-90-411-2809-6).
64. Alina Tryfonidou, *Reverse Discrimination in EC Law*, 2009 (ISBN 978-90-411-2751-8).
65. Mikael Berglund, *Cross-Border Enforcement of Claims in the EU: History Present Time and Future*, 2009 (ISBN 978-90-411-2861-4).
66. Theodore Konstadinides, *Division of Powers in European Union Law: The Delimitation of Internal Competence between the EU and the Member States*, 2009 (ISBN 978-90-411-2615-3).
67. Mattias Derlén, *Multilingual Interpretation of European Union Law*, 2009 (ISBN 978-90-411-2853-9).
68. René Barents, *Directory of EU Case Law on the Preliminary Ruling Procedure*, 2009 (ISBN 978-90-411-3150-8).
69. Yan Luo, *Anti-dumping in the WTO, the EU and China: The Rise of Legalization in the Trade Regime and its Consequences*, 2010 (ISBN 978-90-411-3207-9).
70. Patrick Birkinshaw & Mike Varney (eds), *The European Union Legal Order after Lisbon*, 2010 (ISBN 978-90-411-3152-2).
71. Thomas Gr. Papadopoulos, *EU Law and Harmonization of Takeovers in the Internal Market*, 2010 (978-90-411-3340-3).
72. Bas van Bockel, *The* Ne Bis In Idem *Principle in EU Law*, 2010 (978-90-411-3156-0).
73. Veljko Milutinović, *The 'Right to Damages' under EU Competition Law: From* Courage v. Crehan *to the White Paper and Beyond*, 2010 (978-90-411-3235-2).
74. Amandine Garde, *EU Law and Obesity Prevention*, 2010 (978-90-411-2706-8).
75. Leonard Besselink, Frans Pennings & Sacha Prechal (eds), *The Eclipse of the Legality Principle in the European Union*, 2011 (978-90-411-3262-8).